SERBIA'S GREAT WAR, 1914–1918

ANDREJ MITROVIĆ

Serbia's Great War
1914–1918

HURST & COMPANY, LONDON

First published in the United Kingdom by
C. Hurst & Co. (Publishers) Ltd,
41 Great Russell Street, London WC1B 3PL
© by Andrej Mitrović, 2007
All rights reserved.
Printed in the UK by
Marston Book Services Limited, Oxford.

The right of Andrej Mitrović to be identified as the author of this volume has been asserted by him in accordance with the Copyright, Designs and Patents Act, 1988.

A catalogue record for this volume is available from the British Library.

ISBN 978-1-85065-766-8 *hardback*
ISBN 978-1-85065-883-2 *paperback*

CONTENTS

Introduction by Mark Cornwall	page vii
July 1914	1
Assassination	3
Demonstrations	11
Conspirators	23
The origins of the declaration of war	26
War	38
The Yugoslav Programme	53
A small country in the face of war	55
Perception of war in 1914	59
Austro-Hungarian fronts	63
Emigrés and volunteers	79
War aim	85
Serbia Suffers	102
Exhaustion	103
Political life	113
Undeclared war	121
Unification problems	135
Collapse of defence	144
On Foreign Soil	151
Withdrawal to Corfu	151
Strength returns	161
Schoolchildren, students, teachers	169
Conflicts and strife	180
The issue of unification with Montenegro	190
Occupation	193
Annexation or fragmentation	193
Occupation administration	200

Plans for the Balkans and the Near East	204
Violence and oppression	221
Political and economic circumstances	232
Armed Resistance	245
Uprising	252
Towards a Yugoslav State	278
Signs of community spirit	289
Separate linkages	299
Wartime political problems	304
End of the war	312
Bibliography	327
Notes	340
Index	381

INTRODUCTION

by Mark Cornwall

'It began with an attack on Serbia ...The first bullets of World War I were fired at Serbian soldiers.' In this way the Serbian nationalist writer Dobrica Ćosić introduces his epic series of novels, written in the 1970s and recalling the heroic plight of Serbia in the First World War.[1] Most people know that Serbia was there at the start of the war in 1914—perhaps even causing it by allowing Serb students to ambush and murder Archduke Franz Ferdinand in Sarajevo. Some may also know that, among the belligerent countries and per head of population, Serbia was the country that suffered most casualties in the war. For example, 62.5 per cent of Serbian males aged between fifteen and fifty-five died during the four years of hostilities. But apart from these few facts, what actually happened to Serbia and the Serbians in the war has largely escaped Western audiences. There has been little work on the subject by British or American historians, either those interested in Balkan history or those who research into the First World War.[2] A translation into English of Professor Andrej Mitrović's newly-edited and shortened version of his authoritative study, first published in Belgrade in 1984, is therefore especially welcome.

In view of Serbia's key role at the start of the conflict, the lack of attention to its wartime history is perhaps surprising. It is bound up with the natural tendency of historians to keep to their 'national boxes'. West European historians have usually focused on the Western front, often erroneously perceiving the eastern half of Europe, including the Balkan and Italian fronts, as 'side-shows' that were distractions from the main event in the West. It was a view, of course, taken at the time, and it resulted in Serbia and the Balkans entering West European consciousness only intermittently during the war.

The Serbian experience is in fact of major significance for three notable reasons. First, in the interlocking development of the war–

time continent, Serbia's plight is part of a European jigsaw that cannot be omitted if the whole is to be better understood. At the same time it serves as a valuable case study of the war in microcosm. It contains all the ingredients of the conflict experienced elsewhere—appalling suffering, legendary sacrifice, war aims, political-military tensions, socio-economic and political upheaval—and some more peculiar to itself, such as mass migration, exile, guerrilla resistance and the trauma of three years of foreign occupation. Secondly, the First World War was crucial as a stage in the construction of Serbian national mythology in the twentieth century. It enabled many Serbs to envisage themselves as a martyred people, their blood constantly spilled for the greater good. Out of the wartime Serbian 'Golgotha' (a favourite phrase from the Great War) there finally emerged the dream of a South Slav or Yugoslav state with the Serbian kingdom at its core. It was a national trauma and sacrifice which nationalist Serbs might easily see as being repeated later in the century, in the wars of the 1940s and the 1990s. Thirdly, the Serbian story has a particular resonance for a British reader because of British participation in that trauma. At the time the British role in aiding or propagating or even betraying the Serbian cause was well-publicised across Britain. Since then it has been a rather neglected subject, a sign of the amnesia which can so easily creep into a reductionist official 'national memory'. It is a link worth highlighting here, not least because it demonstrates again the multiple interaction of the world at war.

If we draw out the threads of these three approaches—the European, Serbian and British significance of Serbia's wartime struggle—it is clear that in some minds the first two may be closely interwoven and perhaps inseparable. In the novel by Ćosić already quoted, one of his leading characters announces to the Serbian Prime Minister, Nikola Pašić, in late 1914: 'After several centuries, we are entering Europe with our whole being and with enormous sacrifices. We are becoming part of Europe and sharing her fate. Now we too are helping to draw the map of Europe.'[3] The implication is that the Serbian question had become a European question of concern to all the Great Powers. For Serbians, then or later, it was important to place the Serbian struggle or the role of the Serbian nation on a broad canvas which stretched well beyond the Balkans. Little Serbia's war and destiny had repercussions for the whole of Europe.

For all its inflation in Serbian hands, this perspective has elements of truth. The Serbian question had been on many European minds since the beginning of the century, particularly after the bloody change of regime in Belgrade in May 1903.[4] Many European statesmen viewed Serbia as an irritating problem that seemed to be destabilising the Balkans, weakening Turkey, and exacerbating tensions between Austria-Hungary and Russia over competing influence in the Near East. The view from the Serbian capital Belgrade, as Andrej Mitrović shows well, was one of an Austro-Hungarian imperialist threat, seeking at every opportunity to curb Serbian development and return the kingdom to the status of an Austrian satellite as in the 1880s.[5] The view from Vienna, however, was of an insidious Serbian menace on the very borders of the Monarchy.[6] It was the new Serbian regime which was perceived as the aggressor, with its notorious programme of expanding and annexing South Slav territories of the Monarchy. If such unity was permitted (on the lines of German or Italian unity in the 1860s), then the Habsburg Empire would cease to exist; thus the Habsburg elite itself could argue that Serbia was a 'European problem'. In Vienna therefore, as in Belgrade, there was strong defensive reasoning behind what might otherwise be perceived (notably by Russia) as an offensive agenda.

The year 1913 was crucial, because in the wake of the Balkan Wars Serbia was allowed by the other Powers of Europe to double its territory to the south in Macedonia and Kosovo. The Austro-Hungarian leaders could not prevent it, but they were determined to scotch the Serbian snake before it became an anaconda. The result was Vienna's uncompromising behaviour in the July Crisis of 1914 after the assassination of Archduke Franz Ferdinand. Serbia at this point was certainly no immediate threat to the Empire, its links to the murder being largely unofficial and indirect. For the Austro-Hungarian elite, however, the lesson of 1903–14 was that Belgrade could not be trusted to curb its nationalist ambitions.[7] According to this mindset, the Serbian question had to be 'solved' and the Serbs brought to heel, so that the Habsburg Empire could survive.

Before 1914, therefore, Serbia already figured increasingly on the European stage, itself provoking alarm by trying to redraw territorial borders to its advantage. During the war it continued to be the primary focus for Austro-Hungarian war aims, attracting more attention than Vienna paid to either Italy or Russia. In military terms too the image of 'David and Goliath' is irresistible. Not only could the Serbs proclaim the first victory against the Central Powers in August 1914,[8] as well as ensuring a major diversion of Austrian resources to the Balkans for the rest of the year. Just as important was the Serbian army's role in the final breakthrough in September 1918, when the rolling back of the south-eastern front was a crucial element in Austria-Hungary's disintegration and the Central Powers' overall military collapse.

In the four years between these two exploits on the battlefield, Serbia's strategic significance for the Allies had dramatically shifted. Although in late 1914 Nikola Pašić's government had announced war aims in the form of a Yugoslav programme, and the armed forces had been surprisingly effective, the limits of Serbia's usefulness were equally apparent to its Allied patrons. The latter were quite prepared to bargain away Serbian territory or territorial aspirations in order to ensure that Italy, Bulgaria and Romania joined the Allied side, and that the Central Powers remained cut off from their Turkish ally. Serbia might well protest that its own Yugoslav war aims were a major block to the German or Austrian *Drang nach Osten*, but in 1915 such plans seemed fanciful and unrealisable unless the Habsburg Empire were removed from the map.

Only from 1917 could Serbia successfully begin to reassert its agenda in the Western corridors of power. It now had an increasingly strong strategic profile. After the disasters of 1915–16 its army had been reconstituted and sent to strengthen the Balkan front, and some leaders like David Lloyd George were keen to attack the enemy at a point of weakness away from the Western front. Moreover, as the belligerent mindset on both sides became entrenched and radicalised, so the Yugoslav programme began to appear both feasible and desirable for the Allies in order to achieve victory. Pašić could argue, with a certain justification, that many South Slavs in the Monarchy desired unification with Serbia in order to create a large 'national state' and block German aspirations in the Near East. For the Allies playing the card of 'national self-determination' for European peoples set out a simple moral agenda for their cause. By 1918 it was also an Allied tactic for destroying Austria-Hungary, now increasingly viewed as a German pawn which did not deserve to survive. In the national ideological crusade of 1918, Serbia proceeded to play a major part with its Yugoslav agenda, often competing with Czechoslovak, Polish and Romanian causes for the Allies' attention. In this way Serbia's role in destroying the Habsburg Empire and reordering the map of Eastern Europe in 1918–19 cannot be underestimated.

For the Serbians themselves wartime was the natural environment for breeding nationalist myth and dramatically enhancing their national self-image. Akin to that of the Czechs, the image constructed was of a fundamentally democratic people, forced to undertake yet another struggle against tyranny before, phoenix-like, achieving a glorious national resurrection. Just as Serbians in the fourteenth century had resisted the Turkish menace only to be 'martyred' on Kosovo field (1389), so in 1914 they had taken up their shield again, this time against the pan-European aggression of Germany and its allies. In the elaboration of a modern Serbian national myth, this wartime 'Golgotha' was a crucial stage, which many might view as cyclical—experienced in 1941 against Nazi Germany and in 1999 against NATO. In times of national insecurity, such as the late 1980s, the 'Golgotha and resurrection' of the Great War might easily evoke common memories for ordinary Serbians.[9]

The picture of national martyrdom could be painted in striking colours. In the early months of hostilities the Serbs had stood alone against Austria-Hungary in the Balkans, yet had achieved the 'first complete victory over the common enemy', shattering Vienna's confidence and managing to retake Belgrade.[10] A devastating typhus epidemic then killed 100,000 Serbian civilians. Ten months later Serbia was deserted by its allies and left with Montenegro to fend for itself against renewed German-Austrian aggression. This 'betrayal', almost on a par with the Czech experience in 1938, was duly offset by the behaviour of the Serbian army: in an epic long-march it traversed the inhospitable Albanian mountains to reach Allied sanctuary. While at least 140,000 people were lost during this terrifying winter anabasis, the outcome was otherwise positive.[11] The Serbian nation, though split in two, could renew for itself a strong military and political presence in the Allied camp.

The retreat also shaped further the myth of Serbia's populist democratic struggle. King, cabinet and high command were seen to be participating in the national tragedy alongside the ordinary soldier.

Behind the myth, as Mitrović shows, the picture was rather less edifying. Owing to Pašić's dominance of politics, no broad national coalition had been created to determine Serbia's future. As in other belligerent regimes across Europe, the war served to radicalise prewar political animosities and expose political-military tensions. In Serbia's case it produced a major showdown in 1917 between two factions. Regent Alexander and Pašić moved to eliminate the military clique who had adopted an embarrassingly uncompromising nationalist programme and clustered earlier around the 'Black Hand'. Through a rigged trial and the execution of the *éminence grise*, Colonel Dimitrijević ('Apis'), Alexander and Pašić were able to destroy a rival.[12] It was the climax of the political-military struggle that had bedevilled the country before 1914. It was also a foretaste of what was to come, in terms both of intrigue on the Serbian political scene and of Alexander's later behaviour as Yugoslav monarch.

'Serbia in exile', the story of the heroic retreat and reconstruction of a nation, is one with few parallels in the history of the Great War. But it is only half the myth, half the Serbian national trauma. A mirror-image of sacrifice and resurrection was evident in occupied Serbia from 1916 to 1918. In two chapters of this book Andrej Mitrović describes life under the Austro-Hungarian and Bulgarian regimes of occupation, revealing an enclosed world which has barely received attention in Western historiography.[13] Most striking is his confirmation of the violent repression involved, including atrocities against civilians by both Austrian and Bulgarian troops (a horror well publicised at the time but since forgotten).[14] The Austrian regime, while economically ransacking the region, adopted the principle of crushing the Serbs' spirit and eliminating their intelligentsia from influence. Life in the Bulgarian zone was even more brutal. As the occupiers began a concerted campaign to turn the native population into Bulgarians, those who resisted were often 'sent to Sofia', a euphemism for execution. It was a foretaste of the still greater horrors that would occur under regimes of occupation in the Second World War. But in the circumstances of occupied Serbia it also produced a dramatic reaction which Mitrović has elaborated well elsewhere.[15] The Serbian rebellion of February 1917 in the Bulgarian zone was, as a mass uprising against occupation, the only event of its kind in the First World War. Perhaps 20,000 Serbs died in the revolt and its aftermath. It reinforced a combative Serbian self-image, a legend of active resistance to any foreigner who ever dared to invade the national soil. Again a linear development could be traced between the experience of mountainous guerrilla warfare in 1916–18, the earlier heroic resistance to the Turkish infidel, and what would come later in Serbia's bloody 'national wars' of the 1940s and 1990s.

If the national myth was about martyrdom and resistance, it was also about the realisation of a utopian national ideal. Serbia in the war had selflessly assumed the supreme role of liberating South Slav brothers from the Austro-Hungarian yoke, bringing them together in the kingdom of Yugoslavia. The reality was that this high-minded programme was the radical extension in wartime of a decades-old national mission, now accelerated in order to give Serbia long-term security against foreign aggression. Before 1914 it was precisely this programme, or suspicions of it, that had made the Austro-Hungarian elite feel increasingly insecure. Some might even interpret it as a form of 'Serbian imperialism' quite akin to that of the Habsburg Empire, for while it encompassed both a Greater Serbian goal and the hazy dream of some South Slav or Yugoslav nation, to many Serbs they were the same thing. It was only the war, and the Habsburg Empire's collapse, that made this mission realisable. Serbia's 'survival' in exile after 1915 was therefore essential, ensuring that it still had military and diplomatic leverage with the Allies and could act as a beacon for the South Slav cause.

Yet it would be a gross distortion—gratifying to Serbian nationalists—to suggest that Yugoslavia was created chiefly as a result of Serbia's successful quest for national unity and security. Equally significant were the aspirations of many Slovenes, Croats and Serbs in Austria-Hungary. By 1917 at least they had a similar quest for national and economic security in the face of German, Hungarian and Italian threats to their existence. The complex interaction of motives for unification among South Slavs in Austria-Hungary still requires more research.[16] But what is certain is that nationalist agitation in the Empire in 1917–18, in particular that led by the Slovene clerical leadership, was a crucial complement to the campaign being waged in exile by the Serbian government and by those South Slav émigrés from the Empire who had clustered together in London and Paris in a 'Yugoslav Committee'. By 1918 there were at least three major centres working towards some kind of Yugoslav programme—the Serbian government, the Yugoslav Committee and the South Slav ferment in the Monarchy itself. From September 1918 the advance of the Serbian army and the upsurge in guerrilla activity certainly enhanced Serbia's role in the quickening course of events. The danger now was that the view from Croatia or Slovenia would be ignored in the rush by the Serbian leadership to fulfil Serbia's national mission and redeem its own wartime sacrifice.

Britain and British citizens had participated directly in Serbia's myth-making, both in the nation's 'Golgotha' and later in propagating the Yugoslav mission. Apart from some limited military aid,[17] its main contribution to Serbia's war in the early years came in the form of a stream of medical units and supplies. Already in late 1914, inspired by Serbia's heroic lone struggle, hundreds followed the call of charities like the Serbian Relief Fund, volunteering to travel to the Balkans to minister as doctors or nurses to a small nation in distress. Medical teams such as the British Red Cross Mission, the Scottish Women's Unit and the 'Berry Mission' were attached to the Serbian army and arrived in time to play a key role in combating the typhus epidemic of 1915.

A few of those who volunteered had pre-war links to Serbia. Then there were notable recruits such as the Bishop of London's daughter and the English hymn-writer Percy Dearmer who went out as a chaplain. For many it was a new humanitarian crusade where Serbia's plight matched that of Belgium in the West. It particularly attracted upper-middle-class women, some of them former suffragists who wanted to serve and show they were equal to the task.[18] A few like the 'masculine' Flora Sandes even joined the Serbian armed forces, 'willing to rough it with them and to fight for Serbia'.[19] The gender dimension to these exploits, where cultured British women like Elsie Inglis, Eveline Haverfield and Lady Paget nurtured 'uncouth' Serbian men and shared their hardships, added powerfully to the legend which subsequently circulated back in the mother country. Those who publicised their adventures often wrote in patronising terms of the Serbian natives they encountered. Western civilisation to many Serbs was 'no more than skin deep'. They were 'not as dirty a folk as our own East Enders', but were on the level of England in the seventeenth century or 'of some Central African tribe'.[20] But along with perceived traits of the Serbs as simple, curious and procrastinating, there was always mention of their immense hospitality, their patriotism and spirituality, and their endurance in the face of 'martyrdom'. In the vivid language of Alice and Claude Askew, who experienced at first hand the winter retreat of the Serbian army, 'the tears of Serbia' were 'as the bloody sweat that fell at Gethsemane'. Serbia was 'one of those nations that no conqueror can tame, no brutality subdue. Her flaming spirit of liberty escaped the invader, and a starving army carried the soul of Serbia with them into exile.'[21]

These eulogistic accounts were an extra boost to what became a small industry of pro-Serbian propaganda in Britain. It lay largely in the hands of the Serbian Relief Fund, established in September 1914 by Balkan experts such as the historian R.W. Seton-Watson, the archaeologist Arthur Evans and others dedicated to alleviating Serbia's plight.[22] Their work stretched across the country, encompassing 'flag days' in Glasgow, 'Serbian weeks' in Bournemouth and a collection of cash on the trams of Sheffield. By May 1915 £100,000 had been raised, and in four years £1 million worth of material was secured for Serbs who were sick or wounded.[23]

The propaganda aspect to this humanitarian effort was sharpened considerably after Serbia's winter disaster and Britain's obvious failure to assist. For Seton-Watson it marked the end of his faith in the foreign secretary, Sir Edward Grey. As he wrote in February 1916, 'Our Government betrayed Serbia, disregarded every warning … kept essential information from the Serbs, and then tried to back out of its engagements at Salonica in a manner for which I can find no word.'[24] It resulted in Seton-Watson, Elsie Inglis and others founding a 'Kosovo Day Committee' to publicise Serbia via schools and churches; 2 July 1916 was designated as 'Serbian Sunday' when special sermons were delivered in the pulpits. In August a 'Serbian Society of Great Britain' was officially launched with some prominent patrons. The Society stressed particularly that, because of its geographical position, Serbia like Belgium was of prime significance to Britain as a barrier against Germany's expansion. It was logically essential to promote a large Yugoslav state in the Balkans both for ethnic and strategic reasons. This was the line that had long been trumpeted by Pašić's government, only to fall on deaf ears in the West. But Germany's expansion eastwards was now self-evident, and by 1918—with Austria-Hungary as a 'pawn'—would be even more so. Consequently it was far easier for Seton-Watson and other Yugoslav enthusiasts to make inroads in Whitehall, to argue the logic of the Serbian-Yugoslav case, and present it as part of an overall package for restructuring Europe according to new ethnic and ethical principles.[25] Britain's wartime support for Serbia was certainly uneven, but the need to destroy the Habsburg Empire finally led both countries in the same direction towards creating Yugoslavia.

Serbia's Great War was a traumatic journey, dramatic in its many twists and turns. For those who sought or might seek comparisons, historically or contemporaneously across the European continent, it is a case study which offers much material for analysis. In this spirit Lloyd George in August 1917, when lunching with Nikola Pašić, equated the fate of Serbia with that of Wales; 'the great event in the story of Serbia is not a triumph', he noted, 'it is a great defeat.'[26] In fact by late 1918 it was both. It is that legendary drama with its highs and lows which, through Andrej Mitrović's potent study, is now accessible to a wider readership.

1
JULY 1914

At 11.00 a.m. on 28 July 1914 the government of the Austro-Hungarian Monarchy sent a telegram to the government of Serbia. The telegram, dispatched through the regular post, ran as follows:

> Having not received a satisfactory reply to the note that had been handed to the Royal Government of Serbia by the Minister of Austria-Hungary to Belgrade dated 23 July 1914, the Imperial and Royal Government finds it necessary to see to the safeguarding of its rights and interests and, with this object, to have recourse to force of arms. From this moment Austria-Hungary accordingly regards herself as in a state of war with Serbia.[1]

The next day, 29 July, a declaration of war by Emperor Franz Joseph was announced to the nations of Austria-Hungary. It stated that the 'intrigues of a hate-filled enemy', i.e. Serbia, were forcing the Monarchy to draw its sword in defence of its honour, its reputation, its rank as a Power and its integrity. 'The hatred towards Me and My household is ever greater, and the ambition to sever integral parts from Austria-Hungary is ever more overt.' Serbia was accused of being the architect and fomenter of 'secret dealings' that 'aspired to destroy the fundamentals of state order in the southeast of the Monarchy.' The Imperial government, therefore, having once again endeavoured unsuccessfully 'to put an end to this in a peaceful manner' with the 'note' of 23 July, had no alternative but to go to war: 'This unacceptable activity must be halted; an end must be put to Serbia's infamous provocations.'[2]

That same day Serbia's Regent, Prince Alexander Karadjordjević, made his own declaration of war:

> A great evil has befallen this Serbia of ours. Austria-Hungary has declared war on us.... Our Kingdom's troubles with Austria and those of our nation date back into the past.... In vain have Serb and Croat guards of the march,

like so many other heroes of ours, shed their blood throughout Europe for the glory and benefit of the Court in Vienna.... My Government, in accordance with the wishes of the people and the need for peace, a need felt not only by Serbia but also by the whole of Europe, had wished to avoid conflict at all cost, and that is why it has done its utmost to meet the demands of the Austro-Hungarian Government to the very limit of compliance beyond which no independent state may go.... Unfortunately, Vienna's statesmen have turned a deaf ear to advice urging wisdom and to the interests of mankind. They declared war on us yesterday, thus not shrinking from also provoking the unforeseeable consequences of a European conflict.... I am compelled to call on all my dear and valiant Serbs to defend Serbia's tricolour.... Serbs, defend your hearths and the Serb nation with all your might![3]

Montenegro stood beside Serbia, and on 6 August King Nicholas I Petrović-Njegoš of Montenegro made a proclamation to the nation:

The black and yellow standard, which has long weighed intolerably upon the soul of the South Slav nation, has now unfurled to destroy that nation completely, to trample underfoot its free representatives, Serbia and Montenegro.... Austria has declared war on our dear Serbia, declared war on us, declared it on the Serb nation and on the entire Slav nation.... Whoever considers himself a hero and follows in the footsteps of two ageing Serb kings, let us die and spill our blood for unity and precious freedom.... We wanted peace, but war has been imposed upon us. Accept that as you have always done, accept it as Serbs and as heroes.[4]

The three proclamations embodied two diametrically opposed positions. Franz Joseph's accused Serbia of conspiring against the Monarchy over the years, while not mentioning Montenegro at all; those of Alexander and Nicholas accused the Monarchy of obstructing the Serb nation's development over a lengthy period, while parts of the Montenegrin proclamation spoke of South Slavs in general. Franz Joseph's proclamation interpreted the declaration of war as a natural response to the activities of conspirators; the other two interpreted the same declaration as only part of the Habsburg state's historic subjection of Serbs or Yugoslavs. Franz Joseph cited the right of a Great Power to protect, with war, its honour, reputation, rank and integrity; Alexander and Nicholas cited the need that drives a state to defend its independence and territorial integrity from attackers. Franz Joseph was speaking on behalf of his dynasty and the state it ruled; Alexander and Nicholas spoke as representatives of the nations they ruled. Thus two diametrically opposite worlds confronted one another in the proclamations. The contrasting contents of the two war manifestos highlighted an exceptionally significant historical confrontation that was, on account of its unusual ferocity, to determine the course of events far into the future. Involved here was an essential integral element of the imperialist era, which was made up of sharp contradictions among the Great Power groups and between the Great Powers and small states.

Assassination

The declaration of war had an immediate prehistory lasting a number of weeks. The key event had taken place in Berlin on 5 and 6 July 1914. A special envoy from Vienna—Count Alexander Hoyos, *chef de cabinet* of the Austro-Hungarian Foreign Ministry—had arrived there on the morning of 5 July bearing a letter from Emperor Franz Joseph for Kaiser Wilhelm II and a lengthy intergovernmental memorandum from Vienna.[5] In the two documents Franz Joseph and the Austro-Hungarian government—referring to the recent assassination of the Habsburg heir apparent Franz Ferdinand in Sarajevo, for which Serbia was being held responsible—sought a clear statement by Wilhelm II and the German government as to whether Germany, in accordance with its obligations, as an ally, intended to stand firmly beside Austria-Hungary should it decide to take 'severe and far reaching steps' against Serbia. The word 'war' was not actually mentioned, but the content and tone of those documents clearly showed that the Monarchy intended to deal by force of arms with its small southern neighbour. They also made clear Vienna's conviction that in the existing circumstances Berlin had no choice but to fulfil its duty as an ally.[6]

Count László Szögyény, the Austro-Hungarian ambassador in Berlin, at once sought an audience with Wilhelm II and, carrying the two original documents, was received by him in Potsdam. Hoyos took copies of the two documents to the Foreign Ministry in Berlin. The next day, 6 July, Szögyény and Hoyos held lengthy talks with the German Chancellor, Theobald von Bethmann-Hollweg, and in the meantime Wilhelm conferred in Potsdam with officials of Germany's leading political and military institutions and, also on a special visit to Kiel, with Gustav von Krupp as head of Germany's most prominent arms manufacturer. During these meetings Wilhelm stated that Austria-Hungary intended to exacerbate its relations with Serbia to such an extent that a large-scale war would break out between the Central European empires and at least two of the Entente Powers—Russia and France.[7] He told Krupp that Germany 'would declare war on Russia as soon as Russia ordered mobilisation', and asked the more important of his visitors whether they considered Germany ready to take on such an eventuality. The answer was affirmative on all sides, army representatives being especially resolute. Everyone immediately took the necessary measures.[8]

In the first talks top German figures had not only told representatives of the Monarchy already that the Reich would 'cover the back' of its ally if it attacked Serbia; they also showed themselves unquestionably interested in the Monarchy taking the most far-reaching steps. Wilhelm II even told Count Szögyény that he would personally be 'saddened if advantage were not taken of such a favourable juncture as the present one.' A similar message was conveyed to Count Hoyos in the Foreign Ministry. On 6 July Bethmann-Hollweg officially informed Szögyény and Hoyos that Austria-Hungary could count on Germany's wholehearted support in its intentions against Serbia. Szögyény and Hoyos were able to telegraph Vienna immediately saying: 'We can count with certainty on Germany standing behind the Monarchy as its ally and friend.'[9] As his own personal opinion, Bethmann Hollweg had added: 'As war is already inevitable, the present juncture is more favourable than any later one could be.' He thus repeated what Szögyény had heard from the Kaiser the day before. It is not quite accurate to say that at that time Berlin had given Vienna a 'blank cheque'. A cheque had indeed been given, but one that had been filled out and was valid only if the Monarchy seized the opportunity to go to war against Serbia at the earliest possible moment. Germany was pushing Austria-Hungary into immediate war, and those most responsible were fully aware of the catastrophe towards which they were heading: Bethmann-Hollweg had expressly prophesied on the evening of 6 July that 'action against Serbia could lead to a world war.'[10]

The event that served as a pretext for the two empires to reach their decision so quickly and easily in Potsdam had taken place a week earlier. Emperor Franz Joseph's heir apparent, Archduke Franz Ferdinand, had been assassinated in Sarajevo on 28 June, St Vitus' Day (*Vidovdan*).[11] A young man called Nedeljko Čabrinović had thrown a bomb at the Archduke just before 10.30 a.m. that day, but the intended victim had been unhurt. Then, about half an hour later, another young man, Gavrilo Princip, aimed his revolver, shot twice, and killed Franz Ferdinand and, by accident, his wife Sophie, Duchess of Hohenberg. Both men were immediately arrested.

Investigations soon revealed that as many as six young men had been waiting to kill the Archduke in Sarajevo that afternoon. The police quickly arrested another three of them: Trifko Grabež on 30 June and Vasa Čubrilović and Cvetko Popović on 3 July. The sixth man, Muhamed Mehmedbašić, managed to escape and reach Montenegro. A broader circle of conspirators and their associates was also discovered, leading to the arrest of Danilo Ilić, Miško Jovanović, Veljko Čubrilović, Ivan Kranjčević, Lazar Djukić, Jakov Milević, four members of the Kerović family and others—all members of a national-revolutionary organisation. In all, twenty-five men were arrested and charged. All were Austro-Hungarian citizens and, while the great majority were Serbs, they also included Croats. Most were Orthodox, but there were also Catholics and Muslims.

The investigation established that a centre, headed by Danilo Ilić, existed in Sarajevo which was linked to several places in Bosnia. It had chosen three of the would-be assassins, but the other three—Princip, Čabrinović and Grabež—had recently arrived from Belgrade, where they had actually made the decision to assassinate the Archduke.[12] It was also ascertained that they had been in contact in Belgrade with Milan Ciganović, a refugee from Bosnia, and through him with the Chetnik leader and Serbian army Major Vojislav Tankosić who, the investigation showed, had provided them with weapons. It was alleged that thanks to mediation by Milan Ciganović and Tankosić with their contacts in Narodna Odbrana (National Defence) and the cooperation of some Serbian officers serving on the frontier, they had been smuggled into Bosnia. The bombs found on the would-be assassins, as well as the one used by Čabrinović, had been manufactured in the Kragujevac weapons factory. However, Princip, Čabrinović and Grabež resolutely claimed throughout the investigation and before the court that they had conceived the idea of killing the Archduke completely independently because of their patriotic convictions, and that Ciganović and Tankosić had merely helped them after hearing of their plans. It followed from the conspirators' statements that everything had been done without the knowledge of the Serbian authorities, and they stated expressly that they had taken great pains to conceal their intentions and their journeys to Bosnia from Serbia's civil authorities who, they had been convinced, would have thwarted their designs. Everything that had been discovered led to the conclusion that a group of national revolutionaries had conceived, organised, and carried out the assassination because of their convictions, with the help of some people from Narodna Odbrana in Serbia.

Despite the investigators' determination to find a clue linking the Serbian authorities or other prominent Serbs to the assassination, they failed to do so. Indeed, all made it clear that this was not the case. The Ministry of Foreign Affairs in Vienna sent a senior official, Friedrich von Wiesner, to Sarajevo to collect information and report all that the judicial and police investigation had uncovered concerning the plot that could be compromising for official Serbia. However, on 13 July von Wiesner was only able to telegraph that there were grounds to suspect that the national movement in Bosnia and Herzegovina was supported by some organisations in Serbia that were tolerated by the Serbian government, but that 'it is not possible to prove the Serbian government's involvement in the assassination, its preparation or the supply of weapons.' He went as far as to say, 'There is no cause even for suspicion' since there were 'far more reasons for claiming that it had nothing to do with it.'[13]

Official Serbia's reaction to the first news about the Sarajevo assassination was a customary one to such events in international relations, albeit with a certain haste to point out to its powerful neighbour that the Government in Belgrade not only regretted but also condemned the assassination. The Serbian envoy to Vienna, Jovan M. Jovanović, telegraphed Belgrade on 28 June to say that the assassination of Franz Ferdinand and his wife had been reported from Sarajevo. The government in Belgrade received the telegram at 21.25 and barely an hour later directed Jovanović to express 'deepest condolences to the Foreign Minister on behalf of the royal government', adding that it had itself already 'directly expressed its condolences to the Austro-

Hungarian Ministry of Foreign Affairs.'[14] What had actually happened was that because the Prime Minister and Minister of Foreign Affairs, Nikola Pašić, was in the interior of the country at the time, campaigning for National Assembly (Narodna Skupština) elections, the Minister of Justice and the head of the Foreign Ministry immediately presented themselves at the Austro-Hungarian legation to express their condolences, and the same was done on behalf of King Peter I by the Court Minister and on behalf of the Regent by his *chef de cabinet*. Celebrations marking St Vitus's Day were also halted that same evening, and a six-day period of court mourning was decreed. The government further announced that it would institute an inquiry into any Serbian citizen whom the Sarajevo investigation established as having had connections with the assassination.[15] Immediate orders were issued that authorities in the country should not allow 'manifestations or demonstrations' and should protect Austro-Hungarian representative bodies. And when a guard in Šabac, interpreting these orders literally, prevented the Austro-Hungarian Vice-Consul, whom he did not know by sight, from entering the consulate in that town, he was not only removed but also discharged.[16] Thus the Serbian authorities were making immediate efforts to show goodwill and, probably because of experience with the Monarchy over recent years, to emphasise that they distanced themselves from the assassination, in order to show that they wanted no deterioration in relations that were already bad.

The first articles in the Austro-Hungarian press showed that such fears were well founded. Serbia's minister in Vienna, Jovanović, had to send a telegram on 29 June warning his government, according to press reports, that 'the Sarajevo police were already showing the tendency to direct the investigation as if everything had been prepared in Belgrade' and that it was vital to take note of 'this tendency'. In the following days he was able to confirm that such a tendency did exist.[17] The Serbian chargé d'affaires in Berlin reported, also on 29 June, that 'newspapers here are carrying articles based on reports from Vienna and Budapest linking the Sarajevo assassination to Serbia, thus misleading German public opinion.'[18] Clearly seeing the way matters were leading, Jovan M. Jovanović considerably strengthened both the form and the content of the expression of condolence he delivered to the Ministry of Foreign Affairs in Vienna on 30 June as follows: 'The government of the Kingdom of Serbia most emphatically condemns the assassination in Sarajevo and will certainly for its part most loyally do everything it can to prove that it will not tolerate any agitation or other punishable activity aimed at disturbing our already delicate relations with Austria-Hungary.' He must have judged that some self-defence was necessary even if it meant cautiously placing some blame at the door of the Monarchy: 'The Government of Serbia, despite all the obstructions encountered to date from the Austro-Hungarian diplomacy..., still wishes to lay healthy foundations for our neighbourly relations.... Serbia intends to continue to work to that end.... The assassination in Sarajevo should not and cannot prevent that work.'[19]

Officials in Montenegro were also doing their best to demonstrate their goodwill to the Monarchy's leading figures. When the news from Sarajevo arrived in the Montenegrin capital Cetinje the St Vitus' Day celebrations were immediately halted and the Foreign Minister Petar Plamenac expressed his government's condolences to the Austro-Hungarian chargé d'affaires. King Nicholas was abroad at the time, but hastened home and on arriving in Cetinje on the morning of 30 June lost no time in sending his condolences to Franz Joseph and ordering a two-week period of mourning. He also attended a memorial service for Franz Ferdinand in the court chapel, and a Montenegrin government delegation, headed by the Foreign Minister, attended a memorial service in the Austro-Hungarian legation. The official *Glas Crnogorca* described the assassination as a 'deranged terrorist act perpetrated by lone fantasists' and wrote that it 'had aroused universal sorrow and unanimous condemnation throughout Montenegro.'[20]

However, the public mood in Serbia and Montenegro was different. In the words of a Montenegrin minister, 'This event gave rise to joy and misgivings among the authorities and only to joy among the people.'[21] The same can be said for reactions in Serbia. The Austro-Hungarian chargé d'affaires, Wilhelm von Stork, reported—it would seem reliably—that in private conversations in Belgrade it could be heard that 'a heroic deed has been done and will be continued.'[22] He dispatched the following account on 30 June: 'There is exultation in the streets and in the cafés on account of our misfortune, and it is described as the finger of God and a justified punishment for everything bad that Austria-Hungary has already done to Serbia.'[23] It could not have been otherwise, for there had been widespread belief that Austria-Hungary was hindering the growth of Serbia and Montenegro and preventing Serb and Yugoslav unification; there had also been an inaccurate perception that Franz Ferdinand had hated Serbs and was leader of the so-called 'war faction' in the Monarchy. Nonetheless the authorities, both in Belgrade and in Cetinje, realised the danger they were in and did their utmost to prevent any developments that would increase it. They clearly demonstrated their dissociation from assassination as a means of struggle. Reports from foreign diplomatic representatives in Belgrade at that time reveal a conviction there that 'not only brother Serbs from Bosnia would be held responsible, but the entire Serb nation.'[24]

Von Stork in Belgrade merely registered the Serbian government's efforts to mitigate the situation while constantly stressing what he noted among the public. Although he allowed for the possibility that at the given moment the assassination had not been in line with the 'concepts of Serbia's leadership', he nonetheless openly proposed that the Monarchy should take Serbia to task. He recalled his earlier exhortation to take advantage of the first opportunity to 'strike a destructive blow' to Serbia.[25] 'Our position as a Great Power will be damaged if we do not show our fist,'[26] he claimed; 'we should now bang a fist on the table because that is the only language the Serbian government understands.'[27] He appeared at the Serbian Foreign Ministry on 30 June and demanded to be immediately informed of what measures the Serbian police had taken to pick up the threads of the plot that, he said, 'evidently led back to Serbia'.[28]

The quick and easy agreement reached between Germany and Austria-Hungary on 5 and 6 July was not actually founded on the Sarajevo assassination. Another three facts are striking: first, agreement had been reached when the investigation in Sarajevo was only in its initial phase; secondly, proof of Serbia's responsibility had not even been mentioned in the talks between German and Austro-Hungarian representatives; and thirdly, there had been no real talk of Franz Ferdinand's assassination—at least the subject had been mentioned in general terms and then quickly dropped since the question of how to deal with Serbia was much more pressing. It is evident that the participants in the talks in Potsdam and Berlin had been interested not in who had actually planned the assassination, but only in the fact that the murder provided a 'suitable slogan' for propaganda purposes when setting forward warlike intentions and decisions. No one taking part in those talks needed convincing that the assassination provided Austria-Hungary with a welcome opportunity to wage war on Serbia, so it was not necessary to say anything more about what had happened in Sarajevo.[29]

Franz Joseph replied briefly and clearly to the question of whether Austria-Hungary should enter the war if Germany would back it when he said, in reply to the Chief of the General Staff, Baron Conrad von Hötzendorf: 'In this case—yes.'[30] Unlike Franz Ferdinand, the Emperor himself was among those at the country's head who were keenest on war. That was confirmed by a later statement made by his minister Leon von Bilinski: 'The Emperor was always in favour of war.... He had wanted it a year before.'[31] Nonetheless, the final decision in the summer of 1914 depended on the position of Germany. And when Wilhelm II first heard of the warlike emotions sweeping Vienna as far back as 30 June he had written the telling words: 'Now or never!'[32] A reconstruction of what the most influential members of the political and social elite in Vienna were discussing among themselves and writing to each other on 29 and 30 June clearly demonstrates that those who, as Count Hoyos said, wished to use the assassination 'to fabricate a pretext for settling accounts with Serbia' were in the ascendant.[33] That was heard in Vienna by the Bavarian envoy, who telegraphed the following on 6 July: 'There is also talk of fabricating a pretext for war from the assassination and thus making amends for earlier omissions, as there is no other way to gain the upper hand over Serbia.'[34] And Hungarian Prime Minister István Count Tisza, who was at that time against war, warned of the danger of some people wishing to make use of the event in Sarajevo finally to 'settle matters with Serbia,' to 'provoke a war with Serbia.'[35]

Franz Joseph, his Foreign Minister Count Leopold Berchtold and Habsburg diplomacy in general dramatised the situation immediately after the assassination by such statements as 'The future looks black', describing 'Belgrade's intrigues' as 'insufferable'. Also, it was a case of 'systematic Greater Serb activity of a destabilising nature';

Serbia's 'dangerous endeavours could only be halted by acting ruthlessly' and it was 'necessary to resolve the Serb issue'. German diplomacy was acting in the same way, and ambassadors of the Entente Powers heard in the Foreign Ministry in Berlin that Serbia had to provide 'convincing proof' of its innocence. The Austro-Hungarian ambassador there was told that the Reich 'totally understood any rigorous and resolute move on the part of the Monarchy against Serbia.'[36]

Indeed, the German side had been inciting the Monarchy even before the arrival of Hoyos in Berlin. It did so discreetly and furtively, but nonetheless unambiguously. It is true that the German ambassador to Vienna, on encountering a desire for war 'even among serious persons', at first thought that an attempt should be made to calm tempers. But Kaiser Wilhelm wrote on the ambassador's report: 'Who has authorised him to do that? It is extremely stupid!' The ambassador was immediately admonished, and within a few hours his attitude totally changed. He became from that time on ardently pro-war, manifesting a 'steely consistency', as Count Berchtold wrote. In the Foreign Ministry in Berlin it was considered that the leading figures in the Monarchy should be informed of the matter concerning the ambassador, and Count Szögyény telegraphed from Berlin on 8 July that he had been told that the German ambassador in Vienna had been 'admonished from over here' for acting in Count Berchtold's presence 'in a somewhat conciliatory manner'. In parallel to this, from the beginning of July the Foreign Ministry in Berlin was sending messages to Vienna, using as intermediaries the publicists Viktor Naumann and Hugo Ganz, who were regularly entrusted with important unofficial contacts. The messages were: 'The question of survival is opening up for the Monarchy if it fails to punish the crime and destroy Serbia', 'Germany will support the Monarchy to its length and breadth', 'The sooner Austria-Hungary goes to war the better' as 'yesterday was better than today, and today is better than tomorrow', and so on. The Central European empires were both equally interested in taking advantage of the opportunity offered.

Demonstrations

Jovan M. Jovanović did his utmost in Vienna to work for conciliation, but it was to no avail. Day after day it became clearer to him that public opinion was being dangerously manipulated. He noted, for example, that the conspirators had suddenly started to be called 'Serbs', although they had been referred to hitherto as 'Bosniacs'. Jovanović therefore warned officials in Vienna that the intent was to 'link the nationality of the assassins to Belgrade in order to create the impression that the crime had been planned by Serbia.'[37] He himself condemned the assassination 'most energetically,' saying it was 'a crime no one could approve of', that the murder was 'hateful' to him, as it was to 'both Serbs and Serbia'.[38] Jovanović discovered that the arguments for the accusations came chiefly from the reports sent by the Austro-Hungarian chargé d'affaires in Belgrade. He therefore warned Pašić that the 'unfortunate Mr Stork was simply doomed to report impressionistically'.[39]

When, on 2 July, the bodies of the assassinated Archduke and his wife were brought back to Vienna, Jovanović ordered that the flag on the Serbian legation be flown at half-mast. He also counselled his government: 'Please make sure that there are no demonstrations in our country and that Belgrade newspapers write as moderately as possible.'[40] However, the circumstances in which he found himself are particularly illustrated in the report sent after an incident concerning the flag. On 3 July he reported:

Protests about that occurred yesterday evening. First of all the porter came along, then the rent collector, then the landlord's assistant, and then the landlord himself to take down the flag. Explanations did not avail, and I had to seek help from the police, who asked for the flag to be taken down in order to prevent a breach of the peace. The flag remained, and last night there was noise and shouting around the Legation, which is here called a demonstration.... It was not until two o'clock in the morning that the demonstrators dispersed. Today's newspapers, especially the popular, clerical ones, are carrying articles about the incident, calling it 'provocation on the part of the Serbian envoy', and describing what happened in any manner they wished.[41]

The news of the death of the Archduke and his wife naturally caused great uproar and anxiety in Vienna, as does such news everywhere. However, it provoked far less grief, and even considerable relief, in all strata of the Monarchy's capital except in some naval and, in particular, extreme clerical circles. That could be seen on the streets soon after the news became known. The author Stefan Zweig later recalled: 'People were chattering and laughing, and late in the evening music was playing again in the restaurants and cafés.'⁴² Professor Josef Redlich noted in his diary for 29 June: 'There is no sense of grief in the town. Music has been playing everywhere on both days in the Prater and here in Grinzig!'⁴³ In truth Franz Ferdinand had not been popular, and in leading circles there were few who had not been hostile to him or even hated him.⁴⁴

On 6 July Jovanović accurately reported to his superiors that the Archduke's death had given the people 'a sense of liberation from some kind of pressure and, among a small minority of intellectuals, a sense of relief that something had happened which had been vaguely expected.'⁴⁵ In Budapest, the Monarchy's second capital, there was even joy that a great opponent of Hungarian autonomy and of the great influence of the Hungarian aristocracy on state policy had departed the world. At the court in particular there were no mourners since its members, headed by the Emperor himself, were among Franz Ferdinand's most bitter opponents. The latter had become a counter-ruler to the Emperor, creating some kind of parallel government in opposition to the official government and his own court alongside the Imperial court, and differing fiercely at times with Franz Joseph and his entourage. Thus it was not surprising that the old Emperor greeted the news of his death by saying: 'The Almighty has finally brought order.'⁴⁶ The Bavarian envoy, a man well versed in court matters, felt the need to inform his King that the old Emperor had heard the news of the death of his unwanted co-ruler 'without emotion', and then 'gone about his usual work in the afternoon' and 'slept soundly the whole night'.⁴⁷ In the vocabulary of a courtier this all signified that Franz Joseph had not worried overmuch. The Archduke's funeral, organised by the court, prompted a reporter in *The Times* to wonder 'why they had buried him like a dog'.⁴⁸ The Bavarian envoy reported that the funeral procession 'was short, without a big military escort, without grandeur, without funeral music', and that 'the ceremony lasted for less than a quarter of an hour.'⁴⁹ His next report noted that there was much dissatisfaction with the funeral; the officer corps considered it to have been a serious omission that the 'customary military honours were not paid in Vienna,' and the aristocracy were grumbling because ceremonies befitting the murdered man's high rank had been missing, while the people were sorry they had been deprived of the expected pomp.⁵⁰ From 30 June, anti-Serb demonstrations followed each other on the streets of the capital, while the information media and centres in Vienna and Budapest, which in any case were totally in the hands of the authorities, stepped up their attacks not only on Serbia but on Serbs in general.

Austrian sources later described the circumstances at that time:

> Some kind of frivolous, chauvinistic spirit was evident in all circles of the Viennese population. The *Prinz Eugen* song, which was cheered thunderously, was to be heard everywhere, and strong guards were needed to protect the Serbian Legation from demonstrators.... The press ... daily poured oil onto the flames.[51]

In the summer of 1914 the Austrian people were inundated with chauvinistic propaganda, in which all political parties, including the Labour Party, took part. For years they had been imbibing the poison of German imperialist propaganda, and it was now erupting from them as from a diseased body. An essential part of the intelligentsia, under the influence of governmental actions or the delirium of the masses, reacted with frenzy. Doctors and musicians, economists and philosophers were competing to demonstrate their incapacity for independent thought with their newspaper articles and statements. A particularly terrible wasteland was becoming evident in the sphere of literature. Esteemed authors ... were writing poetry and feuilletons glorifying acts of banditry and the moves of the Central Powers. It is not necessary to describe what writers of little or no reputation did callously and unwittingly.[52]

The dimensions all this assumed could perhaps be shown in a comment, made in a letter dated 26 July on the presentation of the ultimatum to Serbia, even by such an independent spirit as Sigmund Freud: 'Perhaps for the first time in thirty years I feel an Austrian, and would like to try once again with this Empire, for which there is so little hope. The mood is excellent everywhere. A valiant move has had a liberating effect.'[53] Horrified by what was happening around him, Stefan Zweig wrote: 'One sometimes had the impression that one was listening to the raging of a horde of lunatics.'[54]

The Serbian envoy recounted on 6 July:

> The demonstrations and protests that took place in Vienna in front of the Royal Legation and elsewhere two days after the assassination in Sarajevo are not ... a spontaneous expression of the impact made here by the death of the Austro-Hungarian Heir Apparent and his wife.... [They] were gradually prepared by campaigns waged from the offices of clerical newspapers and various associations of a clerical nature.[55]

Jovanović realised from which direction the storm was actually coming. On the evening of 28 June, Professor Redlich had drafted for himself an opinion of the Archduke: 'God himself is probably less clerical in convictions than those creatures at the court of Franz Ferdinand,' adding a remark about Sophie Hohenberg's bigotry.[56] In his diary of those days Baron Ludwig von Pastor, author of a famous multi-volume history of the Papacy, and a protégé of the Archduke, wrote veritable laments on 5 July: 'In Franz Ferdinand Catholics had powerful support and a firm stronghold. He was our pride and our hope.'[57] Those circles were also the most aggressive. Jovanović realised that 'this made it evident [...] that the assassination had been directed against the heir to the throne, that is to the Crown itself.'[58] 'The demonstrators are being incited', he added, 'by the *Reichspost* newspaper and its leading writers Friedrich Funder, Hermenegled Wagner and Leopold Mandl',[59] the most ardent proponents of a 'drive to the Balkans'.[60] However, were not extreme clerics only the most visible leaders? The Serbian envoy noted: 'The same thought predominated among all other circles too.'[61] A member of the Viennese elite, Count Lutzow, stated in his memoirs that the press 'had been given the go-ahead by the government to write in a patriotic sense' and 'pouring oil on the flames' had been encouraged even 'from the highest levels'.[62]

However, while clerics of the most extreme views were acting publicly, the strings were in fact being pulled behind the scenes by inter-linked radical groups, the kernel of which was made up of senior figures in the church the army and the bureaucracy in the Foreign Ministry. Using slogans of hatred towards Serbia and adopting a discourse of extreme warmongering, highly reactionary and militant forces were mobilising, and gradually came to occupy a decisive position in the state. But what was happening on the streets of Vienna was child's play compared with developments in the southern provinces of the Monarchy where, with hatred towards Serbia and threats to all South Slav compatriots as their watchword, with pogroms and intimations of genocide, extreme clerical elements, using the urban under-class as their tool, gathered extreme rightist forces and burst on to the public scene. However, in the background representatives of the civil and, particularly, military authorities were inciting, protecting and even organising them.

Immediately after the Archduke's assassination the focus of events was briefly transferred from Sarajevo to Zagreb. On 28 June 1914 the man who had long been the leader of the so-called 'war faction', the chief of the general staff General Conrad, having spent time with Franz Ferdinand at military manoeuvres in Bosnia, stopped for a short time on his way from Sarajevo at the railway station in Zagreb, and was met there by Baron Adolf von Remen, commander of the 13th Corps, who informed him of the Archduke's assassination.[63] Von Remen had been made commandant in Zagreb, but, sources recount, it was intended that his role should not be confined to the military sphere only. He had been selected back in the autumn of 1912, following the policy adopted at the very top of the Monarchy that it was essential 'for a German general to take over command of the corps and commissariat in Zagreb'; everything necessary had then been done to give von Remen, a German Austrian with origins in the Westphalian aristocracy, the status of citizen of the Croatian *banovina*. In the spring of 1913 Conrad proposed to the Emperor that 'given the vital and immediate need for circumstances to be improved in Croatia, this task should be entrusted not to the *ban* but to a general [Remen] in the capacity of royal commissar.'[64] The Serbian Foreign Ministry had been informed in the spring of 1914 that von Remen had 'links with followers of Ivan Frank' and that he was 'constantly sending Vienna denunciatory reports on the Coalition'.[65] Little is known of the talks at Zagreb railway station on 28 June; it is not known what orders the General Conrad gave to von Remen arising from the assassination in Sarajevo. However, it seems, certain that he did not instruct him to preserve public order and peace, which would have seemed most natural in the circumstances.

A letter written by Conrad that same evening shows he was already pondering the 'profound political significance' of the assassination, which, he claimed, had 'a markedly Serb nationalist nature', and that he regretted there had been no 'resolute action' in the tense circumstances surrounding the Annexation Crisis in March 1909—in other words, that there had been no armed attack on Serbia. It also follows from this letter that Conrad was wondering how to execute a 'well-prepared large-scale action'[66] on the basis of the assassination. In Vienna the next day Conrad informed Berchtold of his programme in no uncertain terms: 'war, war, war'.[67] Whatever was discussed at the railway station, in the early evening of 28 June, just a few hours after Conrad's departure, Zagreb became the scene of anti-Serb demonstrations, which the police and military authorities did nothing to prevent.

Demonstrators chanted slogans in praise of Franz Ferdinand, but they also called out 'Down with Serbia', 'Down with Yugoslavia', 'Hang the traitors' and 'Down with Serb menials'.[68] Headed by Ivan Frank's supporters, anti-social elements and alienated youth made up the greater part of the demonstrators. There were probably also agents of the state's secret services giving direction to the demonstrations. Ivan Frank himself spoke in front of the monument to Jelacić, saying that he simply considered all Serbs responsible for Franz Ferdinand's death, adding that Serbs were 'our alleged brothers who insolently claim to be no different from us'. The demonstrators were even more violent on 29 June and assumed the character of a pogrom. Serb institutions, shops and dwellings were demolished, and individual Serbs were and insulted physically attacked. The pro-Ivan Frank newspaper *Hrvatska* wrote: 'We are infested with all those Serb and Slavo-Serb creatures.... As of today let it be our goal ... to deal with them once and for all and destroy them.' *Dom*, Stjepan Radić's newspaper, was no less emphatic than Ivan Frank's followers.

Pro-Frank representatives reproduced the atmosphere still prevailing in the streets of Zagreb at the *Sabor* (Assembly) session held on 30 June, which was supposed to start with a ceremony in memory of the Archduke. They created a disturbance which prevented the Speaker, Bogdan Medaković, from reading his short memorial address, insulted representatives of the majority Croat-Serb Coalition, and accused them, Serbs and Croats alike, of being 'killers with blood on their hands'. 'Bring Franz Ferdinand back to us,' they clamoured—and 'vengeance meted on the Serb nation in Croatia.' Ivan Frank called Svetozar Pribićević, a Serb leader, a 'traitor and killer' and pointed his finger menacingly at Hinko Hinković, a Croat, claiming that he had personally organised the assassination from Belgrade. All Croats who considered themselves brothers with Serbs were those days being called Serb lackeys and thieves by Frank's followers and their demonstrators. The *Hrvatski Dnevnik* newspaper urged that Svetozar Pribićević, as well as the Croats Mate

Drinković and Milan Marjanović, should all be sent to the gallows. The authorities regarded all this with equanimity and only arrested the Socialist Vladimir Bornemis for criticising in a party paper the state's passive attitude and the suspicious role of the police during the demonstrations.

In Sarajevo too, demonstrations erupted as early as 28 June, but somewhat later than in Zagreb.[69] Around 9 p.m. a group of about 200 people first shouted anti-Serb slogans and then demolished the Hotel Evropa, the largest hotel in Sarajevo, which was owned by Gligorije Jeftanović, a Serb. The police then intervened and quickly restored order. But during the night it was agreed to demonstrate again the next day. Behind those agreements were representatives of the city police and the provincial government, and a significant role was probably played by the principal Catholic bishop of Bosnia, Josip Štadler, and his assistant Ivan Šarić. Posters appeared overnight, issued by the municipal authorities, proclaiming, 'There are subversive elements in this land.' The key message was: 'I call on the people to eradicate such elements.... It shall be the people's sacred duty to purge that shame.' Demonstrations of a far more aggressive nature than those of the evening before started at around 8 a.m. and quickly developed into a pogrom. A Serb school was the first to be demolished, and that was followed by a series of attacks on various Serb institutions, shops and private dwellings. As the mob destroyed and pillaged, its members protected themselves by singing the state anthem, raising pictures of the Emperor and calling the name of Franz Ferdinand. Catholic clerics evidently goaded on the demonstrators, who were Muslims and Catholics, mainly slum-dwellers. The riots were inflamed by rumours in the official and clerical press, among other things, of hidden Serb bombs, haranguing by Serb leaders, hostile Serb pamphlets, and even a Serb role in Franz Ferdinand's murder. Foreign consular representatives in Sarajevo witnessed these happenings with horror. The Italian consul stated that nefarious dealings were taking place 'financed by the government'. The German consul, whom an East German historian rightly described as 'anything but a friend of Serbs', reported on 29 June that Sarajevo was living through its own 'Saint Bartholomew's night', with the 'bribed dregs of society' running wild, and a 'mob of Croat, Muslim [actually Gypsy] boys who had been given a free hand' to commit 'vandalism' under 'military and police protection', adding that this was all a sign that 'Vienna had decided on the last resort'.[70]

Demonstrations soon began in other towns in Bosnia and Herzegovina, including Doboj, Maglaj, Livno, Travnik, Zenica, Mostar, Konjic, Tuzla, Brčko, Vareš, Bugojno, Visoko, Čapljina and Šamac.[71] A Serb church was desecrated, and some Serb houses were burnt down in Metković. In the evening of 29 June the governor, General Oskar Potiorek, declared a state of siege, first in Sarajevo and then throughout the province. However, this did not make matters easier since the forces of law and order behaved in such a way that, while they were able to control irregular circumstances, there was still room for anti–Serb demonstrations. The mob was indeed free to do whatever it liked to Serb property, and there were attacks on individuals. Serb economic activity was boycotted, both overtly and tacitly.

In Croatia outside Zagreb, large-scale anti-Serb demonstrations took place in Djakovo, Petrinja and Slavonski Brod, where graves and churches were desecrated.[72] Attempts to organise demonstrations in Dalmatia failed because not enough people responded; in Sibenik a number of Serb shops were pillaged, and in Split and Dubrovnik small groups people, almost certainly bribed, went around making a noise. In an assessment of the demonstrations in the coastal regions, the *Sloboda* newspaper stated on 13 July that they had been a 'terrible disgrace' to the authorities. There were no demonstrations in the Slovene region, but on 1 July Ivan Šušteršić, president of the Slovene People's Party and leader of the extreme clericals, spoke out sharply against Serbia and accused it of responsibility for the assassination. On 5 July he gave an address in Ljubljana in which he declared his devotion to the Monarchy and the Habsburgs and called for war against Serbia, threatening that the 'heavy fist of the Slovene soldier ... would shatter the skull of that Serb in whom voracious megalomania lived.'

Two facts stand out clearly: first, the demonstrations were supported, organised and led by extremely weak forces on the far right, and second, other political forces not only refrained from participating in them but also condemned the demonstrations, often specifically expressing brotherhood with Serbs.[73] In their newspaper *Hrvat* the followers of Ante Starčević stated that they had truly been 'immunised against the so-called Belgrade influence', but that they would not 'for anyone's sake' act as 'executioner of one and a half million Orthodox citizens in Croat lands'. The coalition newspaper *Hrvatski Pokret* wrote: 'Croats should quash pro-Frank savagery in the name of Croat culture and humanity.' Muslim leaders in Bosnia and Herzegovina did not take part in extreme anti-Serb activity, and on 2 July the *Jenji Mishab* newspaper warned of 'ill-advised and non-Islamic behaviour by ruffians', in whose ranks 'a good percentage of Muslims had regrettably been seen.' In Herzegovina Bishop Fra Alojzije Mišić called on believers to refrain from taking part in the demonstrations, which also met with no support in Dalmatia. In Ljubljana Bishop Antun Jeglić stated that Šušteršić, who was close to him politically, spoke against Serbs 'very severely but well', but condemned the pogroms in Bosnia; two other clerical leaders in the Slovene region, Janez Krek and Anton Korošec, did not join in any way in the anti-Serb activity of their leader and even less in his calls for war. The Liberal mouthpiece *Slovenski Narod* attacked Šušteršić. It was evident that the Monarchy's leadership could only find support for their extreme anti-Serb stand among known reactionaries, whose strength came from the support they received from the state authorities themselves.

During those last days of June and the first days of July 1914 everything indicated that in the depths of political life some kind of solidarity, albeit still undeveloped, existed among the South Slav population regardless of all historical splits, differences in political conceptions, and contemporary circumstances.[74] At that time Starčević's Party of the Right conspicuously stopped harrying Serbs and Serbia, and one of its leaders, Dragutin pl. Hrvoj, while critical of the 'serbomania' that had grown up among the Croat intelligentsia since the Balkan wars, stated in the *Sabor* that 'without any kind of fear of the denunciations that were flying daily to Vienna and Budapest', he personally 'respected the Serb nation' and admired 'its progress over the last century'. Among a narrow circle of acquaintances Janez Krek censured Šušteršić's public activity, and the Liberal leader Ivan Ribar expressed his concern over the fate of Serbia if it were attacked by Austria-Hungary because of the assassination in Sarajevo. The Liberal *Dan*, despite covering itself with expressions of loyalty to the Habsburg state, emphasised that it was not 'thirsty for blood' and had 'always preached the brotherhood and unity of

Yugoslavs'. At that time the clericalist *Straža*, Anton Korošec's mouthpiece in Maribor, wrote of the need to resolve the Yugoslav issue—within the framework of the Monarchy. The youth movement was also evidently in favour of Yugoslav nationhood; a group of Yugoslav students met in Prague at the beginning of July, under the chairmanship of Fran Marinić, a Slovene, and made a proclamation protesting against anti-Serb demonstrations and defiantly proclaiming the ideas of brotherhood and unity.

The social-democratic parties in the Monarchy's southern Slav lands were those that had most resolutely opposed the dissemination of anti-Serb hatred and condemned the demonstrations calling for pogroms.[75] In spite of deploring assassination as a way of conducting a struggle, the Social-Democratic Party of Bosnia and Herzegovina speaking of an act of 'mad self-defence', they saw the causes of that and other plots in the Monarchy as mainly related to the subjugated position of a large number of nationalities in the Habsburg state. The Croat Social-Democratic mouthpiece *Slobodna Riječ* reacted, for example, with articles under the headings 'Against Police Tyranny' and 'Criminal Dealings', while the Slovene *Zarja* reacted with articles headlined '*Furor patrioticus*' and 'Dimensions in Bosnia and Herzegovina'. *Zarja* wrote: 'It is a crime to load the responsibility for an assassination onto an entire nation. The causes are to be found solely in the economic and political circumstances there (i.e. in Bosnia and Herzegovina).... Serbs, Croats and Mohammedans, who are not feudalists, are now able to feel the weight of life under the Monarchy.' All Social-Democratic newspapers agreed that they were witnessing warmongering and savagery by rightists. The Social-Democratic Party of Croatia and Slavonia held an assembly at the beginning of July where it denounced terror and condemned cooperation between the followers of Ivan Frank and the police. It organised citizens' and workers' gatherings in opposition to the 'hue and cry' of 'mobilised riff-raff', and the Party's main committee even threatened a general strike for 17 July. On 3 July the Slovenian leadership decided publicly to censure clerical, i.e. Šušteršić's, attacks on Serbs and Serbia and announced that the Slovene nation was the 'brother of the subjugated nation of the Sarajevo assassins'.

However, anyone capable of seeing the situation as a whole was able to conclude quite the opposite to what was being disseminated by official representatives of the Monarchy, supported by Germany. First, the assassination must, as a conspiracy, have had a narrow circle of organisers and fomenters, and the idea of an entire state or an entire nation being responsible was highly improbable. Secondly, Serbia was a very small and weak country compared with Austria-Hungary, and, given the constant threats from its northern neighbour, it was difficult to believe that such a dangerous undertaking would originate at a high level in the state. Thirdly, Serbia had just emerged from the two Balkan Wars of 1912 and 1913 that exhausted it economically—and from which, and this could not be ignored, it had made considerable territorial gains. It was therefore clear that it needed a pause of several years to gather its strength and consolidate its newly-acquired territories.

The Austro-Hungarian and German propaganda claims were not credible to all members of the broader leading circles in the Reich and the Monarchy, all the more so as some were against starting a war of which the outcome was highly uncertain.[76] One of those people, the German ambassador in London, Prince Lichnowsky, wrote to the Chancellor, Bethmann-Hollweg, in mid-July 1914 that he was opposed to Germany supporting Austria-Hungary's 'gendarme policy', since its authorities had already 'allowed the Heir Apparent to pass along an entire avenue of bomb-throwers.' In May 1915 the German Foreign Ministry received an unsigned copy of a letter, apparently from a prominent German source, in which the following words appeared: 'Pašić's government has absolutely nothing to do with the fact that Austrian subjects killed the Austrian heir apparent as a result of the incompetence of the Austrian police.' But in July 1914 the Bavarian envoy in Vienna wrote that the assassination was 'undoubtedly the result of several years of Belgrade inciting Serbs in the Monarchy', and that Franz Ferdinand 'was killed because he presented an obstacle to the realisation of the Greater-Serb ideal and dominant Russian influence in the Balkans.' Still, he warned: 'Under the Obrenović dynasty, the Serbs did not hate [the Monarchy]. That hatred was sown by autonomous (Hungarian) landowners, nurtured by Austrian industry's exploitation, and allowed to grow by the upstart Ballhausplatz policy.'[77] In Vienna Count Lutzow tried resolutely to act against the assassination being used as a means of starting a war.

Rumours that the true organisers of the plot were to be found in the leading circles of Vienna, Budapest and Berlin were based on a number of factors: the unconvincing nature of the assumption of Serbia's responsibility; persistent attempts to provoke an armed conflict because of the assassination; the fact that a large group of evidently unskilled conspirators and their primitively organised plot had escaped the notice of the Austro-Hungarian police and intelligence service; the presence of many powerful opponents of Franz Ferdinand in both Vienna and Budapest; the fear in Berlin that the Archduke would not be a sufficiently loyal ally once he became Emperor, and finally the fear that the authorities in Vienna had allowed him to go to Bosnia and Sarajevo without adequate protection despite many warnings that, given the mood of the population, an attempt on his life might be made there. On the days following the assassination some of these rumours were to be heard in Vienna, and as early as 30 June the German ambassador went as far as to say in a message to Berlin that 'many are of the opinion that the fomenters of the Archduke's assassination were among those singled out for military command.'[78]

Conspirators

A number of known concrete facts refute claims that either the Serbian government or Serbian constitutional elements were responsible for the assassination, as does a study of Serbia's policy and general circumstances at that time. However, a quite high-ranking figure does seem to have been involved, namely Lieutenant-Colonel Dragutin Dimitrijević Apis, then head of the General Staff intelligence department, for whom the compromised Major Tankosić and Ciganović worked.[79] Only one question seems to stand out: in what capacity did Dimitrijević play a role and, especially, how was he involved? As for the circumstances, Serbia had emerged from making gains in the two Balkan wars more or less divided on the political scene at home. On one side was the Radical Party government and on the other was the secret 'Unification or Death' organisation known as the 'Black Hand'. The latter consisted of relatively young plotters who had been involved in the assassination of King Alexander Obrenović and his wife in 1903,[80] but a group of officers had the main say, the leading figure being Lieutenant-Colonel Dimitrijević.

In the domestic crisis that had reached its peak in the spring of 1914, the Black Hand made up the core of the military opposition in the so-called 'conflict of civilian and military authorities'.[81] Hiding behind the military leadership and cooperating with the opposition, the plotters had persuaded, induced or forced old King Peter to dismiss Pašić's government although it had a majority in the National Assembly. Only with Russian intervention and pressure, and, apparently, injections of French capital had the crisis been resolved in Pašić's favour, which also meant the preservation of the constitutional order. King Peter had been compelled to withdraw, allegedly because of illness, and the executive role was ceded to the heir apparent Alexander Karadjordjević, who became Regent and head of state. To prove his Party's strength and acquire new democratic legitimacy for the civilian authorities, Nikola Pašić called extraordinary Assembly elections, but as this situation was developing, constitutional authorities lost control of the Black Hand plotters, and from that time there were signs of dual authority in Serbia, especially in its policy towards Austria-Hungary.

Dimitrijević and Black Hand members held strong positions in the Narodna Odbrana nationalistic organisation, through which they tried to spread a net of agents in Bosnia and Herzegovina. In this they were helped by the dissatisfaction of the Serb section of the population with the Austro-Hungarian administration, and by the Serb national movement and the growth of Yugoslav sentiments after the Balkan wars. This was quite contrary to government policy, which aimed to avoid a further aggravation of relations with the Monarchy. The government therefore directed its own agencies to continue blocking covert activities in Bosnia and Herzegovina;[82] the Ministry of Internal Affairs, headed by Stojan Protić, gave strict orders to this end. And it was in those first days of June, just after the three would-be assassins had crossed the border, that a sharp conflict over the smuggling of bombs into Bosnia occurred between the prefect and police of the Šabac and Loznica district and the frontier army commander, Major Ljubomir Vulović. The affair came to the notice of the Serbian government and the supreme army command, and Lieutenant Colonel Dimitrijević was required to write a special report explaining what had happened.[83] Stojan Protić then instructed district prefects that 'all similar cases must be prevented on the orders of the Prime Minister'.[84]

That affair was linked to the figure of Rade Malobabić, who was described by Dimitrijević in his report as a 'man to be trusted' and considered 'by some of our best men in Zagreb' as 'a good and upright Serb'. Later too, in April 1917, Dimitrijević identified Malobabić as the man through whom he had worked over Franz Ferdinand's assassination.[85] However, the Serbian police considered Rade Malobabić as not only 'our informant on Austria-Hungary' but also an 'Austro-Hungarian informant on Serbia'.[86] In June 1914 he was also protected by Major Vulović, who acted as if there were no civilian authorities in his command area and took no heed of Protić's orders.[87] There was also conflict between Dimitrijević and Narodna Odbrana members who did not belong to his Black Hand organisation.[88]

In any case the government, despite all its endeavours, was constantly receiving reports that on the frontier 'finance guards [...] were transporting weapons, ammunition and other explosives from Serbia into Bosnia', and that two 'high school pupils' had arrived in Bosnia with six bombs and four revolvers.[89] That almost certainly referred to Gavrilo Princip and Trifko Grabež. The government stepped up its efforts to prevent such occurrences and on 15 June Pašić urged that the Minister of Military Affairs should 'prevent all such activity as it represents a great danger to us'. On 24 June the Ministry of Foreign Affairs, which was headed by Pašić himself, again demanded that the Ministry of Military Affairs should act on the government's orders, and an investigation was started into the activities of frontier officials and Lieutenant Colonel Dimitrijević.[90] It was difficult to get the upper hand against the determined Dimitrijević, who, apart from being leader of the Black Hand, had also become head of Military Intelligence. One of the reasons for this was that he and his men had shown great gallantry at the time of preparations for war against Turkey and during the two Balkan wars. That was how it was possible for the political establishment to be unaware of plans for the assassination of the Archduke while Dimitrijević was aware and may even have participated in some way.

Any possible involvement of Lieutenant Colonel Dimitrijević in the assassination—his subordinates Tankosić and Ciganović were certainly involved—was limited to the provision of weapons and transporting the assassins clandestinely over the frontier. There seems no reason to attribute to him its actual conception and preparation, which were genuinely the result of the conspirators' own initiative. Facts tell us that the conspirators were national revolutionaries and idealists, and that they were also under the influence of anarchist ideas.[91] There is no reason to doubt the truth of Princip and Čabrinović's claim in the investigation that they had first wanted to buy the weapons themselves, but that they did not have enough money and turned instead, for that reason alone, to Ciganović, through whom they also came into contact with Tankosić. From this point the thread is lost, and it can only be assumed that Tankosić communicated with Dimitrijević on the matter. It is not known whether any other Black Hand members knew of the conspiracy, and what is known of the conduct of Major Vulović does not justify including him in the circle of conspirators—possibly he was only carrying out the order to transport Gavrilo Princip and his associates over the Drina, not knowing why they were travelling into Bosnia.[92] It is clear that Dimitrijević's eventual involvement can be reduced to his participation as a member of Black Hand, but not as head of the Military Intelligence Service. As far as we know today, neither the General Staff nor the government knew of this conspiracy. Dimitrijević was undisciplined and a patriot, of a specific kind, and although he used his position as head of the Intelligence Department, he did not act in the capacity of that position. The leadership of Narodna Odbrana also did not participate in the conspiracy, and there are indications that, having been informed of the plot by Dimitrijević shortly before the assassination, they rejected the plan and demanded that it be halted. They tried to force Dimitrijević to do just that,[93] and there are indications that Dimitrijević finally wanted to halt the assassination, but that Princip and the others had not wanted to do so, although it seems that Danilo Ilić was of two minds. But Dimitrijević was not the man behind the conspiracy, although the conspirators could have used him to carry out their plan.

The origins of the declaration of war

When speaking of the decision of the Austro-Hungarian and German leaderships to make a highly dangerous move, it is clear that there were several reasons for this, and these reasons were broader and deeper than the assassination in Sarajevo. They had been accumulating over several years, and had their origins in the particular needs, problems and interests of the two empires, and fundamentally had nothing to do with Serbia.[94]

The Austro-Hungarian Monarchy entered the twentieth century under the burden of a crisis that had arisen from a number of causes. However, they boiled down to the still powerful presence of feudal remnants, especially in social structure, property ownership and ideology, which left an impression on social and political life as a whole and restricted economic development.[95] The Habsburg Empire was only ostensibly a supranational state; it was actually headed by a traditional, hereditary landowning aristocracy. The reorganisation of the Monarchy in 1867 into a complex state comprising two equal parts, Austria and Hungary, revealed that it could not, despite the tenacity of its conservatism, be immune from the general trends of the time, and that each state had been the tool of the leading strata of society that had taken upon themselves the role of representatives of the interests of the entire nation. Here it was a case of two privileged nations: German Austria and Hungary. That is to say that the true joint holders of state authority and social power in the Monarchy were the Austrian and Hungarian aristocracies. The middle class had a certain degree of power in the economy and big business, which was weak by comparison with more developed countries, and represented a part, albeit an inferior one, of the socio-political elite. All the other nationalities in the state were without rights.

The Austrian and Hungarian aristocracies saw themselves as rivals. Driven increasingly by their narrow national interests, they fought, sometimes fiercely. The dualist system enabled the Hungarian aristocracy constantly to stress their own interests and to make the passing of decisions, for the good of the Monarchy as a whole, conditional on these interests being honoured. It also allowed them to threaten Hungarian independence. Thus they virtually had the right of veto and gained a superior position. The Austrian aristocracy could not resolve anything without their consent, but they identified with the Monarchy as a whole and saw themselves as its chief defenders, and felt acute dissatisfaction at the constant emphasis on the separate nature of the Hungarian part of the state.

However, both the Austrian and the Hungarian sections of the elite were united in their concern over the strengthening national movements among the other nationalities of the Habsburg state, as well as the organisation of 'lower' social strata, especially the rallying by Social-Democratic elements. The internal political circumstances in the Monarchy at the beginning of the twentieth century were described accurately in a letter written by Franz Ferdinand himself: 'Conflicts are becoming more and more bitter in the Monarchy. Separatist aspirations are prevailing in Hungary [...] in a terrifying manner. And among the lower classes of the population, particularly the workers, destructive socialist ideas are gaining ground.'[96]

Everything was further complicated by the disarray of Austria-Hungary's foreign policy. Not only was Russia, its rival in the Balkans for over a century, a heavy burden, but the neighbouring German Reich, in spire of being its ally since 1879, was trying to make the Monarchy its satellite. Furthermore Italy, which had been an ally since 1883, was aspiring to annex parts of the Habsburg Empire inhabited by Italians, even including much of the eastern Adriatic coast beyond Italian ethnic borders. Surrounded in this way by Russia, Germany and Italy, the Monarchy was geopolitically trapped, and found itself weakened and unable to compete from a position of strength with other powers and assert its prestige.[97] Despite their mutual rivalry, the Austrian and Hungarian aristocracies had a common interest in self-preservation and hence in saving the Monarchy. Given their internal differences and conflicts, the Austro-Hungarian elite sought their salvation in foreign policy moves aimed at the Empire extending both its sovereignty and its spheres of interest. It would thus achieve two goals: externally it would act independently, show its strength and improve its prestige in the face of all other powers, including Germany, and internally it would create conditions to increase its authority in the face of national and social opponents within the country, with a firm hand if necessary. In view of the international situation the Monarchy's elite saw that the only real possibility for deploying such a policy was in the Balkans, where a number of small and underdeveloped states had emerged in the nineteenth century. For geographical reasons, the first object of this policy was its small neighbour Serbia.[98]

Alongside all that, there was a specific internal policy element that stemmed from the rivalry between the Austrian and Hungarian aristocracies. Despite their being in agreement over the essence of the desired foreign policy, some groups within the Austrian aristocracy also felt a vested interest in increasing the numbers of the Slav population and strengthening Slavs politically within the Empire by annexing new Slav-inhabited Balkan areas, thus creating rivals to the Hungarians. This would undermine the strength of the Hungarian aristocracy as well as the Monarchy's dualist organisation, and lead to a new trialist political system, in which Austria would gain total domination.[99]

The realisation of such a Balkan policy, which concealed a separate hidden vested interest for Austria, immediately met significant external and internal obstacles. One obstacle already existed on the Sava and the Danube. The interpretation of Austro-Hungarian foreign policy given by Count Hoyos in his later writings is revealing:

The tensions in our relations with Serbia started with the murder of Alexander Obrenović and the coming to power of Peter Karadjordjević.... By opting for personal links with the Obrenović dynasty, Austria-Hungary had for many years conducted its relations with Serbia in a way that was contrary to the wishes of the Serbian people. That policy became impossible the moment the throne in Belgrade was occupied by a monarch who was used to being popular both among the people and particularly with the army. As we had given up the idea of intervening against the perpetrators of regicide, only one other policy was open to us that was in accord with our interests.... That was to bind the kingdom along the Sava, i.e. Serbia, to us by economic means in such a way that it would have no interest in working against us politically.... This policy failed because of resistance from Serbian politicians, who would not refrain from their independent plans, and in their wish to be able to conduct a free policy were motivated solely by the desire to free their country from economic dependence on Austria-Hungary.... A radical solution—the annexation of Serbia—was also possible. But such a move did not conform to the intentions of the government in Vienna, and it was not certain whether Russia would allow us to destroy Serbia completely.... To this was added the Hungarian government's resistance to the acquisition of additional Slav-inhabited territories. That was because Serbia could not be permanently annexed to the Monarchy without either a federalist or at least a trialist system.... From the annexation crisis the Greater Serb movement had become transformed into a European issue and thus closely connected with the policy of the Great Powers.... An untenable situation had arisen on our southern borders after the Balkan war. Serbia had emerged from the war with unexpectedly large gains; it had doubled its territory and become a strong military power.... Both in Serbia and in the regions of Austria-Hungary inhabited by South Slavs the conviction became entrenched that the downfall of Austria-Hungary was at hand and that Yugoslavia could only be created with action from Belgrade and the help of the Serbian army.[100]

Given such a perception of the situation, it evidently followed that a solution lay in finding a suitable pretext for war.

Although it had been under Austria-Hungary's hegemony for around two decades, Serbia had, in 1903, become fully independent quickly, strongly and resolutely. In doing so it had sought political support from Russia, and financial support (plus armaments) from France. It was thus emerging as a tough obstacle in the way of Austro-Hungarian plans in the Balkans. In order to remove that obstacle immediately, and given the failure of an attempt to subjugate Serbia with a tariff war, the clear outlines of a plan for the destruction of Serbia through the division of its territories among neighbouring states was created in Vienna—contrary to the claims of Count Hoyos—as early as 1907, even if it meant going to war. The plan, which was fully formed in the spring of 1908, was to divide Serbia's territories mainly amongst Austria-Hungary and Bulgaria, and perhaps Romania too (after its creation in 1913 Albania was also to come into the picture).[101] That was how Austria-Hungary became more and more involved in conflict with Serbia as its goals became increasingly aggressive and therefore dangerous. Over Serbia the Monarchy was clashing sharply with Russia and even with France (with which it could not have the best of relations since the Monarchy was a loyal ally of Germany). In such a situation Vienna had to depend increasingly on Berlin; hence the Monarchy would become a means for carrying out the Reich's policy in southeastern Europe, and also entangled the Monarchy in Germany's growing antagonism with all three Entente Powers over other European and world issues.

Since any plan involving Serbia ultimately implied a trialist state organisation, the realisation of the intended Balkan policy also became complex for internal policy reasons. Although the Hungarian leadership was resolutely in favour of the removal of Serbia as an obstacle in the Balkans, it did not wish to allow its position to be thereby undermined in the Monarchy. Hence Vienna's intentions to go to war with its southern neighbour in 1908–9, 1912, 1913 and finally at the beginning of July 1914 were viewed by Budapest with great mistrust. Only after the Second Balkan War did the Hungarian government conceive its own plan for solving the Serbian problem: to reduce Serbia in such a way that the greater part of the territory would be taken by its neighbours, while the remainder would only appear to be independent since it would be deprived of the economic conditions for an independent existence and placed under the hegemony or even the protection of Austria-Hungary. Essentially, however, the two centres of the Monarchy agreed completely that independent Serbia should be destroyed. That was sufficient reason for the Hungarian leadership to agree quickly in July 1914 on armed action against Serbia.[102]

A programme laid down in 1908 provided for the first two steps in the Monarchy's Balkan policy: the annexation of Bosnia and Herzegovina, and the destruction of Serbia. The first was quickly achieved, but the second proved an insoluble problem. In the course of 1912 and 1913 Serbia became stronger by expanding its territories; it reinforced its political influence, achieved military prestige and entered an alliance with Romania and Greece. All the efforts of Austria-Hungary to prevent the strengthening of its small neighbour were in vain. And then a new and highly important factor emerged: thanks to its successes, and despite the Monarchy's attempts to prevent them, Serbia became the moral and political stronghold not only for Serb independence aspirations in the Habsburg state, but also for the essentially autonomous and autochthonous Yugoslav movement. It thus became a potential threat to the integrity of its large neighbour.[103]

Since the victories of four small Balkan states over Turkey in the autumn of 1912 had caused nationalist movements, particularly the Yugoslav movement, to flourish under both Austrian and Hungarian rule, the leading circles in Vienna and Budapest had began to see Serbia a factor whose very existence meant a great deal to all the internal opponents of the Monarchy and its elite. Failures in Balkan policy gave rise both to despondency and, in some circles, to heightened aggression. Amongst the aggressive circles the most deadly were parts of the high bureaucracy and the military leadership.[104]

Those aristocratic-bureaucratic groups were claiming with ever more urgency that destroying Serbia was the only policy that could save the Monarchy. At the same time they glorified war, saying it was beneficial to all inhabitants of the Monarchy itself as a 'purging' by means of 'steel baths'. That was why they saw the assassination in Sarajevo as offering some kind of convincing propaganda motive for the squaring of accounts.

For the German Reich generally, Serbia was interesting—even in July 1914—only as part of its great pan-European and world plans, and those plans determined its policy towards Serbia. In 1908–9 Berlin supported and encouraged Vienna in its aggressive policy, but in 1912 and 1913 it prevented Vienna from making a move that would lead to armed conflict. Berlin was thus in both cases acting in the way it considered to be of greatest benefit to the Reich's strategic plans.[105] Germany's basic objective was to create a huge empire that would become a world power and if possible a hegemonic world power. What that ultimately boiled down to was Germany achieving expansion and hegemony in Europe (plans known by the name 'Mitteleuropa'), with the Middle East becoming an unchallengeable sphere of interest for the Reich alone (these plans were known as 'Berlin-Baghdad' or 'Mitteleuropa from the North Sea to the Persian Gulf'). Extensive and rich colonies, mainly in Africa (i.e. French Equatorial Africa and the Belgian Congo), were to be acquired. This was to be a 'large economic space', while politically it would be a unique, complex and huge empire, spreading widely over Europe, with the German Reich as its command centre. That empire would include a system of allied and satellite states, spheres of interest and colonies that were linked to Germany as the centre. According to this concept Austria-Hungary, as an essential part of 'Mitteleuropa', had to be linked as closely as possible to Germany.

Such aspirations gradually provoked Britain, France and Russia to form the Entente coalition in order to defend their positions. A great obstacle to its aspirations thus arose on Germany's very borders, and so, in order to achieve its programme, it could not avoid conflict with the other three Great European Powers. The German leadership saw such a conflict as likely to take place, and it prepared the country and the people militarily, economically, ideologically and psychologically for a large-scale war.[106] Between 1912 and 1914

Berlin estimated that the Reich was prepared and powerful enough to be certain of victory in a war against France and Russia together, perhaps even if Britain were to join in too. Germany believed that it compensated for its evident disadvantage in numbers and resources, compared with the Entente, by its 'superiority of military strategic thought' and the strength and readiness of its armed forces. Germany further estimated that it needed to have at least Austria-Hungary alongside it on the battlefield, in line with its 'Mitteleuropa' concept, and in that connection war should be waged on an issue that was of special and direct interest to Austria-Hungary so that it would be among the first, and possibly the very first, to join in the war. Germany could then present its participation as fulfilling its obligation to an ally. To win the war on its own terms, Germany prepared tactics comprising three elements: first, to find a moment more favourable for Germany than for the Entente Powers; second, to find a reason that would be certain to draw Austria-Hungary into an armed struggle; and third, to find a reason that would provide Britain with an excuse, or at least a pretext, for not becoming involved in the conflict.

In the spring of 1914 the German leadership assessed that time was on the side of the Entente; as the Chief of the General Staff, Count Helmuth von Moltke, had stated in February 1913, they should wait for a sufficiently good propaganda pretext for starting war. The assassination of Franz Ferdinand seemed to offer such a pretext. It remained for the authorities in Berlin to start the war in such a way that the Entente Powers might be caught unawares, enabling Germany in a 'lightning war' to beat France and then Russia, and do so before Britain could become actively involved should it decide to join the conflict.[107]

Count Hoyos was well aware that since the annexation crisis the Monarchy's problem with Serbia had become a 'world issue closely connected to the politics of the Great Powers'.[108] Thus the endeavours of the Balkan states to achieve their own independence represented an obstacle to Germany implementing its plans. Serbia's determination to resist the pressure exerted by Austria-Hungary was particularly significant, as was the process of political independence from the Central Powers that was developing in Romania. Russia's traditional aspiration to be the leading power in the Balkan peninsula had then assumed the form of support to Balkan states. French capital, guided by its own interests, made it possible to prevent economic linkage with Austria-Hungary and Germany. Also in the Balkans, behind Russia and France, stood their ally Britain, which was interested in creating on the rivers Drina, Sava and Danube obstacles to Germany's ever growing presence in the Middle East.

The assassination in Sarajevo was understood in the Entente capitals as a possible cause of a new Balkan crisis. All the moves made by the Entente Powers were aimed at calming passions, but they were clearly intended to prevent the Central Powers from bringing about fundamental changes in the Balkans to their own benefit. Since aggravation of the crisis was in the interests of Austria-Hungary and Germany, the Entente Powers logically considered it reasonable to calm the crisis either through readiness to negotiate or by decisive action.[109] Where Serbia was concerned, it had already become a factor in Entente strategy thanks to its independent policy, and was having a positive impact on the development of Romania's independence vis-à-vis the Central Powers.

At a summit in St Petersburg, Russian and French political leaders agreed not to allow the situation to deteriorate, and for that reason decided not to allow Serbia to be at the mercy of Austria-Hungary. On 21 July Raymond Poincaré, the French President, told the Austro-Hungarian ambassador openly: 'Serbia has very fervent supporters among the Russian people. And Russia has an ally—France.'[110]

Because of the Entente Powers' specific interests, it was natural for Russia to assume the task of deterring Germany and Austria-Hungary from taking dangerous steps, while France would have the role of an ally duty-bound to support Russia, and Britain would have the role of mediator, gradually directing the crisis towards negotiations and compromise among the Powers.[111] However, if Austria-Hungary and Germany wanted war at any price, which they did, then clearly Russia had to protect its ally resolutely and to the utmost—a development Berlin was counting on, so that in its propaganda Germany would be able to transfer blame from itself to Russia.[112]

For the conflict they wished to provoke, both Austria-Hungary and Germany had in mind two possibilities: either a local war between Austria-Hungary and Serbia or a war between the Central Powers and the Entente, i.e. a European or world war. Vienna considered the former more desirable, while Berlin considered it good only in that the Monarchy's crushing of Serbia would probably lead to such friction among the Entente Powers that it would be hard for them either to survive as a coalition or to survive war that began at an unfavourable moment. Vienna considered the latter possibility as a necessary evil that should only be contemplated because it would mean a fatal blow to Serbia, while Germany considered a war between Austria-Hungary and Serbia to be a spark that would cause an explosion which, with or without war, could bring the Entente to its knees or destroy it. For Vienna it was important to try to play a skilful game and ensure that all the other Powers remained observers when its troops marched south. For Berlin, however, the important thing was if possible to keep only Russia and France in the arena, and to keep Britain out.

That was why Germany and Austria-Hungary sought the most suitable 'technique of declaration of war'.[113] The leading figures in Austria-Hungary had to try to confine the conflict to Serbia alone and, if that proved impossible, either to provide a pretext for at least one of the rival powers to refrain from entering the conflict, or at least to create the preconditions in which propaganda countering accusations that the Monarchy had been the aggressor would be effective. Because they could count on Russia being the Power to offer the most resolute opposition, their tactics were aimed either at preventing Russia from taking the ultimate step of entering a war or at creating the possibility for claiming that Russia had become involved in the war without a justifiable reason, and furthermore on the side responsible for war.

Two approaches were open for such tactics: either to pass through the entire international legal procedure of declaration of war, or to create an apparently moderate objective for war against Serbia so as to be able to claim there was no intention to destroy it. The first approach was significant in that Austria-Hungary thus demonstrated the independence of its foreign policy from Germany, which was seeking action without any kind of prior international legal process; the second approach was important because it created the impression that Russia had no reason to take up arms. Moreover, the second approach was favoured by the Hungarian leadership because it might prevent from the start any attempt to annex larger Serbian territories.[114]

This was agreed upon in Vienna at a session of the Joint Ministerial Council on 7 July 1914 at which it was decided to go to war, and at a session on 17 July when it was further decided that 'as soon as the war begins the other Powers will be informed that the Monarchy is not waging a war of conquest,' with the proviso that those decisions did 'not exclude strategically necessary border rectifications [to the advantage of Austria-Hungary] or the reduction of Serbia's territory to the advantage of other countries.'[115] Analysis of the views of ministers, the most senior bureaucracy and military commanders shows that it was intended to annex Mačva and Belgrade with their hinterlands, and probably the whole of the Sava basin inhabited by Serbs. The annexation was intended to take place in the course of that summer on the pretext of 'strategically necessary border rectifications'. It is also clear from the activities of the Monarchy's diplomatic service that considerable Serbian territories were to be offered to Romania, Bulgaria, Greece and Montenegro on the condition that they acted in accordance with Austro-Hungarian requirements.[116]

In order to ensure that the international political situation was favourable to Germany at the moment when the war began, Berlin calculated that it would be sufficient somehow to shift responsibility for starting hostilities first to Russia and then to France. It was considered that the shift of responsibility to these two powers could be doubly beneficial: first, by accusing a supposedly aggressive Russia of pushing Europe into an armed conflict (to defend the 'revolutionary stronghold' of Serbia), it would provide Britain with an excuse not to enter the war; and secondly, by claiming that Russia, aided and abetted by France, had forced Germany into a defensive war, it would manipulate German public opinion. In the latter case particular care had to be taken to influence the conduct of German Social-Democrats through propaganda. The reasoning was that Russia would have to take up arms because of an Austro-Hungarian attack on Serbia, since it could not allow the Monarchy to destroy one of its protégés, whereas it was sufficient for Germany to await a Russian proclamation of general mobilisation and then accuse

Russia of intending to attack and declare war on Germany. Such a declaration would induce Russia's ally, France, to mobilise, which was again sufficient for Germany to accuse it of intending to attack and then declare war on France too.

It is revealing that during the preparations for the Austro-Hungarian and German declarations of war the Monarchy officially remained menacingly restrained, while unofficially attacking Serbia most fearfully. Towards Montenegro, however, it showed friendship, goodwill and patience.[117] Austro-Hungarian intelligence quickly learned that Mehmedbašić had escaped into Montenegro, and Vienna officially demanded his extradition. The Montenegrin government then arrested him but he soon escaped from gaol in Nikšić, whereupon an allegedly scrupulous but fruitless search was organised while the fugitive was whiling away his time in Danilovgrad. In Belgrade only the press responded sharply to the Monarchy's accusations, but all remained calm. In Cetinje, however, the authorities and even the King himself had difficulty preventing their nationals from expressing their anger at the Monarchy's conduct. Consequently there were attempts to mount demonstrations on 4 and 5 July, and a meeting was held on 6 July at which hundreds of people showed their solidarity with Serbia and denounced the persecution of their fellow countrymen and accusations against them in the Monarchy. That day King Nicholas had to appear personally before the demonstrators to appeal to them not to approach the Monarchy's legation. But Austria-Hungary persisted in its stand and tried to induce Cetinje's leading figures to distance themselves from Belgrade.

Austro-Hungarian and German diplomatic circles were cautious but nonetheless systematic and consistent in their preparations for a confrontation with Serbia. By waging a covert propaganda war and describing Serbia as a 'nest of revolution' that threatened, 'with its subversive activity', not only peace but also civilisation in Europe, they did their utmost to discredit it in the capitals of the other Powers.[118] In St Petersburg, London, Paris and Rome Austro-Hungarian and German diplomats tried to make these claims believed. Propaganda was introduced into all their personal conversations and circulated by their local agents. The press, meanwhile, was bribed. The claims were slanted according to the sensitivities of the ruling circles in each country. In London, for example, monarchist sentiments were aroused with mention of a 'nation of regicides', referring to the killing of Alexander and Mihailo Obrenović. In St Petersburg stress was laid on 'Serb revolutionary agitation' and anarchist methods. In republican Paris, however, the nuance was different: Serbia's 'subversive activity' was said to be hindering French efforts to 'solve conflicts between the two Power groups by means of agreement'. In Rome emphasis was placed on Serbia's 'unscrupulous and frivolous method' of political activity—its use of 'perfidious murders' was a terrible 'stain on European culture'. Serbia was also spoken of in London and Rome as the forerunner of pan-Slavism and a tool for the 'covert consolidation of Russian hegemony in the Balkans'.[119]

In Vienna Jovan M. Jovanović saw it all: 'Telegrams are being sent throughout the world from here accusing Serbia and the entire Serb nation.[120] ... Even if the culprit is a Serb, that does not mean that the kingdom of Serbia and the entire Serb nation are also guilty.'

War

July 1914 seemed a peaceful month of summer holidays.[121] The individuals and institutions in Austria-Hungary and Germany on whom the attention of statesmen, diplomats and the public was focused did nothing to indicate that they intended anything exceptional. The two emperors and many of their ministers, commanders and civilian officials went on holiday; the German press stopped attacking Serbia; for a time there were no street demonstrations in Austria-Hungary, and only extreme clerical newspapers continued with anti-Serb propaganda. It was soon heard that Baron Giesl, the Austro-Hungarian envoy in Belgrade, was returning to his post, and this was taken as a sure sign that Austria-Hungary did not intend to break off relations with Serbia. Entente ambassadors in Berlin heard only a single message in the Ministry of Foreign Affairs: that it was up to Austria-Hungary what it would do about the assassination and that Germany had no interest in the matter. It was true that their counterparts in Vienna only met with enigmatic silence in the Foreign Ministry regarding Austria-Hungary's intentions towards Serbia, and no serious accusations were being bandied about, but they were unable to discover whether or not anything of exceptional importance was being planned. Jovanović could not make contact with the Foreign Minister Count Berchtold, and the conduct and words of the head of the Foreign Ministry, whom he met regularly, revealed nothing of any looming danger. The conviction therefore reigned that the future could be faced with tranquillity. It would seem that the personnel of the Russian Embassy in Vienna were the most assured on that matter.

But that was an illusion deliberately fostered by officials of the two empires. All those on holiday remained in the closest possible contact, albeit covert, with their institutions, and those on duty were secretly working hard to prepare for the forthcoming war. Where Austria-Hungary was concerned, a rapid, surprise military action against Serbia was planned to give the opposing bloc, especially Russia, insufficient time to become involved in the conflict, thus keeping the war localised. As for Germany, surprise was considered the prerequisite for a victorious military campaign against Russia and France. Well aware that Germany could mobilise and concentrate forces more quickly than France, not to mention Russia, Berlin's strategists planned a surprise attack through neutral Belgium, bringing France to its knees within a few weeks, and then quickly regrouping to strike at Russia. And that was all meant to happen before Great Britain could ship forces in any great number onto the continent.

However, because of difficulties facing the authorities in Vienna, this phase of delusion lasted too long.[122] Despite conclusions reached on 7 July, a whole week passed before Tisza was able to overcome his doubts concerning the true intentions of Austria's politicians over going to war. It was not till 14 July that he gave his full consent. War preparations by the military also posed grave problems. In the crisis during the autumn of 1912 the War Minister at the time, Baron Moritz von Affenberg, had opposed the intended war, warning that the Austro-Hungarian army was not prepared for it. His successor Baron Alexander von Krobatin had claimed from the beginning of December 1912 that the army was ready. He did so together with the Chief of the General Staff, Conrad, who had been reappointed. And it was Conrad who on 29 June 1914 demanded mobilisation for 1 July. Nonetheless, when the decision on going to war was finally made, the army was unprepared, and Conrad consequently sought sixteen more days for mobilisation preparations.

The time thus gained was used to compose the ultimatum to Serbia as carefully as possible, ensuring that it contained credible accusations and unacceptable demands, while at the same time being diplomatic in form.[123] The man entrusted with the ultimatum's drafting, Baron Alexander von Musulin, worked long and hard on his masterpiece and, as someone close to him noted, 'he sculpted and polished it like a precious stone', to 'astound the world' with the 'eloquence of its accusation'. Because there was no real proof of Serbia's responsibility for the assassination, accusations were generalised: 'There is Greater Serbian propaganda in Serbia' and 'Greater Serbian propaganda has been transmitted from Serbia to the Monarchy.' Despite all the facts given in support of such a thesis and the undoubted drafting skill of Baron von Musulin, the fact remained that there were simply not enough reasons to start a war.

The wish to settle accounts was one thing, but according to all realistic estimates a declaration of war on the small state of Serbia was certain in the circumstances to lead to a far more extensive war. And so, having gained full German support, the Monarchy tried to prepare for the decisive move down to the last detail. Hence everything was postponed. In Germany there was evidently impatience to get started, and Kaiser Wilhelm and officials in the Foreign Ministry continually demanded of the Austro-Hungarian ambassador that the opportunity should not be allowed to slip away. Likewise the German ambassador in Vienna repeatedly urged Count Berchtold to start the war as soon as possible, in which he was greatly aided by the German military envoy in his talks with Austro-Hungarian commanders.

On 8 July Count Szögyény reported to his superiors: 'Yesterday and today I have had the opportunity to hear the Undersecretary of State and other Foreign Ministry officials say that our decision is awaited with impatience here as they are convinced that this is a favourable juncture, such as will not come again soon, to act resolutely against Serbia.' On 9 July the Secretary of State for Foreign Affairs said: 'The intended action against Serbia should be undertaken without hesitation.' On 12 July, 'both His Majesty Kaiser Wilhelm and all other officials here not only stand firmly as true allies behind the Monarchy but they also encourage us in the most resolute manner not to miss this opportunity.... Ruling German circles, and His Majesty Kaiser Wilhelm personally, who is certainly no less determined than others, and indeed no less than we ourselves, are exhorting us to undertake action, possibly war, against Serbia.' On 11 July the German ambassador to Vienna telegraphed: 'I again had the opportunity today to talk to Count Berchtold on acting against Serbia, that is to say I again made the Minister aware that the most urgent possible action is necessary.'[124] When the German leadership suspected that the Monarchy was hesitating to take that most hazardous path, it did not shrink from exerting pressure, warning its ally that it had reached the last opportunity to rehabilitate itself as a Great Power—if it did not take advantage of that opportunity, it was 'not capable of being an ally'.[125] Thus, Vienna had to take care not to lose its only and therefore all-important ally.

It was evident, both in Belgrade and in the Montenegrin capital Cetinje, that Austria-Hungary could use the assassination in Sarajevo as a pretext for taking steps that would have far-reaching consequences. There is memoir testimony that on learning of what had taken place in Sarajevo, King Nicholas of Montenegro said to his doctor: 'There will be war.' In Cetinje, Petar Plamenac, a minister, and the Serbian envoy to Cetinje went into a serious examination of the latest situation and the possible consequences.[126] This ended with both believing in the soundness of the Austro-Hungarian leaders—it seemed impossible that anyone could go to war because of an assassination, regardless of its gravity, as the consequences of such a war were unpredictable in view of the aggravated international situation. As a consequence, the government in Belgrade only understood the sharp press attacks in Austria-Hungary and other hostile countries as attempts to take 'the greatest possible political advantage' of the assassination and 'destroy the high moral credit Serbia enjoys today in Europe'. Press articles were regarded as the visible side of the Monarchy's otherwise complex activities, and efforts were made to use diplomatic channels to advance the Serbian point of view. On 1 and 18 July two circular memos were therefore sent with instructions for all envoys abroad, with the exception of those in Vienna, on how to defend their country against the grave accusations to which they were exposed from representatives of the governments to which they were accredited.[127] Otherwise political life in Serbia continued as usual, although it happened that two top officials were not in Belgrade at the time. Prime Minister Nikola Pašić was conducting a pre-election campaign in the interior of the country, and Vojvoda[128] Radomir Putnik, chief of the general staff, was taking the waters at Gleichenberg spa, in Austria of all places.

Serbia had developed a number of lines of defence. Among these were the claim that the Sarajevo assassination 'had met with the broadest condemnation in all strata of Serbian society.' 'It would have been in Serbia's interest to avoid the assassination', which had 'unfortunately' proved impossible because 'both conspirators had been Austrian subjects'. Serbia had 'up to that time been monitoring anarchistic elements and would redouble its control after recent events,' and 'if there were any in Serbia' it would 'take the strictest measures against them.' Belgrade newspapers were only responding to attacks, which the government could not prevent them from doing 'since freedom of the press was guaranteed in the law and in the constitution'. These and other lines of defence were given in the official memos circulated, with the plea that the 'Viennese press should not be allowed to deceive European public opinion and, for purely political purposes, place the grave responsibility for a crime committed by an Austrian subject on Serbia and the entire Serb nation, which could only lose and not benefit from such deeds.' That defence did not draw back from the strongest condemnation of the conspirators and the assassination, calling it 'the mindless act of a young fanatic'. Serbia's recourse to this kind of defence, which resolutely rejected assassination for political ends, demonstrates its fear that the Monarchy not only intended to take 'the greatest possible political advantage' of the assassination, but might also do something more momentous.[129]

As time passed and Europe became lulled into thinking that no serious conflict was impending, Serbia's representatives became more and more concerned. That concern is clearly seen in two telegrams Jovanović sent from Vienna on 15 July. In the first he reported that many people in Vienna wished to interpret Count Tisza's latest address as calming, but that he himself drew attention to the fact that in the speech 'war had not been excluded'. In his second telegram he stated that 'Austria-Hungary could take one of two paths. It could either consider the Sarajevo assassination as an internal matter … or it could put Serbs from Serbia and the Yugoslav nation on trial. Judging by everything being done and prepared, I think Austria-Hungary will choose the second option.'[130] Belgrade was evidently beginning to suspect what was really happening. In its circulated memo of 18 July the government said that it now feared that the Austro-Hungarian government would take steps that would humiliate Serbia in an unacceptable manner—that it was 'preparing some kind of diplomatic course of action that could lead to unfortunate consequences'. That same memo also noted that 'armed conflict is being mentioned everywhere if the Serbian government is not able to give a categorical and satisfactory response.'[131] Around 20 July a sense of deep unease was felt everywhere. Vague news was seeping through to the large political centres in Europe that the Monarchy would make an exceptionally aggressive move in Belgrade.

The hour had struck for the ultimatum to be presented. At 6 p.m. on 23 July 1914 the Austro-Hungarian ambassador Baron Giesl handed the note containing the ultimatum to Lazar Paču, Finance Minister and representative of the Serbian Prime Minister, demanding a response within forty-eight hours. The moment of presentation was timed by Vienna to come after the French President's departure from Russia in order to avoid any top-level discussion of the ultimatum and thus postpone any common stand on it. It had also been decided that the other Great Powers, including Austria-Hungary's ally Italy, should not be informed of the text of the ultimatum until the morning of 24 July, thus shortening the reaction period. And so it happened, although on 23 July the Austro-Hungarian ambassador in Rome informed the Italian government of the contents of the ultimatum orally; however, he had been instructed to do so as late in the day as possible as 'we wish to avoid the news reaching St Petersburg from Rome that same day.'[132] The German government was up to date with the drafting of the document and knew its contents. The final text had been given to the German ambassador on the evening of 21 July, and it had been transmitted to the Foreign Ministry in Berlin through the Austro-Hungarian embassy in the evening of 22 July. In any case, the German government had the final version of the ultimatum a full twenty-three hours before the Serbian government.[133]

Alongside a lengthy indictment of Serbia, the basic assumption was that the idea of the assassination was hatched in Belgrade;

weapons and ammunition were provided by officers and officials who were members of Narodna Odbrana; and officers of the Serbian frontier service had ensured river transport across the frontier into Bosnia. The ultimatum contained ten points.[134] It was demanded that the Serbian government should (1) suppress all publications writing against Austria-Hungary, 'the general tendency of which' jeopardises her territorial integrity; (2) immediately dissolve the Narodna Odbrana and similar societies and prevent them from 'continuing their activities under other names and other forms'; (3) eliminate all propaganda against Austria-Hungary from state education in Serbia; (4) dismiss all officers and officials guilty of propaganda against Austria-Hungary, the names of whom are to be submitted subsequently; (5) accept 'organs of the Imperial and Royal government collaborating in the suppression of the subversive movement directed against the territorial integrity of the Empire'; (6) take judicial proceedings against accessories to the Sarajevo assassination who are on Serbian territory and agree to bodies 'delegated by the Imperial and Royal Government' taking part in the investigation; (7) proceed immediately to the arrest of Vojislav Tankosić and Milan Ciganović; (8) prevent 'assistance to the illicit traffic in arms and ammunition across the frontier' and 'dismiss and severely punish' those frontier bodies that had assisted the three authors of the Sarajevo crime to cross the frontier; (9) furnish explanations of the statements made after 28 June by 'high Serbian officials both in Serbia and abroad' that were hostile in content to the Monarchy; and (10) notify the Imperial and Royal government of the execution of the measures comprised in the previous points.

The ultimatum evidently had the aim of inflicting deep humiliation on Serbia and, what was most important, creating openings through which the Monarchy could harm and even destroy Serbia's independent existence. Points 5 and 6 of the ultimatum and to a certain extent point 10 were aimed at creating such openings. If the Serbian government had allowed Austro-Hungarian bodies to participate in the investigation and if it had undertaken to inform Austria-Hungary of the execution of the measures stipulated in the demands, that would, according to the perceptions of the time, have been more than just degrading to Serbia's independence from a moral and legal point of view, as it might seem at first sight. Austria-

Hungary would also have been able to instigate proceedings against any person in Serbia, infiltrate all institutions of the Serbian state, and ultimately paralyse the independent activity of those institutions. Belgrade was right to interpret those demands as a starting point for destroying Serbia's sovereignty.

In the morning of 24 July, reading the ultimatum to Serbia, the British Foreign Secretary Sir Edward Grey immediately notified the Austro-Hungarian ambassador that it was the most terrible document one state had ever presented to another, indicating point 5 in particular. Moreover, on learning of the contents of the note, the Russian ambassador to Vienna hastened to warn Count Berchtold that it contained demands 'no constitutional state could agree to'. While the Russian Foreign Minister Serge Sazonov was being informed of its contents by the Austro-Hungarian ambassador in St Petersburg, he said—more in despair than in anger, according to the ambassador himself—'I know what you want. You want war with Serbia!... You are lighting a fire in Europe.... You want war and you are burning your bridges behind you.... It is clear how peace-loving you are when you are casting Europe into flames.'[135] As for the French ambassador in Vienna, he informed his government that the 'unexpected and excessive rigour of the demands contained in the Austrian note, i.e. ultimatum, to Belgrade had surprised even Serbia's bitterest enemies.'[136] Reactions were similar throughout the world. An article in *Journal de Genève* dated 25 July expressed grave condemnation of Austria-Hungary, and the Bavarian envoy in Berne informed the government in Munich that 'the press of neutral Switzerland has taken the Serbian side' and claimed that 'the Serbian national idea is the same as that of Italy and Germany, both of which have for centuries also been violating European peace.' Moreover, according to the Bavarian envoy, the diplomatic corps in Berne were unanimous in their view that the Austro-Hungarian note contained totally unsubstantiated accusations.[137]

The Serbian government met the evening the ultimatum was delivered and could only conclude that 'there is nothing left but to die.'[138] Lazar Paču, probably after the first consultations, stated in a memo circulated to all Serbian legations abroad that 'the demands are such that no Serbian government could agree to them.'[139] In Belgrade they clearly realised that it was a fateful moment as the demands were unacceptable, but they nonetheless wanted to meet them as far as possible. They wished, in consequence, to reply within the time limit given and, in the evening of 23 July, in line with earlier statements that an investigation would be instigated immediately against any person the Austro-Hungarian side indicated as being an accessory to the conspiracy, warrants were issued for the arrest of Tankosić and Ciganović. Tankosić was quickly apprehended, but Ciganović had fled Belgrade and was hiding in the interior of the country. On his return to Belgrade Lazar Paču immediately visited the legation of Russia, the closest ally in the Entente Bloc, as did Regent Alexander during the night and Nikola Pašić at dawn. They were seeking advice, and, in an attempt to lessen the pressure at least a little, the Russians were also requested to intervene with Vienna.

Serbia's view of the ultimatum is best demonstrated by Regent Alexander's personal letter of 24 July to Tsar Nicholas II of Russia on the one hand and Nikola Pašić's agitation amongst foreign states on the other. Regent Alexander's letter contained the following:

> The demands in the Austro-Hungarian note humiliate Serbia quite unnecessarily and do not comply with the country's dignity as an independent state.... We are willing to meet such Austro-Hungarian demands as are in accordance with the position of an independent state, as well as those that Your Majesty would advise us to observe. We shall ourselves rigorously punish all persons proved to have been involved in the assassination conspiracy. Certain demands cannot be met without altering our laws, and time is needed. The deadline given is too short.

For his part, Pašić informed the Russian chargé d'affaires that the Serbian government beseeches 'friendly states to protect Serbia's independence, but, if war is inevitable, Serbia will wage it.' Prime Minister Pašić notified the British chargé d'affaires that 'the Austro-Hungarian demands are such that the government of no single independent state could agree to them in totality', adding that he hoped the 'English government will intervene with the Austro-Hungarian government in order to induce it to moderate its demands.' The Serbian envoy in the Montenegrin capital was sent a telegram containing the following: 'Ask the government immediately if, in the case of a conflict with Austria-Hungary, we can count on their support. Reply by telegram immediately.' Through the legation in Athens the same question was put to the Greek government the next day.¹⁴⁰ It is evident that Serbia reacted with all haste, in a conciliatory manner and resolutely.

The Entente Powers wanted to avoid war at that time, and they unanimously advised Serbia to concede to the greatest possible extent. Their governments were playing for time in order to find some peaceful solution. As Britain's position in the crisis was the most independent, its government attempted mediation through Berlin to induce Austria-Hungary to soften its stand and through St Petersburg to induce Serbia to accede to as many Austro-Hungarian demands as possible. On the evening of 24 July Sazonov instructed the Russian legation in Belgrade to transmit its advice to the Serbian government that in the case of an attack by the Austro-Hungarian army 'no serious attempts at resistance should be made.' It was advised from St Petersburg, as shown in the following days, that the Serbian army should withdraw without combat into the interior of the country, and the government should call on foreign powers and European public opinion to prevent invasion and war.¹⁴¹ French diplomatic circles recommended that Serbia should, if absolutely necessary, allow Austria-Hungary to take Belgrade without resistance,¹⁴² which was later proved to be a British idea.¹⁴³ The Foreign Ministry in Rome advised the Serbian envoy that a way should be found to avoid conflict, since anything acceded to would in fact only be of temporary validity.¹⁴⁴

The three Entente Powers and Italy tried to influence Austria-Hungary and Germany to prevent the crisis from deteriorating into war, and to that end made show of resolution as well as offering peaceful solutions. St Petersburg decided to threaten mobilisation, while London, having recourse to more complex tactics, made it clear to Germany that Britain could not stand by if it declared war on France. However, the Serbian chargé d'affaires in Berlin could only report that the French ambassador 'like all the others' was claiming that 'Germany stood resolutely on the side of Austria-Hungary' and was 'working to localise the conflict and leave Serbia alone with Austria-Hungary'.¹⁴⁵ Jovan Jovanović was in no doubt when he reported from Vienna: 'According to the latest information, this matter between Austria-Hungary and us is a very grave one.'¹⁴⁶

The Balkan capitals were cautious, but the replies from Cetinje and Athens were friendly. Replying to a question from Belgrade, the Montenegrin government said it could give no advice and thought 'Serbia should adhere to what Russia and France were advising', but the Serbian envoy was aware that Petar Plamenac had told the Monarchy's representative that he hoped 'Austria had not said its last word', which meant that he was suggesting flexibility. He had told the Italian envoy, who had advised Cetinje to remain neutral, that 'Italy is asking Montenegro to betray Serbia,' and suggested Italy should work for a moderation of Austria-Hungary's demands.[147]

The Serbian reply was finally completed just after 5.30 p.m. on Saturday 25 July. It was drafted by Nikola Pašić and Stojan Protić. They completed the Serbian text promptly, but because of the document's delicacy, the translation into French took longer than expected, and there were also problems typing it out. That might have been the reason why Velizar Janković, Minister of the Economy, appeared in the Monarchy's legation at around 4.30 to ask Baron Giesl for a small favour in connection with a journey his wife was to take. Giesl recorded hearing him say, 'We shall agree to whatever demands we can. But it is impossible to agree to them all,' after which he telegraphed Vienna that it was virtually certain 'integral acceptance of the ultimatum' could not be counted on.[148]

It was Prime Minister Pašić who actually delivered the Serbian response personally to the Austro-Hungarian legation, just before the clock on the Orthodox Cathedral struck 6 p.m. Giesl wrote the following about this moment:

At 5.55 p.m. the Serbian Prime Minister entered my study and handed the government's response to me.... Pašić an elderly man of around seventy with white hair and a white beard, was evidently aware of the solemnity of the moment. The expression in his exceptionally intelligent eyes was one of mournful gravity. In answer to my question what the note contained, Pašić replied in imperfect German: 'Part of your demands we have accepted, for the rest we place our hopes on your loyalty and chivalry as an Austrian general. With you we have always been very satisfied.'[149]

Giesl understood at once that the response was not satisfactory, and as soon as Pašić had returned to the Foreign Ministry a letter arrived from the envoy stating that since Serbia had not accepted Austria-Hungary's demands, relations between the two countries were broken off. Giesl and his legation staff then left Belgrade and travelled to Zemun. Before the ultimatum was even delivered Vienna had instructed Giesl to break off relations and leave Belgrade with his staff if the Serbian government did not agree to every detail of the demands or if the response was at all late in coming. He had been told specifically that he and all his staff should take the train that left Belgrade for Zemun on 25 July at 6.30, only half an hour after the ultimatum's deadline.[150]

The Serbian government's response,[151] while expressing the hope that its note would serve to eradicate 'all disagreement', suggested that since the end of the annexation crisis the Serbian authorities had done nothing against Austria-Hungary and its authorities in Bosnia and Herzegovina. Moreover, the Austro-Hungarian government had not lodged any protest with the exception of a case concerning a school textbook. During the Balkan Wars, it was added, it was 'thanks to Serbia and the sacrifice that she had made in the exclusive interest of European peace, that peace had been preserved.' The note further denied that the Serbian government could be responsible for 'manifestations of a private character...that take place in nearly all countries...and do not come under the sphere of official control.' For all these reasons, it was stated, the accusations had been received with 'pain and shock', especially because it would have been natural for the Serbian government 'to be invited to collaborate in an investigation of all that concerns this crime.'

Having thus explained why the accusations were unjustified, the Serbian government put forward the concessions it was prepared to make. It agreed to condemn, in the official journal *Srpske Novine* and in an order to the army, 'all propaganda directed against Austria-Hungary' and undertook to 'use the greatest severity' towards all found guilty of 'such activity'. There followed the enumeration of ten points: the first session of the National Assembly would introduce a provision into the press law providing for the 'most severe punishment' of all persons inciting 'hatred and contempt' for the Monarchy; the Narodna Odbrana would be dissolved although no proof of its guilt had been produced; everything the Austro-Hungarian side designated as hostile would be eliminated from public instruction; all officials and officers judged before a court to have worked against the integrity of Austria-Hungary would be dismissed; Serbia would agree to 'collaborate with the representatives of the Imperial and Royal Government on its territory' but on the condition that the principles of international law were respected. After those first five points, there followed the key section of the response contained in another five points: the Serbian government 'considers it its duty' to open an investigation against 'all such persons as are, or eventually may be, implicated in the conspiracy of 28 June', but it could not agree to 'bodies designated by Austro-Hungarian authorities taking part in that investigation'. Major Tankosić had already been arrested and a warrant issued for the arrest of Ciganović. Frontier controls would be stepped up to prevent the illicit trafficking of weapons and explosives, and an inquiry would be ordered into the actions of frontier officials in the Sabac-Loznica sector with a view to punishing those responsible; it was 'gladly' agreed that explanations should be given of remarks made by 'officials of Serbia' after the crime as soon as the Austro-Hungarian side made available the necessary evidence; the Serbian government undertook to inform the Monarchy 'of the execution of the measures undertaken'. The note finally contained the promise that if Austria-Hungary were not satisfied with the response, the Serbian government would 'in the interest of precipitating a peaceful agreement' accept a final decision made by the International Court at The Hague or the Great Powers. Serbia therefore agreed to all demands with the exception of that under point 6, while the demand under point 5 was accepted with a proviso, and the arbitration of the International Court at The Hague or the Great Powers was offered.

As far as it is known, this response was received throughout the world as an example of skill and compliance. Even Kaiser Wilhelm was satisfied, and he wrote to the German Foreign Minister: 'Any reserves that Serbia made to the individual points can, I am sure, be totally clarified in negotiations. But contained within is a capitulation of the most humiliating kind that has been published *orbi et urbi*. Therefore, there are no grounds for war.'[152] However, the Kaiser's ministers and generals were not very interested in the content of the response. All that mattered to them was aggravating the crisis to the greatest extent possible with an Austro-Hungarian attack on Serbia, which would in turn lead to a German showdown with Russia and France; however, that was on condition that some kind of pretext of Russia being responsible for the war were received.[153] Therefore, the news of a general Russian mobilisation was awaited impatiently, and even nervously, in Berlin. Vienna, for its part, was only interested in the fact that the Serbian government had not accepted the ultimatum to the letter. It only remained for war to be declared.

In the evening of 25 July, immediately after the Monarchy had broken off relations, the Serbian government moved to Niš, ordered the evacuation of Belgrade and proclaimed general mobilisation, stating: 'As the Austro-Hungarian envoy has this evening declared, on his government's behalf, that he is not satisfied with our response and has finally broken off diplomatic relations, the Serbian government is compelled, for any eventuality, to take the necessary military measures for the defence of the country.... If we are attacked, the army will do its duty.'[154] An accurate assessment of the situation kept the authorities one step ahead of developments. On 27 July King Nicholas of Montenegro sent Regent Alexander the following message: 'The pride of the Serbian nation has not permitted further concessions. Sweet are the sacrifices made for national justice and independence.... Our Serbian nation shall emerge victorious from these great, imposed trials too and ensure a brilliant future for itself. Even now my Montenegrins are ready on the frontier to give up their lives in defence of our independence.'[155] Alexander replied the same day: 'We have done everything possible to save the Serbian nation from new sacrifices and hardships, but we have not succeeded because Austria-Hungary has sought that we sacrifice our cherished independence.... I was filled with great joy when I heard, although I did not doubt it, that Montenegro had made common cause with Serbia in defence of the Serbian nation.'[156]

There are historians who consider that the sluggishness of the Austro-Hungarian bureaucracy was to blame for war not being declared until 28 July. Whatever the case, it was just after 9 p.m. on 25 July that the General Staff ordered mobilisation to start on 28 July, with the stipulation that the first alert should be given on 27 July. Within the government, particularly in the Foreign Ministry, they were dealing with the formulation of the Emperor's war proclamation, the declaration of war and—since it had been agreed that the final move should be made on 28 July—assessments of the current international situation. The text of the declaration of war was submitted to the Emperor for approval on 27 July, and Franz Joseph accepted it without alteration the following morning, after which it only remained to be presented to the Serbian government.[157] Three whole nights and almost two and a half days had passed since the breaking-off of diplomatic relations.

Around noon on Tuesday 28 July an unusual declaration of war arrived in Niš—in the form of an ordinary telegram. The poet Sibe Milačić recorded that he happened to be in the Europa coffee house in Niš, where the Prime Minister Nikola Pašić was lunching, when an official entered and handed him a telegram. Having read it, Pašić rose from the table and said to those present: 'Austria has declared war on us. Our cause is a just one. God will help us.'[158] The suspicion that the telegram might have been some kind of provocation was quickly dispelled: it really was war.

The slogan using the pun '*Serbien muss sterben*' (Serbia must die) was to be heard throughout the Monarchy on 28 July.[159] From that day on trains composed of seemingly innumerable coaches hurtled through Central Europe packed with Austro-Hungarian and German troops singing the hit of the moment: 'Every shot—one Russian/Every stroke—one Frenchman/Those in Serbia have to die too!'[160] Hungarian aristocrats, who were devoted to hunting, went off to war as if going to a hunt where Serbs were to be the game.[161] In Serbia a natural but short-lived period of fear and confusion was replaced by a mood of combined gloom and resolution. The German envoy, who had stayed in Niš at the beginning of August because war between Germany and Serbia had not been declared, observed minutely what was happening around him. He quoted, as being most typical of the prevailing state of mind, what he had heard from a young Serb officer: 'We have finished mobilisation, they can come now. We are waiting for them and we shall win.'[162] Having left Niš after the declaration of war, he arrived in Sofia, where he told an Austro-Hungarian colleague that in recent days in Serbia 'the fear and confusion that had first been felt had dissipated', and 'self-confidence, resolution and intrepidity now prevail.'[163]

2

THE YUGOSLAV PROGRAMME

The localised war the Monarchy had wanted lasted only three days, as the declaration of war quickly produced large-scale armed conflict, for which Germany was responsible.

Even after 28 July London and, to a certain extent, St Petersburg, sought to avert hostilities, but any possible solution presupposed that Serbia would allow the Monarchy to take Belgrade without resistance and thus rescue the shaky peace between the two blocs. Austria-Hungary would then have had the guarantee that its demands would be met as far as possible, the final decision being made by a conference of the Great Powers. Berlin felt that war was at hand. On 29 July the Bavarian military representative informed the War Ministry in Munich that the Prussian War Ministry 'supported by the General Staff' wanted 'urgent military measures'. He added that General von Moltke, chief of the general staff, was 'using all his influence to ensure that the unusually favourable juncture be used to strike a blow'. The next day, he added that the Emperor was 'resolutely on the side of Moltke and the War Minister'.[1] Although political leaders in other countries were playing for time before they entered the war, in Germany they were merely waiting for news of general mobilisation in Russia, and when that news arrived, ultimatums and declarations of war sped from Berlin—to Russia, France and Belgium on 1, 3 and 5 August respectively. German troops had actually attacked Belgium on the morning of 4 August (having occupied the small state of Luxembourg without a declaration of war on 2 August). This triggered a chain reaction of alliances and antagonisms that had nothing to do with Serbia but were based on profound and bitter conflict of long duration. Britain declared war against Germany on 4 August; Austria-Hungary against Russia on 6 August; France and Britain against Austria-Hungary on 13 August, and Austria-Hungary against Belgium on 27 August. Japan joined the Entente with a declaration of war on Germany on 23 August, whereupon Austria-Hungary declared war on Japan the next day. Turkey pronounced itself neutral, but signed a secret alliance with the Central Powers on 2 August and launched hostilities against Russia at the end of October. That resulted in Russia, France and Britain declaring war on Turkey early in November. Thus, in the number of participants, the sheer extent of the battlefronts, and the enormity of European and world issues being disputed, the conflict rapidly assumed a world scale.

Serbia had no contractual obligations creating an automatic *casus foederis*. It had become part of the system by force of events, and, on 6 August, declared war on Germany, the ally of the country that had attacked it. Montenegro, Serbia's traditional ally bound to it by a sense of common national awareness, took up Serbia's cause despite Vienna's efforts to distance it from Serbia and induce it to remain neutral with promises of considerable monetary assistance and the acquisition of Skadar and parts of the Sandžak of Novi Pazar. On the morning of 28 July, that is before Serbia had received the declaration of war, Montenegro ordered mobilisation, and skirmishes took place on its frontiers in early August.[2] But Austro-Hungarian diplomacy did not give up. On 31 July, with the comment that 'Montenegrin neutrality is of the greatest importance to us', Count Berchtold ordered the Austro-Hungarian minister in Cetinje to use his influence to prevent the Montenegrin National Assembly from deciding to go to war. He promised that Austria-Hungary, 'not wishing to annex Serbia's territories, will protect Montenegro's independence and give Montenegro rich financial assistance, as well as territorial gains'.[3]

However, there were too many signs that those promises would not be honoured. Consequently, an extraordinary session of the Montenegrin Assembly held on 1 August 1914, 'lending expression to its justified indignation ... and protesting against surprise attacks on its Serbian brothers and against the outrageous persecution of our South Slav brothers', decided unanimously to declare war immediately on Austria-Hungary, evoking 'war in response to violence and aggression' and 'brothers going hand in hand into a sacred battle'. It was certainly not easy for this small, poor and militarily weak country to make such a decision, but it reflected the broadest sentiments of the time. In a note of 5 August, Montenegro, emphasising that it was 'united with Serbia by strong links of one and the same blood,' broke off diplomatic relations with Austria-Hungary. It officially declared war against Austria-Hungary on 6 August and against Germany on 11 August. Montenegrin army operations started on 7 August.[4]

Four small countries were thus caught up in the maelstrom of a world-scale war—Serbia, Montenegro, Luxembourg and Belgium.

A small country in the face of war

At the time when hostilities began, Serbia's territory extended over 87,300 square kilometres, and its population was slightly over 4.55 million.[5] It was one of a number of very small states in the world at that time. On the Balkan peninsula it was smaller both in size and in population than Romania, Greece and Bulgaria; the only two smaller countries were Montenegro and Albania. In the summer of 1914 the Serbian state's territory consisted of two clearly separate entities: its territory from before the Balkan wars (around 54,000 square kilometres with more than 3 million inhabitants), and that which it had acquired in the wars (around 33,000 square kilometres and 1.5 million inhabitants). By the summer of 1914 those two entities had not merged either economically or culturally, and they differed totally in national composition. The pre-1912 territory was homogeneous and an overwhelming majority of the population practised the Orthodox faith, while the newly-acquired territories were also populated by Macedonians, Albanians and Turks, many of whom were Muslim, residing in compact entities. Moreover, the political and legal system in the newly-acquired territories was affected by the state of emergency still in force, while a constitutional-democratic system providing for broad civic rights held sway within the pre-1912 borders. Over Serbia as a whole there were slightly more than fifty-two inhabitants per square kilometre, which meant that in the Balkans only Romania was more densely populated. The birth-rate was high even by the standards of the time: 17 births per 1,000 inhabitants. From among the Balkan states, Bulgaria alone was ahead of Serbia in that respect with 18.8 births per 1,000 inhabitants, and that was the highest birth-rate in Europe.

The huge majority of the population lived off the land, accounting for 83.6% of the population according to the 1900 census and 84.9% in 1910. Thus Serbia had the highest proportion of peasant population in the Balkans (Romania had 82.84%, Bulgaria 80.88%). The largest town was Belgrade with over 90,000 inhabitants (Bucharest had 340,000, Athens 170,000, Sofia 125,000). The other large towns in the pre-1912 territories were Niš (25,000), Kragujevac (18,500), Leskovac (14,000), Požarevac (13,000), Vranje (12,500), Šabac (12,000) and Pirot (11,000). In the newly-acquired territories a number of towns were large for the time: Bitola (60,000), Skopje (50,000), Prilep (22,000), Prizren (21,000), Štip (20,000), Priština (18,500), Veles (15,500) and Novi Pazar (13,000). However, many of the Turkish and Muslim populations of the towns in the newly-acquired territories were emigrating. Europe's impact had started to be felt in the towns within the pre-1912 border at the end of the nineteenth century, and that impact accelerated at the beginning of the twentieth century. However, in the newly-acquired territories Bitola and Skopje were developed oriental towns, while the others were of the oriental kasbah type.

The pre-1912 regions were incomparably more important parts of the state in all respects. They boasted a stable rural society populated by a free peasantry who were not beholden to a traditional landowning aristocracy or large landowners as in other parts of Europe. Crop-growing and animal husbandry were the backbone of the economy, with peasant households often dealing in both. Despite the backwardness of agricultural production, yields were sufficient thanks in part to the naturally rich soil. Foreign trade was of special importance with exports exceeding imports, especially with the most highly developed countries, including the United States.

Towards the end of the nineteenth century towns were changing more rapidly than villages, and a number of entrepreneurs emerged whose financial power often rivalled that of their European counterparts. The upper classes in urban society were made up of merchants, but despite the existence of small banks and savings banks in all towns, there were few industrialists or bankers. Civil servants and officers also belonged to those upper classes, as did the senior clergy. The social and political role of the increasing number of officers was becoming ever more important. The urban middle classes comprised lower-ranking state officials, secondary and primary school teachers and artisans; this was also true of small towns and villages, where some merchants also lived. At first there were few industrial workers, but their numbers had increased rapidly from 4,000 in 1904 to around 16,000 on the eve of the war. The intelligentsia, mainly secular but with a small number of clergy, formed the cultural and political driving force. Belgrade was home to nearly all Serbia's scientists and artists, the great majority of whom had been educated at foreign universities in Central and Western Europe. These gathered mainly at the Great School (*Velika Škola*), which had become a University in the autumn of 1905. A large section of the wider intelligentsia, also to be found in the towns in the interior of the country, was in state service, while some were members of the independent professions (e.g. lawyers, journalists). The press was free and, given the general level of society, highly developed.

Serbia had its own banks, and these exerted some influence despite their size. With the exception of the military armaments plant in Kragujevac, industry was geared mostly to the production of consumer goods (sugar, textiles, tobacco), and its importance did not extend beyond the country's borders. Moreover, industry was chiefly connected to agriculture and forestry (mills, sawmills, abattoirs etc.). The state did not invest much in industrialisation. A number of large foreign loans were approved at the beginning of the century, and these were mainly used to strengthen the armed forces and develop railway transport: railways were the focus of much attention, and plans for their development multiplied year by year. One German diplomat reported to Berlin that 'a veritable railway construction fever' prevailed in Serbia. Furthermore, mining, which was in the hands of foreign capital (French, Belgian and to a lesser degree Austro-Hungarian), represented the second cornerstone of the country's economic power.

Serbia's economic wealth and potential came to the notice of foreigners. When Austria-Hungary tried to crush the country with a tariff war, the German minister in Belgrade notified his government in August 1907 that Serbia was economically strong and its 'resistance capacity [...] is much underestimated, which is exactly what the Austro-Hungarian authorities have done.' He added: 'Serbia is able to withstand even a very long tariff war with the neighbouring

Monarchy, [since] the diversity of its products, the fertility of its soil and its hilly terrain ensure it has never had a bad harvest.'[6] Foreign banking experts considered Serbia to be of outstanding economic potential and, thanks to considerable surpluses, creditworthy. This was actually a reason for Franco-German economic rivalry:[7] it was for business reasons that the government in Paris used economic means in its attempt to block Germany's drive to the south-east, while German politicians and bureaucrats persistently channelled their country's big business into Serbia to provide Germany with a major foothold in the Balkans.[8] Serbia actually benefited in the 1900s from Franco-German rivalry. It bought weapons for its army and extended its railway lines with French capital, while German goods helped it avoid shortages of industrial consumer products, which neighbouring Austria-Hungary had made available only at the cost of political blackmail. Both countries were unwittingly helping Serbia to consolidate its independence.

Serbia's state finances were founded on a monopoly system (salt, tobacco, cigarette paper, matches, lamp oil and alcohol), as well as on taxes for the use of stamps, and on customs duties. These accumulated earnings grew rapidly from year to year, which made foreign loans possible and ensured their prompt repayment. The monopoly administration had been shrewd in its dealings since the beginning of the century, and more and more remained in the state exchequer even after the repayment of foreign loans. At the start of the war, debts amounted to some 900,000 francs, which represented around 146 francs *per capita* of the population, plus interest of some 10 francs.

Within its pre-1912 borders, Serbia was nationally homogeneous, and members of the Pančić, Weifert, Levi, Bajloni, Ribnikar and other families of foreign origin, including even the Prussian officer Sturm, simply felt themselves to be Serbs living on their own land. In 1910 the two most densely populated areas, one bordered by the rivers Velika Morava, Sava and Drina and the other around the Zapadna Morava and Djetina rivers (23,880 square kilometres in total) were inhabited by 1,595,658 people (67 per square kilometre), which was more than 59% of the total population. Out of this total 1,571,554 were of Orthodox faith (98.6%), while there were 6,702 Catholics (0.4%), 4,734 Jews (0.3%), 3,264 Muslims (0.2%) and 1,213 others. However, at that time religion was not a totally reliable indicator of 'nationality': not all those who pronounced themselves Orthodox were Serbs and, contrariwise, a considerable number of non-Orthodox inhabitants did declare themselves Serbs.

What had actually happened was that two strands of political thought and spiritual belief had become intertwined in the long struggle to gain and preserve independence. On the one hand, there was readiness to defend the country's independence, and on the other the increasingly clear conviction that unification into a larger community of some kind should be sought to ensure future security. Consistent with the insurrectionist tradition dating back to the emergence of Serbia's independence, that desire to secure a safe future through unification presupposed the inclusion of persons 'liberated from foreign rule' into the broad community. Moreover, Serbia's successful struggle for independence had strengthened the belief that a new and broader community should be created around Serbia itself. The examples of large nation states (Italy, Germany) served only to consolidate that belief, and the strengthening of capitalist relations and the construction of a civil society had created the prerequisite for these ideas to take hold. Furthermore, the war had caught Serbia when it was engaged in an upward swing in all domains—economic, political and cultural. The awareness had strengthened in Serbia both of belonging to a broader community and of its own uniqueness.

Perception of war in 1914

When Serbia was attacked by Austria-Hungary, a state inhabited by a large number of persons whose ethnic origin was identical or similar to that of the Serbs, that awareness came to the fore. It provided the psychological basis for resistance and the incentive to achieve the desired broader community. To be more specific, the Serbs in Serbia, who numbered between 3.0 and 3.5 million, saw their broader community as including some 2 million Serbs living in the Monarchy and about 5 million other South Slavs who were inhabitants of the 150,000 square kilometres of Austria-Hungary. The aims and suffering of the terrible war imposed in the summer of 1914 were inordinate and therefore prompted the idea of unification as a lifeline for future survival. But those objectives were so urgent that they allowed little time to ponder the question of how their compatriots would regard Serbia's aspiration to be at the centre of unification.

In a case of dire emergency Serbia considered itself able to call 600,000 men to arms. It mobilised nearly 500,000 men in July 1914, a figure that had risen to over 530,000 in September 1914 and reached 570,000 in August 1915. That was despite the huge losses it had sustained in the meantime. In the period between the summer of 1914 and the autumn of 1915 it had mobilised over 707,000 men, including some volunteers from all the Yugoslav regions. Of that number about 350,000 were probably capable of meeting the demands of the warfare of the time.

In the first weeks of the war a broad realisation emerged in Serbia of what the new circumstances really meant. A doctrine could be said to have evolved containing the outline of Serbia's war aims and practical policies appropriate to the way war was conducted at the time.[9] The perceptions then prevailing can be seen in a series of official acts dating back to that time and recorded at the end of August 1914 by Nikola Pašić, and supplemented by Stojan Protić and to a certain extent by the Foreign Ministry official Jovan M. Jovanović on his return from Vienna. It is only possible to understand the importance of this document if one bears in mind that it contains viewpoints put forward in various talks and many official acts from the very beginning of the war, which were then repeated in various forms up to when it ended. Originally the document had the specific purpose of explaining to the Entente Powers that they were not justified in trying to persuade Serbia to yield part of Macedonia to Bulgaria, which was what they had insisted on from the beginning of the war in the desire to renew the 'Alliance of Christian States' in the Balkans (that is, without Turkey). The document contained the essence of official Serbia's war concept.

The doctrine's premise was that Austria-Hungary had provoked a 'pan-European war' by 'holding Serbia responsible for the assassination in Sarajevo without any legal grounds' and requiring it to 'renounce its independence and become politically subjugated to it'. It was considered that the fundamental reason for Austria-Hungary's conduct lay not only in 'the Serbian nation having, thanks to its own awareness ... and its vital force ... renounced the Obrenović dynasty's dangerous policy', but also in the fact that the Serbian nation had thus also quashed 'the policy of division into spheres of interest in the Balkans.' For that reason the Monarchy 'in a bigger and strengthened Serbia saw [...] the staunchest obstacle in the way of Germanism's drive towards the East,' that is 'a danger to the execution of its plans in the Balkans and to the infiltration of German influence and culture towards the East'. That was why, since the Balkan wars, the Monarchy had been 'doing its utmost to hinder' the consolidation of 'a stronger Serbia' and had 'sought and provoked conflicts ... particularly over issues where Serbia had been isolated in its arguments'.[10] Serbia was facing the disaster of war solely because it wanted to preserve its independence and increase its strength. Thus it had set itself forcefully against intentions to divide the Balkans into zones of foreign interest. Serbia had to fight for independence.

This perception also contained awareness of Serbia's place and role in the broader geographical-political arena, particularly given Bulgaria's policy favouring the Central Powers. The Serbian leadership was clear: if Bulgaria finally joined the Central Powers it would probably obtain territorial expansion at the expense of Serbia, Greece and, maybe, Romania. However, if Austria-Hungary and Germany 'sustained the victory', Bulgaria would soon find that its gains had been 'short-lived'. That was because 'a policy that cannot tolerate an independent Serbia cannot tolerate an independent Bulgaria either.' Bulgaria's alliance with the Central Powers would mean that it had opted for the 'side hostile to the independence of Balkan states, and therefore its own independence.' As for Romania and Greece which, 'due to Russia's pro-Bulgarian policy, had long been separated from their natural allies', they had started to free themselves of unnatural links and friendships forged out of necessity and come closer to the Triple Entente. This they did when the insincerity of Austria-Hungary's friendship had become clear during the Balkan wars.[11]

Another element of the doctrine was thus revealed. What was involved was a conflict between contrasting historical phenomena and political aspirations: a conflict between the desire for a free nation state, as seen in the 'suppression of the policy of spheres of interest', and the desire for more territory. On 5 November 1914

Pašić warned the Allies that Serbia was compelled 'to fight not only for herself but also for the other Balkan nations'.[12]

The document compiled at the end of August stated that 'Germany always stood behind Austria-Hungary,' because it wished to ensure 'the predominance of its interests in the Balkans'. That was why it aspired to 'subjugate Serbia to Austria-Hungary', and in order to achieve that it had 'declared war on Russia and its ally France'. In a Europe divided into 'two camps,' Russia, France and Britain were 'fighting for the independence of small states' only because their alliance was based on a common interest. They were 'opposed to the predominance of Germanism', or rather in favour of 'limiting German predominance'. They supported Serbia only because they saw it as 'the first barrier standing in the way of Germany's drive east', and they 'completely understood what the weakening or destruction of Serbia would mean and what consequences that would have for the further development of German predominance in the East.' They were not defending Serbia for any idealistic or principled reasons, but because 'the interests of Russia, France and Britain were the same as those of Serbia.' Finally, Italy 'immediately realised that an aggressive war against Serbia' meant 'a great threat to itself'. That was why Italy, despite being an ally of Germany and Austria-Hungary, declared itself neutral.[13] Serbia was well aware that Germany was the main enemy and did not delude itself that Russia, France and Britain were waging war for anything but their own interests. It therefore followed that Serbia had no real moral obligations towards the three Entente Powers or Italy.

Another Serb perception was that it was necessary to create a larger state in the Balkans. On 21 October 1914 Pašić made the shrewd observation: 'The creation of small states would be detrimental to peace in the South-East as foreign intrigues would insinuate themselves, sowing mistrust, envy and hatred. A strong state is necessary for peace in the South-East and in Europe.'[14] The division of the Balkans into small states was considered bad since it enabled foreign interests to revive old and incite new dissension. This perception stemmed from the unfortunate experiences of nineteenth-century Balkan history, and the war was seen as a possible means of overcoming the past by making it possible for ethnically similar populations to unify on the basis of the Yugoslav idea, which had been evolving in previous decades.

The thread running through all the perceptions was that Serbia's independence was threatened and had to be defended. In order to rid itself of that threat once and for all, Serbia had to emerge from the war stronger and bigger by unifying its fellow countrymen. To achieve that aim the aggressive Central Powers had to be compelled by force of arms, and the Allied Powers induced politically, to accept Serbia's Yugoslav programme. The realisation that the two power blocs were waging war for their own interests created awareness of the difficult position of small countries, including Serbia. However, it also created awareness that Serbia's independent role was justified and that it could and, indeed had to, insist on its own war objectives *vis-à-vis* the Allied bloc as well. This virtually implied the existence of two battlefronts: an armed front against the enemy and a diplomatic front against the Allies. As for the territory encompassed in this programme of war aims, it could only be that inhabited by the Yugoslav population, i.e. parts of the Monarchy. Serbian foreign policy documents compiled at that time soon started mentioning a future state of Serbs and Croats, or Serbs, Croats and Slovenes. The expression 'Yugoslav state' then appeared.[15] That was the pivot of the defensive-offensive war programme comprising Serbia's right to independence.

Austro-Hungarian fronts

If the outbreak of war had opened up two fronts for Serbia, one military and one diplomatic, the Austro-Hungarian leadership opened up two fronts for itself: an external front against Serbia and its allies, and an internal one against those of its citizens committed to Serbia or the Yugoslav nation.

Austria-Hungary had declared war on Serbia, but it soon became evident that it would take weeks to rally the troops necessary for large-scale operations. It nonetheless set to work immediately, not on the battlefield but internally. The demonstrations that had taken place after the assassination in Sarajevo had been a mere intimation of what was to come after war was declared. Persecution continued, and on 26 July 1914 an order from Vienna deprived the inhabitants of Bosnia and Herzegovina of their constitutional rights, and the military took over. People were arrested in the towns, and not only

Serbs mistrusted by the military authorities were jailed but also young Croats in favour of the Yugoslav idea and pro-Serb Muslims.[16] Among the first to be imprisoned was Savo Ljubibratić, a deputy in the Sabor. That same day the activities of Serb, pro-Yugoslav and also certain Croat national organisations were banned in Dalmatia as well. Many newspapers were closed down, and several Serbs and Croats were arrested, including Grga Andjelinović, secretary of the then banned Sokol organisation in Split; Niko Bartulović and Jerko Čulić, editors of the outlawed *Sloboda*; Oskar Tartalja, editor of the outlawed young people's newspaper *Zastava*, and others. On 26 July between 150 and 200 prominent citizens were arrested in southern Banat. Moreover, in Croatia the Ban's decree of 27 July banned the publication of the Serbian *Srpsko Kolo, Privrednik* and *Sloboda*, the pro-Yugoslav *Narodno Jedinstvo* and *Vihor*, and the Social Democratic *Slobodna Riječ, Oslobodjenje* and *Pravo Naroda*. The extent of the closures can also be seen in the banning on 27 July of a German-language Social Democratic paper in Osijek, and of the Social Democratic *Zarja* and the *Glas Juga* in Slovenia, and a paper intended for revolutionary pro-Yugoslav youth and the trade union mouthpiece *Rudar*. Extreme clerical and rightist groups came up with the slogan *Srbe o vrbe* (string Serbs up on willow trees), and on 27 July the *Slovenec*, a newspaper then close to Šušteršić, published a verse which ran as follows: 'We greet you Serbs with cannon fire/We make a cold home for you by the willows.' It was thus clear that democratic movements in general were being targeted. A kind of counter-revolution was under way under the guise of anti-Serb slogans.[17] It was a case of classic reaction, which had survived the nineteenth century under the wing of the Habsburg state and was now working against national and democratic movements in the name of the policy of the *ancien régime*.

However, the great wave of arrests did not come till the declaration of war, and it then lasted for months and in places for years. And once again it was not only Serbs who took the brunt. Courts-martial were set up in all provinces, with the exception of the Croat Banovina. The repression was conducted chiefly by the military authorities, and everyone arrested was simply accused of high treason. In Dalmatia and Boka all leading Serbs and pro-Yugoslav Croats still at large were arrested, including Božo Vukotić, a Serb, and Josip

Smodlaka and Ante Tresić-Pavičić, both Croats. All three were deputies in the Austrian parliament. Prominent Croats of different political convictions were jailed, including Ivo Krstelj, Mate Drinković, Melko Čingrija, Prvislav Grisogono and Ivan Lupis-Vukić.[18] Those jailed in Dalmatia included the young Ivo Andrić, a writer from Bosnia, and among the hostages was the celebrated writer Ivo Vojnović. Some fifty people were executed in the province of Dalmatia in the first days of the war. These were ordinary people—a teacher, merchants, seafarers and peasants. Among the hundreds jailed in Vojvodina was Jaša Tomić, while two people were killed in Sombor. Bunjevci leaders were placed under police surveillance. Inscriptions in Cyrillic were torn down in several places; the windows of houses belonging to Serbs were broken; people were attacked and insulted; all Serb associations were banned, as were the *Zastava, Branik* and *Srpstvo* newspapers. The leaders of the Serb National Radical Party were ordered to dissolve their organisation. Moreover, the wave of violence swept into Istria, and Idrija miners were targeted.

In Croatia mass persecution took place only in Srem, while there were individual incidents elsewhere.[19] Svetozar Pribićević was first arrested, as was his brother Valerijan; Svetozar was then carried off to Budapest to be interned for over a year. Many people suffered harassment, and some were sent to the front. Social Democrats were targeted, as were members of the then ruling Croat-Serb Coalition. Nothing worse happened because the Hungarian government had preserved the constitutional order in Croatia—evidently it knew that the main instigators of extreme activity were Greater Austrian army leaders who intended to limit Hungary's independence and particularly its significant role in the Monarchy. The Hungarian Prime Minister Count Tisza publicly protested against pogrom-like demonstrations in Bosnia and Herzegovina in the wake of the assassination, and in September 1914 he provided a degree of protection to Serbs in Vojvodina. Among the prominent politicians only Srdjan Budisavljević was arrested (August 1914). All in all, some 200 people were jailed in Srem in the first days of the war, and eight people were executed in the village of Klenak.

The reign of terror in Bosnia and Herzegovina was more cruel than elsewhere, and the authorities tried to divide the population as much as possible. This was evidently aimed at crushing the growing pro-Yugoslav movement. Advantage was taken of the many potential sources of dissension in a multi-confessional and multi-national environment such as Bosnia and Herzegovina.[20] Following on the pre-war arrests, Serbs were jailed in huge numbers after 28 July. Coming from all walks of life, they were accused of political misdeeds and suspicious conduct, and many were taken hostage. The authorities, particularly the military, first held sway, but irregular troops, the so-called 'protection detachments', quickly sprang up. These numbered several thousand men from among the Muslim population of Bosnia and Herzegovina. These detachments had the official task of assisting the gendarmes, but it soon became evident that they were there to perpetrate illegal repressive measures. The fact that 'loyal Serbs' headed by Danilo Dimović were spared repression was probably at least partly due to an intention to implant a sense of mistrust among Serbs themselves. However, the complaint made by General Stjepan Sarkotić, who replaced General Oskar Potiorek as governor of Bosnia and Herzegovina early in 1915, that Dimović was a suspect seems to point to extremists wanting a decisive confrontation with all Serbs. This is also illustrated by the analogy of complaints made by extremists against Ivan Šušteršić in the Slovene region, a man far more devoted to the Monarchy than Dimović. Those who wished to target all Slovenes indiscriminately even claimed that Šušteršić was 'the leader and future fighter for the realisation of the Greater Serb idea and the downfall of the Monarchy'.

Up to the spring of 1915 the pretext of security measures could not be used in the case of Slovene territories because those territories were not close to the front. However, arrests began immediately, with accusations of people being 'pro-Serb' or 'anti-patriotic'. Regardless of whether such measures were justified or not, their aim was to suppress Slovene national self-awareness. Things came to such a pass that the Austrian Minister of Internal Affairs had to warn the authorities in Styria that they should not 'regard every member of the Slovene nation as *a priori* politically suspect'. By 1 September 1914 at least 450 people had been arrested in Styria, while over eighty were jailed in Primorska and Trieste in the first ten days of the war alone. The latter included the writer Ivan Cankar.[21]

There were dual causes for the 'internal front'. Extreme forces were exacting an extreme policy and even more extreme conduct, but the fact remains that Austria-Hungary could not rely on the loyalty of all its South Slav citizens, especially those of Serb nationality. The persecution carried out in the Monarchy's southern provinces revealed two things. First, the authorities were trying to destroy the bond which, despite their considerable differences, existed among Yugoslavs. It was a twofold bond, being both ideological (the 'Slav South') and political, as manifested in national movements linked by the common desire for independence. Secondly, despite the differences the war had created among Yugoslavs, the ensuing persecution created a new integrating element of common suffering and the sense of a common enemy. In this way, generally the war, contrary to the intentions of those who started it, strengthened the links that already existed among the Yugoslav peoples. Serbia and Montenegro on the one hand, and Yugoslavs in the Monarchy on the other, were increasingly parts of the same historical trends, thus forming the new phenomenon of their mutual links.

To take full advantage of the war as a means of inducing dissent, Austria-Hungary adopted even the most extreme tactics. It sent units made up chiefly of South Slav or other Slav soldiers to attack Serbia and Montenegro.[22] In the Balkan army under the command of General Potiorek, governor of Bosnia and Herzegovina in the autumn of 1914, the forces were largely made up of the 15th Corps stationed in Sarajevo, the 16th Corps stationed in Dubrovnik, the 13th Corps stationed in Zagreb, and the 8th Corps stationed in Prague. Those units contained a large number of Monarchy Serbs who accounted in some cases for a quarter of the total, while Croats sometimes accounted for over half. One of the reasons for the haste to go to war in the wake of the Balkan Wars was the perception that circumstances in the Monarchy could lead to Slav regiments refusing to fight under the Habsburg banner. As Baron von Musulin insisted on several occasions at the Foreign Ministry in Vienna, the intention in July 1914 was to take advantage of probably the last opportunity to use Croat troops against Serbia.[23] The Serbian supreme command was aware of that. Seeing the composition of the troops the enemy was amassing on the frontier, it realised that the intent was, in the case of Austro-Hungarian victory, to claim that South Slavs loyal to the Habsburgs had beaten the Serbs and, if there were a Serb victory, to foment hatred among those defeated. Austria-Hungary was then still able to make such a move because, besides the tradition of allegiance to the Monarchy, the coercive state laws were still effective and indeed especially severe in war conditions. Moreover, war indoctrination, as developed mainly by ideologies of extremist clerical circles, was still strong.[24]

Although at the beginning of August 1914 larger and more important fronts opened up in Western and Eastern Europe, the Central Powers deemed a rapid victory over Serbia vital to ensure favourable political developments in the Balkans, that is to say the territorial expansion of the war front, and to secure land links with Turkey. The subjugation of Serbia was also necessary for moral, political and propaganda reasons. Hence on 30 July large-scale forces comprising the Austro-Hungarian 5th and 6th armies started to concentrate on the front against Serbia and Montenegro. The 2nd Army was mustered in Srem and Banat, but it was actually intended for the Russian front.[25] The main direction of the attack was meant to come from the west, from positions in Bosnia and across the Drina. The Serbian army, then numbering around 400,000 men under the command of Regent Alexander and Vojvoda Radomir Putnik, head of the supreme command, was composed of three armies and some separate troops. The Montenegrin army, numbering 45,000 men under the command of King Nicholas and Serdar Janko Vukotić as chief of staff (he was Prime Minister and Minister of Military Affairs), was made up of the Pljevaljska division and the Herzegovački, Lovćenski and Starosrbijanski detachments. These faced Austro-Hungarian troops incomparably better armed and equipped than the Serbian army, not to mention the Montenegrin army.

Dialogue between Serbia and Montenegro on military cooperation had started on the eve of the outbreak of war.[26] The initiative had come from the Montenegrin side because King Nicholas believed that close and comprehensive cooperation with Serbia and its army was vital. Towards the end of July he sought 'instructions on the direction of the movement of military operations', and shortly thereafter he sent his delegate Brigadier Jovo Bećir to the Serbian supreme command to urge the creation of a joint general plan of operations that would make maximum use of the Montenegrin battlefront in particular. He also requested aid in cannon and ammunition. On 4 August Pašić supported the Montenegrin requests before the Serbian supreme command, pointing out that Serbs and Montenegrins should work together and not separately. And on 6 August Vojvoda Radomir Putnik completed the elaboration of the 'Joint campaign plan for the Serbian and Montenegrin armies in the war against Austria-Hungary'.

Although the concentration of the 5th and 6th armies was not complete, the Austro-Hungarian army launched an attack on Serbia on 12 August. The 5th Army went into action first and, in the course of fierce fighting, drove back the Serbian 3rd Army. The 6th Army with its 16th Corps attacked the Serbian and Montenegrin front on 15 August, whereupon the 2nd Serbian Army hastened to join battle on the march in the night of 15/16 August. Fighting then flared up on Mount Cer, to end on 20 August with the rout of the Austro-Hungarian 5th Army. Vojvoda Putnik notified King Peter of the victory in a telegram saying: 'The main enemy army has been defeated in Jadar and on Mount Cer, and our troops are in hot pursuit.'[27] Reports from the front announced: 'The enemy is withdrawing in the greatest disorder.'[28] Under the date 19 August an Austro-Hungarian soldier wrote in his diary: 'The army is beaten and is in headless, wild and chaotic flight.... An unruly mob bolted in mad fear towards the frontier.... Men were trampling over one another in their haste.'[29] On 24 August the liberation of Šabac, the largest town in Mačva, marked the final defeat of the first Austro-Hungarian incursion into Serbia. That was actually the first Allied victory in the First World War.

On the Montenegrin front, parts of the Austro-Hungarian 16th Corps, despite valiant resistance, took Pljevlja on 19 August, but the offensive was quickly halted because of the defeat suffered on Mount Cer.[30] On 21 August a Serbian army mission, headed by General Božidar Janković and Colonel Petar Pešić, arrived in Montenegro at the invitation of King Nicholas, and brought with it Putnik's 'joint campaign plan'. Taking advantage of the slackening of enemy pressure on the front, Montenegrins regrouped their forces and reorganised the command set-up. On 24 August King Nicholas created a supreme command, on which the recently arrived Serb General Janković was appointed chief of staff, Colonel Petar Pešić his deputy, and the three other Serbian military mission officers and two Montenegrin captains were made members. Strong new units were created—the Sandžak Army and the Drina Detachment. Moreover Prince Peter, a son of King Nicholas, took over command of the Lovćenski detachment. On 26 August the Sandžak Army went over to the offensive and counterattacked, liberating Pljevlja on the very first day. At the end of August and the beginning of September the Montenegrin army recovered the territories lost and, in some places, crossed the frontier.

And so began long months of constant and exceptionally fierce fighting where attacks were interspersed with counterattacks, advances with retreats and border river crossings with withdrawals. But the result was that Serbian and Montenegrin units had successfully defended their state territories.[31] The Serbian 1st Army breached the Sava on 6 September and, despite the heavy blow sustained by the Timok Division I at Čevrntija, managed to dig in on the left bank. Belgrade defence units entered Zemun on 10 September. However, on 8 September the Austro-Hungarian 5th Army had again started exerting pressure on the Drina, and the Serbian army had to withdraw from Srem.

The short break in large-scale operations was only the calm before the storm. The Austro-Hungarian Balkan Army filled its ranks, replenished equipment, reinforced its artillery and rested.[32] Its third major attack started on 6 November with continuous artillery fire and determined pressure from the 5th and 6th Armies, which advanced over the entire front. The Serbian army was found to be powerless, its equipment worn out and artillery rounds in short supply. The 1st Serbian Army suffered a severe blow. The state of affairs on the front became so critical that on 8 November a joint session of the government and the supreme command was held, chaired by Regent Alexander. Vojvoda Putnik stressed the critical nature of the juncture and even mentioned a separate peace, but Prime Minister Pašić urged further resistance and threatened the government's resignation. Nonetheless the final outcome of that dramatic session was agreement that the fight should go on.[33]

The enemy took the towns of Valjevo, Obrenovac and others,[34] and the Serbian army was in even greater disarray. Pašić sought help from the governments of the Allied Powers, ordering envoys abroad:

'Urgent help is required. Beg and plead.' Equipment, artillery ammunition and troops were all in short supply. The Allies expressed understanding, but help was not forthcoming. However, France provided the necessary ammunition. In the mean time, the enemy had taken Belgrade without a fight and on 3 December 1914 held a triumphal military parade there.

The people retreated alongside their army. On 4 December Albin Kutschbach, the German agent in Niš, reported to his command: 'More refugees are arriving by the day, and despite many people being sent on south, there are certainly still 60,000 people here. The accommodation is full to overflowing. I myself am sharing a room with three others, and I have to be doubly cautious. Many refugees are sleeping out of doors.'[35]

According to Kutschbach, the inhabitants of Niš had received the news of the fall of Belgrade 'impassively, because it had been expected since the beginning of the war',[36] but reactions abroad were strong. Germany sent delighted congratulations to its ally.[37] The Austro-Hungarian leadership estimated that victory was at hand and started to prepare for the administration of occupied Serbia; the Austrian and Hungarian leaderships even started to quibble about whether a larger or smaller part of Serbia should be annexed. General Stjepan Sarkotić was appointed Governor General in Bosnia. However, on 3 December the Serbian 1st Army launched a surprise counterattack from its position west of Gornji Milanovac, and before that General Živojin Mišić had shortened the front line, allowed the soldiers some rest, received and distributed the artillery ammunition that had finally arrived and decided on a counterattack, whereupon the other two armies also received orders to attack. The Austro-Hungarian front faltered, crumpled and then collapsed.

The Bulgarian minister in Niš started his report of 8 December with the following words: 'The most improbable news from the battleground, sweet to the Serb ear, has been going around since this morning.' He had heard that in the past three to four days Serbia had taken prisoner one general, ninety-four officers and 20,000 soldiers, as well as capturing forty cannon and huge quantities of war matériel.[38] Two days earlier the British Minister had informed his government that the Serbian offensive was progressing brilliantly.[39] Serb commanders again reported from the front: 'The enemy is withdrawing towards the Sava and the Danube.'⁴⁰ 'The roads are strewn with discarded ammunition (particularly for artillery) and different matériel. One officer and 620 soldiers have been taken prisoner.... On 10 December alone this Division confiscated seven cannon and one heavy machine-gun.... Three officers and 600 soldiers have been taken prisoner. Six field cannon and six hill cannon have been confiscated, as well as many ammunition wagons, ... two regimental standards, a large amount of discarded ammunition and other matériel.'⁴¹

The Austro-Hungarian soldiers who had not been taken prisoner did not stop until they crossed the Sava and Danube rivers into Srem or Banat, and only a small number of them returned to their positions in Bosnia. One Austro-Hungarian soldier's diary read: 'We could not even have imagined that the Serbs were on our heels, after all we have recently been victorious' (9 December 1914); 'Toppled field kitchens, wagons knocked over ..., dead horses in ditches, all over the place discarded goods, clothes, harnesses, tins, barrels' (10 December); 'I have crossed a pontoon bridge over the Sava ..., there are no words to describe how the bridge swayed with the teeming crowds on it, the way men were pushing and elbowing their way forward, the agitation and the disorder.' (14 December)⁴² On 17 December Kutschbach reported:

The final days of my stay in Niš were not joyful for me. Victory celebrations rang out night and day, and I had to take great care not to reveal my true identity. The Serbian 1st and 2nd armies have vigorously continued their counterattack against Austro-Hungarian troops and, given their delight and their spirit of combat and courage, the Serbs will prevail.... Mišić is considered to have a fine and capable mind.⁴³

An elderly citizen of Belgrade, who as a boy witnessed the Austro-Hungarian withdrawal, has said: 'The withdrawal did not resemble retreat, but rather flight.'⁴⁴

On 16 December a directive was issued by the Serbian supreme command, containing the following: 'The recapture of Belgrade marks the successful end of a great and magnificent period in our operations.... The enemy is beaten, dispersed, defeated and expelled from our territory once and for all.'⁴⁵ According to an order issued by the Supreme Commander on 17 December, 270 Austro-Hungarian officers and over 40,000 non-commissioned officers and soldiers were taken prisoner during the fighting, and more than 130 cannon, seventy heavy machine-guns and a large quantity of matériel were captured.[46]

And when the news of the fighting on the Balkan front reached the wider world, the German publicist Maximilian Harden wrote: 'Serbia has once again risen from its grave on the field of Kosovo.... From the source of the Kolubara river it will draw courage for the greatest battles for a whole century.'[47] The way General Živojin Mišić, who was promoted to the rank of Vojvoda, conducted the battle has entered the textbooks of military schools and academies.

All three Austro-Hungarian incursions into Serbia were notorious for the cruel treatment that was inflicted on the civilian population. That was particularly true of the first incursion. Although only the elderly, women and children had remained in the occupied territory, and there had been relatively few of them because part of the population had withdrawn together with the army, the invading forces—on the pretext that the population was offering resistance—rounded up and shot large groups of people, regardless of age.[48] Later, when the Serbian army freed these territories, it found evidence of terrible crimes. After the battle on Mount Cer, General Paul Jurišić-Sturm, a Prussian by birth who had come to Serbia as a young officer, reported:

> The Austrian army has committed frightful atrocities in our territories. A group of nineteen (men, women and children) has been found by the Krivajica tavern. They had been roped together and then horribly massacred. Such a group of fifteen people was found in Zavlaka. Small groups of slaughtered and disfigured people, mostly women and children, are to be found throughout the villages. One woman had belts of skin cut off and another had had her breasts cut off.... Another group of twelve women and children has been found who had been tied together and massacred. Peasants say such sights are to be seen everywhere.[49]

That same morning the commander of the 2nd Army Cavalry Division reported that the enemy had 'slaughtered men and women',[50] and the commander of the Combined Division that 'atrocities have been perpetrated in Ljesnica. Men and children aged ten have been hanged or shot, and the women dragged off into slavery.'[51] Reports arrived of even more heinous acts. On 22 August the commander of the Cavalry Division reported that he had personally seen 'five male and three female bodies that had been disfigured', and that 'the village of Prnjavor has been destroyed' and 'according to the locals, enemy soldiers (Hungarians and German-Austrians) had butchered and burnt alive women, children and the old.'[52] Reprisals were also carried out against the civilian population in the occupied areas of Montenegro.

A communiqué of 8 August from the Austro-Hungarian supreme command to the command in Sarajevo stated: 'There have been repeated reports that the population of Srem and Banat are quite unreliable.'[53] The veracity of those reports was soon forcibly demonstrated by the inhabitants of the village of Borča near Pančevo. On hearing that Serb units were crossing rivers that marked frontiers, the inhabitants of Borča bedecked their village with Serbian flags, sang Serbian patriotic songs and even sent envoys to Belgrade to seek unification with Serbia. Something similar happened in Zemun, and the commander of the Austro-Hungarian Danube flotilla notified the War Ministry in Vienna that the people there had 'welcomed Serbian troops with great enthusiasm, throwing flowers and waving flags', adding that 'Serbian flags were flying throughout the town' and the population had 'stayed awake the previous night in expectation of the entry of Serbian troops'.[54]

The claim that 'the subversive element was predominant among Serbs' served to justify repressive measures, but it contained an element of truth. Dissatisfaction was increasingly obvious among the Serb population and those who did not wish to renounce the idea of brotherhood. Thus the vicious circle spiralled: the authorities mistrusted the people, terrorised them, which in turn provoked ever-increasing hostility; anti-Serb propaganda led to crimes that only served to strengthen pro-Serb and pro-Yugoslav feelings. Extremism thus gained new impetus and caused ever more religious and national hatred, which in turn consolidated the commitment to liberation from Habsburg authority and the creation of a unified and free state. It is difficult in individual cases to determine whether the reign of terror spread because of the nature of extremist policy itself or because of popular defiance.

The remote mountains and forests of Bosnia and Herzegovina saw both arbitrary terror and the spirit of resistance. Police documents record that a certain Djuro Gudelj was hanged in the Trebinje gaol for sending signals to Montenegro, and Vid Parežanin, a priest, suffered the same fate for sending signals to Serbia. Police reports affirm that Parezanin stood 'at the gallows with a noose around his neck and shouted repeatedly "Long live Serbia. Long live the Serbian army. Long live great Russia!"'[55] In the district of Bihac three retired gendarmes—Stojan Rapaić, Stojan Brakus and Jefto Grubor—were arrested for propagating the Serb idea; the same happened to retired gendarme Ilija Princip in Grahovo, who was accused of insulting the Emperor. Pensions were immediately withheld from their families. In August a certain Petar Radoman, whom the police had considered one of their own, greeted the Montenegrin troops entering the village of Lastva: 'Welcome, Montenegrins. I wish you good fortune. Long live the King and Montenegrins!' Petar Radoman was supported by two former gendarmes, Todor Mileusnić and Djuro Djenderac.[56] On 22 August General Potiorek complained: 'Our Serbs fight on Serbia's side not only in Herzegovina but also at Višegrad, where the population worked covertly against our troops when they were withdrawing successfully and the enemy troops were infiltrating.'[57]

The authorities in Slavonia, Lika and Gorski Kotar received reports that some households kept Serbian insignia, that people were praising Serbia and its ruler and criticising the Monarchy. Serbian flags were also unfurled, the reports added. The Austro-Hungarian army's incursions into Serbia also had an unexpected effect, unwelcome to the Austrians: Yugoslavs from different regions became better acquainted. Besides heightening respect for Serbian military skill, which had been an important element in consolidating the Yugoslav movement since the Balkan wars, the awareness also grew, according to Milan Marjanović, that there were 'no nobles or large landholdings' in Serbia. Consequently 'the peasants changed their views of Serbia' and 'particularly those from Zagorje [soon became] more pro-Serb than some of the intelligentsia.' A similar mood also existed in political circles. In the spring of 1915—while stressing Croatian singularity—Starčević's *Hrvat* wrote of 'the glorious past and even more glorious present of the Serb nation', and of the 'classic heroism' shown by Serb mothers. In Dalmatia, similar convictions, which had been expressed earlier, strengthened with the reverses suffered by the Austro-Hungarian army in Serbia. In Ljubljana, on the first day of the war, some students handed out leaflets with the words 'Down with the war! Down with the clericals! Down with Šušteršič!' A secondary school pupil, Alojz Klemenčić, was among the 'many young people' who called on mobilised Slovenes 'not to shoot at Serbs', and the police arrested several people for shouting 'Long live Serbia!' In October 1914 a verse was to be heard in Carniola that ran as follows:

> The great Slovene day approaches
> A Russian and a Serb are bringing it
> We shall be the masters here
> Woe upon you German dogs!
> Long live Serbia![58]

The authorities continued with their reprisals. Arrests were quickly followed by mass internment in camps that were located mostly in ethnic German or Hungarian regions of the Monarchy. Trials and executions on charges of high treason quickly followed. On 28 July 1914 transporters carrying internees had already set off to a camp at Arad, the first prisoners having been arrested during the previous two days in the Banat towns of Pančevo and Bela Crkva. And for months to come many such travellers were to journey from all the Monarchy's Yugoslav provinces to an ever-increasing number of camps. In mid-August 1914 those arrested in Dalmatia were mostly sent to Styria via Zagreb and Budapest. On 10 August the first transports from Bosnia and Herzegovina were sent to Arad, where over 3,300 people were interned during the war. It is impossible to say exactly how many died there; one list puts the number of dead at 355 and another at 470,[59] but it is certain that there were many deaths among the internees. According to the diary of the internee Damjan Djurić,[60] there were fifty-eight deaths in the Arad camp on 21 January 1915, thirty-two on 22 January, twenty-eight on 23 January, forty-six on 24 January, twenty-one on 27 January, twenty-seven on 28 January, thirty-eight on 29 January, forty-seven on 2 February, twenty-five on 3 February, thirty on 6 February... Death was probably due to exhaustion and infectious diseases. Internees from Bosnia and Herzegovina were also sent to camps in Sopronyek, Komoran, Kecskemet, Talersdorf, Turonj and Graz. Some internees were quickly mobilised, and it is not known how many of them died as Austro-Hungarian soldiers. A large camp was set up near Doboj in Bosnian territory, in which there were 46,000 internees, of whom nearly 17,000 were women and children—mainly the families of men who had signed up as volunteers for Serbia. There was also a camp in Žegar near Bihać. Most of the Slovenes arrested were also sent to camps or interned.

Living conditions in these camps were exceptionally difficult, and prisoners lived in constant fear and deprivation.[61] In those first days some were in danger of being lynched; for example, those arrested in Pančevo on 27 July spent many hours in mortal fear when Hungarian nationalist demonstrators tried to fight their way into the prison and mete out their own justice on them. When being transported from southern Banat to Temišvar, internees were waylaid by enraged mobs which pelted them with stones. Josip Smodlaka later recalled that 'furious Hungarian soldiers wanted to massacre' him and his comrades in Budapest, and the prominent writer Svetozar Ćorović was forced by guards to run without food or water beside the railway transport carrying prisoners. It also seems there were hundreds of trials before extemporised courts-martial.[62]

All kinds of judicial procedures and trials were taking place, particularly in Bosnia and Herzegovina. The largest was held in Sarajevo in October 1914 to try those who had been involved in the plot to assassinate Franz Ferdinand.[63] Sixteen sentences were handed down, ranging from three years' hard labour to death by hanging. On 3 February Danilo Ilić, Veljko Čubrilović and Miško Jovanović were executed in Sarajevo. Death sentences had also been pronounced on Nedeljko Kerović and Jovan Milović; these were commuted to life imprisonment, but according to official reports both men died in prison from tuberculosis in April 1916. The other conspirators, including the actual assassin Gavrilo Princip, avoided the death penalty because they were minors. Gavrilo Princip, Nedeljko Čabrinović and Trifko Grabež were each sentenced to twenty years' hard labour, Vasa Čubrilović to sixteen years and Cvetko Popović to thirteen years. Only Vasa Čubrilović and Cvetko Popović lived to see the end of the war. Disease took the lives of others. Nedeljko Čabrinović died on 23 January 1916, Trifko Grabež on 21 October 1916 and Gavrilo Princip on 28 April 1918. Among the others given prison sentences, Lažar Djukić, Mitar Kerović, Jakov Milović and Mirko Perin all died in gaol. Hence eight of the thirteen sentenced to imprisonment died while serving their sentences. Their trials had been regular and legal, but they were ill-treated in gaol.

Serbs from all walks of life found themselves under attack, and the rich lost the social status they had previously enjoyed.[64] Nevertheless, it was the ordinary people—mainly peasants, the lower clergy and teachers—who suffered the worst reprisals in Bosnia, Herzegovina and Srem. At the beginning of the war peasants from Bosnia and Herzegovina were hanged in large groups. Some were sentenced by courts, both regular and irregular, but others were killed without any trial, and many were tortured. This occurred in particular after Serbian and Montenegrin units had entered and then left eastern Bosnia, Srem and southern Banat. Around fifty people were hanged or shot in Zemun after the withdrawal of Serbian troops, while 250 people were shot without trial in twenty-seven villages of Srem. A total of twenty men and ten women were accused of high treason in Srem and given prison sentences of between three and thirteen years. As a result of pro-Serb behaviour in Borča, the Austro-Hungarian military authorities immediately jailed fifty-three men and twenty-five women on their return to the village, and a court martial in nearby Pančevo sentenced ten of them to death and nineteen to prison sentences of between ten and fifteen years. Those convicted included sixteen poor peasants, nine farm workers, two village artisans and two apprentices.[65] Furthermore, over 170 peasants from Banat were interned in the camp at Arad, and a huge number of peasants were deported from Srem and Bosnia. Around 20,000 people were deported from Srem, their homes settled by Hungarian and German peasants. Approximately the same number of Serbs were deported from Slavonia, although that region was far from the front line; these were mainly women and elderly men, proving that the measures taken were not for security reasons.

Culture was also targeted in this war 'on the internal front'.[66] Serb Cyrillic script immediately came under attack. According to orders issued on 3 and 13 October 1914, the use of Cyrillic in schools in Croatia was limited to religious instruction. A decree passed on 3 January 1915 abolished the right of inhabitants (in force since 19 August 1911) to address the authorities in either Cyrillic or Latin script, and it repealed the obligation on first instance authorities in areas with Serb majorities to respond in Cyrillic to missives submitted in that script. The decree of August 1911 was repealed in Dalmatia by a decision of the Provincial School Council on 22 October

1914. Finally an imperial order of 25 October 1915 decreed that Cyrillic script could not be used publicly in Bosnia and Herzegovina except 'within the scope of Serb-Orthodox Church authorities'.[67] Attempts were also made to suppress the use of the expression 'Serbo-Croatian' in a linguistic context, as well as the related concept that 'Serbian' or 'Croatian' were merely synonyms referring to the same language.

Social Democracy was also under constant pressure.[68] Some of the leaders and most of the members in Bosnia and Herzegovina, Croatia and Slavonia were mobilised and sent to the front; their organisations were not allowed to function, and their newspapers and all political activity by them were banned. Those Social Democratic leaders, members and sympathisers who remained at home were under police surveillance and accused of lacking patriotism. This state of affairs lasted till 1917.

Emigrés and volunteers

Before the war and during its first few months several prominent pro-Yugoslav political figures—mainly Serbs, but also Croats and a number of Slovenes—left or fled from Austria-Hungary.[69] Among those who fled immediately on the outbreak of war, three men—Ante Trumbić, Frano Supilo and Hinko Hinković—were to play an important role in the Yugoslav movement. They started their lives of voluntary exile in Italy. Though isolated at first, they were able not only to put forward Yugoslav ideas but also to work politically.

From the very beginning of the war it had been demonstrated that Serbia and Montenegro were the moral and political pillars of the Yugoslav idea and thus a gathering point for those favouring unification and against the Monarchy. Such people fled to Serbia and Montenegro from Austria-Hungary or came there from other parts of the world. A broad, unorganised and heterogeneous movement linked itself to those two states for the very reason that they were in the forefront of the armed struggle against the Monarchy and therefore interested in and capable of bringing together, supporting and defending pro-Yugoslav opponents of the Habsburg Empire. That was particularly the case with Serbia because it was a larger, more developed and more powerful country. The more Serbia proved itself capable of facing all dangers on the main Balkan front, the more it was seen as—and indeed became—the central factor of the political Yugoslav front. Serbia thus demonstrated the renown it had achieved, especially during the Balkan Wars. On 14 February 1915 Frano Supilo, who had long been active in the Yugoslav movement, wrote to Ante Trumbić about Serbia from Niš: 'The army is doing wonders. The people are true martyrs to work, suffering and sacrifice.... It seems to me that Šumadija will be able to carry out its task in the creation of a South Slav nation...'[70]

On the outbreak of war there were hundreds of South Slavs in Serbia. Some had come in previous years, mostly during the Balkan Wars, in which a number of them had fought as volunteers.[71] After hearing of Franz Ferdinand's death many of the several hundred guests at the St Vitus' Day celebrations in 1914 decided not to return to the Monarchy. From July onwards even more people came to Serbia from Banat, Srem and Bosnia, a number of them arriving with the Serbian army after its brief incursions into southern Srem and eastern Bosnia. There were therefore large numbers of refugees in Serbia. A letter, dated February 1915, from the Serbian Finance Ministry to Prime Minister Pašić states: 'We had 200,000 people who had fled from Bosnia and Srem together with their livestock.'[72] Scores of people from European and Mediterranean countries, not only Yugoslavs, set off immediately for Serbia. A group of twenty-two volunteers—including five Russians and one Lithuanian, while most of the others were from the Bay of Cattaro—gathered in Salonika at the beginning of August and travelled quickly to Serbia.[73] Some wanted to help on the war front, while others wished to assist in the political or propaganda spheres. Volunteers and refugees also arrived in Montenegro, especially from Herzegovina, Dalmatia and Lika.[74]

A number of politically active émigrés were quite powerful in Serbia.[75] These included the Slovene ethnologist Niko Županič, who had been in Serbia for some time, and the prominent Ribnikar family, which already considered itself Serb. Moreover, Nikola Stojanović, a distinguished Bosnian Serb leader, had come to Belgrade to join in the St Vitus' Day celebrations and had decided to stay there. Dušan Vasiljević, another prominent Serb from Bosnia, happened to be in Switzerland at the outbreak of war, and he travelled to

Serbia in the autumn of 1914. However, Jovan Banjanin, editor of a Serb newspaper in Croatia and deputy in the Croatian Sabor, was among the prisoners of war in Serbia, but he immediately informed the Serbian authorities that he was prepared to 'go to France and England wearing the uniform of an Austrian officer' and personally inform public opinion in those countries of 'Austrian crimes'. He would also, he declared, 'as a representative of Croatia', together with other émigrés, 'seek support from Europe for the unification of our entire nation'. Also in Serbia at that time were Ivo Ćipiko, Jefto Dedijer, Josip Milačić and others, all of whom said they were ready to make the Yugoslav programme a reality and set to work politically. Especially remarkable was the revolutionary activity of pro-Yugoslav young people, such as August Jenko, Dragotin Gustinčič and Vladislav Fabjančič (Slovenes), Milan Marjanović and Milostislav Bartulica (Croats), Pera Slijepčević (a Serb from Bosnia), and Veljko Petrović (a Serb from Vojvodina) among others.

The volunteer movement emerged at the very start of the war. Its core consisted of experienced Serb *comitadji*, Serbs from Serbia who were not conscripts, and inhabitants of the South Slav provinces of the Monarchy who wished to fight on Serbia's side. These were soon joined by émigrés of Yugoslav origin living in allied or neutral countries, particularly the United States, and more and more Austro-Hungarian soldiers who had been taken prisoner on the Serbian or Russian fronts. The wish of Austro-Hungarian subjects to become volunteers for Serbia stemmed from their pro-Serb, pro-Yugoslav or, more rarely, pan-Slavist convictions. Most firmly believed that there was no difference between Serb and Yugoslav nationhood.

On 28 July the Serbian Minister of Military Affairs had ordered that 'volunteers should not be formed into separate volunteer commands.'[76] Such a decision could have reflected ideological belief in the unity of Yugoslavs, but in fact political reasoning prevailed: first, the creation of separate Yugoslav units would have provided the Monarchy with proof of its propaganda claim of Serbia's 'subversive activity' against it, and secondly, the creation of another unification factor might have made the political situation even more complex. That was why volunteers, both from Serbia and from abroad, were attached either to Serbian military units or to *comitadji* detachments as auxiliary units.

On 3 August the government issued to the Supreme Command a general ruling concerning *comitadji* activity. It provided, 'in the case of our offensive', for *comitadji* disrupting the enemy rear, attacking transport lines and compelling the enemy to 'disperse its forces'. In the case of an Austro-Hungarian offensive, the *comitadji* on the Monarchy's territory were to serve as the 'core for inciting a people's uprising in areas inhabited by Serbs'. If the Austro-Hungarian army were to penetrate deeper into Serbia, the *comitadji* were to lie low in areas denoted in advance and 'having let the enemy troops pass', attack the enemy rear with the greatest force, form troops made up of 'the most reliable persons', and create 'terrorist groups', with the aim of carrying out attacks on several enemy army commanders, 'spreading fear and panic on enemy territory.'[77] A Supreme Command order of 4 August 1914 created four *comitadji* detachments,[78] all commanded by leading Black Hand figures.[79] Volunteers included Serbs from Serbia and men from all the Yugoslav areas, including Montenegro, although Montenegro was also at war and had its own volunteer detachments. Among them were Orthodox, Catholics and Muslims: it was a time when individual differences were erased in the interests of the community as a whole.

From the very beginning, both as Serbian soldiers and as *comitadji*, the volunteers fought with exceptional courage and self-sacrifice, and suffered huge losses.[80] Among the first of them to die in battle was August Jenko, leader of the Slovene pro-Yugoslav national-revolutionary youth; his comrade Vladislav Fabjančič was wounded. In all, their losses amounted to over 60%. Moreover, the enemy were merciless in their treatment of captured volunteers, especially those who were Austro-Hungarian citizens.

Among Austro-Hungarian soldiers of Yugoslav origin the wish to enter the Serbian regular army as volunteers was spontaneous.[81] On 27 September 1914 the head of the command dealing with prisoners of war informed the Serbian Ministry of Military Affairs that 'as is well known, there are many Serb prisoners,' and 'there is also a considerable number of prisoners who are good Serbs and would like to fight against Austria.' He ended his report: 'It would be a sin to leave those people idle, mixed together with other prisoners of war, when even the slightest help is welcome to our army [and] those men themselves wish to make great sacrifices for our common liberation.' Vojvoda Putnik himself informed the Minister of Military Affairs that 'some Austrian prisoners of war, who are Serbs or Croats by nationality, declare under interrogation that they wish to join our army and fight with them against Austria for the liberation of their homeland.' He further stressed the need for 'a decision in principle on this matter', in order that 'those prisoners of war might be of use.' On 21 October the government made a decision on the issue of prisoners of war: 'Prisoners of war may not be forced to take part in military operations against their homeland, but they may take part in such operations of their own free will. Military deserters may, if they wish, serve the country to which they have fled.' The government elaborated an official stand on this: 'These prisoners of war and military deserters can be used for military operations (1) if they apply voluntarily to do so, and (2) if they are made aware that from the moment they enter the ranks of the Serbian army they will be considered as traitors if caught by Austrian troops, and they stop being prisoners of war the day they enter our ranks.' On 22 October the Ministry of Military Affairs issued orders to the supreme command accordingly, but it further stipulated that every prisoner of war who wished to become a volunteer had to 'give a written statement that he was joining the volunteers of his own free will'. The volunteers were to be used for service in the newly-acquired territories (Kosovo and Macedonia), which meant that they would not be sent to the Austro-Hungarian front where, if caught, they would have been punished immediately for high treason. Through the Legation in Petrograd the government informed those taken prisoner in Russia and wishing to serve as Serbian volunteers that they would be used 'only for guarding the frontier with Albania and for maintaining law and order, but not in the war against Austria-Hungary'.[82]

At the end of 1914 there were some 70,000 prisoners of war in Serbia, of whom 20,000 were of Yugoslav origin.[83] A lenient approach was actually being used towards all Yugoslav and Czech prisoners of war. By that time they were being quickly separated from the other prisoners of war and were given complete freedom of movement—foreigners were surprised to see prisoners of war enjoying such freedom. The American journalist John Reed wrote that in Niš Austrian prisoners in uniform wandered freely everywhere, without a guard—some drove wagons, others dug ditches, and hundreds were idle and merely loitered about. 'Now and then an Austrian officer passed alone, in full uniform and with his sword.'[84]

A Yugoslav volunteer movement emerged spontaneously in Russia too.[85] In mid-September the Serbian minister in Petrograd informed the government in Niš that he was being approached by 'many Serbs from Bosnia and other areas, Austrian soldiers taken prisoner by the Russians', who were begging him to send them to Serbia.[86] At the beginning of that month a group of prisoners from Bosnia and Herzegovina had made contact with the Serbian Legation and asked to be sent to Serbia 'to take up arms against the enemy of the Serbian nation with our brothers there'. They wrote that they wanted to contribute at least something 'to their own liberation'. Although the Serbian and Russian authorities quickly agreed that such wishes should be granted, the necessary procedures took a long time. That was because the war was not expected to last long. By the summer of 1915 about fifty volunteers had been transferred from Russia to Serbia.

In the United States too, according to an article by a member of the Croatian National Community administration in the *Zajedničar* paper dated August 1914, the news of the war had caused questions to be asked by 'our people as to when and how they could travel to Europe to join the Serbian army'.[87] On the eve of the outbreak of war, the secretary of the *Sloga* Association of United Serbs announced publicly that all Serb émigrés to the United States were ready to travel to Serbia and fight for it if Austria-Hungary decided to attack. In August 1914 several Serbs and some Croats arrived in New York intending to cross the ocean and join the Serbian army, but they could not find passage. When Mihailo Pupin, the Serbian Consul General in New York and a professor at Columbia University, secured transport in British and Italian ships, several thousand came forward and declared themselves ready to go to the Serbian or Montenegrin battlefront; they had acted spontaneously or in response to a Montenegrin appeal made in the meantime. In the following months around 4,000 men crossed the Atlantic with that objective.

Between the end of October and the end of December 1914 a total of 452 prisoners of war in Serbia applied to join the volunteers.[88] The number of volunteers grew constantly, particularly with the arrival of émigrés from abroad. In January 1915 volunteers were regrouped and supplemented by new applicants and new arrivals into the 1st Volunteer Battalion headed by Major Vojin Popović. Another two volunteer battalions were created later, bringing the number of volunteers up to 3,500. All these battalions were deployed on the frontiers with Bulgaria and Albania. Meanwhile, four volunteer battalions had been formed in Montenegro.[89]

The great majority of volunteers were undoubtedly Serbs—in December 1914 there were only twenty-six Croat volunteers and a few members of other Slav nations among them. However, the national "labels" at that time should not be taken as totally accurate, since with the upsurge of Yugoslav idealism the identify of one's nation was not important.[90]

War aim

The first months of the war revealed two contrasting historical aspirations and two completely divergent war aims—those of Austria-Hungary and those of Serbia.

Austria-Hungary embarked on the war to punish the independent Serbian state and to halt the upsurge of the Yugoslav movement within its own borders. Owing to internal friction, its leaders were unable to state categorically if they would totally destroy the Serbian state or not. During his mission to Berlin on 5 and 6 July 1914, Count Hoyos told German statesmen that 'Serbia must cease to exist', that Serbia 'has to be divided between us, Romania and Bulgaria.' He was thus expressing what was evidently a widespread opinion.[91] Even before the autumn of 1914 certain individuals, including General Conrad, had been claiming that the Monarchy should annex Niš, or rather the whole of the Morava river valley. However, the Hungarian leadership continued to resist large-scale annexation of Serbian state territory, as a result of which the actual Austro-Hungarian war aim at that time was that Serbia should be territorially decimated so that it would be unable to exist independently. According to the decision made in July, Austria-Hungary would annex the territory around Šabac and Belgrade, i.e. the entire Sava river valley. It was also prepared to offer Serbia's neighbours, mainly Bulgaria, considerable additional territory. On the afternoon of 28 July, when the news of the declaration of war reached Sofia, the Austro-Hungarian minister there notified Vienna that 'the mood of the people was in favour of war against Serbia and Romania', which had been 'confirmed by the Prime Minister' Vasil Radoslavov.[92] During covert preparations for war around the middle of July, a draft treaty of alliance with Bulgaria was drawn up in which the Monarchy offered Bulgaria all of Macedonia that fell within the Serbian state.[93] Thus in the autumn of 1914 there was a minimum Austro-Hungarian war aim regarding to Serbia: namely that Serbia, reduced by at least the territories of the Sava river valley and Macedonia, should ostensibly remain a free state, while it would actually become a satellite of Austria-Hungary. However, the more aggressive forces in the Monarchy also hoped that victory would bring about a more comprehensive annexation of Serbia's territories.

In their public addresses in the first months of the war, Serbia's representatives were mainly concerned with the defensive nature of their country's tasks. In the proclamation of general mobilisation issued late in the evening of 25 July 1914, the Serbian government identified its war aim as follows: 'We consider it our duty to call on the nation to defend the Homeland.'[94] The orders given to the army by the supreme command in the summer and autumn of 1914 only repeated this aim, in more emotive terms echoing the sentiments of the time. It was stated in August 1914 that the enemy had 'ruthlessly attacked our honour and our lives', demanding 'our lives and our independence', and that 'there is no more sacred duty in the world than to defend one's state, one's nation and one's faith, one's hearth, one's old and one's weak.'[95] There were a number of reasons for stressing the purely defensive nature of the war. At the start of the armed conflict, the basic aim had indeed been the country's defence; the enemy had fabricated a pretext for war by accusing Serbia of directly threatening its integrity. But in fact Serbia had been attacked and forced into a war at a time when it was not ready, either materially or from a political or ideological point of view. And although the Yugoslav idea was present among the public, it had not elaborated any programme for armed conflict with Austria-Hungary. In fact, such a programme did not exist in independent Serbia's practical state policy even in draft form.

If we examine what was happening behind the scenes when political decisions were being made, it becomes evident that a clear commitment existed in August to base the war aim on the Yugoslav idea. It was not till the second half of 1914 that attempts were made to fill in the gaps. It is mentioned in the memoirs of that Nikola Pašić had spoken at the end of July of a frontier somewhere on the line Klagenfurt-Marburg (Maribor)-Seged (Szeged).[96] And in the Regent's order of 4 August, besides a predominantly defensive tone, there was also an offensive inflexion when he mentioned the laments of 'millions of our brothers' being heard 'from Bosnia and Herzegovina, from Banat and Bačka, from Croatia, Slavonia and Srem and from our sea of stony Dalmatia'.[97] In the light of these facts, it can thus be understood why, in his proclamation of 29 July, the Regent had mentioned not only Serb but also 'Croat guards of the march' who had shed their blood in vain for centuries for the ungrateful foreign Habsburgs.[98] Still, there was hesitation in the first months of the war over whether to include Slovenes in the programme because it was not known whether the mood in favour of entering a Yugoslav state was widespread among them. Hence two variants existed: Serb-Croat and Serb-Croat-Slovene.

It was not till the end of the summer of 1914 that the Ministry of Foreign Affairs called on a broad circle of politicians, diplomats and university professors to look into the exact geographical extent of lands that were ethnically Yugoslav and elaborate possibilities for the internal organisation of a new state.[99] In parallel to this, preparations were carried out for practical political work, and the first diplomatic moves were made. Such a war aim then entered into state acts, and the community of the 'Serb-Croat tribe' was already taken into account in the programme document compiled at the end of August.[100] It was felt that a the clarification of the Yugoslav idea was needed, and Professor Jovan Cvijić, one of the government's most important advisers, stated that 'we need to crystallise views on the Yugoslav entity and to strengthen our knowledge and awareness of it.'[101] Professor Cvijić had been assigned the task of precisely determining ethnic Yugoslav territories, thus identifying the borders of the desired state as well as consolidating the Yugoslav idea scientifically on geographical-anthropological grounds. On 30 October 1914 Professor Božidar Marković, one of the leading figures in the Independent Radical Party, wrote to Professor Ljubomir Stojanović that it had been agreed that 'activity had to be geared to the creation of an integral, independent Yugoslav state comprising, besides Serbia, Croatia and Slovenia.'[102]

But what actually happened was that everything was overshadowed by the battles being fought and developments in the diplomatic sphere. Everything else had to take second place—the programme's elaboration, its presentation on the international scene and, from October onwards, the preparation of broader activities for Yugoslavs who had fled the Monarchy and the inclusion of prisoners or war among volunteers. The Entente Powers were trying to win over new allies, mainly with promises of territory that was part of the Yugoslav programme. They were trying to tempt Bulgaria by offering it large parts of Macedonia, Romania by agreeing to its demand for Banat, and Italy by agreeing to its aspirations regarding the eastern Adriatic coast. Italy suggested that the Entente should introduce the idea of an independent Croatia into its plans for the political future of the Balkans, in the hope of preventing the creation of a Yugoslav state that would be an obstacle in the way of Italian ambitions in the Adriatic and the western Balkans.

Serbia responded with the Yugoslav programme, which it had built up in the face of diplomatic opposition. On 29 August Jovan Jovanović, representing the Foreign Minister, wrote that the Yugoslav programme should be elaborated 'in connection with the issue of compensation to Bulgaria'.[103] On 4 October he sought to hasten the progress of the programme's elaboration, pointing out that, at Italy's insistence, 'some diplomatic circles are already examining the idea of an autonomous Croatia, to include Croatia, Slovenia and part of Dalmatia, as well as perhaps part of Bosnia.'[104]

The more the major Allies tried to tailor the Balkan peninsula to their needs in the World War, the firmer the Serbian side became in its defence of the entire Yugoslav programme as a permanent solution in the post-war period. In response to Entente pressure to induce it to cede part of Macedonia to Bulgaria, the Serbian government made what it called its 'ultimate concessions'[105]—on the condition that similar concessions would be made by Greece and Romania, and only if in the event of an Entente victory Serbia were to become united with the Serb and Croat lands of Austria-Hungary, while Bulgaria should remain not only neutral and accommodating to Serbia and the Entente Powers but also part of the

Balkan bloc. Clearly Serbia intended to make the offer as unacceptable as possible. It further warned that 'to take from Serbia and give to Bulgaria, which is extorting gain and is supported by Austria and Germany, means weakening one's own policy. That means facilitating, to a certain extent, Germanism's drive to the east.'[106] Besides, the 'ultimate concessions' were so small compared with Bulgarian demands that they must have known in advance that Bulgaria would not accept.

By 4 September, as a reaction to agreements among the Allies themselves and between the Allies and some neutral states, a war aim had been formulated providing for 'turning Serbia into a strong south-western [sic] Slav state comprising all Serbs, all Croats and all Slovenes'.[107] This was claimed to be based on the 'sound concept ... of the great importance of the Serb-Croat tribe for the survival and further development of the independence of Slavs and the Balkan nations.' The views were therefore founded on the internationally significant strategic concept that 'the Balkans need a strong central state' that would always be a 'reliable basis for peace in the Balkans', and would preserve 'balance in the Adriatic and to some extent in the Mediterranean.'[108] According to a circular memo sent by the Prime Minister on 4 September to diplomatic representatives abroad, 'that state should be Serbia together with Bosnia, Herzegovina, Vojvodina, Croatia, Istria and Slovenia.'[109]

According to a draft composed by 22 September, the Yugoslav state was to include the entire plain of Banat, all of Baranja, Medjumurje and Slovenia, and probably a large part of Carinthia. An essential element of this demarcation lay in the ethnic Yugoslav basis, but strategic reasons were also mentioned ('Serbia needs Banat with its geographic-strategic border, as otherwise it can not defend either Banat or the capital Belgrade'), as well as historical reasons ('It is the greater part of old Serbian Vojvodina with the Military March frontier') etc.[110]

Pašić's circular memo of 4 September also stated that Bulgaria 'may enter the community on a federal or other basis'—Serbian-Bulgarian brotherhood had been created in the nineteenth century and was still alive in Serbian public opinion. That was despite the fact that the most important ideologue of Yugoslav unity, Jovan Cvijić, had evolved the ethnographic-territorial programme of the future state in the autumn of 1914, and his ensuing ideology had excluded Bulgarians. Despite noting that Bulgarians were a 'nation akin' to Yugoslavs, he had mentioned the characteristics that set them apart.[111] Unlike Cvijić, Aleksandar Belić classified Bulgarians as 'Slav South' ('On the basis of the history of Balkan and Slav nations, it can be concluded that four nations inhabit the Slav South: Slovenes, Croats, Serbs and Bulgarians').[112] The historian Stojan Novaković also mentioned links with Bulgarians ('There are really two concepts of Yugoslav nationhood: one broader and more comprehensive, and the second narrower; the first includes Bulgarians'). He further spoke of the possibility of a confederation 'from the Black Sea to the Adriatic'.[113] Diplomats also discussed Bulgaria as being part of a united state. On 7 November the Bulgarian minister in Niš heard from his Montenegrin counterpart Lazar Mijušković that in the opinion of a Serbian diplomat 'an agreement should be reached with Bulgaria, and in fifteen years those two countries [Bulgaria and either Serbia or the Yugoslav state] should form a union that will be bordered by three seas and will dominate the Balkan peninsula.'[114] The fact that Pašić always addressed that same Bulgarian minister in a spirit of friendship and even, as the Bulgarian noticed, endeavoured to show him close personal attention[115] should doubtless be seen as a tactic directed at eliminating the danger of an attack from the east. However, while the links among Serbs, Croats and Slovenes were being stressed, both deliberately and spontaneously, the bridges between Serbs and Bulgarians were being brought down.

Little is known of the ideas for the internal system of the future state. However, it is certain that the section of the programme dealing with that had been drawn up by the mid-autumn of 1914. It is difficult to enumerate all those involved in its elaboration, but they certainly included Nikola Pašić, Professor Božidar Marković as representative of the Independent Radical Party, and, at least in one phase, distinguished university professors, social scientists and historians.[116] At one point Nikola Stojanović and Dušan Vasiljević, Serbian émigrés from Bosnia, also played an important role, and the opinion of the Slovene Niko Županič was also, to a certain extent, taken into account. A number of discussions took place on this issue, at least one in Valjevo and one in Niš.[117]

The key solution is contained in what was agreed in Niš on 27 October: that the new state would 'preserve the national characteristics of each tribe without separate organisation'.[118] As Božidar Marković wrote to Ljubomir Stojanović on 30 October, a 'simple' state was desired 'without any kind of separate state-legal autonomies'.[119] It was further agreed that 'confessional equality' would be ensured, which would be manifested as necessary in the ranks of the heads of the churches, 'equality of scripts'[120] (Marković's letter stipulates that 'the complete equality of Latin and Cyrillic scripts is guaranteed'[121]) and 'total civic equality'. It can be concluded from available sources that what was envisaged was a constitutional and centralist monarchy with a common government and assembly. That concept opened up the possibility for unification, envisaging that Serbia would 'guarantee that capable and correct administration staff would retain all their previously acquired rights',[122] that is the rights they had enjoyed in Austria-Hungary. There was readiness to agree to many Croat demands, and it was agreed that 'Croatia be mentioned in the name of the state', that 'if necessary' the Yugoslav ruler be 'crowned with the Croatian crown', that the 'historical individuality of Croatia be expressed in emblems (coat of arms and maritime flag)'. 'In the extreme case' there could be 'negotiations on a separate Croatian provincial *sabor*'. Those concessions were considered to be ones that 'do not harm the state's unity or hinder the final crystallising of the nation's unity'. Marković wrote to Stojanović: 'It is greatly desired here that Croats should enter into a state with us, and more concessions will probably have been made.'[123] Consistent with this, it was envisaged that Slovenes could obtain 'similar concessions, with a separate guarantee for their language'. Unification was to be implemented in such a way that the Serbian constitution would be valid for all the territories until the passing of a new constitution. Furthermore, Marković wrote, the 'new regions will be represented in the central administration', and 'elections will be held promptly for a Great National Assembly, which will bring into being a new constitutional order' in which 'everyone will be represented.' This evidently meant representatives of Slovenes, Croats and Serbs and those of the populations of all the historic territories united in the Yugoslav state.

Clearly based on the idea of 'one nation', the concept aimed at creating a unitary parliamentary and civic-democratic monarchy in which particularities would be honoured. This can be construed as meaning the cultural particularities of the Serb, Croat and Slovene populations. It should be noted that a discrepancy could already be felt between the basic idea of 'one nation' and the realisation that it was necessary to honour the particularities of the three recognised 'tribes'. Alongside the presupposed cultural particularities, the concessions created the possibility for a degree—if necessary, a considerable one—of political autonomy. The ultimate solution was left to the future constituent assembly made up of freely elected representatives of the country's inhabitants. It was also agreed that guarantees should be provided that all agreements reached previously on internal order would be honoured. However, everything was imbued with the awareness of Serbia as an independent democratic factor, which as such had the central place and a determining role.

The issue of unification with Montenegro was considered integral, but nonetheless a special part of this programme.[124] There were several reasons for this. First, it was considered that Serbia and Montenegro, as two independent states, should decide on that issue themselves and thus limit the involvement of the Great Powers as much as possible. Belgrade and Cetinje had, after all, started negotiations on unification back in the first half of 1914, before the start of the war. And, given the fact that both the Entente Powers and neutral Italy had their separate vested interests in parts of the Austro-Hungarian territories inhabited by South Slavs, as a result of which the Yugoslav programme was therefore constantly in a state of flux, it seemed inadvisable to broach the issue of the unification of the two states as an international one.

In the official notes on what had been agreed at Niš on 27 October 1914—immediately after the aim of creating 'a single Yugoslav, possibly Serb-Croat state' had been stipulated—the following was written: 'As negotiations on a real union (army, foreign policy, trade and communications, finances) are already under way with Montenegro, the unity of the Serb tribe has been assured.' The expression 'real union' denoted possible unification on the basis of honouring the existence of two states with each preserving a considerable amount of its own individuality, while of course unifying the most important areas such as the military, foreign policy, transport, trade and monetary affairs. The foundations for such a 'real union' had already been laid in the negotiations in the first half of 1914, when the incentive had come from the Montenegrin side (although that was actually on the basis of what had been begun in 1913), because it was considered such a small and poor country as that Montenegro had to seek its future in a community with Serbia. However, another reason was the growing dissatisfaction in Montenegro with the rule of King Nicholas.[125] Talks conducted in the pre-war years inside the Montenegrin political leadership indicated that those in favour of unification understood that the Petrović-Njegoš family should abdicate. The Serbian government had been informed of that, and Pašić, the Prime Minister announced the possibility of a perpetual apanage for the Montenegrin dynasty. However, the idea of abdication soon proved unattainable, at least for a time, since it was impossible to persuade King Nicholas and his family to renounce their rights as rulers.[126] Montenegrins also hesitated over whether simple unification or a union with Serbia on 'special terms' should be undertaken. As for Serbia, it wanted Montenegro to propose a specific method of achieving unification, which Pašić explained as necessary to avoid any criticism that the stronger Serbia was imposing its own ideas. It seems that Belgrade's belief that it was essential for the Montenegrin side to declare what would happen to its ruling family was of key importance in this.[127]

In a lengthy letter to King Peter of Serbia dated 15 March 1914 King Nicholas underlined his desire for links with Serbia at the earliest possible moment, but he particularly did not use the word 'unification', and stressed the need for agreement to be reached 'on the independence and equality of our states and dynasties' and for the exact identification of 'mutual obligations in military, diplomatic and financial matters'. The impression is that he did not want unification, but if it could not be avoided, then he preferred a confederation of two states headed by two equal dynasties, with the merging of military, foreign policy and customs matters. Nor was King Peter's response sufficiently specific, which seems natural given the nature of the proposal he had been given. However, the Serbian King did use the word 'unification' when he remarked, seemingly *en passant*, that it was an undertaking 'that had had such a fortunate outcome in Germany'. It seems that Serbia was indicating its readiness to accept a solution like that reached in Germany, namely unification on a federal basis, with each member of the federation retaining its traditional ruling family with their titles, as well as its government with local jurisdiction. This meant that an offer had been made to the Montenegrin King whereby he and his family would remain in power, while Serbia, which was bigger and more developed, would take the leading place in the future state. That would have followed the German pattern where leadership had gone to the strongest member, Prussia.[128] The views of unification still remained different, but the two sides presupposed that both dynasties would remain, and the solution could be seen in a 'real union'. That was the state of affairs when war was declared.

In the autumn of 1914 the concept of Yugoslav unification, taken as a whole, was both incomplete and riddled with contradictions. We have seen that, if in principle the state had been conceived as a unit, it could also have had federal components, and even confederal ones in the case of Serbia and Montenegro. And in the case of the Croats and Slovenes it could also have had elements of institutional singularity within itself (possibly regional autonomy). The final solution therefore depended on developments as a whole and on the political strength of the individual participants in the movement for unification of the Slav South. In parallel to this, practical work was under way. In August the Entente Powers had been made aware that Serbia wished to emerge from the war unified with the Croats or, at best, with all the other Yugoslavs, and they were officially informed of this, albeit cautiously and indirectly, in September 1914 (circular memos of 4 and 22 September). Particular attention was given to the organisation of joint activity by the Serbian government and individuals from Austria-Hungary itself who favoured the idea of Yugoslav unity. By the beginning of October a clear concept had emerged. Pašić wrote: 'We should ... hasten to form a Yugoslav Committee in London, in which Dalmatia, Bosnia and Herzegovina, Croatia, Slavonia, Slovenia, Banat with Bačka, Baranja and Srem will be represented.' The Committee's task was to represent and defend 'Yugoslav interests' and 'inform public opinion in England and Europe' of those interests.[129]

At the end of October it was decided to start implementing that concept, and the meeting in Niš agreed to go ahead. The notes from that meeting contain the following:

> The Committee should be made up of members who are convinced of the need for such a united state and prepared to work hard to bring it about.

The Committee president does not have to be a Serb. The Committee will communicate with the King's government through Serbian envoys, and is free in its internal activity. It will function as an independent and autonomous propaganda body *vis-à-vis* the public.[130]

On this subject Božidar Marković wrote to Ljubomir Stojanović that it was for Croats to determine who else should enter the Committee, that one Serb from Vojvodina (if possible from Banat) should join the Committee, and that there should also be some members from Serbia. Marković added that it had been decided that the Committee should function independently on internal matters and in relation to the public, and should specify 'where and what each member should do'. It had also been decided that the Committee could publish a newspaper. Marković also set out the first steps to be taken: 'We now know that among Croats there are those in favour of unity (Trumbić, Supilo, Hinković), and when they have been found … we should listen to them, speak with them, and, if they agree, organise further activity with them.' 'An attempt should be made through them to obtain links with other Croats' as well as Slovenes.[131]

One can only conclude that, in line with the idea of unification, the Committee was a means of unification only and not conceived with any narrow political aims. It was then decided to entrust the first talks to Nikola Stojanović and Dušan Vasiljević, who were to travel to Italy to reach agreement with Croats abroad on 'all matters of urgency'. Professor Marković would also travel there if necessary. On 29 October Stojanović and Vasiljević set off on their journey.[132]

After all these preparations and activity it was officially announced that the Yugoslav programme determined Serbia's war aims. The new Coalition government, which in the mean time had been created from among the strongest parties and was headed by Nikola Pašić, made a statement before the National Assembly at a session in Niš on 7 December 1914. The statement, read by Pašić, was as follows: 'The government is sure that it will retain the trust of the National Assembly as long as it works for great causes, the Serbian state and the Serb-Croat and Slovene peoples.' The government further bowed 'with limitless respect … before the illustrious sacrifices made bravely and willingly on the altar of the homeland.… Confident peoples of the determination of the entire Serbian nation to persist in the battle to defend its holy hearth and freedom, it considers its most important and, at this fateful time, its sole task as being to secure a successful end to that great war which, at the moment of its inception, also became a struggle for the liberation and unification of all our brother Serbs, Croats and Slovenes who are not free.'[133] That short and formal document, known as the Niš Declaration, sounded a cautious note, given the delicacy of its contents during a war whose outcome was uncertain, but it was clear and resolute. It totally equated the government's duties in Serbia's defence with those affecting the creation of a Yugoslav state, and it was in that context that the sacrifices made hitherto were interpreted. The National Assembly voted in favour of this statement, opposed only by two Social Democratic deputies. The contents of the Declaration were quickly reported officially to the envoys of France, Britain and Russia, although only excerpts were quoted. The Montenegrin government resented the fact that it had been overlooked in the passing of that document.[134]

It was around the same time that Jovan Cvijić, using the pseudonym Dinaricus, completed his theoretical treatise on the Yugoslav nation, which was printed in Niš in December 1914 and appeared at the beginning of 1915 with the title *Jedinstvo Jugoslovena* (The Unity of Yugoslavs). The treatise resembles a kind of theoretical rationale of the Niš Declaration and, despite all Professor Cvijić's independent work, it was based on his understanding of the war as it had been evolved in written form by Pašić, Protić and Jovanović in August. The introduction to the treatise contains the following:

Serbia's geographical position is significant but difficult: it lies in the centre of the Balkan peninsula, around the Morava-Vardar valley, with communications linking Central Europe with the Middle East, the Mediterranean and Suez. In addition, areas around the Adriatic Sea and around Trieste are inhabited by fellow countrymen of Serbs who, by the very nature of things, aspire to prevent the foreign, Central European drive towards the Adriatic and Trieste. In short, Serbia, together with the Yugoslavs in Austria-Hungary, is the main obstacle in the way of the southward drive of Germanism and Austro-Germanism, and thus its geographical position makes it the main fighter for the freedom and independence of the Balkan peninsula.

It should be noted that Cvijić equated the historical role of Serbs from Serbia with that of other Yugoslavs. Only then did he add that the war Serbia was fighting at that very time was 'for a noble cause, for the freedom and unification of Serbs and other Yugoslavs.'

Cvijić's real intention was to justify those political convictions by providing deeper reasons, geographical links and anthropological bonds that bound Yugoslavs into a single entity, despite the visible differences. Many migrations in recent times had had the effect, Cvijić wrote, of 'dispersing and homogenising national characteristics'. Furthermore, he said, 'Serbs, Croats and Slovenes have become strongly intermixed, better acquainted, and accustomed to one another.'

Maps of the future borders of the Yugoslav state date from the end of 1914. They were drawn up on the basis of respect for the political decision that 'all Serbs, all Croats and all Slovenes' should enter the new state.[135] They provided one project in two variants and with several alternatives. Both variants contained broadly the same northern border encompassing Temišvar (Timisoara), Subotica, Baja, Pečuj (Pecs), Maribor, Celovec (Klagenfurt) and Beljak (Villach); only the first variant also included Velika Kanjiža (Nagykanizsa). In both variants Prekomurje remained outside the Yugoslav state. In the west the valleys of Pontebba and Trbiž stayed on the Italian side, and the border ran along the left edge of the Soča valley and met the Adriatic at Aquilaea, i.e. it followed the demarcation line between Italy and Austria-Hungary at the time. The first variant provided for a zone 'pending agreement with Italy' (Kranjska [Carniola] Gora, Tolmin, Gorica, Trieste, Kopar, Poreč, Rovinj and Pula). There was hesitation over the border with Romania: the minimum requirement was for a border that ran immediately east of Bela Crkva and Temišvar and reached the Moriš (Maros) at Lipova (Lipe), while the maximum requirement provided for a border starting east of Oršava (Orsova) and encompassing the whole of the upper Tamiš river basin and then returning to Lipova and the Moriš river. Temesvar was included in the future Yugoslav state in all cases. The basis of all the solutions was the line the government put forward in its circular memorandum of 22 September 1914.

Serbia thus combined the struggle for its state and national Serbian aims with that for Yugoslav aims. However, the Yugoslav programme offered the best prospects both for victory in the current war which had been forced on Serbia and for the future. Thanks to the Yugoslav programme it was able to see the struggle as one for broadly based national liberation, and an opportunity to strengthen its own psychological and ideological resistance forces with a great ideal and to gain a strong propaganda tool for weakening Austria-Hungary from within. Moreover the realisation of the Yugoslav idea would place Serbia in a community of similar nations and indeed, according to that notion, make it the pivot of that community. Such a state would have a long coastline and, from Serbia's point of view at that time, the nearest large countries would be far from its territory—Italy to the west, some kind of possible Austrian-German state to the northwest, and an Austro-Hungarian state, if it survived, to the north.

Given the time when all this was taking place, only a national ideology could ensure that a corresponding political programme could be successfully worked out. The developments of previous decades had brought Yugoslav ideology to the fore, but that was in conditions where Serbs, Croats and Slovenes had clear national characteristics. In the circumstances of the early months of war in 1914 and at the beginning of 1915, many different concepts and definitions were put forward to describe the fundamentals of unity: the 'Serb-Croat-Slovene tribe', 'brother Serbs, Croats and Slovenes', 'Serb, Croat and Slovene—one single ethnic nation', 'Croats, Serbs and Slovenes are the same nation with three national names', 'Serbs and Yugoslavs', 'Serbdom and Yugoslavism', 'the Serb tribe and Yugoslavism', 'members of the same tribe', 'Serbo-Croats', the 'national programme of Croats' that is 'quite feasible in our new state', 'the Yugoslav nation or the South Slav nation', the 'southwestern Slav state' and so on. This confusion was a clear result of the immaturity of Yugoslav ideology at that time, and the reasons for it lay in highly developed national singularities.

Nonetheless, a basis existed for the thesis of ethnic kinship that was manifest in the slogan 'tribes of one nation' and the word 'brothers'. The almost identical literary languages of the Serbs and Croats and their similarity to the Slovenes' literary language did not represent the essence of that concept. The concept of brotherhood overrode national, cultural, religious and political differences and nullified the centuries of separation and the divisions drawn by the trenches of the war. For Serbs that concept was based on two interests: Serbia's interest in ceasing to be a tiny state at the mercy of international politics and in finally coming together, though dispersed and mixed among other nations, in one independent state. The realisation of these two interests was only possible through association with other nations ethnically related to them. This all went counter to national movements in the Balkans that stressed individuality and had separate aims that were often opposed to each other.

The key thesis of Yugoslav ideology in Serbia—one nation with 'three tribes'—contained the acceptance in principle that these 'tribes are equal among themselves,' and excluded the possibility of the existence of some other 'tribe'. Still, when preparing his address to the Entente in response to the demand that Serbia should yield part of Macedonia to Bulgaria, Nikola Pašić wrote that the territory in question was 'inhabited by Macedonian Slavs, a tribe that is closer to Serbs than to the Bulgarian tribe'.[136] Pašić therefore used the word 'tribe' for Macedonians in the same way as for nationalities such as the Serb and Bulgarian, and (as recorded in other documents) Croat and Slovene. It is evident that this was not only Pašić's opinion but also that of a broader circle among Serbia's leading echelon, and that Macedonians were considered internally to be separate in the same sense as Serbs, Bulgarians, Croats and Slovenes. However, there was no wish that this separateness should be recognised.

Frano Supilo's views give an indication of what Yugoslav émigrés from Austria-Hungary thought of the Yugoslav programme during this phase. Several times in 1914 and early 1915 he spoke at length of Yugoslav unification, stressing that common threats necessitated all Yugoslav peoples uniting into an independent state. He put the threat of Pan-Germanism first among these, although having been born on the Adriatic coast he was particularly sensitive to danger from Italy.[137] In a letter to Gina Lombroso-Ferero on 20 September 1914 he underlined the need for '*un beluardo contro Drang nach Osten*' (an obstacle in the way of the German drive east), but feeling danger threatening from elsewhere he once told Trumbić that if Croatia remained alone 'Italy would swallow us up like macaroni'. He saw the reason for strengthening the unification front in the fact that 'Austro-Hungarian politics has done everything to cultivate separatism and antagonism …, with the aim of *divide et impera*'. He stressed the ideological platform of defence as being 'that we Croats,

Serbs and Slovenes from Triglav [Slovenia] to Timok make up one and the same nation with one and the same language, and with only three names for the nations.... It is not important what a nation is *called*, but how that nation *lives.* What is important is that it answers to itself, is free, united and makes progress.'

In contrast to the historical divisions among Yugoslavs, Supilo presented the thesis of the profound links binding them and the identity of language.

Serbs and Croats are divided by two pasts and to a certain extent by difference in confession. But their language is one and the same. There are almost no differences in dialect, with the exception of the Slovene dialect.... Our common man from Triglav to Timok, regardless of the dialect he is speaking or listening to, can make himself understood without any difficulty.

The territorial part of Frano Supilo's programme was identical to Serbia's. In November 1914 he gave the following enumeration:

1. Southern and eastern Carinthia.... 2. Southern Styria.... 3. Austrian Primorje ... consisting of Gorica, Gradisca, Trieste and Istria. 4. Dalmatia. 5. Bosnia and Herzegovina. 6. Croatia and Slavonia with the town of Rijeka and its district. 7. Southern Hungary including the frontier in Styria, north of the River Mura eastwards to just south of Pecs ... to Mohacs, where it crosses the Danube and climbs north of Subotica ... right to the Tisa south of Szeged. It then follows the River Maros to near Arad and then loops down to the Danube at Orsova. 8. Today's Montenegro. 9. Today's Serbia.

Finally, on the basis of 'fusion with Serbia and Serbs', and stressing that 'we as Croats must resist all separatism', Frano Supilo considered Serbia as the centre of unification and named it Piedmont.

The representatives of Serbia and of Yugoslav émigrés from Austria-Hungary had the same views on the essentials of the programme consistent with the motto 'one state one nation'. That was in the conviction that unity was the solution to threats from foreign powers. The vital element of the programme that came to the fore in 1914 was 'unity above all'. Some uncertainties arose owing to the concept of Serbia being the 'pivot of the Yugoslav state', but were left to be resolved later. For example, Jovan Jovanović warned in that context that such a programme was feasible only if 'all Croats felt liberated and not absorbed'. Meanwhile Ante Trumbić was thinking of the liberation 'of our nation in two groups, Croat and Serb'.[138] What was actually happening was that putting the Yugoslav programme into effect was creating two sets of problems for its proponents—foreign policy problems and those concerning internal relations within the hoped-for state. The foreign policy problems were being solved by fighting with the enemy on the battlefront and by diplomatic struggles with the Allies. As for internal relations within the unified state, these had to be solved by the proponents of the Yugoslav programme themselves. Resolution of foreign policy problems lay in securing international recognition and recognition of borders for the Yugoslav state, while internal problems could only be resolved by organising mutual relations among the Yugoslav peoples. The former were tackled immediately, while tackling the second group was postponed.

By the emphasis placed on the Yugoslav programme in the War, the issue of creating the Yugoslav state was placed on the agenda of international politics. How relations within the state were to be arranged remained an internal policy issue to be tackled by the Yugoslavs themselves.

3
SERBIA SUFFERS

When the American journalist John Reed wrote in the spring of 1915 that Serbia was a 'country of death' he was both right and wrong. Seeing Serbia's economy shattered, Reed recalled something an official had told him: 'All the men of Serbia are in the army—or dead—and all the oxen were taken by the government to draw the cannon and the trains.' After visiting the Drina river front some months after fierce fighting had taken place, he wrote, 'An awful smell hung over the place', adding that he 'walked on the dead, so thick were they—sometimes our feet sank through into pits of rotting flesh, crunching bones,' and holes that 'opened suddenly' ... were 'swarming with grey maggots'. Yet he was amazed at the 'extraordinary lack of bitterness ... everywhere in Serbia', where everyone thought 'that the crushing Austrian defeat avenged them for all those black enormities, for the murder of their brothers'. And he recorded, translating roughly into English, the simple verse sung by soldiers: 'The Emperor Nicholas rides a black horse/The Emperor Franz Joseph rides a mule.'[1] He was in the strangest of lands, a land both dead and full of life, a land ravaged by war but still bursting with fighting spirit.

In those first months of 1915 Serbia was truly at a peak of military glory and basking in the moral and political victories of the battles it had fought to defend its territory over the previous six months. It had nonetheless suffered huge losses. The Serbian army had inflicted 273,804 casualties on the 450,000-odd enemy troops, 7,592 of whom were officers. However, its own casualties had numbered 163,557 of its 250,000 combatants, 2,110 being officers.[2] A total of 69,022 men had died on the battlefield of wounds or disease.[3]

Exhaustion

It only remained for the military leaders of a defeated Austria-Hungary, and those of a Germany confused and irritated by its ally's debacle, to analyse the reasons for Serbia's victories. Albin Kutschbach, a German agent in Niš, said in his report of 15 January 1915: 'Serbian officers are militarily irreproachable.'[4] Austro-Hungarian military intelligence concluded that Vojvoda Radomir Putnik was 'extremely popular and enjoyed the trust of the entire nation', adding that he was 'highly influential both at court and in government circles', that he had a 'cool, sober head' and was 'highly gifted militarily'. It also noted that Vojvoda Putnik, who was elderly and ailing, was surrounded by exceptional assistants. That same source of military intelligence also collected information about Vojvoda Živojin Mišić—a 'highly trained military leader' who was the 'heart and soul of Serbia's Supreme Command' and 'certainly the most competent Serbian officer and the most capable Serbian leader'. Vojvoda Stepa Stepanović was also praised and said to be 'one of the most capable leaders of the Serbian army... calm, resolute, extremely forceful and possessed of an exceptional understanding of matters necessary for supreme command'.[5] These assessments were remembered by the German general staff during preparations for a new, large-scale offensive across the Sava and the Danube in September 1915.[6]

Enemy experts during the Balkan wars had written that the Serbian officer corps, especially its younger members, had proved themselves in a remarkable way, and described them as 'pillars of strength'. They claimed that it could rightly be argued that Serbia's army owed its successes mainly to its officers. As for its infantry, intelligence reports noted their exceptional marching capacity and tenacity and persistence when attacking, but the greatest praise was reserved for the qualities they showed in defence, when they fought 'stubbornly', 'unyieldingly' and 'successfully'. The artillery were considered the elite of the Serbian army since they had 'well trained and highly intelligent officers'. They were said to aim very accurately, and the heavy artillery were singled out for their excellent performance. Thus the enemy army could only rely on the huge losses the Serbian army had suffered. According to German general staff estimates, during the autumn of 1914 'the core of the [Serbian] army had fallen' and huge numbers had then fallen victim to diseases that had swept through the ranks in winter and spring.[7]

Serbia and Montenegro were therefore enjoying considerable renown among Allied and neutral countries, and world public opinion viewed them with sympathy. The battle of Mount Cer represented the first Allied victory, and the landmark victory at the Kolubara drew much attention to Serbia.[8] Foreigners flocked to the country in late 1914 and the first eight months of 1915. Some came to see what was happening and to relay that information to their governments and the public in their own countries. Others came to offer humanitarian or political aid or indeed to fight alongside Serbs in their battle for independence. It was a motley group of people. There were political envoys, journalists, intelligence agents, humanists, pacifists, the merely curious and those in search of adventure. Individuals, groups of people and organisations throughout the Allied and neutral countries started to give moral, political and material support to Serbia, Montenegro and the Yugoslav movement.

Moreover, the visits made by the British General Paget, and the French General Pau had considerable military and political impact as propaganda and in raising morale. The Swiss forensics expert Archibald Reiss came to Serbia to investigate both the way Austro-Hungarian troops were waging war on Serbian territory and the crimes they had perpetrated against civilians. He published his findings, lambasting the Austro-Hungarian army, while the war was still under way.[9] Two Americans, the left-leaning publicist John Reed and his fellow traveller Boardman Robinson, journeyed to Serbia to become better acquainted with the Serbian people, and similar curiosity also motivated J.D. Rockefeller Jr.

A group of prominent and influential public figures in Britain lent support in the media to the struggle being waged by Serbia and Montenegro. These included the publicists Henry Wickham Steed and R.W. Seton-Watson, the archaeologist Sir Arthur Evans, the historian George Trevelyan, the historian Sir Charles Oman and many others. On instructions from the Foreign Office, Seton-Watson and Trevelyan travelled to Serbia at the end of 1914 and spent two months there. During that time they learned what was happening, held talks with the Regent and the Prime Minister, and made a number of other acquaintances.[10] In France Victor Bérard and the university professor Emile Haumant were among the Paris intellectuals who spoke out for Serbia and the Yugoslav programme.

There was also activity elsewhere. In many towns in Russia—Petrograd, Moscow, Odessa, Kiev and others—'Slav committees' were set up to collect aid of all kinds for Serbia and Montenegro. The Russian Red Cross and the Slav Charity Society in Petrograd set themselves the same task. As early as September 1914 the Serbian Relief Fund was set up in London, and the British government became its patron in March 1915. Articles in defence of Serbia and Yugoslav unification appeared more frequently in the London press, although a considerable number of people had sided with Austria-Hungary at the beginning of the war. That support became even more evident after the battle of the Kolubara, when the London press wrote warmly of the small Balkan nation of Serbia.[11] 'Serbia Day' was declared in Paris at the end of March 1915, and there were donations to the cause. Half a million francs were collected in March 1915 alone.

Serbia and Montenegro were held in such high esteem that certain cultural circles in Italy went so far as to advocate that Italy should also enter the war, citing the two as examples. Presenting their convictions visually, Marinetti and his Futurists created a graphic vision of the warring nations with the title *A Futurist Synthesis of War*. This listed all the parties to the war, each with three or more attributes. Heading the first column was 'Serbia' and in second place on the second column was 'Montenegro'—both on the positive side—and both were accompanied by the same three attributes: 'independence', 'ambition' and 'intrepidity'.[12] Gabriele D'Annunzio wrote his *Ode to the Serbs* in the autumn of 1915.[13]

In reality both Serbia and Montenegro were totally exhausted; economic life had ceased, and the costs of continuing the war were spiralling. Serbia gloried in its military victories and the prestige it had gained, but it was also appalled by its losses and the travails which still loomed. In his reminiscences an elderly citizen of Belgrade likened the situation to a football match, the takings of which were to go to the Red Cross, between Belgrade students and allied artillerymen, while monitors were taking careful aim from Austro-Hungarian positions on the Danube.[14] As eyewitnesses John Reed and Albin Kutschbach spoke in almost identical terms of the state of mind they encountered everywhere. Reed recorded an anecdote concerning a certain Djordje Stanojević, who, after a few drinks, complained: 'What are those French and English doing? [...] Why don't they beat the Germans? What they need there are a few Serbs to show them how to make war. We Serbs know that all that is needed is willingness to die—and then the war would soon be over...'[15] Kutschbach reported that Russian doctors were withdrawing from Serbia because they could no longer tolerate Serb officers constantly telling them that their army would already be in Austria and on the verge of peace if the Russian army had won as many victories as it had—as it was, 'Serbia was heading towards great danger.'[16]

On 15 January 1915 Kutschbach informed his superiors that the army's fighting spirit had not weakened, adding on 6 March: 'The army again numbers between 250,000 and 260,000. After a break of three months, which was necessary after the latest battles, it has recovered totally.' His report dated 10 March stated: 'The people want peace more and more, but the army is still firm in its determination to fight to the bitter end, and the newly mobilised troops have that same feeling.'[17] Still, he had noted in his report of 15 January that the ruling circles were worried about the immediate future and were 'preparing to withstand a new Austrian offensive with all their might.'[18] Despite all that it had endured, Serbia still had the strength to fight, but the people knew very well how much blood had already been shed and were afraid for the future.

War was therefore experienced as a huge misfortune and it was resented, but there remained the conviction among many people that it was no use bewailing their fate, which was something they had to wrestle with. In their talks with Albin Kutschbach, that same attitude could be seen in the bearing and the words of the Regent and the Prime Minister. Both showed self-assurance but were concerned. On 9 February Regent Alexander was 'full of pride and joy' when he spoke of the Serbian army's recent battles; the Serbs had 'fought with incomparable gallantry', the people and the army were as one in their determination 'to prevail or fall', and 'every foot of land would be defended to the last breath'. However, according to the report of 10 February, the Regent also 'bitterly regretted the war, which Serbia had truly not wanted'.[19] In a conversation on 13 February Pašić blamed Austria-Hungary for the war having come about at all.[20] Given the determination to continue fighting despite the losses that had been suffered, Serbia's ruling circles had to figure out how to reinforce the army's ranks. At a session on 25 June the government therefore decided to deploy Serb and other volunteers from Russia in southern Serbia (Kosovo and Macedonia), while 'only those who expressly stated that they so wished should be deployed on the Austrian front.'[21] That was because such combatants, if taken prisoner, would immediately be executed as traitors by Austria-Hungary. The recruitment of volunteers accelerated from then on. By the end of September a special mission dispatched from Niš to Russia had resulted in 3,500 volunteers going to Serbia.[22]

In order to continue fighting a war against a numerically far superior enemy, Serbia was obliged to mobilise over 707,000 men by the spring of 1915, which represented one sixth of its population, while Montenegro provided 50,000—nearly the same proportion. This meant that far too few people were left to produce anything at all, and those who remained were usually of limited capability. The *Radničke Novine* newspaper wrote: 'Only old people, small children and the sick can be seen in the villages of Serbia.' German intelligence received the information that in the spring of 1915 around 10,000 women and children were working in the military and technical institute in Kragujevac.[23] Military matériel was lacking, as it had been since the very beginning of the war. As early as 21 August 1914 Vojvoda Putnik had instructed the Ministry of Military Affairs that recruits should be ordered to bring from home clothing, footwear and other necessary articles ..., as it was certain 'there would be no uniforms, at least initially.'[24] The army had requisitioned all available draught animals.

Military expenditure was also too high for Serbia and Montenegro, and in Serbia had reached a sum equal to the turnover of the entire economy over several peacetime years. State debts to French, British and Russian banks were colossal, but new loans had constantly to be sought. In February 1915 the Ministry of Finance asked the Prime Minister to take the necessary steps to ensure that 'an allied state perform our financing'; the allied states should together undertake to bear those costs until the war was over and a final settlement of Serbia's costs had been made. It also sought a new loan of 150 million dinars for 1915, cautioning that 'if Serbia does not receive that support it will not be able to maintain its army and will therefore be in no position to continue the war.'[25]

Serbia was desperately short of food, draught animals, raw materials, money and manpower. The areas where fighting had taken place remained desolate, and enemy troops had laid waste and set fire to everything in their path.[26] On 18 February 1915 the Ministry of Finance officially submitted a document to the Prime Minister informing him that the state's financial capacities had been totally destroyed as a result of Austria-Hungary's attack, and after nearly seven months of war financial circumstances were deteriorating day by day. Owing to the total lack of exports, the document continued, there was no way to import gold into the country from any quarter, and gold was vital to pay for the purchase of articles urgently required. It was further impossible, the document went on to say, to meet the army's needs given the underdeveloped state of industry and virtually total mobilisation of the adult male population. The country's centres of economic life had been hit the hardest, and trade and economic life had been brought to a total standstill. 'Belgrade, the trade and banking centre, has been completely eliminated from economic life as a result of constant bombardment,' the document emphasised, as a result of which 'trade and loan transactions have halted in the entire country.'[27]

The green and fertile Sava valley had also been laid waste. This was how John Reed described Mačva: 'All this country had been burned, looted and its people murdered. Not an ox was seen, and for miles not a man. We passed through little towns where grass grew in the streets and not a single human being lived.'[28] Some 2,000 rural dwellings had been destroyed. The 18 February Ministry of Finance document also stated that Mačva was 'desolate', which was why the quantity of food and fodder had been reduced considerably, and 'some foods normally sufficient in quantity are having to be brought in from elsewhere.'[29] Ministry of Finance experts explained the reasons for the sorry state of the economy as follows:

Around 400,000 mobilised Serb troops have been on the move during the war, not counting over 100,000 mobilised military personnel in the rear. Around half a million enemy troops, together with field supply carts and livestock, have swept through, laying waste to the areas they occupied.... Moreover, huge numbers of displaced persons have placed a further burden on the rest of the population.... Up to 200,000 refugees have fled from Bosnia and Srem with nothing but the clothes on their backs.... To compound the misery, around 60,000 prisoners of war have had to be fed at the people's expense.[30]

That was why in mid-February the commander of the Combined Division reported that in the region where his unit was deployed there was no food to be had at all; reserves had been exhausted.[31] Colonel Živko Pavlović later recalled: 'The country lacked food, animal fodder and firewood.'[32]

John Reed wrote that after the victory of December 1914, when the refugees who had retreated with the Serbian army earlier returned home and got out of the train, they 'stood there beside the track, all their possessions in sacks over their shoulders, gazing silently at the ruins of their homes.'[33] So bad was the situation that the Serbian authorities decided not to let the refugees return to their ruined homes that could not provide a living for them, and detained them for a time where they were. In April 1915 the Belgrade daily *Politika* wrote of distress, lamentation and protests; cripples, orphans, the barefoot and the hungry everywhere in the country.

The government sought and received assistance from the Entente Powers, but, owing to war operations and unreliable transport routes, that assistance was neither sufficient nor able to arrive regularly. In February 1915 the Ministry of Finance summed up the transport problems: 'The sheer weight of movement through the kingdom of Serbia has ruined all the roads. Communications are therefore extremely difficult.' Only the railway to Salonika remained open for exports, but it was too busy carrying imports. However, even if it had not been so busy, the Ministry said, it could not have been used to carry exports since it was single-gauge and the country did not have sufficient rolling stock: 'All available carriages are constantly on the move carrying the wounded, the sick or troops and transporting material needed by the army.' It was impossible to transport fodder owing to bad roads and the shortage of draught animals.[34]

Supplies from Allied countries had to take long and perilous land transport routes from Salonika and the Mediterranean or travel by river along the Danube from Romania and Russia. Greece, not yet in the war, to a certain extent hindered the transporting of war material from the port of Salonika—partly to demonstrate its neutrality and partly because of the influence of King Constantine and his entourage who favoured the Central Powers. It was difficult to transport food acquired in Russia because of the bad links between the Danube port of Prahovo, the reception centre, and the interior of the country. The head office of the Serbian railways assessed that 'the tracks are busy carrying supplies for the military, particularly transports from Russia,' adding that there was insufficient rolling stock for either narrow-gauge or normal track.[35] Colonel Pavlović wrote: 'Our narrow-gauge railway could not able to carry more than 400 tons of food daily into the interior, which was only half of the army's daily requirements.' Where food was concerned, the population on the whole fared worse than the army. Inflation was high,[36] and speculators were taking advantage of the war and the shortages.[37]

The government's efforts to revive economic life could not succeed—mainly because all effort was focused on preparations for the resumption of fighting. For a long time the defeated enemy, engaged in exhausting operations on the Russian front, could not recoup enough strength to renew operations on the Serbian front, which gave Serbia an unexpected ten-month break from war. But even those months did not pass without other ordeals.

In his report of 15 January 1915 Albin Kutschbach stated that spotted typhus had spread alarmingly, and some other epidemics had emerged, such as dysentery, and cases of cholera. Many people were suffering from pneumonia. These diseases mainly affected the army, thus inevitably weakening it. Alongside the many hospitals for those wounded in action, all kinds of premises were being turned into hospitals to treat infectious diseases.[38] Eyewitnesses, particularly foreigners, were distressed by what they saw and gave moving accounts of their experiences. A Swedish economic expert stated in his report: 'The greatest losses were, of course, in human lives. Those who did not die in battle later succumbed to various diseases.'[39] Colonel Hunter, a British doctor, had only just arrived in Niš at the beginning of March when he informed his superiors that the situation was extremely grave and asked for further medical aid to be sent urgently.[40] The British military attaché called on his Minister in February to provide emergency aid to Serbia in the form of medical personnel, medications and equipment, warning that the epidemic had taken such a firm grip that the Allies would not be able to count on Serbia as a member of the group of countries fighting the war if prompt aid was not forthcoming.[41] The Russian Minister telegraphed his government several times with the same message. In his memoirs Archibald Reiss from Switzerland recalled: 'Spotted typhus was yet another threat. Gangrene set in among the wounded, and killed the poor fellows who managed to avoid typhus.'[42] At that time Kutschbach was informing Berlin that disease was rapidly spreading throughout Serbia and causing many deaths.

The epidemics had started in the second half of December 1914 and reached their peak in February and March 1915, when innumerable corpses were piled up on all sides. The Russian Minister reported: 'The dying lie on straw alongside the dead in outhouses and fields.'[43] Hospitals were places to chill the blood. The town of Valjevo was described as being 'a vast lazaretto where the living are indistinguishable from the dead'.[44] John Reed wrote of the hospital in Valjevo: 'Here was a horrible room full of men with post-typhus gangrene, that awful disease … in which the flesh rots away and the bones crumble.'[45] Reiss described what he saw on the streets of Serbian towns: 'Carts passed by one after another laden with rough coffins quickly knocked together out of a few planks. To save wood the coffins were bottomless except for a few laths between which the legs of the dead dangled.'[46] It is estimated that over 400,000 people were infected and some 100,000 civilians died, as well as 30,000–35,000 soldiers and 30,000 prisoners of war.[47] When he asked where all the people in a Mačva village had gone, John Reed was told that they had 'all died of the spotted heat'.[48]

Schools closed down, and on 9 March the supreme command banned military and civilian transport for the 16–31 March period except for medical purposes.[49] At the end of 1914 aid on a large scale in the form of medical personnel, equipment and money started to arrive from abroad. It came from governments, national Red Cross organisations, various charities and individuals.[50] The new arrivals included specialist doctors and their ancillary staff, the necessary equipment and medicines. Among the first to arrive were the British mission of Lady Paget,[51] who opened a large hospital in Skopje, and the Russian mission of Countess Trubetskoy, wife of the new Russian Minister to Serbia. The Russians brought two field hospitals, a surgical unit with 350 beds and an epidemiological unit with 120 beds, as well as four complete mobile kitchens. Mme Hartwig, wife of the former Russian Minister to Serbia, brought a field hospital that was set up in Niš. The Slav charity organisation was headed by a certain Mme Savinyin. The British humanist Tom Lipton provided transport to Salonika on his yacht for a thirty-strong British Red Cross mission led by the Berrys, a married couple both of whom were surgeons. Lipton and the mission immediately travelled on to Serbia, and he soon arranged for the transport of sixteen field hospitals, eight field ambulance vehicles and 230 tons of medical equipment. Mrs Stobart's mission arrived in April, comprising fifty women doctors and nurses and equipment that included fifty-five tents, 250 beds, three cars, two ambulances and two mobile kitchens. St John's charity from London, headed by Professor Bennett of Oxford University, opened a hospital in Vrnjačka Banja at the beginning of April.[52] Lady Wimborne, a member of the British aristocracy, brought 30,000 francs of her own money and another 50,000 francs donated by the British government. France, for its part, sent at least 100 doctors, including the prominent bacteriologist Dr Nicolle from the Pasteur Institute in Paris. Edward Ryan from the American mission also made a notable contribution, and he later fought alongside Serbian soldiers on the Salonika front. The Rockefeller foundation and the American Red Cross sent two prominent bacteriologists headed by Richard Strong, director of Harvard University's Institute of Tropical Diseases. A Swedish mission of four doctors worked in Kragujevac. The greatest aid came from Russia, Britain and France, but considerable assistance also came from neutral countries such as the United States, Greece, Switzerland, Italy, Denmark and the Netherlands. Material aid also came from countries as distant as Japan, Argentina and Chile. In all, at least 2,000 people came to Serbia as part of the various missions and assistance initiatives.

However, doctors were not immune from the diseases they were fighting.[53] The first head of the American medical mission succumbed to typhus at the beginning of March, and Lady Paget and Edward Ryan both became ill. According to Archibald Reiss, 'One in four Serb doctors, already few in number ... lost their lives on their own fields of battle, alongside their patients.' On 9 February 1915

Dr Sichev from Russia informed Petrograd that twenty-two Serb doctors had died on that single day because of an epidemic; Albin Kutschbach wrote in his memoirs that out of 440 Serb military and civilian doctors about 200 had died from to that disease;[54] the director of the Serbian hospital in Niš, Vladimir Stanojević, recorded that 157 doctors had died from various infections, and 124 from spotted typhus alone. Stanojević reported that 383 members of the medical staff in the Niš hospital had fallen ill and forty-one had died. Nadežda Petrović, a celebrated painter, died of typhus while she was working as a nurse in Valjevo in April 1915.

Although the start of spring weather caused the epidemic to tail off, foreign aid was still decisive in beating it. Seen as part of the whole picture, the epidemic can be seen as yet another misfortune for Serbia, but it also caused immeasurably important humanitarian solidarity to develop internationally.

Political life

Despite the woes of war, people continued to discuss politics as if they were living in times of normality and peace. Foreigners could not believe their eyes when they saw people arguing in the streets, in cafés and on railway platforms about their political concerns. This covered the social spectrum—from officers, civil servants and priests to the ordinary man in the street. They would argue and often complain about the government, especially the Prime Minister. Gerhardt Gesemann found one such conversation so interesting that he described it in his diary. It was with a Serbian non-commissioned officer, a peasant whose views on political issues were acute and who did not mince words in his criticism of Prime Minister Pašić.[55] John Reed recorded that a coachman who had driven him from Krupanj to Valjevo was very proud of his team of horses and had named one of them Vojvoda Mišić and the mare King Peter.[56]

The British Minister reported to London from Niš that 'everyone is interested in politics here.'[57] The National Assembly was functioning almost normally. The leading state figures—the ruler, the government and the supreme command—were acting in an exemplarily united manner, with the occasional natural differences in assessments and views. Pašić was right when he said: 'Total harmony reigns between the supreme command and the government.' In the middle of January 1915 Albin Kutschbach, whose job it was to know what was happening, reported to his base that the Serbian government had powerful support, notably from its officers.[58] Nevertheless, a customarily sharp political struggle was being fought out on the main political scene, and Nikola Pašić and his government were bombarded with constant criticism from both left and right. Newspapers continued to appear as they had done before the war, and John Reed concluded that Serbia was 'one of the most democratic countries in the world'. The atmosphere in the country was in fact one of spontaneous popular defence. In Kutschbach's view, the Serbs believed that they were 'defending the independence of all Balkan nations' and that 'an Austro-Hungarian victory would mean the end of Balkan nations' independence.'[59]

Censorship was stricter than before, especially in the case of *Radničke Novine*, the mouthpiece of the Serbian Social Democrat Party, which was banned in the spring of 1915 in the territories acquired in the Balkan wars and closed down completely that same summer.[60] However, the Social Democratic leadership soon started publishing a newspaper with the same content but under a new name *Budućnost* (*The Future*). The crisis on the battlefront in November 1914 led to considerable political upheaval, sharp criticism of the government, and acrimonious political tension. In an obviously well-informed message the Bulgarian Minister reported to Sofia that 'passions against the present government are aflame in the opposition camp.'[61]

Little is known of the Black Hand's relations with members of the Radical Party on the one hand and with Regent Alexander on the other.[62] Black Hand members certainly held politically sensitive posts in the army, particularly in voluntary detachments. General Damnjan Popović, a prominent member, was commander of the troops in the New Territories (those acquired in the Balkan wars) and was responsible for Serbia's more radical line in Albania. He was in favour of occupying Albania as a whole[63] and, unlike the government which relied on Esat Pasha, he supported Esat Pasha's opponent Ahmed Bey Zogu.[64] It is not known whether Popović was acting in compliance with or even on the orders of Lieutenant Colonel Dragutin Dimitrijević Apis. In the meantime Dimitrijević had been relieved of the post of head of the supreme command's intelligence service and given other military duties. In the crisis of late November and early December Black Hand members are believed to have induced members of the Radical Party to agree to a coalition government, and there are many indications that relations between the Radical Party, which was the strongest at the time, and Black Hand members in the army were tense. The Bulgarian Minister in Niš was informed, as he said, by 'reliable sources' that there was 'great political agitation in the army against Pašić', and great difficulties were being encountered in the creation of a coalition government because the Black Hand was 'trying to take the Ministry of the Interior into its own hands'.[65] The government's relations with the supreme command and officers were good, but the same cannot be said of its relations with Dimitrijević's Black Hand group.

Regent Alexander did not become involved in any major political activities in the first months of the war. Twenty-six years old at the time, he was overshadowed as commander in chief by his much older, celebrated generals, especially Vojvoda Putnik, while as head of state he was overshadowed by the experienced Prime Minister, Nikola Pašić. Sympathisers with Austria were few in number in Serbia and to be found among the ranks of older-generation Liberals and Progressists rallied around Professor Živojin Perić. They had no great influence.[66]

The importance of the Social Democrats, who were totally opposed to the system in force at the time as well as to the Serbian leadership's overall political orientation, lay in their stubborn fostering, despite all the misfortunes of war, of a basic political ideal that differed totally from the prevailing one. As part of the pre-war European Socialist movement, Serbian Social Democrats sought a world without capitalism, a world of cooperation among free and equal nations and nation states, and that was why they were against war. Serb Social Democrats and Russian Bolsheviks were the only parties to vote against their governments' war loans, thus keeping faith with the Second International. In Austria-Hungary and Germany, however, Social Democratic leaders supported their governments' policies. War was a hard blow for European social democracy as a whole, but especially so for Serb Social Democracy since Serbia had been attacked and had to fight for its independence.[67] The Social Democrats were faced with a head-on confrontation between their principles and reality. Many actually took part in the country's defence, and many died fighting for their country including Dimitrije Tucović, the most prominent Serb Socialist, who was killed serving as an officer fighting for the national cause. This conflict of principle as experienced on the personal level can be seen in letters Zdravko Todorović, a Social Democrat, sent to Dragiša Lapčević, one of the party's deputies:

Recent events have … left a deep mark on the feelings and thoughts of all of us, but we should not allow them to break us. I think it is only after them that we should act. Our cause should not weaken; our deeds must not be in vain. It is the duty of this generation to survive the crisis. I know of no higher or nobler goal than to renew our lives and our struggle after the war.… The blow, I admit, is a hard one. But is it fatal? I do not think so. A red phoenix will rise from the ashes.… That hope is my life.

In those complex circumstances Serb Social Democrats were seeking to discover what to do in the spirit of Tucović's declaration—'We want our nation's freedom, but not to destroy the independence of others'[68]—and that of Dragiša Lapčević's statement in the Serbian National Assembly that for him and his comrades the war was a continuation of the struggle against chauvinism in all countries 'and primarily Serb chauvinism'.[69]

Almost everyone in Serbia, regardless of social level, shared the view of their country as a 'vanguard' of unification, but that concept was simplified among many people into the idea of a struggle for the liberation of their 'subjugated brothers'. And that idea, or rather ideal, acted in Serbia as a powerful ideological and moral unifying force and enabled the war to be seen as a battle for survival. Valentine Chirol, a British special envoy who visited the Balkans in the summer of 1915, informed the Foreign Office that Serbs were subject to almost fanatical idealism and that they clearly differentiated between the Kingdom of Serbia and the Serb nation, of which they considered themselves the protector. For them, therefore, any talk of the interests of the Kingdom of Serbia was of no interest if it was detrimental to the interests of the Serb nation.[70] Summing up his impressions after a talk with Regent Alexander, R.W. Seton-Watson reported on 12 January 1915 the Serb 'enchantment with the dream of Yugoslavia'.[71] The American John Reed, evidently ill acquainted with all the nuances of the issues he was talking about, concluded on the basis of everything he had heard and seen while travelling around Serbia: 'The secret dream of every Serb is the uniting of all the Serbian peoples [sic!] in one great empire ... an empire fifteen millions strong reaching from Bulgaria to the Adriatic and from Trieste, east and north, far into the plains of Hungary.... Every peasant soldier knows what he is fighting for.'[72] The *Politika* daily of 30 April 1915 accurately described that same collective ideological and political thought: the war was actually about 'the liberation and unification of our nation into one entity, into one state' and 'that ideal alone is motivating our people, and for that ideal alone so many people have been willing to die.'

Among the projects for the future there was also the Social Democratic idea of a Balkan federation.[73] On 9 January 1915 *Radničke Novine* demanded that the government should conduct a policy that would persuade other states in the Balkans to unify into a federation. This would be, not least, in Serbia's interest, since its international position would thus no longer be hopeless. In its edition of 27 August 1915 *Budućnost* sharply attacked government policy in the name of the Balkan ideal: 'It is high time to abandon the idea of Serbia's hegemony in the Balkans [and] accept that the idea ... of a democratic and republican Balkan federation, that will be the source of life and pride for all Balkan nations represents the sole salvation.' On 14 July *Radničke Novine* had written along the same lines that the aim should be the 'merging of Serbia, Bulgaria and Macedonia into one economic and political entity'.

No favourable prospects for the Yugoslav programme on the international scene presented themselves in 1915. Not only did the two warring power blocs not accept such a programme, but they also had their own plans—plans that depended on Yugoslav territories within Austria-Hungary as well as those already within the Serbian state. The Entente merely acknowledged the Niš Declaration, which is to say that it did not destroy its future prospects, but also did not agree with it. What was actually happening was that the Entente Powers were trying to gain new allies by offering them territories inhabited by Yugoslav peoples that were then within the borders of Austria-Hungary and also parts of Macedonia that belonged to

Serbia. For example, the Entente tried to win over Italy by promising it the eastern Adriatic coast. In this it was successful. According to a secret treaty signed in London on 26 April 1915, Italy obtained Istria, the Kvarner islands and northern Dalmatia together with Zadar, with the exception of Brač and some smaller islands.[74] Bulgaria was offered the part of Macedonia south of the line going through mountain Golemi Vrh, north of Kriva Palanka and then southwest to the Gubovci monastery on Lake Ohrid. It was for this that the three large Allies were putting pressure on the Serbian government. The Entente's first joint step in that direction was taken as early as 30 August 1914, and more followed in notes of 29 May and 3 August 1915. They were trying at the same time to bring Romania around by promising it Banat after the war.[75]

Serbia's Yugoslav programme was *a priori* unacceptable to the Central Powers. Austria-Hungary and Germany first tried to win over Bulgaria by promising it the whole of Macedonia, and they soon started promising it other Serb territories. They finally managed to make Bulgaria their ally by promising it Macedonia, the Juzna Morava valley together with Toplica, and the whole of eastern Serbia up to the Velika Morava river, all of which represented 59 per cent of Serbia's territory at that time. They did so in a secret treaty on 6 September 1915.[76]

Serbia's response to the pressure exerted on it by the Allied Powers to cede Macedonian territories to Bulgaria, as well as the news that the Entente was negotiating not only with Bulgaria but also with Italy and Romania, was to refuse to yield to demands and compromises made without its knowledge.[77] Official Serbian documents from confidential archive dossiers are full of attempts to reason with the Allies. To cite one example, 'The Serbian government, which finds itself in a difficult position because of its high esteem for the assistance provided by the Triple Entente, ... is nonetheless compelled to state that it cannot give the Triple Entente states the authority to propose and promise territories that are within the Serbian state.... We cannot make concessions to the detriment of our nation' because 'we seek ethnographic i.e. national borders.'[78] Foreigners travelling around Serbia met the same determination on all sides. John Reed recounts that in reply to his question what would happen if Italy were to take Dalmatia, an official had replied: 'It is very exasperating. For it means that after we have recovered from this war, we must fight again.'[79] Military leaders were particularly vehement in their opposition to Allied demands. In a conversation with Valentine Chirol, Colonel Živko Pavlović said resolutely that Serbia would never be able to agree to Bulgaria cutting off its only railway line to the Aegean. He further rejected any political argument, with unconcealed disdain, and said that the issue of Macedonia was a military one and could only be settled by the army in battle.[80] The British envoy listened to complaints from Regent Alexander that the Entente was negotiating with Italy behind Serbia's back. That, he was told, was the reason for Serbia's suspicions that the Triple Entente could act in a similar way concerning the claims of Bulgaria and Romania. Alexander warned that the effect of such conduct by the Allies could be to crush the Serbian army's morale.[81] The Serbian government's readiness to agree to some concessions on Macedonia in the summer of 1915 was just enough to provide evidence of good will but not enough for the concessions to be accepted.

Germany offered Serbia a separate peace and Austria-Hungary first supported that offer, but on discovering that Berlin had interests detrimental to its own, it then decided to obstruct it. Germany was in fact trying to open up another political front that would jeopardise both the integrity and independence of Balkan states and the Yugoslav movement.[82] By offering Serbia territories belonging at that time to Albania, to Montenegro and even to Bosnia and Herzegovina, which was then under Austro-Hungarian sovereignty, Germany was aiming not at extracting Serbia from the war and securing itself a land link with Turkey, but at a territorial reorganisation in the Balkan peninsula ensuring that the region would ultimately fall politically into German hands. Serbia would, in fact, in return for promised but uncertain gains, have had to concede a large part of its territory to Bulgaria and certain regions to Austria-Hungary.[83]

Germany used a number of covert and unofficial channels to achieve this end. One contact was set up through Professor Adolph Strauss and his associate Janos Dada, both Hungarian citizens resident in Budapest, and these were joined by Otto Follberg, a German from Berlin.[84] However, that contact was broken in the summer of 1915, partly because it was uncovered by Austro-Hungarian intelligence and partly because the men involved were discovered in Berlin to be mere fraudsters interested only in financial gain. A second unofficial contact was set up through a representative of the Berliner Handelsgesellschaft bank; this was Karl Dürenberger, who had worked for the bank in Belgrade for many years before the war and happened to be in Niš in 1915. The third contact was through Albin Kutschbach, who had resided in Niš from October 1914 with the approval of both the German and Serbian governments. He was able to travel freely through Serbia and met and conversed with many prominent Serbs including Regent Alexander and Nikola Pašić. He kept Berlin informed of what was happening in Serbia and his conversations through the intelligence centre in Bucharest. The fourth contact was through King Constantine of Greece. All these contacts were directed from Berlin and financed by the Deutsche Bank with the knowledge of the German Foreign Ministry.

Official Serbia did not refuse to listen to Germany.[85] Janos Dada visited Niš in 1915 and talked with Minister Milorad Drašković and, according to Dada's reports, which were not always reliable, with Professor Ljubomir Stojanović, after which he received Pašić's reply through an intermediary. Dürenberger too had high-level contacts in Serbia, and he informed the Foreign Ministry in Berlin of Serbia's views through Karl Fürstenberg, owner and executive director of a bank. Kutschbach discussed the offers of a separate peace with Nikola Pašić personally. As for King Constantine, it was on his initiative and through a member of the Greek royal family that the Serbian Minister in Athens was informed of the offer of a separate peace, which he transmitted to his government.

There were those in Serbia in favour of negotiating with the Germans. These could even have been among ministers of the coalition government who did not belong to the Radical Party. Nonetheless, the official Serbian response was always determinedly negative. Although Dada, like his associates Strauss and Follberg, persistently claimed to have been successful, he could only report that Pašić had not received him and had conveyed the message that he could not 'negotiate with anyone personally'. Dürenberger— who, unlike Dada, was not trying to make money out of this— reported: 'The position and mood of the authorities has not changed … although the Russian retreat has given rise to some doubts. That is why there cannot yet be any thought of a separate peace with Serbia, regardless of how favourable it might be for that sorely afflicted country.' Kutschbach reported that Pašić was holding 'only academic conversations' with him—Pašić was convinced that 'he would win if he adhered to the Entente'.[86] In September 1915 Kutschbach told Pašić that far stronger forces of the Central Powers would attack Serbia if it did not agree to a separate peace. In his report of 20 September he described how the Serbian Prime Minister had behaved on that occasion: 'He was visibly impressed. He told me it was his great responsibility both to his country and to history to find the right path, while a great deal of often contradictory information rained down upon him. He places his trust in Russia, and it is evident he does not expect the other Entente Powers to abandon Serbia militarily either.'[87] According to the message from Athens, the prospects for acceptance of the German proposals were not favourable either.[88] Pašić declared later during the war that acceptance of such offers would in practice have meant 'surrendering to Austria'. That was because Austria-Hungary and Germany, if victorious, 'would unhesitatingly take everything back they had given, and also destroy Serbia's independence'.[89]

Undeclared war

While rejoicing swept through Serbia in the second half of December 1914 because of the great victory over the Austro-Hungarian army, dangers were looming on the eastern and southwestern borders, where war had not been declared.

Reports and information from Bulgaria and Albania indicated that the enemy was successfully winning over those two neutral countries and organising and equipping troops for *comitadji* (guerrilla) incursions into Serbian territory. Representatives of Serb military and civilian authorities in Macedonia and Kosovo repeatedly sent reports warning of ever-increasing danger. In his report of 24 December, General Damnjan Popović wrote: 'All reports concur that Austria-Hungary and Bulgaria are preparing new troops equipped with regular and heavy machine-guns and including men particularly skilled in the use of explosives. These troops are led by officers.' Four days earlier Popović had communicated: 'According to a report from the head of Ohrid district, proclamations are being circulated among Muslims advocating a holy war against Serbs and Montenegrins. Those proclamations are signed by prominent émigrés from our territory.' Popović's report of 22 December sounded the alarm; he called for his troops to be reinforced with artillery, machine-gun units and infantry, specifically mentioning threats from Bulgarian and Turkish *comitadji* organisations, the activity of Austria and Young Turks in Albania, and the preparations being made by Serbia's enemies. The effects of those preparations could already be felt, he said, but their full impact was expected in the early spring.[90]

Austria-Hungary was behind those actions aimed at facilitating its army's operations in Serbia. Relying on behind-the-scenes activity that it had conducted for years before the outbreak of war, Vienna had made its first such move the night before the ultimatum was presented to Serbia. Orders signed by Leopold Count Berchtold had been delivered to the Austro-Hungarian legation in Sofia at 11 p.m. on 23 July 1914, a full two days before Serbia's response to the ultimatum and four and a half days before war was declared. The orders ran as follows: 'Whatever the case, we are extremely desirous of rigorous work starting immediately with the main objective of destroying communications (bridges, railway lines, telegraph lines), thus cutting Serbia off from other countries, i.e. from Salonika in the south and Bulgaria in the east.'[91] At 6.30 p.m. that same day, that is only half an hour after the ultimatum had been presented, Berchtold gave the following instructions to the Austro-Hungarian commissioner at the International Control Commission in Durrës and diplomatic-consular representatives in Constantinople, Skadar, Salonika and Vlore: 'In the case of war between Austria-Hungary and Serbia it would be absolutely desirable from our point of view if the Albanian population there [in Serbia] were to rebel.'[92] Long before war broke out Austria-Hungary had further found Turkey to be an eager associate. On 9 August 1914 the Grand Vizier had elaborated a plan to the German Ambassador on the creation of 'a new Balkan alliance that would include Turkey and be headed by Germany and Austria' with the aim of 'hermetically sealing Serbia from all sides'.[93] This plan further presupposed taking of territories. Alongside his orders concerning preparations for Bulgarian *comitadji* activity,

Berchtold added that the Bulgarian Prime Minister should be clearly informed that Austria-Hungary would honour 'the historic (territorial) claims of Bulgaria in Macedonia'.[94]

From the moment the ultimatum was presented, Serbia had to reckon on Bulgaria joining the enemy. Just after its defeat in the Second Balkan War in the summer of 1913 Bulgaria had sought an alliance with Austria-Hungary, which would include Germany.[95] The basis for such a policy had been laid by Austria-Hungary during the Bosnian crisis of 1908–9, when it cautiously and secretly offered friendship to Bulgaria on the basis of a division of Serbia's territories, but Russia, through diplomatic activity and by extending a large long-term loan to Bulgaria, had succeeded in halting those negotiations at an early stage. In the period from the end of 1912 to the first half of 1913 Austro-Hungarian diplomacy had done all in its power to transform the Serbian-Bulgarian dispute over Macedonia into a conflict—at the end of June 1913 it even encouraged a Bulgarian military attack on Serbia. However, Germany at that time had rejected closer links with Bulgaria in the desire to preserve its alliance with Romania and friendship with Turkey, while at the same time trying to draw Greece and Serbia closer. Berlin had calculated that the four small states were mutually linked by a common interest regarding Bulgaria. But whenever a large-scale war had seemed likely, Germany had been prepared to ally itself with Bulgaria as it had done in the 1908–9 crisis, in December 1912 and in July 1914.

Although it postponed any decisive moves to a later time, the Austro-Hungarian leadership quickly opted to form an alliance with Bulgaria after the assassination in Sarajevo, and particularly after the agreement with Germany in Potsdam on 5 and 6 July. The Austro-Hungarian Minister in Sofia had been called to Vienna for consultations in the first half of July, and was given the Austro-Hungarian version of the treaty of alliance with instructions to start work on it as and when ordered. The very day the ultimatum was presented to the Serbian government, the Austro-Hungarian Minister was instructed to indicate the possibility of negotiations on alliance, with the promise of gains in Macedonia. However, he was further instructed to take care to 'avoid Bulgaria entering the war prematurely', because 'our primary attention must at first be directed towards localising the war, that is avoiding other Balkan states becoming involved.' Nonetheless, the Bulgarian *comitadji* were required to be ready for action, and the government of Prime Minister Radoslavov was advised to organise that activity covertly.[96]

Negotiations got under way in Sofia on 28 July, the first day of the war. The Austro-Hungarian version of the treaty of alliance that had been drafted earlier was probably presented on 31 July. The German government also started to make haste. On 29 July Count Szögyény reported that in Berlin he was being asked almost daily how negotiations with Bulgaria were progressing.[97] Events accelerated. On 2 August the German Chancellor instructed his Ambassador in Vienna to remind Count Berchtold constantly of the need for the prompt conclusion of a treaty with Bulgaria. On 3 August the German envoy in Sofia was authorised personally to start negotiations,[98] and on 6 August the Bulgarian government was presented with the German draft treaty.[99] Nonetheless, the Austro-Hungarian leadership was then still convinced that its army would defeat the Serbs quickly and easily, and political reasons dictated that Bulgarians should enter the war somewhat later, which meant that Austria-Hungary would be under less of an obligation concerning the Bulgarian military contribution to the war. The German leadership, on the other hand, wanted Bulgaria to become fully engaged in order to allow Austria-Hungary to deploy as powerful forces as possible on the Russian front in those weeks when the greater part of the German troops were trying to destroy France with a lightning strike.

The Bulgarian government immediately agreed to negotiations on an alliance.[100] On 2 August Radoslavov submitted letters to the ministers of Austria-Hungary and Germany presenting his government's terms: Bulgaria was to be guaranteed, first, that it would keep all the territory it held at that time, and, secondly, that it would acquire new territory from those Balkan states that were not allies of Austria-Hungary and Germany. Radoslavov then explained to the two envoys that Bulgaria counted first on the parts of Macedonia that were in Serbian hands and then on the sectors of Kavalla and Dobrudja 'if Greece and Romania became enemies'.[101] The German Minister estimated that Bulgaria could be sent into war against Serbia in the interest of Germany. Thus Austria could send against Russia those troops it would otherwise have sent against Serbia.[102]

When, on 2 August, Radoslavov presented Bulgaria's terms, the news had not yet arrived that Germany had declared war on Russia. A few days later Austria-Hungary and Germany found themselves at war with the powerful Entente coalition, and their allies Italy and Romania declared themselves neutral. The awaited Austro-Hungarian offensive was days in coming and when on 12 August it did finally begin, it was not much more than a week before news was heard of the Austro-Hungarian army suffering a heavy defeat. In parallel to this the Entente Powers were exerting diplomatic pressure on the Bulgarian government, rousing their friends in Bulgaria and also offering parts of Macedonia held by Serbia if Bulgaria maintained at least a friendly neutrality. The Bulgarian government started putting off signing an alliance with the Central Powers.

Although Bulgaria's negotiations with Vienna and Berlin were soon broken off, King Ferdinand of Bulgaria and Radoslavov's government maintained an accommodating neutrality towards Germany and Austria-Hungary. An alliance with Bulgaria was becoming increasingly necessary to the two powers the longer the war continued, and they tried to foster the best possible relations by giving Bulgaria increasingly large loans and exerting pressure on Turkey, Romania and Greece to improve their relations with Bulgaria. On 19 August they managed to bring about a secret treaty between Turkey and Bulgaria, which had been deeply divided till then.

The longer an alliance was postponed, the more feasible an 'undeclared', i.e. subversive war against Serbia seemed. On 6 August the German Ambassador in Vienna stated that high-ranking representatives of the Austro-Hungarian Foreign Ministry were saying that the Monarchy did not at that time need Bulgaria to attack Serbia and the 'creation of guerrilla troops was sufficient'.[103] That was exactly what Germany and Austria-Hungary had wanted from Bulgaria even before the ultimatum was presented to Serbia, as Berchtold's instructions of 23 July testified.[104] A firm agreement was also reached between Vienna and Berlin to authorise a certain Falko Šup to organise *comitadji* activity in Macedonia, each of the guerrillas to be given 25,000 marks. It was on such a mission that Šup spent some time in Sofia in the second half of October 1914.[105] It was around the same time that the Foreign Ministry in Berlin came up with a plan to use the successful businessman Mannesman (an agent who had operated earlier in North Africa) and the coffee and grain merchant Rozelius (head of the intelligence centre in Bucharest) to overcome possible communication problems in the future. This was because it was evident that Turkey would soon enter the war, and transport links with the Middle East were becoming harder because neutral Romania, being unwilling to cooperate like Bulgaria, was creating problems for transit traffic, and Serb artillery had halted shipping in the central part of the Danube. Mannesman and Rozelius prepared a plan to attack from the direction of Banat with 5,000 Austro-Hungarian and 5,000 German troops and 30,000 Bulgarian *comitadji* and take the north-eastern part of Serbia together with the town of Negotin. They would then, via this territory, create a corridor linking Austro-Hungarian and Bulgarian territories. This would ensure unhindered transport links to Turkey via Bulgaria.[106]

Although the German general staff welcomed the idea of Bulgarian *comitadji* and agreed to arm them, they did not believe in a corridor across eastern Serbia or want to deploy 5,000 soldiers for that purpose. Moreover, all available forces were then being used to win decisive victories on the French front and restore the already tarnished credibility of a 'lightning war'. General Erich von Falkenhayn, then War Minister and head of the general staff, wrote to the German Chancellor: 'The use of Bulgarian *comitadji* against Serbia is the only practically viable element in Mannesman's undertaking. If 30,000 guerrillas could be armed and induced to attack eastern Serbia from Bulgaria, then Serbia would have to deploy part of its forces against them, thus facilitating Austro-Hungarian operations.'[107] The Austro-Hungarian military leadership did not agree to the idea of providing 5,000 soldiers either, because it was finding difficulty in maintaining its front against the Russians and because all other available forces were being used in the initially successful and promising offensive against Serbia in the Drina river valley. In the meantime the German leadership had reached agreement and concluded that Bulgarian *comitadji* activity should be encouraged. Mannesman therefore arrived in Sofia at the beginning of November.[108]

The fundamental weakness in the idea of using Šup and Mannesman was that the Bulgarian government could not permit foreign powers to create its guerrilla troops in addition to the country's existing *comitadji* organisation, and it wanted to determine when and where its own *comitadji* should be used. On 9 August 1914 Radoslavov had, in no uncertain terms, told the Austro-Hungarian Minister that he was waiting first for Austro-Hungarian army victories in Serbia before provoking disorder in Macedonia that would force Serbs to take repressive measures. The Bulgarian army would then have a pretext to enter Serbia. Radoslavov told the German Minister that when his government decided to use *comitadji* forces it would do so in groups of at least 1,000 men.[109] The plan was evidently first to wait for a decisive Austro-Hungarian victory, and then, by provoking disorder, to obtain a pretext for using a large number of *comitadji* in anticipation of a general Bulgarian army attack. Awaiting that moment, Bulgaria was strengthening and reinforcing its *comitadji* troops on its own territory, while expanding its subversive organisation in the territory of Macedonia within Serbia. It was also cooperating with Turkish agents working on the creation of Muslim *comitadji* troops and encouraging inhabitants of that part of Macedonia to flee to Bulgaria to recruit new *comitadji* from their ranks.

Meanwhile only small-scale guerrilla activity was allowed, so that for the time being it was left to Muslim troops to have a prominent role (Serb units were at that time pursuing and destroying Muslim troops led by Mehmed Bey and Haki Bey). In parallel to this, Bulgaria was conducting what the German envoy called a 'press war', accusing Serbia of crimes in Macedonia.[110] The government in Sofia otherwise had good reasons not to get involved prematurely since Entente representatives were keeping an eye on the Bulgarian *comitadji*. Furthermore, the fact that Serb guerrillas and the Serbian army were ready to counterattack could not be ignored, and it had to be remembered that Greece had threatened to respond to any Bulgarian act of armed aggression against Serbia by acting similarly against Bulgaria. Hence there were only minor incursions in the first months of the war, the largest of which was in November 1914 when a bridge over the Vardar river was demolished near the village of Udovo.[111]

In the spring of 1915 the Bulgarians decided to go a step further. Although no alliance with the Central Powers had been concluded, rapprochement with them had been rapid, and the Bulgarian government began to expand its territorial claims to the Južna Morava valley and parts of eastern Serbia. It was at that very time that

Germany and Austria-Hungary paid the second instalment of a large loan to Bulgaria conditional on a clear commitment to alliance. Serbia meanwhile was at the limits of its endurance because of war and disease.[112] Bulgaria launched a massive *comitadji* attack,[113] and there was intense fighting around Strumica and Valandovo, but in a fierce strike on 3 April Serb troops with reinforcements forced the attackers back over the border.[114] According to Serbian estimates, around 3,000 Bulgarian *comitadji* took part in the attack.[115] Although the threat of Bulgarian attack remained, there was no further major action till mid-October 1915.

In response to a message from Vienna advocating that Albanians in Serbia should rise against the authorities, Austro-Hungarian consular representatives replied on 24 and 25 July 1914 (this was before Serbia had replied to the ultimatum);[116] only the consul in Vlore considered a rebellion impossible to organise. The director of the Consulate General in Skadar, Karlo Halla, was convinced that a rebellion could easily be provoked, since he had already been approached by Bairam Cur, who had sought the 'support' of 5,000 gold napoleons (10,000 francs), and by Cerim Bey from Peć, who claimed to have 2,000 men at his disposal. The most resolute was the Austro-Hungarian commissioner at the International Control Commission in Durrës, Consul General August von Krall, who stated that 'rebellion in New Serbia' should best be directed 'certainly and inconspicuously from here', adding that a powerful movement 'could be got under way if the necessary support were provided from our side'. They could rely, he said, on Hasan Priština, who had already promised help, even going so far as to 'insist with determination'. The Consul General concluded his report: 'At the given moment, this objective is worth financial sacrifice by us.'

Subversive activity then got under way, and it accelerated with the outbreak of war. Krall repeatedly sent telegrams to Vienna asking for money and 'a large quantity' of rifles and ammunition' to be sent to him urgently. He reported on 28 July that Hasan Priština 'had demanded resources in an exceptionally resolute way' to create a *comitadji* movement in the districts of Debar and Luima. On 29 and 30 July Hasan Priština and Isa Boljetini, accompanied by Krall, stayed secretly in Herceg-Novi and conducted talks at the Austro-Hungarian command there on activity in Serbia. On orders from

Count Berchtold himself in Vienna, 2,000 rifles, 100,000 rounds and 50,000 crowns were immediately placed at Krall's disposal. During the night of 13 August, in the presence of two Austro-Hungarian representatives, a shipment of 1,900 Mauser rifles together with ammunition was unloaded in the Albanian port of Medua, and then sent by horse and cart to Albanians preparing to make a raid into Serbia.[117] Serbian border posts had already been attacked twice on 1 August 1914, and there had been similar incidents on the following days.[118]

By inciting Albanians to rebellion, the leading figures in Austria-Hungary evidently considered them pawns in Austro-Hungarian politics.[119] This is demonstrated by instructions to August von Krall, signed by Berchtold on 26 July 1914, to spread the news among Albanian rebels that Austria-Hungary and Serbia were already at war, the Serbian court and government had abandoned Belgrade, the Serbian army had left Kosovo, and Austro-Hungarian troops had already crossed the Serbian border. All this was untrue, except that the court and government had indeed left Belgrade, and that was only because the capital was close to the country's border. Vienna was pushing Albanians into a perilous venture on the basis of false information a full forty-four hours before war was declared and seventeen days before the Austro-Hungarian army actually crossed the Serbian border.

In talks conducted in Constantinople on 31 July and 1 August 1914, the Austro-Hungarian Ambassador Janos Count Pallavicini, the Grand Vizier and the Turkish Minister of Internal Affairs also agreed to cooperate in fomenting rebellion among Albanians in Serbia, thus combining activities that the two powers had conducted separately and with a degree of friction up till then.[120] From then on all basic strategy was agreed at government level through regular diplomatic channels. Austria-Hungary had the task of inciting, organising, arming and financing preparations for rebellion.[121] The centre for operations in Albania was located at the war command headquarters in Herzeg-Novi, in Austro-Hungarian territory, and it was there that Lieutenant-Colonel Spaits performed his tasks in line with an order given on 10 August 1914: 'Incite Albanian activity against Serbia as soon as possible.'[122] Intelligence officers in Albania itself were active in the supply of weapons and ammunition. Cash to pay Albanian leaders came from the military command in Herzeg-Novi, the Legation in Durrës, the Embassy in Constantinople and the Foreign Ministry in Vienna.

Turkey was responsible for propaganda activity, military organisation and directing the rebellion.[123] The actual work was entrusted to the Young Turks' Committee in Constantinople, particularly its executive. 'Emissaries' were designated in Constantinople, and these often included leading figures in the Committee, one of whom was the executive committee chairman Nazim Bey. They were sent to Albania on political, propaganda and command assignments carrying money obtained from the Austro-Hungarian Ambassador. According to information received by Count Pallavicini in early February 1915, sixty-eight such 'emissaries' had travelled to Albania while another five were to be sent to each of the Debar and Scutari-Djeme-Malesiia sectors and eight to the Ohrid-Struga-Tirana-Elbasan sector. In Albania they contacted Bairam Cur, Hasan Priština, Isa Boljetini, Ahmed Mat, Mufti Brus Cazim, Mustafa Endroko and Camil Elbasan, through whom cash was conveyed to other leaders. Turkish officers, mainly of Albanian origin, were also sent to command troops. In the case of a large-scale rebellion on Serbian territory, the Turkish government intended to send a high-ranking officer to take command. A third group was made up of 'volunteers', i.e. individuals forming the backbone of the pro-Turkish *comitadji* forces, and in January 1915 400–500 such men, already divided into groups both large and small, were ready in Constantinople.

The 'emissaries' first travelled to Albania from Constantinople by sea via Brindisi, but that soon proved dangerous when Turkey entered the war.[124] Towards mid-November French naval vessels intercepted a ship between Brindisi and Corfu that was carrying two prominent members of the Young Turks' Committee, Fuad Bey and Ayub Sabri, the latter being of exceptional importance for subversive activities in Albania. The men were taken prisoner and the 500 gold napoleons they were carrying were confiscated. That was probably why it was planned, in January 1915, to send a new group of 'emissaries' and guerrillas by land via Bulgaria, Romania and the Hungarian part of the Habsburg Monarchy to meet in Sarajevo, from where they would be sent to Albania.

However, the objectives of Austria-Hungary and Turkey in Albania were totally different.[125] The supporters and opponents of Esat Pasha Toptani had held centre stage in the huge political upheavals and many armed conflicts that had been under way since Albania gained independence and after the rapid departure of the first ruler, Prince William of Wied, on 4 September 1914. Esat Pasha, who was supported by Serbia, was at first stronger than his opponents. However, when Turkey and Austria-Hungary stood together behind his opponents, the scales started to tip the other way. Those two empires agreed that Esat Pasha's movement should be crushed and an Albanian uprising fomented in Serbia. However, while Austro-Hungarian agents wanted first an uprising in Kosovo and Macedonia, evidently because the Monarchy was mainly interested in weakening Serbia's military resistance, Turkish agents insisted first on the downfall of Esat Pasha, evidently because it was Turkey's objective to bring Albania under its influence.

Austria-Hungary's consuls and intelligence agents could rely on a dozen Albanian notables with their followers, in all perhaps a few hundred men. In January 1915 Consul Halla assessed that 'present circumstances … for an incursion into New Serbia are very favourable, and certainly more favourable than ever before.' Consequently the Foreign Ministry in Vienna sent sums of money to be divided among the Albanian leaders.[126] In April 1915, when the situation had changed owing to orders from Vienna that action should be halted so as to reduce friction with Italy, Halla presented a new list of those who had to be paid within three to four months in order for them to be counted on in the future.[127] However, István Baron Burian, who replaced Berchtold as Austro-Hungarian Foreign Minister in January 1915, provided Halla with only 5,000 crowns for this purpose—far less than had been requested. Nonetheless, he also approved a loan of 100,000 crowns to be used if circumstances deteriorated.[128] All these efforts by Austria-Hungary and Turkey placed Esat Pasha in a very difficult situation. However, the Kosovar Albanians did not rebel, and activity was limited to a few border incidents.

Most of these incidents took place on 9 February 1915.[129] Hasan Priština claimed that he could foment an uprising in Liuma and Malesia, and with some 200 men he launched a surprise attack on the border post of Zhur and entered Serbia. According to Austro-

Hungarian data, he took two Serb officers and six soldiers prisoner and killed about forty Serbs. As soon as news of this reached Scutari, a 'committee for support to the uprising' was immediately created that presented Halla with a demand for 800 gold napoleons. Halla considered the attack to have been a dangerous venture that could provoke the Serbian army to strike back in such a way as to 'exclude totally the possibility of a second uprising in the foreseeable future'. But because the venture had already begun he considered that it should be on the largest possible scale, and he contacted his superiors in Vienna calling for the Austro-Hungarian army to attack from the north—a request Burian immediately passed to the supreme command,[130] which was not able to take action on it.[131] Meanwhile Priština's advance had been halted, and there was no uprising, although the attackers had been joined by the inhabitants of three Albanian villages near the border. Priština's forces encountered a Serbian army unit and were quickly dispersed, while Hasan Priština and his men had to flee for their lives and free the officers and soldiers taken prisoner. Serbian troops then crossed the border and, on discovering that the attackers would not return, went back to their positions. Halla informed Vienna that Hasan Priština was fleeing, that Albanians from Liuma had been hostile to Hasan Priština, and that there was peace in the Albanian border zone.

Despite all the effort exerted and money spent, little came of these attempts to stir up a rising. This was not only due to Serbia's efficient border defences. Albanians themselves also played an important role. Esat Pasha was a trained and skilled soldier; he knew how to handle himself in Albania's complicated affairs, and had his own stronghold in the country. Moreover, a group of Albanian notables, who could not be said to have been supporters of Esat Pasha, considered that nothing could be gained by serving Austro-Hungarian and Turkish interests, and either guessed accurately or knew for a fact that Serbia could undertake to occupy Albania by force. Further, those on whom Austria-Hungary and Turkey relied were seen by the Grand Vizier and Count Pallavicini as men whose mentality 'excludes the struggle for higher objectives'. For them 'the personal goal, most often prompted by the desire for revenge' was the highest objective. They were said to 'take part in fighting and disorder only to plunder'.[132]

From various quarters the Serbian government quickly started to receive accurate information about Austria-Hungary's intentions and Turkey's involvement in Albania. On 28 July at the latest it had been informed by its Legation in Bucharest that Vienna had instructed prominent Albanians who had fled from Kosovo into Albania that they should immediately start an uprising in Serbia. On 29 July a report arrived from Durrës with the information that Albanians in Serbia were making hurried preparations. On 7 August the Serbian Ministry of Military Affairs had information that hostile Albanian refugees from Kosovo 'had obtained 800 rifles and money from Austria-Hungary'. The Serbian head of the Ohrid district reported at that time that 'Albania was flooded with foreign agents', while a report from Durrës on 15 August stated that weapons and ammunition from Austria-Hungary had arrived by ship at Medua. On 18 October it was already known that Fuad Pasha and Eyub Sabri had travelled from Constantinople to Albania; however, there were border incidents in the Prizren district around 1 August, and Albanian guerrilla activity was in evidence on the border in the Ohrid district in November, when the Austro-Hungarian army was advancing.[133]

The Serbian leadership allocated sufficient military forces to guard the border, and inhabitants of Serb villages also armed themselves. Albanian leaders were told that, if forced, the Serbian army would have to enter Albania. Moreover, Serbia found support in Albania itself in the person of Esat Pasha.[134] Nonetheless, the Serbian leadership considered that it would be best to occupy parts of northern Albania in order to have 'better strategic lines'. The supreme command disagreed, believing that everything else should be subsidiary to the war with Austria-Hungary, but the officers in command of the New Territories thought differently. General Damnjan Popović even wrote in official documents of the occupation of Albania as a whole. At the beginning of September 1914 Pašić had raised the issue of the Serbian army's entry into Albania with the aim of removing the threat of the 'combined impact of Albanians together with Turks and Austrians'. He claimed that if Serbia had new 'strategic' lines it could defend itself with far fewer troops. The Allied governments rejected that idea, partly in order to maintain Serbian military strength focused on the main enemy, Austria-Hungary. Fearing that Serbia's entry into Albania would have serious political circumstances and provoke discontent on the part of Italy and the Balkan states, they did not allow the Serbian government to implement its plans concerning northern Albania.

As time passed, the situation in Albania was becoming more and more confused. In October 1914 Greek troops marched into southern Albania; Italian forces landed on the island of Sazan at the beginning of November and at the end of December near Vlore. In December the anti-Esat Pasha movement flared up, and in Niš at the beginning of 1915 it appeared necessary to 'secure Serbia and its interests with the most effective means possible'. All efforts were then made to prepare the ground diplomatically for the entry of Serbian troops into Albania.[135]

On 6 January the Serbian government instructed the supreme command to make all necessary preparations and 'order all previously occupied strategic positions in Albania to be taken immediately'. This evidently referred to the line reached in the First Balkan War. Because of Vojvoda Putnik's opposition to having the supreme command involved in this, a separate unit was created and entry into Albania was entrusted to the command of the troops in the New Territories.[136] However, that action was constantly postponed, probably because the Allied governments continued to oppose such a step by Serbia. Hasan Priština's incursion was therefore a welcome development, being small in scale but providing an excellent excuse to move the army. The Serbian government informed the Italian government, which was monitoring developments carefully, that 'thousands of Albanians had attacked, armed with machine-guns and cannon'[137]—this seemed an over-dramatisation designed to justify military action. It is also revealing that Albin Kutschbach, reporting to Berlin from Serbia, said: 'the Albanians' attack has been at the focus of attention for some days…. Everyone is happy with this development because they think a suitable pretext has been created for Serbia to enter Albania and occupy areas extending to the Adriatic coast.'[138]

The Serbian Foreign Ministry then explained to Kutschbach that 'Serbia is refraining from advancing to the coast because it wants to avoid fresh complications, particularly with Italy, and it will therefore limit its occupation to certain points in Albania to ensure its own security.'[139] On 27 March the commander of the troops of the New Territories was ordered to prepare units to 'take some strategic places that will make it easier for us to protect our territory'.[140] By the beginning of May three detachments with over 20,000 men, thirty-four hill and field cannon and sixteen heavy machine-guns were therefore deployed on the Albanian border, and on 29 May they were finally ordered to advance. Resistance was determined in places, but the Serbian army reached Elbasan on 4 June and Tirana on 9 June.[141] Somewhat later those three detachments were merged into one unit under the name of Albanian Troops with their headquarters in Debar: it comprised 26,694 men and its command was entrusted to the commander of the New Territories.[142] The Allies, who by then included Italy, protested strongly at Serbia's entry into Albania, but the Serbian army remained on the territory it had taken.[143]

The Serbian government's move to order the army into Albania was justified by real threats resulting from the activities of Austro-Hungarian and Turkish agents, but it was actually trying to secure for itself access to the sea through Albanian territory with its own forces. It was a purely Serbian programme, independent and separate from the Yugoslav programme. It was not explicit, but it remained constantly in all the territorial plans of Pašić's government.

Unification problems

Even in the midst of the fiercest battles and in the tense periods between fighting much thought was given in Austria-Hungary and Serbia to the political future of the central and western Balkans.

Secret state plans were elaborated in Austria-Hungary, and the increasingly uncertain outcome of the war and disagreement between the Austrian and Hungarian parts of the empire caused Serbia's future in the autumn of 1914 to be put into the hands of officials.[144] Consequently, between November 1914 and May 1915 a large number of 'strictly confidential' memoranda appeared, their approaches reflecting the differences between the Austrians and Hungarians: the Austrian annexationist approach and the more moderate version of the same on the Hungarian side. One group was of the opinion that Austria-Hungary should aspire to gain as much of Serbia's territories as possible, and proposed the annexation of Belgrade, Mačva, Djerdap and the Morava River valley together with the town of Niš, i.e. important areas of the Serbian state before the Balkan wars. That was because Niš, together with Mount Jastrebac, would be 'an ideal border' for the Monarchy in the Balkans. There was also a demographic proposal: first, the ethnic structure should be changed in the annexed lands by settling a large number of Hungarian and German colonists, and secondly, the Serbian intelligentsia should be destroyed and Serbs reduced to a population of peasants. The second group favoured the annexation of the Sava river valley, mainly Mačva, with the demand that Mount Maljen should be on the border. Both groups agreed that large parts of Serbia's remaining territory should be annexed by Bulgaria, but the opinion prevailed that, wedged between an enlarged Austria-Hungary and an imagined Greater Bulgaria, 'some kind of highly reduced Serbia' should continue to exist, which would be closely linked economically, politically, militarily and culturally to the Monarchy.

In Serbia the ideological links among Yugoslavs were further elaborated. This was done to overcome the deeply-rooted and historically developed perception of Serbia and Serbs as having a specific character of their own. The task fell to prominent social scientists who presented their views in the press. Their common starting-point, which was the generally held view at the time, was that Serbs, Croats and Slovenes were members of the same nation, while it was recognised that Slovenes had certain features peculiar to themselves. The historian Stanoje Stanojević wrote: 'Serbs and Croats are absolutely identical,' and 'There are insignificant differences between them and Slovenes.'[145] However, writers differed greatly over the definition of where the focus of the problem lay and what facts formed the basis for such thoughts. Jovan Cvijić tried a Pan-Yugoslav approach, while Stanojević took the history of the Serb nation as his starting-point and saw the crux of the problem as being the Serb issue: 'In the conviction that the Serb nation, divided into several states, constantly fighting its enemies …, has not been able to concentrate all its strength as a nation on its cultural and economic consolidation and progress, we want all the Serb, Croatian and Slovene people, who are of the same origin and have the same language and mentality, to be gathered together in one state entity.' He saw the solution of the Yugoslav unification issue only in the context of solution of the Serb unification issue.[146] The philologist Aleksandar Belić founded his observations on both a historically-constructed cultural community (literature, folk poetry) and the existing awareness of unity. He saw unification as justified not only by the common aspirations of long-separated Serbs, Croats and Slovenes, aspirations rooted 'in national-ethnographic unity personified in the same language or very close dialects', but also in the greater need for defence against surrounding states. He was sure that 'the Serb people in Serbia' had been required 'by the very nature of events' to assume the role of 'Yugoslavia's' leader against Austria-Hungary and its protector 'before the entire world'.[147]

Serbia was thus assumed to have the leading role, and, in line with the system consolidated there after 1903, the principle was advocated of civic rights in a parliamentary state. What was most often promoted was the creation of a 'single, united state' (Stanoje Stanojević). However, the historian Stojan Novaković warned that it would be better to have a 'confederative state of Southern Slavs' (*Jugo-Sloveni*), and called for an examination of the experiences of the Swiss Confederation and the German, Austrian (*sic!*) and American systems.[148]

How the entire international community could gain from the creation of a Yugoslav state was also discussed. Novaković envisaged gains from the consistent implementation of the national principle, and others claimed that the unification of Yugoslavs would serve to consolidate peace. Belić said unification would secure peace and order in the Balkan peninsula, stressing that 'there can be no European peace without peace in the Balkans.'[149] However, Stanojević took the issue into higher spheres with his claim that Yugoslav unification was a step towards 'the realisation of Mankind's great ideal, that all people and all nations should be free, healthy, materially secure and, if at all possible, happy and contented.'[150] However, all this was based on the assumption that it was a unification of 'brothers', and that those 'brothers' living in Austria-Hungary were fellow-sufferers in that terrible war. That idea took no cognisance of any divisive factors such as religion or the front lines at any given time. In no single official document discovered to date, in no single article and in no single autobiographical source that appeared during the war are there any critical observations, reproaches, attacks or ugly words directed against Yugoslavs from Austria-Hungary. There was no criticism of the supporters of Ivan Frank, nor any mention of the pamphlets published in May 1915 dealing with the demonstrations, persecution and terror that had taken place the previous year.¹⁵¹ The sole enemy was Austria-Hungary itself.

The movement based on the Yugoslav programme strengthened and expanded, but it also became increasingly complex, filled with different, contradictory aspects, all of which resulted in a degree of internal friction. Relations between Serbia and Montenegro, an essential part of the programme, were typified by the awareness that 'we share good and evil', as the Montenegrin government put it on 24 July 1914. However, in the official politics of the two states conflicts arose, multiplied and occasionally became highly aggravated.¹⁵² The Montenegrin leadership was faced with renunciation of its statehood, and the Petrović-Njegoš dynasty with loss of rule. Still, among the people, in political circles, the army and the government the unification movement in Montenegro was strong. It further dominated the Montenegrin National Assembly; in Jovan Djonović, Todor Božović and others it had increasingly influential advocates and in Andrija Radović a potential leader. The movement formulated the simple idea of one state consisting of one nation, and Montenegro's losses in the war were taken as proof that a safe future should be sought exclusively in a common state, be it Serbian or Yugoslav.

King Nicholas of Montenegro and his entourage had misgivings about unification and tried to secure a special status for Montenegro in any future common state, thus consolidating the position of the Petrović-Njegoš dynasty as a ruling family. In 1915 such an idea was put forward in a number of variants.¹⁵³ Consequently, in America in the spring of 1915 Jovan Matanović, in his capacity as King Nicholas's emissary, elaborated on the trialist concept of a Yugoslav state, with Serbia, Montenegro and Croatia forming three separate units. In May the Montenegrin Heir Apparent, Danilo, told Colonel Petar Pešić that he intended to travel to Serbia to resolve the Serb issue because 'we must be one state along the lines of the German system.' On another occasion he was more explicit: 'I shall do as the Bavarian king did at Versailles.... I shall be the happy king of Montenegro in the Greater Serbia of dear Sandro [Alexander].' This meant that the Petrović-Njegoš dynasty would accept the overlordship of the Karadjordjević dynasty on the model of the Wittelsbachs of Bavaria, who had agreed to the sovereignty of the Hohenzollerns in January

1871. That is to say it would remain the ruling house of Montenegro while retaining broad autonomy. Montenegro would further maintain the right to its own diplomatic representatives, and diplomats of other states would be accredited there; it would have independent command of its army in war and a degree of administrative autonomy. Meanwhile, foreign policy and the supreme command of the army would be in the hands of the central state authorities. However, in August 1915 Colonel Pešić was to hear from King Nicholas that there could be no mention of unification without preserving the position of the Petrović dynasty and that unification would only be possible after his death on the condition that 'Montenegro, together with its dynasty, remains equal.' Evidently the example of Bavaria was not to be followed to the letter.

By making some independent foreign policy moves King Nicholas tried to consolidate his increasingly unsure rule and ensure that Montenegro, with himself at the helm, would be on an equal footing with Serbia.[154] He therefore presented a separate territorial claim in which Montenegro sought the Skadar district (perhaps with part of Albania up to the Mata river), the Adriatic coast up to the mouth of the Neretva (and perhaps even including the town of Split), all of Herzegovina and part of Bosnia, including Sarajevo. He looked into the possibility of cooperating militarily in an Italian attack on the Dalmatian coast as soon as Italy joined the Entente.[155] And he attempted to become somewhat independent militarily by appointing General Mitar Martinović as his permanent emissary to the Russian high command. At the end of June 1915, after Serb troops had occupied part of Albania, he sent a detachment under Brigadier Radomir Vešović to the district of Skadar despite the Entente's indignation and behind the back not only of the Serbian supreme command but also of his own chief of general staff, General Božidar Janković. The detachment took Skadar on 27 June. However, King Nicholas' sons, Princes Danilo, Peter and Mirko, were showing ever greater affinity with Austria-Hungary and Germany, and Danilo, the heir apparent, did not hide his belief in the victory of the Central Powers, even in front of Entente representatives. He left the country, allegedly for medical reasons, in the middle of August.[156]

The Montenegrin king and his followers looked on Serbia's self-confidence over unification with the greatest distrust, which grew into a conviction that the Serbs would attempt to realise unification 'by force' and that they simply intended to depose the Petrović dynasty with the help of the Montenegrin unification movement.[157] At that particular time the Serbian leadership was not raising the question of unification, but working on it by consolidating cooperation and community spirit in the conduct of the war. Within the limits of its capacities, which were very limited, Serbia provided Montenegro with essential assistance in the form of officers, men, weapons, ammunition, other military equipment, food and money. There is no evidence that it helped or fostered the unification movement in Montenegro, but it is known that Serb officers were expressly forbidden to discuss or campaign for unification. However, it was intended that Montenegrin politics and the Montenegrin army should be directed in a coordinated manner towards the common objective of realising the Yugoslav programme, and Montenegrin dependence on Serbian aid emerged as a practical means for connecting the two.

The speed and content of Regent Alexander's response to Prince Danilo's offer, as well as his reminder to the Prince of his own offer, demonstrate his desire to achieve unification as early as possible, that is, during the war.[158] Alexander then said he was convinced that 'the issue should be settled promptly in the interest of the entire Serb nation' because that would make it possible 'to know in advance what policy to conduct in the interest of the general Serbian-Croatian issue.' Repeating, at the end of May 1915, that he accepted Prince Danilo's offer and stressing that he thought there should be no hesitation, Alexander pointed to the need to 'take the wind out of the sails of a certain faction' that wanted to bring about an agreement between Montenegro and Italy, which would have had a detrimental impact on the joint war effort. Thus Serbian-Montenegrin unification was perceived as part of the Yugoslav programme (which at the time was called 'Serbian-Croatian'), the resolution of which could further help to establish the political concept of unification. He accepted the offered form of unification 'along the lines of the German system'.[159] Prince Danilo did not continue the dialogue at that time.

Meanwhile, Serbia's supreme command proposed that cooperation with and assistance to Montenegro should be halted if it deemed the moves of the Montenegrin leadership out of harmony with the overall war effort. There are indications, albeit few, that the Black Hand also had its own plan. Nikola Pašić stated that the Montenegrin government should be made aware that 'conversations involving irresponsible elements' had caused the conflict at that time, and there are reasons to believe that he was thinking of Black Hand members. It is further known that Dragutin Dimitrijević Apis intended to become involved in his own fashion by organising the assassination of King Nicholas, thus creating the conditions for a revolution by unification supporters in Montenegro. But the Black Hand did nothing, partly because its members were engaged in military affairs and war, but mainly because Pašić's government was firmly entrenched.

Despite the many conflicts and aggravated suspicion, relations between Serbia and Montenegro did not deteriorate, and the two countries continued to live together. The Montenegrin side stressed its intention to resolve any conflict through dialogue and explanation with the 'brother kingdom', while the Serbian side declared its readiness to act 'openly and always in agreement with Montenegro'. Indeed, after every crisis cooperation was revived, which was how the conflict over the entry of the Montenegrin army into Skadar was resolved.

Yugoslav émigrés in Western Europe began to organise themselves in the first months of 1915. On 8 November 1914 Nikola Stojanović and Dušan Vasiljević had conducted their first dialogue with Ante Trumbić and Julije Gazari in the Serbian Legation in Rome, and had agreed to an initiative from Niš to create a body that would promote Yugoslav aspirations for an independent unified state. Other prominent émigrés soon started to gather, including Frano Supilo, Hinko Hinković and Ivan Meštrović, who were joined by Jovan Banjanin and Niko Županič; Franko Potočnjak from Croatia and Bogumil Vošnjak from Slovenia emigrated from Austria-Hungary in December 1914, Milan Srškić did so from Bosnia in February 1915 and Gustav Gregorin from Slovenia in May 1915. A Yugoslav Committee was formally set up in Paris on 30 April 1915, with Ante Trumbić, a Croat, as chairman, and this became the centre of activity to show the world that the Yugoslav population in Austria-Hungary wished to unite into an independent state with Serbia and Montenegro. On 7 May it moved its headquarters to London, where it stayed till the end of the war. Offices were also opened in the other Entente capitals and Geneva.[160]

Even before the creation of the Yugoslav Committee these émigrés had been politically active and promoted the concept of a unified Yugoslavia. For example, when they learned from the Italian press that Count Tisza had praised Croatia's conduct in the war, Trumbić and his associates wrote, in the prominent *Corriere della Sera*, that the war was 'a Hungarian and Austrian war, but not a Croatian or Slovenian one at all', and that Croats and Serbs were one and the same nation and had 'the same ideal which is one and indivisible throughout the sacred entity of motherland, blood and tongue'.[161] In January 1915 they decided that it was necessary to form a volunteer army consisting of Yugoslavs from Austria-Hungary and thus contribute, at least morally, to the struggle for a Yugoslav state.[162] They also visited Entente capitals and tried to persuade French, British and Russian ministers and influential public figures to support the object of their struggle. Franko Potočnjak was sent to the United States, where he induced representatives of Yugoslav émigrés at a gathering in Chicago to publish a proclamation asserting that 'Croats, Serbs and Slovenes are one nation with one language.' On 23 March those émigrés addressed the Russian Ambassador in Washington with a petition calling on Russians to 'support and help our native lands—Croatia, Slavonia, Dalmatia, Istria, Carniola, Styria, Carinthia, Bačka, Banat, Medjumurje, Bosnia and Herzegovina—that are now fighting to cast off the Austro-Hungarian yoke and its tyranny.'[163]

However, it could be seen even then that unification would open up issues that would cause friction.[164] Hence the decision to create a volunteer army aroused the Serbian government's suspicion that the Committee wished to play the role of a totally independent organisation. A disagreement over autonomy also arose between the Committee and the Serbian Minister in London, while in the summer the ailing Frano Supilo began to distance himself from both the Serbian government and the Yugoslav Committee.

In the summer of 1915 both sides in the war redoubled their efforts to bring Bulgaria over to their side. The Central Powers were striving to destroy Serbia's independence, but the moves of the Entente Powers were such that they could have undermined all prospects for the achievement of Yugoslav unification. Russia, France and Britain demanded that Serbia should cede Macedonia south of Skopje, but offered in compensation Bosnia, Herzegovina, Slavonia, Srem, Bačka, part of the Adriatic coast from Cavtat in the south to the Planka headland in the north, and the part of Albania between the rivers Drin and Vojusha.[165] Trumbić then supported the Serbian government, claiming: 'The loss of Macedonia would break Serbia's spine, and with the separation of Slovenia from Croatia and the western regions the role of Serbia in the liberation of all Yugoslavs would come to nothing, thus ending the hopes of national unity.'[166]

However, Serbia's defences were only sufficient to preserve the vital friendship of the Entente Powers.[167] Having received a joint note presenting the resolute Allied demand that Serbia should agree to renounce part of Macedonia, Serbia started to play for time by showing goodwill, but secretly trying to ensure that the Allies' plan would fail. The Serbian note of 1 September 1915 was an example of diplomatic skill. It expressed agreement to renounce territory as demanded, but far less was renounced than had been sought under the pretext of the need to solve the border issue with Bulgaria. The Allies could not but admit that Serbia had demonstrated considerable flexibility, but it was nonetheless clear that Bulgaria, whose aspirations were far greater, would do all in its power to thwart the Serbian proposal. Furthermore, the Serbian government's supposed flexibility had created the opportunity to put the entire Yugoslav programme to the West. It therefore demanded, in addition to everything else that had been offered, that 'Croatia together with the town of Rijeka' be 'united with Serbia', that 'Slovenian regions' be liberated and obtain 'the right to decide their own destiny freely', and finally that 'the western part of Banat be united with Serbia'. Southern Macedonia and the entire Yugoslav programme were thus defended.

In this way the Yugoslav movement was broadening and becoming increasingly complex, as witnessed by some covert developments among Slovenian and Croatian political forces, which otherwise acted on the public scene of Austria-Hungary's southern provinces within the bounds of the existing system. In the early spring of 1915 there were in fact some secret exchanges of opinion and adjustment of views among leading political figures from Slovenia, Trieste, Istria, Dalmatia and Croatia. The initiative came from the Slovenian side.

The clerical leaders Janez Krek and Anton Korošec had become estranged from their leader Šušteršič and started to gather Yugoslavs in Austria-Hungary to resist the hegemony of Vienna and Budapest.[168] In March 1915 Krek met some Dalmatian clerical representatives and the Istrian leader Matko Laginja in Rijeka, and as the result two emissaries were sent to Rome to inform the Russian embassy there that the gathering in Rijeka had 'expressed in secret the general desire that Croats and Slovenes should enter with Serbs into one Yugoslav state under the Karadjordjević dynasty' and the most important 'Yugoslav parties [should] aspire to the complete and final liquidation of Austria-Hungary'. Similar exchanges of opinion took place in Trieste, where sixteen politicians from various parts of Slovenia and Croatia gathered. A joint movement of Croats and Slovenes was then founded with the aim of achieving self-determination during the war. It should be noted that Bogumil Vošnjak and Gustav Gregorin had belonged to these circles and entered the Yugoslav Committee with mandates from them. With Krek's talks in Zagreb in the summer of 1915, in November that same year and at the first session of the Croat-Slovene Club in Maribor on 28 October the Yugoslav movement was showing itself to be broad, varied and polycentric.

Collapse of defence

However, for Serbia the greatest trials of war were still to come. In September 1915 the Austro-Hungarian 3rd Army was in Srem and north-eastern Bosnia, the German 11th Army was in Banat, and the Bulgarian 1st Army was in western Bulgaria, with the 2nd Army to its south. Commanded by Field Marshal Mackensen, who had proved himself one of the most capable German commanders in the war, the troops involved in the entire operation numbered, according to some estimates, 800,000 men. They had modern equipment and air cover. On 6 October the combined German and Austrian armies attacked with a powerful artillery barrage, and the first small groups were sent across the Danube and Sava. The main operation of forcing those rivers took place the next day.[169] Serbia, for its part, was able to counter with 300,000 troops at the most, and these were mostly either newly mobilised or older soldiers drawn from the approximately 1,000-kilometre front and deployed all over to await attacks from the north, west and east.

The sector of Belgrade was the first to come under heavy attack, mostly from Austro-Hungarian troops. On 6 October at 7 a.m. Belgrade came under unremitting artillery fire, and 3,000 to 4,000 shells, including exceptionally destructive 420mm. shells, poured down on it.[170] The city was also defended by civilians—old people, women and children—who took weapons from dead soldiers. General Živković's report of the morning of 8 October read: 'Battle is still under way; there has been no respite at all. Our troops are still attacking the enemy.' The report also states that the enemy had 'silenced our heavy armaments' in the first phase of combat, using 'over 15,000 shells of various calibre, even 30.5cm.', and then the enemy had introduced 'artillery from monitors into the battle'.[171] The same was happening on other parts of the front; for ten whole days the Serbian 1st Army held the enemy virtually at its initial positions in the northwest and the west. Mackensen's chief of staff noted that 'resistance is strong' and 'the Serbs are fighting heroically.'

Things continued the way they had begun; the enemy advanced, but slowly and with great losses. After two weeks of fighting Mackensen's armies had advanced only 30 kilometres into Serbian territory, far less than had been planned.[172] Three days late on 14 October, the Bulgarians attacked from the east, virtually striking at the back of the Serbian defence. However, the Serbian 2nd Army quickly halted Bulgaria's 1st Army. Hearing of this, the German general staff concluded that it was necessary 'to create a breathing space' by bringing reinforcements into Serbia, despite the shortage of troops that was felt on all the other fronts. The Alpine Corps was brought from the French front, and it joined battle towards the end of October, while the Austro-Hungarian 10th Mountain Brigade was also brought to the Serbian front.

Under constant pressure from strong enemy forces, the Serbs withdrew step by step, and civilians continued to fight alongside the army.[173] For example, the commander in chief of the German 11th Army wrote that he had been engaged in a battle for a long time around the village of Selevac and that women had joined in on the Serbian side. Moreover, tens and tens of thousands of civilians had fled south, taking with them everything they could carry, not knowing where their journey would take them. The Russian Minister reported that Serbia was a moving mass of refugees without food or shelter. They were making their way through wind and rain, their goal unknown; he feared that the terrible epidemics that had raged in the spring would reappear. The Socialist leader Dragiša Lapčević wrote the following description of what he saw in Jagodina: 'Since the beginning of the war Jagodina has been full of refugees, especially from Belgrade. Now, when the enemy has started to infiltrate from all sides, refugees have been arriving constantly, night and day, in trains, carts and on foot, and then going on.... Many are homeless, without food, and the poor, barefoot and in tatters, are unable to withstand the cold October weather.'[174] Military units, supply cars and especially artillery had great difficulty getting through because of the huge number of people. General Jurišić-Sturm informed the supreme command that 'there are so many refugees that the roads to Ćuprija are impassable.' A German war correspondent reported that Serb soldiers were trying to clear the roads of women and children to let the army pass, but 'they just keep going!' The enemy too started to catch up with them. Lapčević described what he felt when enemy forces reached Jagodina: 'It was the worst moment in my life. Bitter pain engulfed me; tears streamed from my eyes. I was struck by the awareness that from that moment our independence and freedom had ceased and we had become occupied slaves.'

One month after the start of the offensive the attackers could see that they had advanced, but as many as a fifth of their troops were out of action. Nonetheless, the country's defence, already weakened, declined totally. When the Bregalnica division could not halt the incomparably stronger units of the Bulgalnian 2nd Army, the state of affairs on the Macedonian front soon became critical. The Bulgarians reached the Vardar River on 19 October, entered Kumanovo on the 20th, reached Skopje on the 22nd and took the strategically important Kačanik gorge on the 26th. That led to Petar Bojović taking over from General Damnjan Popović as commander of the New Territories.

That successful attack by the Bulgarian front's southern wing cut off Serbian communications with the Aegean. After the German attack Serbia first lost contact with Romania, and therefore also with

Russia, and now it lost its link with Salonika, where French and British forces had been landing from 5 October. The danger loomed of ammunition and food running out totally. More and more Albanian rebels were fighting with the Bulgarian units. The Allies in Salonika offered a certain ray of hope; Vojvoda Putnik sent a telegram to the Allied command there saying that if they wished to help they should do so as soon as possible.[175] French forces did move along the Vardar valley to the north, and some of their units replaced Serbian troops in positions near Strumica and Krivolak and engaged the Bulgarians. However, that manoeuvre had no major military impact as French and British forces in the Balkans were still few, their landing was progressing slowly, their command in Salonika was indecisive, and the pro-German King Constantine of Greece had succeeded in keeping his country neutral. And Russia was a long way off. The Serbian government asked the Allies to send urgent assistance of 120,000–150,000 troops within ten days, warning that it would later need at least a million men for combat in the Balkans if that contingent were not sent. But it was in vain. Moreover, the few sympathisers of Austria-Hungary in Serbia took on a fresh lease of life. A former minister from the time of the Obrenović dynasty, Vukašin Petrović, even appeared at Field Marshal Mackensen's headquarters to offer his cooperation, and a group of prominent politicians including Stojan Ribarac, Vladan Djordjević and Vojislav Veljković awaited the enemy's arrival in Vrnjačka Banja.[176] At that time Serbia could really only count on Montenegro, whose army was still successfully holding down Austro-Hungarian forces. In order to protect the Serbian army's rear and its flanks the Montenegrin commander (*Serdar*) Janko Vukotić constantly expanded his front with the Sandžak army and even undertook the defence of the sector of Čačak-Ibar River gorge-Ivanjica-Mount Javor. That helped the Serbian army to make an orderly withdrawal and avoid being surrounded.

However, despite all the misfortunes the government, army and most of the population of Serbia did not weaken in their resolve to persevere, and the leadership showed itself equal to the task. For example, the front at Pusta Reka had started to collapse, but at the most critical moment Vojvoda Stepanović arrived together with old King Peter. The unit took strength from that and managed to hold its position, which was then vital for a successful retreat. This episode was also interesting because the Austro-Hungarian Foreign Minister Baron Burian told the German Chancellor Bethmann Hollweg that the Serbian King had been seen near the front, and he regarded this as a sign that Peter I was seeking an opportunity to surrender.[177] Austro-Hungarian aristocrats, whose aged Emperor was spending his time far from the carnage of the war in Schönbrunn and Bad Ischl, simply could not comprehend that peasant and king were in the same ditch on the other side of the front, and that all the Serbian people were engaged in the war. It is revealing that Field Marshal Mackensen had already received instructions to accept a Serbian offer of capitulation, while the Austro-Hungarian leadership was concerned that the Field Marshal should not accept the capitulation on behalf of Germany but as commander of the coalition army. But they waited in vain for Serb negotiators to appear.

On 29 October, at a government session in Kruševac attended by Regent Alexander, it was decided to 'persevere to the end in the policy conducted up till now.'[178] Despite this, the increasingly untenable situation was causing rumours that Serbia would have to capitulate and agree to a separate peace.[179] The Entente Powers too were taking account of such an eventuality, but Serb morale prevailed over all tribulations. The Serbian government informed the Allies that 'Serbia, although in an extremely grave position and liable to face an even graver one, is determined to persevere to the end in its battle against the occupiers.' Solutions were therefore sought in all directions except capitulation. First of all, an attempt was made in November to get through to Skopje and join with the Allied army in the south, but French units started to retreat to a bridgehead established at Salonika on 11 November. Consequently Serb troops descended into Kosovo in mid-November accompanied by many civilian refugees. A testimony to the state of mind at the time was given by French Deputy Auguste Boppe: 'Arriving at a place from which there is no way out, the multitude feels caught in a trap.'[180] In their wake soldiers and refugees left innumerable bodies, each one evidence of a human tragedy and immeasurable suffering. Velimir Rajić, a poet, could not stand the physical and mental suffering: 'he died of a broken heart,' wrote the dramatist Branislav Nušić, who was himself with the retreating multitude. Losing all hope, the writer Milutin Uskoković drowned himself.

Collapse of defence

The government and the supreme command then decided to retreat to the Albanian coast, informing the Allies of their decision and asking for food and equipment to be sent to the places where the Serb troops were heading. Pašić telegraphed Serbian envoys abroad, saying that after the retreat 'we shall in one month have an army of 250,000, well equipped, properly dressed and armed, which, together with the Allies, will be able not only to force the enemy out of the Balkans but also to destroy him.'[181]

The order for retreat issued by the supreme command on 25 November 1915 wars as follows:

> The moment has come when a combination of circumstances is forcing us to retreat through Montenegro and Albania.... The state of the army is generally unfavourable.... Capitulation would be the worst possible solution, as it would mean loss of the state.... The only salvation from this grave situation lies in retreating to the Adriatic coast. There our army will be reorganised, supplied with food, weapons, ammunition, clothing and everything else necessary that is being sent by our Allies, and we shall once again be a factor for our enemies to reckon with. The state lives; it still exists, albeit on foreign land, wherever the ruler, the government and the army are to be found, whatever its strength may be.... In these difficult days our salvation [lies] in the endurance, patience and utter perseverance of us all, with faith in the ultimate success of our Allies.[182]

Milutin Bojić wrote prophetically: 'I shall return the same, once again joyful, risen, fearless/... I will be proud as you once knew me/ on glory-gilded fields.'

That same unbreakable fighting spirit also produced a totally opposite reaction. Major Dušan Simović, commander of the Šumadija division, had received an order on 27 November from Vojvoda Stepanović, commander of the 2nd Army, instructing him to go over to the attack.[183] Vojvoda Mišić, commander of the 1st Army, had the same reaction, particularly when he received the news that German troops were withdrawing, which was actually happening. At four meetings in Peć between 29 November and 1 December Vojvoda Mišić tried to persuade the highest-ranking army commanders who were in action—Stepanović, Jurišić-Sturm and Živković—to counterattack.[184] At the meeting on 1 December he said: 'There are two solutions in such circumstances; to go on to the offensive and see who we are running from, and if we succeed so much the better; if we do not succeed then we send representatives to the enemy and start negotiations on a cessation of hostilities.'[185] That was evidently contrary to the government's decision and the orders from the supreme command. The other commanders probably hesitated for some time but concluded that an offensive counter-strike would have failed at that moment, and at the fourth meeting on 2 December there was agreement that the supreme command's orders of 25 November should be followed.[186]

This was truly the most critical moment in the whole war, with the army in a more or less chaotic state. Having seen the gravity of the situation Mišić, Stepanović, Jurišić-Sturm and Živković had halted in Peć. Reports described the situation at that time:

A huge number of soldiers are fleeing; food and fodder are scarce and it is impossible to acquire anything to give the troops. Communications are difficult; the weather is biting cold; clothing and footwear are worn out; men and livestock are totally exhausted as a result of constant fighting (!) and movement; there is no food at all in the directions determined for retreat [...]; it is dangerous to go via Rožaje because of rebel Albanians. These are the causes for the desperate state of affairs in the army.[187]

In line with all the reports they had received, the commanders described the situation on 1 December as follows:

The morale and the material state of our troops are desperate. Despite all the measures to prevent desertion, the number of troops is plummeting, and they are fleeing en masse. Deserters are fighting against our troops to clear their way to the villages of Istok and Mitrovica. They are selling weapons to Albanians. Regiments number only a few hundred men. There is only enough food for the troops for another four to five days. All efforts to acquire food have proven useless.[188]

These were signs of profound disorganisation and demoralisation caused by withdrawal, shortages of food and equipment, disappointment caused by false reports of Allied troops coming to their help, and difficulty in accepting the fact that the struggle had to be continued on foreign soil. Some of the refugees and scores of thousands of soldiers decided to return home. They turned round and set off in the direction of occupied territory.[189]

4

ON FOREIGN SOIL

The withdrawal through Albania has gone down in history as 'Serbia's Golgotha.' The government set off on 24 November 1915 and reached Skadar four days later, while the supreme command took longer, leaving on 26 November and arriving there on 6 December. The army first had to assemble and then, having buried the cannon or thrown them into the River Drin, and having destroyed their means of transport at the beginning of December, set off for the inhospitable mountains of Albania and Montenegro. Many civilians accompanied the army, including most parliamentary deputies, political party members and university professors.

Withdrawal to Corfu

The suffering of the army and civilians withdrawing to the Adriatic was indescribable. The mountains of Albania became graveyards for tens of thousands of people who died of hunger, exhaustion and cold, or were killed by Albanian bullets. Some units withdrew in disarray, and the Montenegrin and especially the Albanian populations en route were prey to looting and banditry. Refugees started arriving in Skadar and on the Adriatic coast towards mid-December. As one foreign eyewitness wrote, they arrived 'one by one, in small groups, in massed squads, on horse, on foot—all mixed together …, in a state of extreme exhaustion, walking corpses …, emaciated, haggard, despairing, with black faces and hollow eyes.' Yet, he added, 'there was no sound of complaint to be heard from the those who had suffered so terribly …, they walked silently, and one word— "bread"—was uttered by those with enough strength to speak at all.' However, the same eyewitness noted that 'the occasional detachment still bore itself in a military manner.'[1] According to supreme command records, there were nearly 110,000 soldiers and 2,350 officers on the Albanian coast at the end of December 1915.[2] But those numbers may have been an underestimate. It has been calculated that of those who started to withdraw at the end of November, 70,000 went missing; and of more than 27,000 recruits, fewer than 15,000 still remained during the withdrawal. Moreover, according to lists drawn up later in Bizerta in Tunisia, only 7,192 of them were left. Of the 6,000 young men born in 1897 and 1898, only 500 remained alive.[3] It should nonetheless be recalled that the support and assistance provided by the Albanian troops under Esat Pasha in the Durrës-Tirana sector helped the Serbian army and the refugees considerably, and mitigated the losses. Esat Pasha and his supporters also provided the Serb units with a certain number of weapons, a few cannon with ammunition, and gave valuable intelligence concerning the movement of enemy troops.[4]

But that was only the first stage in the ordeal of suffering and death. Neither food nor shelter awaited them on the Albanian coast. There were no Allied ships, and weapons were in short supply. They had only seventy-two cannon, 173 heavy machine-guns, 50,000 rifles and carbines and 707 sabres.[5] The Serbian government had informed the Allies of the withdrawal through Albania in a circular dispatch on 20 November and had asked them to 'send food for the army, as well as fodder, to Durrës and Skadar'[6] by 29 November. It was then still thought that the Serbian army would be able to reorganise and rest on Albanian territory. The food sent by France and Britain had started to reach Brindisi, but its onward dispatch was slow because the Italian navy had not allocated enough ships, and those it had allocated were too small. Moreover, the food dispatch was being carried out hesitantly, and that was partly because of the danger threatening communications from enemy submarine activity. The only food to arrive on time was in Durrës. The Serbian government sent telegrams from Skadar warning the Allies that they would ruin everything if they did not send sufficient food, and Regent Alexander wrote to the Russian Tsar that the survival of the Serbian army was at stake. The situation became desperate when Austro-Hungarian warships sank an Italian convoy carrying a cargo of food bound for Medua. The Allies then decided that ships should take safer routes and head for ports around 100 kilometres south of the positions of the enfeebled Serb refugees. That meant more marches and more hunger for people already almost half-dead.

The French deputy Auguste Boppe, who was with the Serbian government in Skadar, later recalled that the government had first been able to give the hungry only a piece of bread each, and was soon unable even to do that.[7] Nor could food be obtained from the local population. As usually happens in such situations, food and fodder prices rocketed. The commander of the Timok Division reported, for example, that 'it is impossible to buy food and fodder for cash locally because of the incredibly unrealistic prices set arbitrarily by the sellers,' adding that 'our money is worth only as much as Albanian speculators put on it.'[8] Those selling food started refusing banknotes and demanding payment in gold and silver coins.[9]

The victories of the Central Powers and Bulgaria meant that the Albanian authorities loyal to Esat Pasha lost much of their power and their control over the local population. Moreover, the wretched state of the Serbian army made the population think that a new state of affairs was emerging, as a result of which they started to disobey the local authorities, particularly when they were required to help the hungry and exhausted refugees and troops. In some cases those very authorities had not wanted to help in the first place. The Serb military commands had to avoid 'requisitioning', being aware that such measures would 'inevitably lead to conflict'. That was why Italian commanders warned that Serb soldiers were 'selling' rifles, bullets and hand grenades, which probably meant they were being exchanged for food.[10] The supreme command was receiving reports describing the state of affairs as 'desperate'. One commander pleaded: 'It is high time to take our troops out of this hostile country and send them somewhere that they will be able to concentrate on getting better without this spiritual and physical torture.'[11] During the night of 16–17 December alone as many as forty-six soldiers died from hunger.[12] The sufferings of civilians from these adversities were even worse than those of the soldiers. On 18 January a request was sent from Medua that 'special ships be sent immediately for [civilian] refugees' as they were 'dying en masse'.[13] A report dated 15 January stated:

> Over 3,000 refugees, mainly old people, women and children, have been queuing in the port for over twenty days waiting to be evacuated. They have no food or shelter. They are afflicted by all kinds of infectious diseases,

and even the healthiest among them are helpless in the face of the cold wind and storms.... The commission can no longer look on in the face of the misery of these people and therefore beseeches the most rigorous possible action to ensure that two or three ships be sent to Medua as soon as possible for the exclusive use of refugees, as they will all soon be dead if there is no help.[14]

On 24 December the Russian envoy Trubetski telegraphed: 'It is difficult to imagine anything more tragic than the Serb nation, which, at the cost of huge losses, has won through to the sea and is now suffering hunger there. These people have no shelter, no fires to warm themselves, they are barefoot and have little hope for the future.'[15] When the French General Pierron de Mondesire, the head of a special French military aid mission, arrived there he saw 'wretched men, women, children, old men and women, wounded and maimed soldiers, even the dying'; he said they were barely alive 'without shelter, in rags, hungry, crying out for help'. King Peter, himself wracked with rheumatic pain, awaited him with the words: 'The Allies should have done something to get us out of these straits before things came to such a pass.... Even if Serbia survives, I fear there will soon be no more Serbs.'[16]

The French government headed by Aristide Briand had decided at its session on 27 November 1915 to do everything in its power to save the Serbian army, and towards the middle of December it sent a mission headed by General de Mondesire. The Serbian Minister in Paris telegraphed the government that 'France is our greatest friend in the West and it has decided to help us to the limit, with all resources.'[17] More and more food and medical material started to arrive. The Allies also realised that the Serbs had to be evacuated from the Albanian coast, and preparations for this operation began on 29 December. On 8 January the French and British decided to ship the Serbian army to Corfu, and on 11 January French troops landed there to carry out the necessary preparations. They did so without seeking permission from the Greek government or from King Constantine.

With the weakening of the Serbian army's resistance, the Montenegrin army was receiving the brunt of enemy pressure. That pressure had increased after 10 December, when the Serbian 1st Army, which had remained as the rearguard, started to withdraw. In January 1916 Montenegrins were alone on the battlefield.[18] On 5 January the Austro-Hungarian 3rd Army attacked Montenegro, with a superiority in numbers of between three and three and a half times, in addition to which its men were better armed and equipped. The Montenegrin soldier was hungry; he had insufficient ammunition; his artillery was incomparably weaker than the enemy's; and he was exhausted by the fighting. He was now required to defend a 500km. front with barely 40,000 men. The Montenegrin King and government persistently sought troops, food, ammunition and equipment from the Allies but to no avail. Nonetheless, the Montenegrin army, at the time of the enemy's strongest offensive, was to fight its most glorious battles of the World War.

Austro-Hungarian troops started to exert pressure on the sector of Mojkovac on 5 January 1916; the next morning they attacked with all their forces, and by the evening they had penetrated deep into the defences of the Sandžak Army.[19] However, during the night of 6–7 January General Janko Vukotić ordered his troops to counter-attack, starting at dawn on the 7th. In the battle attacks were interspersed with counterattacks which lasted from dawn to dusk on icy mountainous terrain, and the Sandžak Army not only rebuffed the enemy but thrashed him in such a way that, although it could not crush him completely, it made an Austro-Hungarians attack impossible. The Sandžak Army then held the Berane-Andrijevica-Mojkovac-Tara river line till 18 January, when it its supreme command ordered it to withdraw. The enemy attack was also halted on the front towards Herzegovina. All this was of immense importance for the Serbian army, which was still waiting in vain to be evacuated from the Albanian coast.

The situation on the Lovćen front was different.[20] The Austro-Hungarian infantry outnumbered Montenegrin infantry by six to one, and the artillery by as much as twelve to one—not to mention the hugely superior quality of the Austro-Hungarian weaponry. Austro-Hungarian troops started attacking at dawn on 8 January and took the key Montenegrin defence positions on 9 January, the highest peak—Štirovnik—on 10 January, and finally Lovćen on 11 January. Such a rapid advance gave the impression that the defences were disgracefully weak, an impression that quickly spread through Montenegro and caused a general feeling of dejection. However, the enemy had lost 1,260 men in their attack on Lovćen, which meant that the Montenegrins had fought valiantly. Nonetheless, enemy infiltration on that very front was of crucial importance in that phase of the war on Montenegrin territory. The commander of the Austro-Hungarian 3rd Army estimated that the Montenegrins could still offer resistance if King Nicholas decided to encourage them to do so. The Kučko-Bratonožička Brigade did indeed manage to hold the Austro-Hungarian advance from Cetinje to Podgorica in a battle on 16 January, and on the 18th General Vukotić was considering giving orders for a decisive battle, but he was also prepared to order a withdrawal like the one ordered by the Serbian army.

However, high-ranking Montenegrin officials acted totally differently from the army, probably because they were not sure about unification and the way it should be achieved. Hence they were out of step with the prevailing mood among the people and were unable to reach clear solutions for the future.[21] The Montenegrin National Assembly was convened on 25 December for the first time since the outbreak of war, and it did so to find a solution to the grave situation. It was decided, despite everything, that Montenegro should act as Serbia had done, i.e. it should prolong the battle by withdrawing, and it forced the vacillating government to resign. King Nicholas then barely managed to form a new government headed by Lazar Mijušković, who till then had been Minister to Serbia. On 3 January that government won the confidence of the National Assembly, having announced that it would continue to fight whatever the cost. However, because of the enemy's advance on the Lovćen front, the government hastened to persuade the King, on 10 January, to send negotiators to ask the Austro-Hungarian commanders for a truce. King Nicholas once again maintained that he was personally only intent on fighting a decisive battle with the enemy, but such a battle was never actually prepared, which has given rise to the suspicion that all he wanted was to prevent his army from withdrawing from the country. On a number of occasions, the last being on 13 January, the supreme command proposed that the King, the government and the army should withdraw, but to no avail. In a report of 14 January it told King Nicholas that 'such a sense of demoralisation has arisen in the army that any further resistance is absolutely impossible', and a truce should therefore be sought from the enemy. Evidently the King had decided earlier on a truce, and on 13 January Montenegrin negotiators had presented enemy commanders with the government's proposal for a halt in fighting, as well as a personal letter from King Nicholas I for Emperor Franz Joseph.[22]

The Austro-Hungarian response was to demand unconditional capitulation. On 16 January the Montenegrin government gave its reply, agreeing that the entire Montenegrin army should 'lay down its arms unconditionally', but refusing to hand over Serb troops still on Montenegrin territory.[23] Such a response meant a final decision had been made. That was despite efforts by certain leading figures, mainly General Janko Vukotić, to continue fighting. The diplomatic representatives of the Allied states left Podgorica on the day that the capitulation was accepted, and on 17 January the remaining Serbian units and Serb officers in the Montenegrin army set off for Skadar in accordance with orders from their supreme command. On 18 January the Montenegrin Prime Minister Mijušković left for Skadar never to return to the country. But worst of all, on the afternoon of 19 January, without informing the members of his government or leaving any instructions as to what should be done in the future, King Nicholas himself left his country in secret. Moreover, he did not sign the order that the army should withdraw into Albania that General Vukotić had submitted to him on 18 January. The King first travelled to Skadar, where the Serbian supreme command was still located, and then to Medua where he sailed to Brindisi aboard an Italian ship on 21 January. All the indications are that Nicholas wanted to go abroad alone, and not with his army that had been nurtured with the idea of unification with Serbia.

The King was followed abroad by some Montenegrin military officers and around 300 exiles.[24] About 2,500 Herzegovinan volunteers who had emigrated from Austria-Hungary also fled at that time. However, some of the Montenegrin units in Skadar and Medua, who had accompanied their King through Albania, returned to Montenegro, thus demonstrating the confusion prevalent at the time. Prince Peter of Montenegro also went into exile, while Prince Mirko stayed in the country—for reasons that are not known. Only three ministers remained in Montenegro, including the Minister of Military Affairs Radomir Vešović; Minister Andrija Radović had travelled abroad earlier. General Janko Vukotić remained in the country with his army. The three remaining ministers took over the running of the country as a 'skeleton government', an eventuality stipulated in the Constitution. Although it was still possible for the troops to withdraw, since the enemy did not sever communications with Albania until 21 January, it was decided to halt resistance and disperse the army on 20 January.

From that moment the real fight against the enemy passed from the Montenegrin state to the Montenegrin people. The Austro-Hungarian supreme command was aware that this was happening even on 20 January 1916, when General Conrad wrote to Baron Burian that 'we should count on the probability of the Montenegrins waging guerrilla warfare.'[25]

The weaker Montenegrin resistance became, the more dangerous was the position of the helpless Serbs on the Albanian coast. According to Allied plans, evacuation should have started on 2 January 1916, but the first small-scale embarkations in Medua and Durrës did not take place until 6 January.[26] Transport slowed down again in the following days, and slightly over 1,200 people were shipped to Bizerta in Tunisia. Then, despite the danger threatening from Bulgarians in the east and Austro-Hungarians in the north, the evacuation came to a total halt. The exhausted Serbs were in danger of being encircled because the Allies were working too slowly: steps taken on 7 January led to the larger-scale evacuation of Serb troops to Corfu beginning only in mid-January. As the state of affairs on the Albanian coast was becoming more and more desperate, the Serbian government, the supreme command and diplomatic representatives inundated Allied representatives with requests for haste. Telegrams flew for weeks between the Allied capitals calling for urgent action to save the Serbs and, when all were claiming they were doing the best they could but no results could be seen, the Serbian government could only beg and accuse. On 11 January, Pašić ordered the Serbian Minister in Paris to transmit the following to the French government:

Montenegro is facing a catastrophe, which will lead to the Serbian army suffering a catastrophe.... From everything that Italy has done in this month and a half concerning food for the army and the army's transport from Albania, we have become convinced that it does not wish to give actual help but is willing to let our army be destroyed and capitulate.... At this last and desperate hour, we beg the French government to ... send its ships and take our army.[27]

That same day a similar declaration was given to all Allied envoys to the Serbian government, and in response to their offer to evacuate only the Serbian government because of the limited number of places available, it was stated that the government would not leave until the greater part of the army had itself embarked.[28]

The foreign envoys had shared the fate of the Serb people and army and recognised that Serbia was justified in its accusations. On 12 January they jointly communicated that they would stay with the Serbian Government and said it was up to their commands as to whether they, their own diplomats, would fall into enemy hands.[29] The Serb demands were supported most energetically by Tsar Nicholas and his Government. The French Government, headed by Aristide Briand, and the French supreme command, headed by Joseph Joffre, started working increasingly resolutely to perform rescue operations, relying mainly on their own forces and their own resources. In parallel to this, Prime Minister Briand was warning that the Serbian army was in danger of 'total collapse' and, for the sake of the war itself, 'everything must be done to preserve the remnants of the Serbian army,' this being the Allies' 'human duty'.[30] On 14 January, after it had received firm assurances that the actual evacuation of the army and the refugees was underway, the Serbian Government was finally transferred to Brindisi,[31] and on 18 January it arrived in Corfu from there. The first Serb units had been shipped to Corfu on 15 January, but in the course of two weeks only 15,000 troops arrived there, and Pašić had to warn again that another 140,000 people were waiting on the Albanian coast. Suffice it to say that on 23 January, the day when the Austro-Hungarian forces entered Skadar, barely one tenth of the people waiting to be rescued had been evacuated.[32] In the meantime the exhausted and hungry Serb troops had to move from northern Albania to the safer and more secure ports of Durrës and Vlorë, which meant marching up to 250 kilometres through inhospitable terrain. However, the fact remains that the French government was doing its utmost to bring the evacuation to a successful conclusion. Towards the end of January large Allied ships—French, British and Italian—started to sail with increasing frequency into the ports of Durrës and Vlorë, and the number increased at the beginning of February. By 15 February 90,000 soldiers and about 5,000 civilians had embarked in the port of

Durrës alone. On 6 February the Serbian supreme command and Regent Alexander were evacuated to Corfu, where around 120,000 evacuees had arrived by 15 February and around 135,000 ten days later. Up to 10,000 evacuees had been taken to Bizerta around the same time. Most of the Serb troops had been evacuated by 19 February, but some units still remained on the Albanian coast. The cavalry division did not embark till 5 April 1916, which marked the end of the operation.[33]

A French eyewitness described the disembarkation in Corfu: 'They were all totally exhausted and frightfully thin.... Those poor Serbs. Sailors helped them out of the boats, and they made their painful way uphill using their rifles as supports. They finally dropped to the ground, prostrate, virtually unconscious.'[34] At least 15,000 of them were gravely ill, but Corfu could not be transformed into a gigantic hospital for the sick and convalescent all at once. It was a poor island and everything, even food, had to be shipped in for the 140,000 weak and sick newcomers. The French troops who had arrived had only been able to make the most basic preparations for the huge number of long-suffering evacuees, who first had to be helped to build shelters for themselves. In addition, the weather at the beginning was very bad. Heavy rain fell unremittingly, so that the Serb soldiers started to liken their plight to the biblical Flood.

The situation continued to be catastrophic. The French eyewitness recorded: 'Huge numbers died every day.... From 23 January to 23 March there were 4,847 deaths.'[35] A French nurse later recalled: 'Corpses, piled up like planks of wood one on top of the other ..., four in a row, sometimes six.... An arm, a leg or a convulsed face stuck out here and there.' The sick were quarantined on the island of Vidos near Corfu, where, after so much torment, many died; the island became engraved in the memories of both Serbs and Allies alike as the 'island of death'. Around 5,400 people died there. Another 1,000 Serb soldiers died in Bizerta. And disease struck many of the survivors. General de Mondesire reported to his superiors that on 24 February, some five weeks after the first Serb units had landed, there were some 6,000 sick people on the island of Corfu.[36]

But even the worst of misfortunes have to end. The weather finally improved; and the lull in fighting and rest worked their cures. The Serbian army was gradually able to provide better conditions for itself. Under the leadership of the French mission and with the cooperation of the British mission, the Allies were able to deliver more and more food, tents, clothing, medication and other requirements. Soon even those evacuees who had been close to death on arrival started to recover. 'The Serbs are setting their camps to order and embellishing them.... It was a pleasure to go and see them.' Men only recently prostrate with exhaustion and illness could be seen lined up in impeccable ranks, 'healthy, well-armed, equipped from head to toe'. Auguste Boppe reported to his Foreign Ministry: 'Such a rapid and complete transformation seems miraculous.'[37]

Strength returns

The situation in the first months of 1916 was totally changed. Serbia, with a reduced population, and Montenegro were in Austro-Hungarian hands. The Serbian King, Regent, government and most deputies were in exile, as were most able-bodied soldiers and thousands of civilians. Also in exile were the Montenegrin King with most of his family, some officers and politicians, and some soldiers and officials. A total of 140,000 Serb exiles, mostly soldiers, were in Corfu, while around 11,000 were in Bizerta. Some 2,000 of the sick had been shipped to hospitals around France, some of which were in Corsica. Several thousand people had fled to Salonika and Epirus in Greece. Civilian refugees had been taken to France, Switzerland, Italy and Britain, but most had actually gone to towns in France and in the French colonies of Tunisia, Algeria and Morocco. A few of them had found refuge in Russia.[38]

The Serbian army had lost nearly 400,000 men in the period from the beginning of the war to the end of the evacuation, but it still numbered 150,000 men, a force to be reckoned with. The total number of civilian refugees was over 20,000. All those people needed food and rest, and the army needed to be reorganised and re-equipped. Corfu became a temporary political centre for Serbia, with the government staying there till the end of the war, accompanied by foreign diplomatic missions. France had invited Regent Alexander and the Serbian government to stay at Aix-en-Provence, but the offer was declined: the latter proved an important political decision because it meant that the most important figures in the state thus stayed with their army or, when the army was sent into battle again, relatively near it. It also meant that they were not under the direct pressure of the politics or interests of a single Great Power. King Nicholas and his followers journeyed through Italy to France, where they first settled in Lyons, but were soon relocated by the French authorities to Bordeaux, where the exiled Montenegrin officers, politicians, officials and diplomats accredited to King Nicholas soon started to gather. At the end of May 1916 King Nicholas moved to the Paris suburb of Neuilly, and from August the Montenegrin government made its headquarters there too. The King and his entourage continued to represent the Montenegrin state on the side of the Allies, but they did not have armed forces in any considerable number.

The Serbian leadership had emerged from the crisis-laden autumn and winter virtually intact: the King, the Regent, the government, most of the deputies, leaders of political parties (all except certain Social Democrats) and the army commands were on foreign soil. There had been certain changes in the government with Božidar Terzić being appointed the new Minister of Military Affairs. But the supreme command had been subject to a fundamental change: its head, Vojvoda Radomir Putnik, had been dismissed in December 1915 in Skadar, and on 12 January 1916 his place was taken by General Petar Bojović. Putnik went to live in Nice, where he became ill and died in the spring of 1917. Putnik's deputy, Živko Pavlović, was also dismissed in January 1916. As for Vojvoda Živojin Mišić, he was dismissed from the post of commander of the 1st Army and sent to recuperate in Italy. He later went to inspect the front in France, and was finally returned to Corfu.

There were probably political reasons for the changes in the military leadership, but their exact nature has not been discovered. Radomir Putnik was certainly sick, but it had been Regent Alexander's decision to dismiss him and Pavlović. It would seem that the Regent made those changes because the officers in the supreme command had been keeping him in their shadow, in his capacity as both ruler and commander-in-chief. It could also have been that both Putnik and Pavlović, although they did not belong to the Black Hand, supported Colonel Dragutin Dimitrijević, while Regent Alexander was regarding the secret organisation with ever greater misgivings.

Members of the Black Hand were already asking who was to 'blame' for the collapse of the country's defence and accusing the government and the Regent of incompetence. It would seem that Alexander considered that the government, or rather its Prime Minister Nikola Pašić, should take the blame, but he rejected outright the accusation that he himself was responsible. Justified or not, the dismissals in the supreme command were interpreted among the ranks of the Black Hand, and perhaps in broader circles, as attempts by Alexander and the government to shift responsibility onto the army. From the beginning of exile the question of who was to 'blame' had assumed major political and psychological dimensions. The fact that Živojin Mišić was kept far from a command position for a long time suggests that he was somehow involved. Could that have been because of Mišić's hesitation to carry out the order for withdrawal through Albania, or was it because of his warning that a separate peace should be concluded if the offensive failed? There are many such questions, but still no real answers.

With its decision not to capitulate but instead to evacuate its top politicians, most of its armed forces and other representative figures in the population, including the country's most prominent intellectuals, Serbia created the conditions whereby it could continue to have a political and military impact on the World War. Consequently its most important task was to equip the remaining armed forces to return to the battlefield so that Serbia could demonstrate the continuity of its role and confirm its identity by adhering to the war programme it had laid down. At the end of winter and the beginning of spring, despite loss of territory, the Serbian leadership took new steps in Paris, London and Petrograd, and at the Allied Conference in Chantilly, to make known clearly, to both the enemy and the Allies, that Serbia was continuing the fight. This was thanks to activity by political and military representatives, particularly the Regent and the Prime Minister.[39]

In Corfu the Serbian army was reorganised in such a way that it essentially retained its old form of organisation.[40] Volunteers from Herzegovina, the Bay of Cattaro and Montenegro became part of the 2nd Army. Weapons and equipment were French, and the units were also armed according to French regulations, although the artillery was not so powerful as its French counterpart. The Serbian army was finally ready to fight again. The form of its inclusion in war operations was important not only from a military point of view but also politically. The Serbian authorities had rightly assessed that their army could fight both as part of the Allied army and as a separate entity, and that it therefore had the right to obtain its own operational area on the Salonika front and have independent command within the general plans of the Allied command in that province. France's intentions were just the opposite: it wanted the Serb units to be at the disposal of the Allied, or rather French command in Salonika.[41] As a consequence, general disagreement lasting four to five months ensued, but the Serbian side got its way in the end.

In the period from March 1916 to the end of May Serb units were transported to the northern Aegean coast, with the bulk of the troops being moved from mid-April.[42] The transport was organised by France and carried out mainly in French vessels, although the Italian and British navies also took part. There were no losses in transit. Around 127,000 Serb soldiers were concentrated at the end of June in camps prepared by the French on the Halkidiki peninsula. In July their number grew to 152,000. They received additional armaments and a certain period of extra training, after which they returned to the battlefield during June and July, mainly taking up positions in the area from Mount Kozuf to Lerin (Florina) in the central section of the Allied front north of Salonika. French and British troops formed the bulk of the Allied forces on the Salonika front, but there were also strong Russian and Italian units for a short time, compared to one Montenegrin battalion under French command.

When the Allies had at last successfully completed negotiations on the entry of Romania into the war on their side, their commands were given the task at the end of August of preparing and launching an offensive on the Salonika front. The Serbian army had a prominent role in these plans. The offensive was to start on 20 August, and Romania was to attack Austria-Hungary on 27 August. However, the Central Powers and Bulgaria had noticed the concentration of hostile forces on the southern front as well as Romania's increasingly suspect behaviour. Therefore, in order to thwart Allied intentions at Salonika and at the same time discourage Romania, they decided to take the initiative.[43] On 17 August the Bulgarians launched a fierce offensive, thwarting and surprising the Allied commands. The main

Bulgarian strike was in the sector of the Serbian 3rd Army, which was forced to retreat, and for a certain time the situation was grim both for the Allies and for the Serbian army. But a counter-strike was prepared. Vojvoda Živojin Mišić was urgently recalled from Corfu, and at the beginning of September he again took over command of the 1st Army. On 14 September the Allied counter-attack began, Serb troops bearing the main brunt. In three days of fighting, most of it hand to hand, the Serbian 1st Army beat the Bulgarians in the battle at Gornichevo and forced them to retreat.

Fierce fighting lasted for longer than two months, particularly around the Kajmakčalan peak, and on 30 September, after a number of attacks and retreats, the Serbian army was victorious and set foot once again in its own homeland.[44] Battle-weary veterans were to say that never had they seen so many dead over such a small area; one Serbian division alone lost 3,320 troops, and total Serb casualties amounted to 4,643. Among those who lost their lives was the commander of the Volunteer Detachment, Lieutenant-Colonel Vojin Popović (Vojvoda Vuk). The Serb advance was slow but constant in other sectors too. Another major battle was fought around the Crna Reka river, where the 1st Army penetrated deep into Bulgarian defences and forced the enemy to retreat more than 40 kilometres, after which Allied troops were able to enter Bitola on 19 October. When the Bulgarians and the Germans managed to halt the advance north of Bitola, the front was stabilised and trench fighting began—a situation that remained the same for nearly two whole years. The Serbian army had confirmed its worth, but the cost had been extremely high—as many as 28,000 casualties. In return, however, the Bulgarians and Germans had suffered 68,000 casualties at the hands of the Serbs, and 7,700 of their troops had been taken prisoner. Because of the extent of its losses, the Serbian army was reorganised to comprise only the 1st and 2nd Armies.

One can gain an insight into both the collective psychology and the morale at the time from a song that was sung from the time of the army's collapse up to its re-entry into the battlefield. It is nostalgic, but the principal idea is one of optimism. The singer is from the land 'where the lemon tree blooms yellow', and directs his thoughts 'far away in the distance, where the sun shines brighter', where the village lies in which he was born. He sings of the sea lapping the shores of the island of Vidos, where the dead were buried, echoing that 'there lie the graves of the valiant, brother alongside brother', who are 'the Prometheus of hope, the Apostles of suffering'. The folk poet piled rhyme on rhyme, singing bitterly and defiantly of the restless Serbs who fall because God is asleep and knows nothing of their suffering. Nonetheless, the nostalgic air with its sorrowful melody finishes with the thunderous 'Long live Serbia!' The poet was truly singing a requiem to the 'tomb of blue', but one 'the like of which the heavens have not seen'. He demanded silence so that even the dead might hear 'the roar of battle'—'over the father peace reigns, over the son history is being made.' In the bittersweet song the poet said he would still awaken the sleeping God.

Soldiers and officers alike were longing to return to their homes from which they were separated by the battlefront. The diary of the army artist Dragomir Glišić tells us:

I dream of my dear little Mara grasping hold of my moustache, and mother tapping her lightly on the hand, remonstrating and telling her not to touch daddy's whiskers. Milica and Vlada are laughing. When will God let us all embrace one another and never part again? Christmas came and went.... My heart is not here, my soul ... is with my fatherless children. I wonder whether they are eating well and thinking of me as I am of them. But I comfort myself with the thought that their good mother will prepare a fine meal for them, however lowly. And my son will take his father's place, he will light a candle, and Milica and little Mara will join him in a hymn to Christ's birth, with mother's help, of course. Enough now, but what can I do when I am so sad. I can write at least to myself when I can't write to them; I am making some paintings at the front, but I find no enjoyment in it. My heart and soul are with my family and my fatherless children. I don't know how they are, and there seems no end to our separation.[45]

Generally, the Yugoslav unification front was constantly spreading and expanding, which was demonstrated by the ever larger volunteer movement. That movement was encouraged to some extent by the Serbian government and to some extent by the Yugoslav Committee, but it was certainly also growing spontaneously. Work on the recruitment of volunteers became especially important at the beginning of 1916, owing partly to the huge losses sustained and the impending battles. The Yugoslav Committee, which worked to expand the volunteer movement, was inspired primarily by political motives; this was because the participation of the Yugoslav population of the Monarchy in the armed struggle on the side of the Entente could not but have the effect of strengthening the Committee's role in the unification process. Volunteers comprised Yugoslav émigrés in the United States and in the British dominions of Canada, Australia and New Zealand, as well men from among the tens of thousands of Yugoslavs taken prisoner as Austro-Hungarian soldiers by the Russians and, to a lesser extent, the Italians.

During the summer of 1916 the Serbian government and the Yugoslav Committee stepped up the recruitment of volunteers from North and South America. Where Serbia was concerned, it would seem that the idea was first discussed by the Serbian and French supreme commands. After that, at the beginning of August at the latest, the government worked to secure, for that purpose, money from the French and means of transport from the British. On 25 November 1916 the Serbian, French and British supreme commands signed a convention[46] on the recruitment and transportation of Yugoslav volunteers from America, Australia and New Zealand. In December a Serbian legation was opened in Washington with the special task of continuing to recruit volunteers, and special personnel were sent for this purpose to North and South America.[47] As a consequence, around 4,200 volunteers came to the Salonika front, the huge majority being Serbs, while there were around 200 Croats and even fewer Slovenes. Men were showing willingness to become volunteers in Australia and New Zealand too, but no organised recruitment ever took place there. Still, by February 1918 seventy-eight Dalmatians had managed to make the long journey from those distant countries to Salonika. They came on their own initiative and with the help of the British military authorities. There were tens of thousands of Yugoslav prisoners of war in Italy, and the Serbian government tried to recruit volunteers from among them, but the Italian government blocked almost all such attempts and only 260 volunteers arrived on the Salonika front from Italian prisoner of war camps. However, the prisoners of war in Russia could be recruited more quickly, more easily and in greater numbers.[48]

Already in January 1916 the Serbian government had sent a note to the Russian government asking for permission to recruit volunteers. The request was been granted, and a recruitment centre was set up in Odessa. The result was described by an eyewitness: 'A huge number of prisoners, former Austro-Hungarian soldiers, mainly Serbs, came from all corners of Russia's vast territory from the most distant prisoner of war camps. They removed their grimy Austrian uniforms and donned new uniforms, albeit Russian ones; however, the Serb military cap gave them a distinctively Serb appearance.'[49] The 1st Regiment of the Serb volunteer detachment was soon formed. The number of volunteers continued to grow, and in February the 1st Serb Volunteer Division was formed. At the end of February Colonel Stevan Hadžić was named commander of the Volunteer Division by the government in Corfu. That Division soon numbered 9,733 volunteers, almost exclusively Serbs from Bosnia, Vojvodina and Lika. Volunteers continued to flow in, and in mid-August their numbers reached nearly 18,000. When Romania entered the war at the end of August, the volunteers went into battle as part of the Russian 47th Corps and were sent to the front in Dobrudja to fight the Bulgarians. Made up of combatants who were firmly committed ideologically, the 1st Division fought with great courage, despite the fact that it had been sent into battle without sufficient equipment or training. Hence its losses, of around 8,000 men, were appalling.

In the meantime, the Russian authorities were simply recruiting Yugoslav prisoners of war from the camps, no longer asking if they wanted to join the volunteers or not. That made possible the formation of another division, but it also sowed the seeds of new problems. Because of the large number of volunteers, on 26 July 1916 the Serbian supreme command in Salonika issued an order that a Serb volunteer corps should be formed in Russia. The 2nd Serb Volunteer Division was then created in Odessa. Among the 20,000 men in that Division 11,169 had specified their nationality; there were 6,200 Serbs, 3,144 Croats, 1,556 Slovenes, and from among the non-Yugoslav nations Czechs numbered the most—193. The initial enthusiasm among the combatants soon declined, partly because of the huge losses in Dobrudja, and partly because they were not sufficiently motivated to wage war on fronts far from their own homelands.[50] Hence the idea was born of the Corps being concentrated north of Djerdap (Iron Gates), and then attacking towards the Ključ area and infiltrating into north-eastern Serbia. That operation would have represented an important manoeuvre within the broader Allied activity in the Balkans, and was in fact intended to hold down part of the enemy forces at the time when Allied offensives were taking place on fronts at Salonika and in Dobrudja.

To a certain extent the Russian intelligence service was already working in that direction. It created a centre in Turnu-Severin and managed to establish links with the population of occupied Serbia.[51] A Serb guerrilla detachment was also set up in Turnu-Severin which already had nearly 160 men in the second half of September. It was commanded by Lieutenant-Colonel Aleksandar Srb, an officer sent from Salonika who had previously been a *comitadji* and a member of the Black Hand. He was soon joined by Lieutenant-Colonel Božin Simić, an experienced intelligence officer and guerrilla combatant, who had also been sent from Salonika and was a member of the Black Hand. That detachment, a special task unit, was to be the first to cross the Danube and start activity behind the enemy lines. However, an order came from Corfu banning the guerrillas from crossing into Serbia—partly, perhaps, because a settling of accounts with the 'Unification or Death' (Black Hand) organisation was being prepared. However, Central Power forces quickly defeat the Romanian army, and before the Serb volunteer corps could become concentrated the sector north of Djerdap was lost.

Schoolchildren, students, teachers

With the first signs of the collapse of Serbia's defence, France, Britain, Russia, Italy and neutral Switzerland showed readiness to help educate the country's youth by giving them places in their schools and universities. The Serbian authorities in exile invested great efforts in educating as far as possible the young people who had left the country because of the war. The war itself naturally created a deeply contradictory situation: on the one hand, it required as many young men as possible to fight on the front, but on the other the huge losses meant that as many youngsters as possible had to be educated for the sake of the country's future. This led to a difference of opinion between the military and the education authorities: the army demanded that medical students should help the sick and wounded because of the shortage of medical staff on the battlefield, while the education authorities had to ensure that as many medical students as possible finished their studies and became qualified physicians. Nonetheless it was agreed in principle that the Ministry of Education should have the final say in these matters.[52]

Serb schoolchildren and students continued their education in France, Switzerland, Britain and Italy. Plans for education in Russia came to nothing; according to Professor Jovan Žujović, this was because 'neither Mr Pašić nor the students wanted to leave "sweet France".'[53] Of all the countries where Serb students continued their education and studies, France was the most important.[54] In November 1915 the French Chamber of Deputies made a decision on this subject, and the French government did so at the beginning of December.[55] The rectors of the French universities were then informed of the arrival of Serb schoolchildren and students and of the necessary preparations. They were also informed that resources had been secured to cover the costs of both education and medical treatment. In December 1916 approximately 1.4 million francs were allocated for this purpose.

A mixed Franco-Serb 'University Committee for Serb Youth' was created to coordinate all those matters in December 1915. It was chaired by Professor Louis Liard, rector of the University of Paris, and included the department heads of the relevant French institutions, including the Ministry of Foreign Affairs. Serbia was represented in the Committee by Professor Jovan Žujović, president of the Serbian Academy of Sciences.[56] The sum of 50,000 francs was placed at the disposal of the Committee by the French Foreign Ministry, 15,000 francs by the French Ministry of Education, and 50,000 francs by the Serbian legation; the initiative of the rector of the University of Paris resulted in voluntary donations being given to the value of 8,000 francs. By mid-June 1916 the Committee had 130,000 francs at its disposal. On 21 January 1916 a special Serbo-French charity organisation named La Nation Serbe en France had also been set up, which had two presidents, one Serb and one French. Moreover, the 'Franco-Serb Committee' comprising the wives of prominent French figures was set up in March 1915 to collect clothing and other necessities for young people who had fled Serbia.

The evacuation of Serb schoolchildren from the Albanian coast progressed painfully slowly, although perhaps around 100 embarked at Vlorë on 28 December 1915 and were shipped to France immediately.⁵⁷ But the majority had to wait, and it was some weeks before larger groups started to arrive by way of Italy. A number of schoolboys and schoolgirls who had withdrawn to Greece had been transported with greater ease from Salonika to Marseilles at the end of 1915. Moreover, in the spring of 1916 a certain number of schoolchildren and students reached France in smaller groups or individually. All in all, it is calculated there were around 3,000 primary and secondary school pupils and students in France in mid-March. Around 300 of them quickly left for Britain, and a considerable number went to Switzerland. There were 1,606 schoolchildren, of whom were 288 girls, and 431 students registered in France in the summer of 1916.⁵⁸ With the passage of time that number was to increase to 1,151 Serb secondary pupils (306 of them girls) in schools throughout France, 193 primary school children in Corsica, and another ninety children in Nice in the 1917–18 school year. That same academic year there were 1,164 university students (including eighty-four girls) in France and another thirty-one attending special courses.

To deal with these matters concerning the Serbian government opened a Department of Education, headed by university professors Jovan Žujović and Sava Urošević, at the Legation in Paris, under the direct supervision of the Serbian Ministry of Education. Furthermore, international legal issues were settled through a special convention.⁵⁹ The convention stipulated that special French language courses and teaching of the Serbian language, national history and literature should be provided for those children, while the Serbian government was granted the right to appoint teachers for those national subjects. It also regulated the enrolment of Serb secondary school graduates in French universities. The various courses were given by Serb civilian and military teachers, as well as French teachers. All known facts indicate that the first intake studied extremely diligently and passed the examinations with good marks. In October 1916, out of the 108 matriculation candidates in a school near Grenoble, thirty-two did so well that they did not have to take the matriculation examination, and fifty passed. A total of 202 candidates matriculated there and twenty-five passed the teachers' training examination. The authorities were delighted with the diligence of the pupils and the results they obtained. In mid-August 1916

Professor Jovan Žujović wrote that his 'sole satisfaction' lay in seeing 'that all the possible matriculation candidates are carefully studying', that 'in these matriculation courses the pupils see the most positive object of their work ... and they work hard.' He added that for him, who 'sometimes felt like weeping for the future of Serbia', the 'work and success on the part of the huge majority of our young people' actually encouraged him to carry on living.[60] All those who monitored the October examinations in the Schoolboys' Battalion in Jausiers were also very satisfied with the results.[61]

In parallel to this, the Serbian government was considering the possibility of opening special Serbian secondary schools, and after vacillating between mainland Greece, Corfu and France it finally opted for France. In July 1916 a higher trade school for Serb pupils was opened in Aix-en-Provence. Work was also under way on opening a grammar school. In August 1916 the Minister of Education Ljubomir Davidović wrote: 'A special grammar school is being opened for our pupils who for various reasons cannot be enrolled in French schools. This school will be maintained exclusively with our resources, and the teaching staff will be from Serbia.'[62] This grammar school would be transferred to Serbia 'as soon as a part of our territory is liberated.' The government allocated 250,000 dinars for that purpose at its session on 8 September 1916.[63] A grammar school was opened in Nice in the autumn, and the first examinations were held there in December. The school was later transferred from Nice to Saint-Jean-Cap-Ferrat, where classes were held during the 1917–18 school year. It was attended by around 1,000 pupils, and about 700 matriculated there while some fifty passed the teachers' training examination. Moreover, 153 secondary school pupils and forty-six primary school pupils were educated in Algeria. The charity organisation La Nation Serbe en France provided scholarships for 250 secondary vocational school pupils.

The first students to arrive, numbering 431, were immediately divided into groups and sent to several universities in southern and central France: ninety-seven to Montpellier, sixty-nine to Bordeaux, fifty-seven each to Poitiers and Grenoble, thirty-six to Clermont-Ferrand, thirty to Paris, twenty-seven to Lyons, twenty-five to Toulouse, twelve to Rennes, ten to Dijon, nine to Besançon and two to Nancy. A total of 129 students enrolled to study law, 229 to study natural sciences, sixty-one in the faculties of philosophy, and twelve to study medicine.[64] The young men who had not been exempted from military service had first to report to the recruitment service. The number of students at French universities quickly multiplied. Belgrade University Professor Jovan Radonjić, who was the Education Board's inspector at the matriculation examinations in the spring of 1918, wrote: 'Everyone rushed to study at the universities. It is evident that a very small number of pupils enrol in vocational schools ..., and the state desperately needs such persons. As it provides education in entirety, the state should have the right to influence what they study taking account of the country's requirements.'[65] There may have been around 1,200 students from Serbia (including 100 girls) in France at the end of the war.

Many young Serbs were suffering from the grave consequences of the diseases and exhaustion they had endured during the fighting and the withdrawal from Serbia. This was aggravated by the fact that scholarships were meagre. The economic conditions in France, exacerbated by the war and particularly by the constant inflation, hit Serb students hard with the result that some diseases spread, especially tuberculosis. Serbian authorities tried to help as much as they could. In 1917, and maybe earlier, the Department of Education in Paris had allocated a considerable sum for treating 'our pupils', and a sanatorium had been established in Menton, helped by an association of Scottish women. At its session of 7 February, the government in Corfu decided 'to increase the scholarships for our students to 180 dinars because tuberculosis had started to spread suddenly due to difficult living conditions.'[66] One student, Ljubomir Stojiljković, requested on 21 August 1917 that he receive more caring treatment for the tuberculosis he had contracted because he first caught typhus in Serbia and then pneumonia in France. A students' collective in Rennes, asked the Department of Education in January 1918 to send a law student, Milivoje Ilić for treatment immediately because his 'state of health is critical.'[67] The request was granted. It was because of the bad material conditions of the students at the University of Rennes that they held a meeting on 31 March 1918, as a result of which they sent a petition to the Department of Education on 10 April stating that they had received an increase in their scholarships in October 1917, and that since that time their value had been 180 francs, which was of little help.[68]

At the beginning of the summer of 1916 a group of 300 schoolchildren, ranging in age from six to seventeen, travelled from France to Britain.[69] The costs of their journey and their further education were borne by the Serbian Relief Fund in London, which in the autumn of 1917 allocated around £2,000 a month. On their arrival in Britain, these schoolchildren were first divided into two groups, one going to Oxford and the other to Cambridge; they were later sub-divided again sent to fourteen 'colonies'—nine in England, four in Scotland and one in Wales. However, the largest number remained in the two university cities, with the result that in November 1917 there were forty Serb schoolchildren in Oxford and forty-two in Cambridge. The schoolchildren and students in Britain lived in incomparably better conditions than those in France, probably because there were far fewer of them and because Britain was not directly exposed to war operations. It also seems that the Serbian authorities concerned themselves less over the young people in Britain than they did over those in France. However, in Britain too the care of the children was entrusted to a distinguished university professor, the celebrated literary historian Pavle Popović, a member of the Yugoslav Committee.

At the beginning of 1918 the Serbian Ministry of Education in Corfu decided to send a large number of students who had been exempted from military service to universities in Italy, in line with a government decision to discharge schoolboys and students from the army to enable them to complete their education. An Education Committee was therefore also set up at the Serbian Legation in Rome,[70] headed by Professor Vladimir Mitrović, who taught technical studies at the University of Belgrade. The candidates were chosen from among soldiers who had already studied technical subjects. This initiative demonstrates that Serbia was in need of graduate engineers. Moreover, the idea of establishing a separate Serbian technical faculty in Italy was also mooted in the Ministry of Education.

There was also a large number of refugees in Switzerland. One of them wrote in his memoirs that 'nowhere in Europe, nowhere in the world, could one live more freely and in a more cultured manner' than in Switzerland.[71] This was thanks largely to the level of economic development and social stability and the country's democratic system, but it was also due to Switzerland being neutral in the World War. As a result of this, it was host to individuals of different and sometimes even opposite political affiliation, which came to light in all fields of life. A large number of Serb war orphans had been sent to Switzerland, and two committees were responsible for their care—one, with twelve members, chaired by Professor Alfred Mayer, while the other, with eleven members, was made up exclusively of distinguished Swiss women. In the autumn of 1916 Professor Jovan Cvijić informed the Ministry of Information that 'our children are well looked after, thanks to the parent-like care of the committees here, which deserves all praise.'[72]

The first person to provide care for schoolchildren and students in Switzerland had actually been Professor Cvijić himself: when he arrived there from Serbia in December 1915 he had encountered a number of Serb children who had been 'in a wretched state'.[73] They had been attending schools in Switzerland earlier, but since the fall of Serbia they had lost touch with their parents and had no means of maintaining themselves. Refugees—schoolchildren and students—soon started to arrive too, and Professor Cvijić asked the Serbian Relief Fund in London for assistance. Twice in 1916 he received 25,000 Swiss francs from the Fund, with the right to dispose of the money as he saw fit—he sent it in the form of scholarships to schoolchildren and students via school and university administrations. When he moved to Paris at the end of 1916, having been invited to lecture at the Sorbonne, Cvijić continued to manage those resources. From his reports to the Serbian Education Minister at the beginning of August 1917 it can be concluded that 'pupils have now been helped for sixteen months.' Furthermore, by June 1917 'a total of 87,300 Swiss francs have been given to students,' while 'the number of students ranged between thirty and eighty,' and 'the largest sum of assistance given was 120 francs, not counting school fees.' According to other sources, there were fifty-two such scholarships in 1918. Cvijić himself considered the scholarships 'quite inadequate', and he asked Minister of Education Miloš Trifunović to provide assistance with 'school fees amounting to at least 12,000 Swiss francs a year.' Cvijić's reports further noted that small children were forgetting the Serbian language, and he therefore allocated a scholarship recipient and a school inspector to teach children Serbian language, history and religion on Saturday afternoons.

The composition of the schoolchildren and students in Switzerland was, in fact, Yugoslav.[74] Many of the young men who had fled Austria-Hungary for Serbia in 1914 or decided as prisoners of war to join the Serbian army knew German, and therefore, having been exempted from military service, they wanted to study in Switzerland. In mid-1918 there were also 159 Montenegrin students who had gathered there. As time went by, there were more and more students in Switzerland and France. There were just over sixty students at the universities of Geneva, Lausanne, Berne and Zurich in 1916, but at the end of 1917 there were around 180 (including thirty-nine girls) receiving scholarships from the Serbian Ministry of Education. In fact there were more: it has been calculated that around 300 Yugoslavs were studying in Switzerland at the end of the war. At the University of Geneva alone there were 232 of them (including 112 from the Yugoslav lands of Austria-Hungary). There were also students at the Universities of Lausanne, Zurich, Berne and Neuchatel.

It is almost impossible to say exactly how many Yugoslav schoolchildren and students were studying in these countries. Some data tell us that different Serbian institutions alone were providing scholarships for some 5,500 youngsters, the Ministry of Education accounting for 4,896, while in September 1916 King Nicholas' scholarships were being received by 183 schoolchildren and students. During the three years of exile, of course, a number of children reached school age, primary school children reached secondary school age, and secondary school children started higher education. There was also an influx from the army. At the beginning of 1918 significant steps were taken to exempt refugees, volunteers and prisoners of war from the Yugoslav regions of Austria-Hungary from military service with the political motive of demonstrating practical commitment to the Yugoslav programme. Pašić made a decisive move on 28 January when he wrote to the Ministry of Education: 'Among the Yugoslav volunteers, both those from Russia and the others, there is a considerable number of undergraduates. According to the regulations for our own students, these too would have the right to continue their education.... For political reasons ... Yugoslav schoolchildren should receive the same treatment as schoolchildren who are Serbian subjects.' The Minister of Education agreed, and consequently on 27 February the Minister of Military Affairs decided to extend the exemption of Serbian schoolboys and students from military service, so that they could continue their education, to include 'all schoolboys and students who were volunteers or foreign subjects, regardless of where they came from before entering our army', stipulating that they should be treated in the same way as Serbian subjects.[75]

The organisation of education and the teaching of national subjects created the possibility of gathering together and providing work for most teachers in exile, a number of whom had been given army exemption and withdrawn from the front.[76] When the Government agreed in August 1917 to a grammar school being set up in Volos in Greece, Minister of Education Miloš Trifunović concluded that at least thirty grammar school teachers should be seconded from the army. In the autumn of 1917, when the issue of training of engineers in France was being considered, seven professors and assistant professors of the Technical Faculty in Belgrade were seconded from the army and placed at the disposal of the Education Committee in Paris. Moreover, when, at the beginning of 1918, students were to be sent to Italy to study technical subjects, also with the aim of providing the country with more engineers, Miloš Trifunović requested that the Ministry of Military Affairs should exempt assistant professor Petar Bajalović from serving in the army. The teaching staff of the University of Belgrade bore the brunt of educating of schoolchildren and students abroad, and some of them were at the same time teaching students of the host country. In Clermont-Ferrand, for example, Nikola Vulić, a professor of ancient history, taught Latin to both Serb and French students, but as he himself said, he spent part of his classes teaching French students 'the history of Yugoslavia (not only of Serbia) in ancient times.' Moreover, he gave public lectures every Tuesday on the Yugoslav issue.[77]

Serbia's teachers and academics gathered mainly in France, which helped the Ministry of Education to revive in Paris, in February 1918, the work of the Serbian Education Council which had not been able to meet since the beginning of the war. It needed to function for several reasons, the main one being that curricula had to be prepared for all schools in anticipation of the moment when the country would be liberated.[78] At its first session the Council placed on the agenda 'the issue of the standardisation of schooling for our young people who have stayed in Serbia, are interned, are prisoners of war or are still at the front with that of their counterparts who are now receiving education.' Discussion also focused on 'the way to organise curricula and schoolbooks for the period of transitional teaching ... in Serbia between the time of war and that of normal peacetime,' thus anticipating the return to Serbia.

Serb intellectuals devoted much of their time to school and educational activities, but they were also politically active. They were often encouraged in such activity by the government, but a number of them were following their own convictions. For example, Jovan Cvijić withdrew from public life at the end of 1915, evidently not trusting the politics of Pašić's government. Devoting himself to his own work in those years, he made an immense contribution to knowledge and to the elaboration of the basic principles of the Yugoslav programme. Besides a number of minor works and several lectures, he wrote at that time his substantial work La Péninsule Balkanique (*The Balkan Peninsula*), published in its French version in Paris in 1918.[79]

Indications exist that research work was supported officially, albeit unsystematically and always in ways geared to political requirements. The idea was born in exile of writing and publishing what would become a Yugoslav encyclopaedia: Jovan M. Jovanović explained the need for it by saying that in Europe 'few know about this entire issue of ours', and that anyone who wanted to know more about it had to read 'between ten and fifteen tracts' instead of finding all the information 'in one place, in one book'. *The Balkan Peninsula* evidently met with understanding among high-ranking political figures both as a book in its own right and as one with a political value. In a telegram supporting Cvijić sent to Pašić on 25 April 1918, Milenko Vesnić wrote:

Both in the writer's renown and in the value of the book itself, this work will be of great importance for the discussion of political and diplomatic issues.... In this sphere Cvijić is doubtless the greatest and most recognised authority not only in Serbia but also throughout the entire educated world. It is in our interest to encourage and support him in this work, and it is our duty to do so.[80]

Cvijić's *The Balkan Peninsula* is a voluminous study that analyses one geographical area by encompassing many essential natural-geographical and social-historical elements. The author proved himself not only an outstanding authority and researcher in several areas of a number of key sciences dealing with man, society and geographical space, but also a thinker who examined links between phenomena regardless of the separate paths of their scientific perception.[81] Consequently the author did not elaborate his synthesis only on the basis of his overall research experience, but also introduced his own general political and ideological views—those stemming from his own time and place in history. Hence the result was both an original scientific work and a unique political document.

On the basis of his truly extensive analysis of ethnic circumstances and population movement, Cvijić concluded:

Serbs and Croats barely knew one another up to the great population movements, and Serbs and Slovenes knew one another even less. As a result of migrations during the Ottoman Empire, Serbs became greatly mixed with Croats.... Our national unity does not rest solely on the original kinship of our tribes; nor does it rest, moreover, solely on one single Serbo-Croatian literary language or, to a certain extent, on common literature, as is usually thought. A long period of ethnic and ethno-biological melding and merging at the times of Ottoman and Venetian rule preceded the common literary language. Because of that, national unity has deeper roots, true national roots.... Our nation's migrations to Srem, Banat and Backa or Slavonia had another impact. That migration-populated national belt was an obstacle to foreign influence.

An analysis of the specific features of geographical borders in the Balkan peninsula, Cvijić said, provides a geographical basis for the entire 'Eastern question', which makes the deeper reasons for Austria-Hungary's attack on Serbia more understandable:

As Turkey was collapsing rapidly, Central Europe, represented by Austria-Hungary, first wanted to take advantage of its favourable position to occupy the central and western parts of the Balkan peninsula. Its northern border, completely open, was exposed to attacks from the north or from along the Morava and the Vardar river valleys and the valleys of the Sava and Danube tributaries.... The Balkan peninsula attracts conquerors thanks to the fertility of the northern regions, the mild climate of the Aegean region, the huge Salonika gulf, which is open to the Aegean and thus to the Mediterranean, and finally the immense, unforeseeable possibilities in the Middle East. And all that was luring the Central Powers.

Cvijić also pointed to the other direction from which the Balkan peninsula was threatened for geographical reasons:

> Russia, a vast country without any reliable maritime communications, was also highly attracted to Constantinople and the straits.... It is natural for Russia to be interested in the region of the straits for communications and economic reasons.

Conflicts and strife

The hub of Serbia's political life was in the island of Corfu. Part of the provisional state leadership was located there, the other part being in the zone of the Salonika front together with Regent Alexander and the supreme command.[82] However, political life became most important and colourful in the countries where large numbers of civilian exiles had settled, notably in Western Europe, mainly France and Switzerland. Serbs and Montenegrins mingled in those countries with Yugoslav émigrés from Austria-Hungary, and political exile circles became the centre of a new movement for state unification. The Yugoslav Committee had its headquarters in London, but Switzerland, a neutral country, gathered émigrés of the most disparate opinions. Moreover, the Serbian government had a propaganda centre in Switzerland, where the Yugoslav Committee also had an office, King Nicholas had his own centres, and the Serbian and Montenegrin opposition factions had created their own bases. Switzerland was also a rallying point for representatives of those in the Yugoslav lands of the Monarchy and in Serbia who were in favour of joining the Central Powers, as well as confidential envoys of supporters of Yugoslav unification from among the political forces of Austria-Hungary's southern provinces.

It is clear that, despite its exceptional circumstances, Serbia was basically continuing to exist within its pre-war constitutional framework, albeit with limited scope. Complex political life continued within this democratic framework. Moreover, internal political struggle was waged openly and sometimes quite fiercely, behind the scenes, at one point assuming the characteristics of a merciless underground war. The collapse in the autumn of 1915 was certainly overcome by the determination to continue along the same path, but there was also a renewal of the former constitutionally and non-constitutionally formed internal policy fronts and a radicalisation of their conflicts. To this was added the uncertainty brought by a war that was continuing with no end in sight.

The Serbian Assembly started functioning again relatively quickly.[83] In response to a call from the government, 123 out of the total of 166 deputies had gone into exile, which meant that forty-three had remained in the country. A small number of them had at first gone to Greece, while most had travelled through Montenegro and Albania to Italy. Demonstrating a wish to avoid party division at a time of crisis, many of the deputies in exile met first in Rome and formed the Joint Club. They quickly moved from Rome to Nice, where the Joint Club headquarters was relocated and where on 24 February 1916 eighty-nine of them met to discuss whether or not to resume the Assembly in the new circumstances. It was decided unanimously that the Assembly should, 'in agreement with the government, start work as soon as possible'.[84] In response to this initiative, the Regent's edict of 29 July 1916 convened it to meet in Corfu on 10 September. It did indeed convene on that day, and sat until 22 October. A total of 108 deputies attended, which was sufficient since the Constitution established that eighty-three deputies constituted a quorum. However, inter-party conflicts had erupted in the spring of 1916, and with the passage of time they grew in magnitude and animosity.[85] The first sign of the crumbling of the initial accord was seen in April 1916 when the Old Radicals, Pašić's deputies, distanced themselves from the Joint Club and created their own Club of Radical Deputies. However, that move led to a division among the Old Radicals—thirty opting to leave the Joint Club and fourteen disagreeing with that decision. The latter then formed their own separate Club of Independent Radicals. The Independent Radicals went on to form their own Main Committee and Deputies' Club, and representatives of the Progressive and People's parties also started to act independently.

This conflict led to long intervals between sessions of the Assembly, which, together with the government's refusal to allow the formation of Assembly committees for the individual political sectors (only an economic committee had been approved), was seen as proof of the intention of Pašić and the Old Radicals to retain power for themselves. Consequently all large-scale conflicts among Serb politicians centred around the figure of the Prime Minister. Some were eloquent in their praise for him, while others blackened him totally. He was described in Assembly sessions as a 'national treasure' and the 'embodiment of the national and state programme.' But other voices were heard saying he was the 'demon of Serbia', even a 'bandit'. Both sides insisted on the creation of a Yugoslav state as part of their own programme, but they nonetheless fought fiercely over the issue. The Government persistently claimed that, under the given circumstances, it was following the programme in the best possible way, but the opposition claimed that the Government was not following the programme sufficiently 'rationally and vigorously' and was relying solely on the uncertain Allied 'belief in the justification of our cause.' The opposition further maintained the Government was achieving virtually nothing, concluding, in short, that 'it had not succeeded in assuring the Allies of the justifiability of the Yugoslav issue.'

But the hidden political battle was incomparably more vehement and more ruthless. Three power factors can be said to have emerged in this battle, each of which had been in conflict with the others previously, and these differences had sharpened immediately after the withdrawal through Albania.[86] In December 1916 all the bitterness came to the surface when Colonel Dragutin Dimitrijević Apis was arrested. He was then deputy chief of the 3rd Army general staff. There followed the arrest of another nine high-ranking officers who had been founders and members of the secret nationalist association 'Unification or Death' (the Black Hand), which had only allegedly ceased functioning when armed conflict with Austria-Hungary began. Besides the arrests, investigation proceedings were instigated against another 124 officers, some twenty of whom were threatened with court-martial. A number of civilians and volunteers from the Yugoslav regions of Austria-Hungary were also arrested. The officers under suspicion were interned in camps in Greece and in French colonies in North Africa.

In the spring of 1917 charges were brought against eight of the officers, one of the civilians and two of the volunteers who had been arrested. They were charged with fomenting revolution and attempting to assassinate Regent Alexander near Ostrova in September 1916. They were tried before a military court in Salonika between

2 April and 23 May 1917, the main defendant being Colonel Dimitrijević. Deliberations were rapid, and sentences were read on the last day of the trial. Death penalties were meted out to Dimitrijević, Colonels Milan Milovanović, Radoje Lazić, Čedomir Popović and Vladimir Tucović, Lieutenant-Colonels Velimir Vemić and Ljubomir Vulović, Vice-Consul Bogdan Radenković and volunteer Rade Malobabić. Prison sentences of fifteen years were passed on retired General Damnjan Popović and volunteer Muhamed Mehmedbašić, one of the six men involved in the conspiracy against Franz Ferdinand. All of them appealed against their sentences within the forty-eight-hour appeal period. The High Military Court commuted the death sentences on Colonel Popović and Vice-Consul Radenković to twenty years' imprisonment, but it increased the sentence passed on General Damnjan Popović to the same. Regent Alexander then used his right and commuted the death sentences passed on Colonels Milovanović, Lazić and Tucović and on Lieutenant-Colonel Vemić to twenty years in prison, while he reduced the prison sentences of Čedomir Popović and Vice-Consul Radenković to ten years. Dragutin Dimitrijević, Ljubomir Vulović and Rade Malobabić were executed near Salonika at dawn on 13 July 1917.

The Salonika trial was rigged, its aim having been the forcible removal of a dangerous political rival. The executions of Dimitrijević, Vulović and Malobabić were in fact political assassinations under the cover of a judicial sentence.[87] Such drastic measures are proof of the ferocity of the political conflict which arose from the overall circumstances after the departure from the country—which in fact had their roots in events that had taken place over many years. A chain of events had led up to this, whose links comprised the assassination of King Alexander Obrenović in 1903, the so-called conflict between civilian and military authorities in 1913–14, the Sarajevo assassination and the collapse of the country's defence at the end of 1915. Having gathered force, the conflict reached its peak in Corfu because the defeat had naturally made relations among the most important state figures extremely tense. It had already been felt in Albania that there were three factions which were starting to fight among themselves: one was around Regent Alexander, the second around Pašić and the Government, and the third around the Black Hand organisation.

It would seem that the twenty-six-year-old Regent Alexander considered the crisis an opportunity to take the leadership of the country completely into his own hands, even if it this would violate constitutional provisions. The first step in that direction was the removal of Old Radicals from positions of authority. And there are several indications that the Regent did indeed intend to remove Pašić's government. Pašić and the Old Radicals, a decisive factor in political life despite the Coalition government, found themselves compelled to defend their authority by keeping the Regent's actions within the bounds of the constitution. The Black Hand considered the wielders of power in the country responsible for the defeat and thought they should therefore be removed. The Black Hand leadership had been dissatisfied ever since 1913 with the Old Radicals, accusing them of not conducting national policy resolutely enough, despite being the leading party. What was actually the case was that the country's home and foreign policy was in the firm grip of constitutional elements, which prevented Black Hand members from imposing their ideas from the shadows. As Regent Alexander was demonstrating ever more clearly that he considered himself the sole decisive factor and was for that reason suppressing Black Hand influence, Dimitrijević and his adherents turned against him too. In short, the Regent wanted to use monarchical power; the Old Radicals wanted to retain the monopoly of decision-making; and Black Hand members wanted to make the decisions themselves.

The Regent gathered around him a group of officers opposed to the Black Hand, including Colonels Petar Živković, Josif Kostić and Petar Mišić, and thanks to his constitutional position he could also rely on all military officers devoted to their duty and otherwise politically uncommitted.[88] Regent Alexander thus created a kind of military junta around the constitutional position of the Regent, which was called the White Hand; Pašić had the Old Radicals on his side and was transforming the police increasingly into his own political tool. Besides members of their own organisation, the Black Hand also had volunteer detachments from which it mobilised agents, using the motive of 'the exceptional interests of the nation and the homeland', while the organisation's striking force comprised a group of officers. Here too one could speak of a kind of military junta. All three groups had their unquestioned leaders, and the personal characteristics of Regent Alexander, Prime Minister Pašić and Colonel Dragutin Dimitrijević played key roles. Whatever the case, each of those groups violated to a certain extent the country's constitutional provisions, although the Old Radicals did so least, simply because they were in power constitutionally—in contrast to the White Hand which abused the constitutional powers of the Regent, and even more the Black Hand since it acted totally outside the Constitution.

As the three sides became more and more mutually antagonistic, the possibility arose for the Regent and the Black Hand to act concertedly against the Old Radicals. The few facts at our disposal would indicate that an attempt at conciliation took place under the high-sounding name of 'reconciliation in the army'.[89] However, it soon became apparent that another combination was far more likely—of the Regent and the Old Radicals against the Black Hand—and that was what happened. It is difficult to say exactly what caused this, but certain elements can be discerned. Dimitrijević and his men, believing that the state authorities had been conducting the wrong policy in the war and were therefore responsible for the collapse in the autumn of 1915, threatened to topple the Regent and the government, and probably even took steps in that direction. Here matters are not quite clear. It would seem that in this the Black Hand did not make much progress, but other reliable sources indicate that the assassination of Regent Alexander and Prime Minister Pašić was discussed and that some of volunteers had even been selected to carry out the task. Whatever the truth of the matter, it was sufficient to induce the Regent and Pašić to take action against the Black Hand together.

Two elements seem of importance in this entire matter: first how the members of Black Hand saw themselves and their role, and secondly what methods they were ready to use. The way they saw their role can best be discerned in letters written by General Damnjan Popović. He wrote that Black Hand members considered themselves 'ideal patriots', the true representatives of the nation and, as such, best qualified to act in the interest of the nation and the state. They deemed that they alone knew what policy was best for the nation. This was expressly stipulated in the Black Hand statute, where it was specified that the secret organisation was founded 'with the aim of the realisation of national ideals—the unification of Serbdom' and that the organisation, by its very nature, influenced all official factors 'in Serbia as Piedmont.' Black Hand methods comprised pressure on all state factors, the consideration of each and every Serb as a tool for its concept of politics, the creation of a network of secret organisations in Serb regions outside Serbia, and the use of force, hence also assassination, against state representatives.

However, it remains that, despite all its efforts, the Black Hand had not succeeded in having any essential impact on the conduct of state policy since the Old Radicals had been elected to leading positions. Since 1914, moreover, Black Hand members had not been satisfied with the parliamentary state either, not to mention their dissatisfaction with the Old Radicals. Hence they kept attacking the 'internal evil' and claiming that it could not be uprooted until 'this regime' had been toppled, further maintaining that the regime—personified by the Regent and the Prime Minister—would otherwise 'destroy greater Serbia'. Dimitrijević and his associates belittlingly called Regent Alexander 'that little man' and Pašić 'Judas'. They considered the Regent immature and the Prime Minister to be prepared to betray national and state interests.[90] Evidently the Black Hand targeted the Regent and the government purely because they were not conducting a relentless Serbian expansionist policy and insisted on taking account of limiting factors domestically and on the international scene.

It is difficult to say if the issue of a separate peace with the Central Powers played any role in all of this.[91] If it did, it would be necessary first to clarify whether the Regent and the government executed Dimitrijević to facilitate that peace or because Dimitrijević himself wished to conclude a separate peace. There are no grounds to believe the former supposition because peace offers had already been rejected in 1915, and the idea that a separate peace was desired during a time of exile and dependence on the Entente is absurd. Moreover, the actions of official Serbia totally discounted such a possibility. German sources contain no data on any negotiations with Serbia in 1916, and Austro-Hungarian sources from 1917 and 1918 expressly state that it had hitherto been impossible to negotiate peace with Pašić's government. As far Dimitrijević's involvement in the Sarajevo assassination, it was he himself who wrote about it during the Salonika trial, at a time when his fate had already been sealed. However, there are grounds for the second allegation—that Dimitrijević wished to conclude a separate peace. Although he and his group were the most resolute opponents of Austria-Hungary, they did have a certain affinity with the Prussian-German Reich. Besides, their claim that 'bad politics' had led to defeat leads to the assumption that, for them, 'good politics' could have been acceptance of German proposals in 1915.[92] Their otherwise rather simplistic concept of politics supports this assumption. In addition, two figures from Serbian diplomacy who were close to the Black Hand were in favour of a separate peace. German sources (reports from agent Albin Kutschbach) mention a diplomat Boško Čolak-Antić, though not specifically enough, and it is known that Vojislav Bogićević had broken with the Serbian government and, according to German sources, was looking for contacts with the German leadership when he was in Switzerland. But none of this proves anything. Finally, the fact that Milorad Drašković negotiated with Janos Dada in Niš, while he had earlier had contacts with Colonel Dimitrijević, in the capacity of an opposition leader offers for the present only the possibility of substantiation of the second, still unfounded allegation.

Dimitrijević and his associates, morally and psychologically confused and politically discountenanced, had threatened the Regent and Pašić. They had been devising something and had even made plans, but had done nothing. However, they had shown themselves to be a threat for the future. So the situation had continued to deteriorate where the Black Hand was concerned. But refugees and exiles had been feeling less dissatisfaction with it as time went on, and when fighting restarted Black Hand members had been deployed and in effect dispersed in different units. Some of them had even been sent to Russia. Then came the Volunteer Detachment's attack on the Kajmakčalan peak, in which it suffered huge losses and Vojvoda Vuk, one of the Black Hand's leading members, had been killed.[93] All in all, the Black Hand had been growing continuously less capable of any action on the home political scene.

Regent Alexander seems to have taken advantage of these developments to strike a fatal blow at the rival group. A narrative source tells us that he was encouraged to do so by White Hand officers who were opposed to Dimitrijević and his supporters, and Regent Alexander had received information, both accurate and inaccurate, to drive him to action.[94] The police too were reporting all kinds of things about the conspirators' activities, intentions and statements. Historians have noted that Regent Alexander had sought the adoption of a law on courts-martial for officers at a session of the National Assembly in Corfu in the autumn of 1916, but it had proved impossible because the entire government and all the deputies had been against it. The Regent and the White Hand had therefore decided to conceive and stage an assassination plot in order to have an excuse for liquidation on the basis of false indictments. They were helped in this by Pašić and his party members, as well as the police.

This, as far as it is known, was the political background of the Salonika trial. After sentences had been passed and the executions carried out, the Black Hand was disbanded and the army and state institutions purged of its members and supporters.[95] The struggle lost its edge, but the Salonika trial and the execution of the three condemned men served to sharpen the public political struggle. It was because of the executions that the Coalition government actually collapsed because ministers Davidović, Drašković and Marinković, members of the government who were not Old Radicals, refused to take responsibility for them. Before this Davidović and Drašković had addressed the Regent with a request that the death sentences should be commuted to 20 years' imprisonment, but their request had been denied. The stability of the homogeneous Old Radical Government then created was based, from that time until the end of the war, on the 'pact' reached with the Regent that was aimed at destroying Black Hand. Members of Black Hand who had then been abroad, and in that way had escaped the persecution, quickly launched a campaign lambasting the trial and the sentences passed in Salonika. Similarly, *Srpski List*, the organ of an obscure group in Geneva, participated wholeheartedly in the attacks on the Regent and the Government. And in Russia, Lieutenant-Colonels Aleksander Srb, Božin Simić and Vojislav Gojković, and Major Radoje Janković, all of whom were members of the Black Hand who had been sent to create volunteer units, rallied opposition to the government from there. The campaign against the trial and its sentences was therefore directed against the Regent, Pašić and the

Old Radicals. Pašić responded by ordering government services to tell the Allies that his attackers were 'Austro-German government agents'.

Meanwhile the country's collapse in the autumn of 1915 had put the Serbian Social Democratic Party in a worse position than any other Serbian political party.[96] A number of leading Social Democrats stayed in occupied Serbia, including the Party Secretary Dušan Popović and Committee member and National Assembly deputy Dragiša Lapčević. Triša Kaclerović emigrated but soon returned to the occupied country via Switzerland and was imprisoned in Kragujevac from January to April. Under the occupation administration political activity was impossible. Some Social Democrats were sent to internment camps, including the prominent biologist Nedeljko Košanin and Filip Filipović, who had earlier been a member of the Bolshevik faction of Serbian Social Democracy. But most of the Party's leadership, members and sympathisers left the country and remained in exile.[97] Since the Social Democratic Party recruited its members mostly from the working class, the majority of its members outside the country were in the army, deployed in different units and with tasks at the front and in the rear (it is calculated that there were around 200 of them on the Salonika front in mid-1917).[98] In May 1917 Petar Radovanović, a Social Democrat soldier who served in the front line, wrote, 'We have to keep silent about politics', and it only remained for him and his fellow Social Democrats to wonder 'what century are we living in'. A number of Social Democrats also lived in exile in different European countries. Thus for the Social Democrats no serious political activity was possible.

Up to the outbreak of the Russian Revolution, Social Democrats generally believed that an imperialist war was being waged and that opposing it by voting against war credits gave them moral prestige. They further stressed that they were citizens of a country that had been attacked by a Great Power and was therefore a victim of imperialism. This viewpoint was expressed by Dragiša Djurić in a letter written in the summer of 1916:

We consider it necessary to stress the following: (1) The working class, like Serbia itself, has for its part done all it could to avoid this terrible war. (2) forced to defend her freedom by force of arms, Serbia has done her duty as a freedom-loving nation in this war *imposed* upon her, and that is why she has also had the right to the active help of the working class in the defence of freedom. (3) The Serb nation, awash in the blood of her children ..., has had to lend her struggle a general revolutionary nature too. She has had to proclaim the right and freedom of her brother Serb-Croat and Slovene nations in the face of Austro-German imperialism. Most of the socialist parties of Germany and Austria-Hungary, by voting for war credits have helped and continue to help Austro-German imperialism.[99]

The issue of unification with Montenegro

The issue of unification with Montenegro became exacerbated in exile, and Pašić's government evidently considered that the time was ripe to resolve it. That was because King Nicholas was in a foreign country without real political power, while most prominent Montenegrin politicians believed that the creation of a common state should not be postponed. However, Nicholas I still represented independent Montenegro to the Allies.[100] Despite there being no public conflict, which is of course important, relations between the two states were not good. Pašić was resolute: 'The unification of Montenegro with Serbia must be carried out, whether there will be a Yugoslavia or not.' This statement contained the belief that for official Serbia unification with Montenegro was an issue separate from the general unification programme and a particular objective that it wished to achieve in any case. But King Nicholas was no less resolute in his declarations: 'There can be no mention of any unification with Serbia. I cannot permit it.... I say Serbdom shall not be unified, that is just an idea for hotheads. It cannot happen without the eradication of one dynasty [i.e. either the Karadjordjević or the Petrović].' But King Nicholas' evident need to stress that 'no one alive in Serbdom can say that he was, before me, the actual instigator of that national ideal of mine' demonstrated that his resistance to unification was actually groundless. This was mainly because King Nicholas did not have much support among Montenegrins. However, Pašić could find support for his resolution in the general desire for unification, a desire that was strong even among Montenegrins, and in Serbia's actual greater strength and its more powerful political position in the Allied bloc.[101]

King Nicholas tried to consolidate his position in various ways. Only in Italy did he encounter a high level of support among the

The issue of unification with Montenegro

Allies—not merely because he was King Vittorio Emmanuel's father-in-law, but because Rome wished to use his dynasty to hinder the birth of a Yugoslav state and thus facilitate Italy's aspirations on the Adriatic.[102] He tried to win over a group of a few hundred Montenegrins who were interned on the Lipari islands, but did not succeed. Moreover, the Allies, particularly the French, were encouraging the inclusion of Montenegrins in the Serbian army. King Nicholas further tried to obtain the support of the Russian imperial government for his foreign policy objectives. In March 1916 Lazar Mijušković sought, on King Nicholas' instructions, to persuade Russia not only to guarantee Montenegro's independence but also to agree to its territorial demands, the minimum of which was determined as follows: northern Albania with the mouth of the river Drin up to Prijepolje, Sarajevo with its environs and the Neretva river valley to the Adriatic, and hence the coast from the river Neretva to Medua, including the area of Dubrovnik and the Bay of Cattaro.[103] This was a variant of the programme put forward in the spring of 1915.

Nonetheless, King Nicholas' position did not improve, and the unification of Montenegro with Serbia was the most important political issue encountered by Montenegrin émigrés. Those émigrés were further divided among themselves between the few supporters of King Nicholas and the ever broader opposition. It was because of that issue that King Nicholas found it very difficult to create a stable government.[104] As a result of conflicts first with some members of the dynasty and then with the King himself, Lazar Mijušković had resigned as Prime Minister. In a letter explaining his resignation, he accused King Nicholas of creating problems that would obstruct unification with Serbia. He also stated his belief that the Montenegrin people would succeed in entering 'unsullied and worthy' into 'a great Serb community, which it has otherwise also deserved thanks to its centuries-old struggle for freedom and the unification of the Serb nation.' Andrija Radović then formed a government in May 1916. He actually managed to consolidate significantly the international position of the King and the government. However, Andrija Radović was one of the leading proponents of the idea that the state of Montenegro had already played its historical role. Small and poor as it was and as it would stay even if it greatly increased its territory, he considered, Montenegro should take advantage of the war that was under way to become unified with Serbia. In a memorandum on 18 August 1916, Radović suggested that King Nicholas should immediately unify with Serbia by abdicating in favour of Alexander. He proposed that the eldest male members of the Petrović and Karadjordjević dynasties should take the throne of the unified state on an alternate basis. The King continued to state that he was in favour of unification, but he was actually stalling in his reply to several demands from his Prime Minister. As a result Andrija Radović resigned in January 1917. A new government was formed by Brigadier Milo Matanović, but, suspecting the King's intentions, he wrote on 15 May 1917, on behalf of his entire government, warning King Nicholas that it was high time to start negotiating with the Serbian government on unification, and advising that 'the idea of unification, has become the religion of the masses' and that 'anti-national separatism' could erupt in Montenegro because of Nicholas' vacillation. But it was all in vain, and Matanović's government also resigned.

King Nicholas then entrusted the formation of a government to Evgenije Popović, who for many years had been the Montenegrin Consul in Rome. He was known to be a great admirer of Italy and things Italian, and to enjoy Italian support.[105] King Nicholas thus succeeded in securing for himself acquiescent ministers right up to the end of the war.

5

OCCUPATION

Triumphant in November and December 1915, Germany, Austria-Hungary and Bulgaria insisted that Serbia should be vanquished once and for all. The German Kaiser was visiting Vienna at this time, and the Emperor Franz Joseph and high-ranking officials were heard to declare that 'Serbia must be destroyed' and 'vanish'. Within the circle of his dignitaries Franz Joseph was heard to agree with the generally accepted belief that 'nothing should be allowed to remain of sovereign Serbia'. And the Bulgarian King Ferdinand, and his ministers and commanders, spoke with determination when they told their allies that Serbia had to be 'wiped from the political map'.[1]

Annexation or fragmentation

In Austria-Hungary extreme ambitions were aroused and annexation appetites whetted, but rivalry also sharpened between the Austrian and Hungarian leaderships, between the proponents of two different perceptions of the Monarchy's Balkan aims. The differences then emerged. Both concepts were annexationist, but the Austrian concept was more extreme. Official policy had until then been vacillating and limited to specifying minimum war aims, but it became clear that, despite the differences between Austria and Hungary, the Monarchy truly had major annexation aspirations regarding Serbia.[2]

In late November 1915 General Conrad, the leading proponent of the extreme annexationist option, sent four lengthy memoranda to the Foreign Minister, Baron Burian. Furthermore, on 1 December he reported to Burian and the Emperor in person. General Conrad's memoranda and his personal reports sought the destruction of Serbia. His second memorandum, dated 26 November, contained the following: 'Annexation should encompass all other Serbian territories [i.e. those not promised to Bulgaria], as well as Montenegro and Albania.' He allowed that Albania should either be divided between Austria-Hungary and Greece or remain an independent state under the Monarchy's protection.[3] In the latter case it could also be expanded to include some Serbian territories, but with the stipulation that 'the entire Nova Varoš-Novi Pazar-Mitrovica-Kačanik line should remain within the Monarchy as a future important normal-gauge railway line.' He also proposed another possibility for Montenegro. If it were to remain a state 'for the sake of facilitating a peace agreement', its territories would not extend beyond the Tara river, the Petrović dynasty would retain the throne, and Montenegro would be included in the Monarchy as a federal unit 'without customary sovereign rights'. The third memorandum of 29 November contained a far more specific proposal:

> Serbia is to be removed from the ranks of European states with a single coercive diplomatic [sic!] act that would be ratified to a certain extent by the military situation; its criminal culpability for having provoked a World War should thus be accentuated. To this end it should, in agreement with the German and Bulgarian governments, be declared that: first, Serbia has ceased to exist; secondly, the Karadjordjević dynasty has accordingly ceased to rule; thirdly, the area of today's Kingdom of Serbia comes under military administration as agreed by the three allies that retain the right, also to be agreed upon mutually, to decide on the future division of the entire territory.[4]

It can be seen from Conrad's notes of the talks in Vienna on 1 December that he told the Emperor and Burian that it was 'absolutely vital to annex western Serbia and Montenegro' and that 'Serbian-Montenegrin-Albanian territories should be organised as a military march', as that was the way to destroy Hungarian hegemony in the Monarchy itself.[5]

However, others favoured more moderate aims, including an option propounded by István Count Tisza, who, in his capacity as Hungarian Prime Minister, was able to exert great pressure on the highest-ranking elements in the Monarchy. In a memorandum sent to the Emperor on 4 December 1915,[6] he argued that 'radical' solutions were not feasible because they were based on an 'underestimation of our enemy's strength' and because 'the possibility of concluding a peace with the upper hand is still extremely distant'. Disputing Conrad's views, he tried to prove that annexation should not encompass too large a part of what remained of Serbia: it was desirable to retain a diminished Serbia. Hence he showed a degree of flexibility and envisaged the possibility of negotiations of some kind with the Entente. He was in fact reiterating his old forebodings, which had been evident back in 1913 and were felt not only by him. He feared that total annexation would allow 'close contacts between Serb inhabitants in Austria, Bosnia, Croatia and in Hungary itself with Serbs in the newly-acquired territories', as a result of which it would 'only be a question of time before a concentrated force ... would be created in the south of the Monarchy, that would succeed in reviving national aspirations'. He added:

…another one and a half to two million Serbs will not only change the numerical balance of forces but will also revive the national aspirations and hopes of Serbs in our state, and the Hungarian state will be threatened with the loss of its true identity. If ascendancy is gained by centrifugal elements, or even those elements that do not actually oppose the state but are indifferent, Hungary will lose its coherence, and the entire Monarchy will lose the most important living strength that is essential for it to withstand victoriously the gigantic shift of power in this World War.... The inclusion of all Serbs would certainly not kill off the Greater Serb idea—on the contrary! An increase in the number of Serb subjects in the Monarchy by unifying all Serbs under the sceptre of one ruler, an increase in the Serb element as compared with others from the same tribe, or the creation of a huge majority of Orthodox Serbs *vis-à-vis* Croats will intensify Greater Serb propaganda. Thus any concession to nationalism will only be a new weapon in the battle for the ultimate goal—secession from the Monarchy.[7]

He advocated the following aim:

Serbia should lose its eastern and southern parts that have been promised to Bulgaria. We should also annex its north-western corner and thus cut it off completely from the rivers Sava and Danube.... A third possible annexation would include territories inhabited by Albanians. For its future existence Serbdom would then comprise a reduced Montenegro cut off from the sea, and the western part of central Serbia, a mountainous region far from river routes and largely infertile. It would thus be crushed between stronger neighbours and economically be totally dependent on the Monarchy. I am persuaded that it is in our true interest not to annex those territories but to link them to the Monarchy in a way that would best serve our economic interests.

He also advocated an independent Albania, but on the condition that it should have a land border with the Monarchy in order for the Monarchy to have control over it.[8] Tisza's views show that Hungarian ruling circles were seeking to have Serbia (as well as Montenegro) diminished in such a way that it ceased to be completely independent.

As for the territories that would remain as a semblance of a state, Tisza offered the following solution:

> The remainder of Serbdom, isolated from the world, will depend on the Monarchy for its existence as a state. The question whether there should be a separate Montenegro and a separate Serbia or whether Montenegro and Serbia should be unified into one organism under either the Montenegrin ruling dynasty or another ruler friendly to us could remain open for some time. In any case the entire area would be linked to the Monarchy economically and militarily.... We would thus make the further economic existence of the remnants [of Serbia and Montenegro] dependent on us, and in addition we would supervise their independence in such a way that they would not participate at all in the political life of the Monarchy.

As for the territories to be annexed, Tisza anticipated that they would be attached to Hungary, with the stipulation that 'probably for a lengthy transitional period' they would be under autocratic rule, while 'at the same time a large-scale colonisation of Hungarian and German elements should be conducted.' Such a colonisation would create 'a patriotic majority completely loyal' to the Habsburg state on the territory of the Sava valley in Serbia, including Mačva. That would 'drive a wedge between the Serbian state and the Serb population' in Vojvodina and Slavonia. Tisza concluded: 'The planned increase in the Hungarian and German population in Srem, Bačka and Banat will represent a solid rampart to protect our southern border and prevent the Greater Serb infection from reaching the Serb population within our borders.'[9]

Official policy as represented by Baron Burian was, of course, a compromise between the two opposition factions, although Burian, allegedly 'Tisza's man', wanted the Monarchy to 'swallow up' as much territory as possible.[10] In his attitude towards Serbia, and soon towards Montenegro too, he was not personally in favour of the Hungarian government's demands. He was actually a pro-Habsburg legitimist. Hence Burian not only left Tisza to deal with the proposals put forward by Kaiser Wilhelm II during his visit, but also advocated a stand diametrically opposite to Tisza's before members of the Kaiser's entourage. On 29 November a German diplomat reported: 'When I asked him what he, Burian, intended to do with what remained of Serbia, he showed his true colours by agreeing that it only remained for [Austria-Hungary] to place Serbia under its rule; any other solution was impossible, if only because of Bosnian Serbs.'[11] Moreover, Burian's notes in the margins of Tisza's memorandum of 30 December also demonstrate that he did not agree with what Tisza had put forward. To the proposals from Conrad Burian had clearly replied in a note of 25 December: 'I have long believed that the Yugoslav issue must be resolved within the scope of the Austro-Hungarian Monarchy, and now is probably a unique opportunity to do so.'

At a session of the Joint Council of Ministers held on 7 January 1916 in Vienna[12] Burian stated that 'the Yugoslav issue must be resolved within the boundaries of the Monarchy' and that 'now is the time to do it.' All the ministers except Tisza agreed with him, but Tisza's political power and his exceptional personal prestige resulted in the session ending in a compromise. It was agreed that 'as a matter of principle those territories that, depending on the outcome of the war, could be annexed to the Monarchy on the northern [Russian] battlefront should be unified with Austria, while the occupied territories in Serbia should be annexed to Hungary.' Burian did in fact try to take advantage of the somewhat unspecific conclusion and continued for some time to conduct a policy of annexation of all Serbian territories that had been occupied by Austro-Hungarian troops, striving thereby to obtain Germany's prior agreement. However, no solution was found even when Count Czernin became foreign minister in December 1916 or when Burian returned to that post in April 1918.[13]

While Burian was in office a new element was introduced into Austro-Hungarian policy: if official policy could not aim at large-scale annexation of Serbia because of Hungarian opposition, then the whole of Montenegro should be annexed. In the course of 1916 that idea was developed: it had always been agreed that Montenegro should lose its independence, but once again varying solutions were put forward. One of these was that Serbian territories should be attached to Montenegro, with the stipulation that Montenegro should have some kind of subservient status to the Monarchy; a second solution mooted was that it should lose its territories north of the Tara river and the coastal regions, while the remainder—some kind of fictive state—should be attached to the Monarchy. A third solution put forward was that Montenegro should be included in the Monarchy as a federal unit. The solution of attaching parts of Serbia to Montenegro headed by the Petrović dynasty but under Habsburg hegemony, an alternative that had never been seriously considered, was finally abandoned at the Joint Council session of 7 January 1916. Given the collapse of Montenegro's defence at the beginning of 1916, the Central Powers, and particularly Germany, considered that for propaganda purposes concluding a separate peace with it would be useful. On 19 January in Vienna the following fundamental principles for such a peace were elaborated:

Montenegro remains a kingdom with its already existing dynasty and king still ruling. Losing the coastal belt, Lovcen and some militarily important territories, it will be reduced to its borders as stipulated in the Berlin Congress agreement [1878]. It will be drawn into our sphere of political, military and economic interest although, as stated, it will certainly retain its independence.[14]

The clearer it became to Burian that Tisza and much of the Hungarian nobility would not allow large parts of Serbia to be annexed to the Monarchy, the more radical his plans concerning Montenegro became. When in the summer and autumn of 1916 the Central Powers decided to call openly on the Entente Powers to conclude a peace, Berlin and Vienna intended, behind their fine-sounding, pacifying words, to achieve great gains. Among those most desired Burian wanted 'Montenegro to be included in the Monarchy'. Point five of the official list of gains drawn up contained the annexation of Montenegrin territory to Austria-Hungary 'with the exception of territories inhabited by Albanians.'[15] This never actually happened because Germany and Austria-Hungary were not able to achieve peace either by force of arms or by diplomacy. When, in 1917 and 1918, the war was going so badly for the Monarchy that it could not count on even a slightly decisive victory, its leadership returned to the idea of Serbia and Montenegro being reduced and seemingly independent. Hence the idea came about of a Habsburg archduke becoming the ruler of either a territorially reduced Serbia or the unified remnants of Serbia and Montenegro (i.e. the parts of those states that had not been annexed by Austria-Hungary or Bulgaria).[16]

It was evident even in early December 1915 that Bulgaria's aspirations towards Serbia's territory were greater than stipulated in the agreement signed on 6 September 1915.[17] On 4 December the Bulgarian plenipotentiary at the German supreme command produced a letter from his Prime Minister from which it could be concluded that the Bulgarians 'placed exceptional importance on the Smederevo-Niš railway line belonging to them in its entirety above and beyond the borders guaranteed by the agreement'. This meant that they were looking to see if circumstances were favourable for them to demand the left bank of the Morava river, i.e. to move the border even further west. An official step was taken in that direction when King Ferdinand, Prime Minister Radoslavov and General Zhekov, chief of the general staff, visited the German Kaiser. During the talks that took place on 10 February 1916, the Bulgarian side submitted a request for territories on the left bank of the Morava, for the parts of Kosovo and of Albania that had been occupied by Bulgarian troops. Consequently the Bulgarians were actually demanding the towns of Smederevo and Kruševac, Mount Kopaonik, Kosovo and eastern Albania.[18] Although the Germans tended to agree to most Bulgarian demands, the issue was not resolved, owing to Austro-Hungarian opposition.

Germany itself had no territorial claims on Serbia and Montenegro, but it did have its own plans, dictated by the way the war was going, regarding what should be done with the two countries. The Germans always sought solutions by means of redrawing borders, first those of Serbia and Albania, and then those of Montenegro.[19] Their ideas ranged from the total cession of Serbia and Montenegro to Austria-Hungary, through attempts to preserve something of the territory and independence of those states, to the unification of the reduced Serbia and Montenegro into one state under the hegemony of the Monarchy. A constant element in the German plans was that Bulgaria should be expanded at Serbia's expense, at least to the borders stipulated in the agreement of 6 September 1915, while Austria-Hungary could annex considerable parts of Serbian and Montenegrin territories.

Occupation administration

After the collapse of Serbia's defence the victors were faced with the task of organising administration in the occupied territories. At the beginning of 1916 the Germans decided not to seek occupied territory in Serbia for themselves despite their troops having played a decisive role in the autumn offensive, and the task of ruling it thus fell to Austria-Hungary and Bulgaria, whose leaders considered holding the occupied territories and thus enabling the implementation of their far-reaching plans of vital importance.[20] However, the formation of occupation zones proved a complex task, partly because Austria-Hungary and Bulgaria had different interests and partly because Germany had revealed that, although it did not want its own occupation zone, it refused to remain empty-handed in the Balkans owing to its (mainly economic) vested interests in the region. Organising the administration therefore continued until the mid-spring of 1916. Moreover, disagreements arose between the three allies as early as November 1915, and by the beginning of December grave problems were on the agenda. The disputes concerned the railway line in the Morava river valley, the mines east of the Morava, exploitation of the agricultural resources of western Serbia and the use of the arsenal in Kragujevac. The situation became very tense when the Bulgarians came up with large new territorial demands at Serbia's expense. Germany, the strongest partner in the alliance, used, for their sake, the tactic of creating a *de facto* situation by promising them support for their further territorial aspirations and issuing appropriate orders through Mackensen's command. In return, the Germans in early December secured for themselves the temporary exploitation of mines and railways in the Bulgarian occupation zone, albeit without signing any agreement, and the right to use the agricultural resources in a broad belt east of the Morava river and in the valleys of the Južna Morava and Vardar rivers at the time when their troops were at the front at Salonika.

Bulgaria divided the territories occupied by its troops into two zones. One zone, centred on Niš, was called the 'Morava Military Inspection Area'. It encompassed the territories of Serbia as laid down in the agreement of 6 September 1915, which meant the Južna Morava river valley east of the Morava river. A second zone, encompassing Macedonia, was centred in Skopje and called the

'Macedonia Military Inspection Area'. The Bulgarians intended to include all parts of Kosovo occupied by their troops into the second zone, and if possible parts of Albania. They therefore endeavoured to create a *de facto* state of affairs in this sense. As for Austria-Hungary, it hastened to place under its administration all territories west of the line drawn in the agreement of 6 September 1915—haste was necessary since the latest indications were the Bulgarian government had extended its demands. On 1 January 1916 the Austro-Hungarian supreme command ordered the formation of a 'Military Governorate General' in Serbia on the territory of the previous Serbian districts of Belgrade, Šabac, Valjevo, Gornji Milanovac, Kragujevac and Ćuprija. According to a new order of 11 February, that governorate was extended to the districts of Užice, Čačak and the western parts of the Kruševac district.[21]

Austro-Hungarian diplomats and military representatives in Sofia and Custendil, the headquarters of the Bulgarian supreme command, were constantly making demands, both spoken and written, that the Bulgarians should stop setting up their administration in parts of Kosovo and Albania. Moreover, when in mid-February 1916 King Ferdinand, Prime Minister Radoslavov and General Zhekov visited Vienna and the Austro-Hungarian supreme command in Teschen, they heard those same demands from the mouths of Franz Joseph, Burian and Conrad. Matters became so exacerbated that a fierce quarrel erupted in Teschen between King Ferdinand and Conrad. Austro-Hungarian troops then crossed the line dividing them from the Bulgarian army at a number of points and started occupying territories already held by Bulgarians. The crisis came to a peak when the Bulgarian commander in Kačanik offered armed opposition and forced the Austro-Hungarian troops to withdraw.

As in March, it had become evident that Austria-Hungary and Bulgaria could not reach agreement through negotiations, and Germany in the meantime was indicating openly and increasingly resolutely that it did not intend to remain a mere observer. Vienna accepted the proposal that Field-Marshal Mackensen, or rather the German general staff, should act as intermediary. At the same time the Austro-Hungarian side continued to create a *de facto* state of affairs wherever it could, and in an order issued on 15 March attached the districts of Prijepolje, Novi Pazar and Kosovska Mitrovica to its already established governorate.²² These were the three districts that Serbia had acquired in the First Balkan War, and the fact that they were not attached immediately could have been due to some political reason, such as preparation for their annexation to the Monarchy. In January 1916 Baron Burian had actually stated to the German ambassador that 'the Sandžak must belong to the Monarchy'. Annexation plans also included Kosovska Mitrovica. However, because circumstances were not favourable for the implementation of these plans, Vienna abandoned them temporarily and awaited developments. The Bulgarians at first resisted German mediation, while trying nonetheless to secure as much territory as possible for themselves.

Finally, Mackensen visited Sofia in person for talks with King Ferdinand and Prime Minister Radoslavov. He obtained Bulgarian consent to the proposed German compromise plan and on 1 April an agreement on a demarcation line was signed between the Austro-Hungarian and Bulgarian commands. This specified that Bulgaria would retain the district containing Prizren and Priština, while Austria-Hungary would keep Elbasan. Both sides accepted that the agreement was 'exclusively military in nature' and that the two governments could, if they desired, reach another agreement later.²³ Bulgaria succeeded in retaining the administration of territories in the central Balkans far to the west of the line drawn in the agreement of 6 September 1915, but its new gains did not come without cost. As well as the railways and mines it had already yielded to the Germans, it had to cede the valleys of the Morava, the Južna Morava and the Vardar as 'stage zones' for supplying the German army on the front north of Salonika. In practice, however, the German stage zone encompassed the whole of Macedonia and the part of Kosovo in Bulgarian hands, as well as Europe's then richest copper mine in Bor and the railway line running along the valleys of the Morava and the Vardar right up to the new battlefront north of Salonika.

The internal organisation of the Austro-Hungarian Military Governorate General recognised the conflict between Austrian and Hungarian interests and their disagreement over Serbia. Count Tisza had already stipulated the basic principles of organisation, fearing that the pro-annexation military leadership would try to take advantage of the occupation to create a state of affairs not in line with Hungarian aspirations. Since Austria was responsible for administration of the occupied territories in Poland, the Hungarian Prime Minister insisted that Hungarians alone should administer Serbia, which in any case had to be in army hands for the duration of the war. Hungary and Serbia were neighbouring countries, he explained, also claiming that Hungarian administration was in the interest of the better, integral functioning of the Monarchy leadership. Tisza also advocated that a high-ranking functionary of Hungarian nationality should be appointed as civilian commissioner to assist the military governor-general in Serbia. General Johan Count Salis-Seewis, a Croat, was appointed the first governor at the end of 1915 and took up his post on 3 January 1916. On 17 January Ludvig Count Thallóczy, a prominent Hungarian historian and expert on Balkan affairs, was named civilian commissioner. A sharp dispute soon arose between the military and civilian authorities because the military commanders were implementing measures evidently preparing for annexation. Tisza lodged a complaint with the Emperor and with the commander-in-chief, Archduke Friedrich. As a consequence General Adolf Baron von Remen (a German) was appointed the new governor-general and assumed the office on 26 July, which he held till the end of the war. After the untimely death of Ludvig Thallóczy in a traffic accident near Budapest in November 1916, Teodor Kušević, until then a high-ranking functionary in the Bosnian-Herzegovinan provincial government, was appointed as civilian commissioner in January 1917. The governorate was divided into the city of Belgrade and twelve districts ruled by district commanders.[24] The municipal authorities were administered by the Serbian population.

Although it already occupied Montenegro, Austria-Hungary hesitated for a month before introducing an occupation regime there.[25] The 'skeleton government' represented the continuity of the Montenegrin state, and civil (primarily fictitious) authority was still in Montenegrin hands in February 1916. At that time Vienna still counted on Montenegro concluding a separate peace and hoped that the 'skeleton government' would obtain authorisation from the ruler in exile both to conduct negotiations and to sign a peace treaty. However, weeks passed and there was no change in a state of affairs that had originally been considered temporary. On 28 February 1916 the occupation forces' command informed the 'skeleton government' that it had ceased to function, and on 1 March Montenegro was finally declared occupied. A military governorate general of Montenegro was organised along the lines of the military administration in Serbia, and Victor Baron von Weber was appointed military governor general for Montenegro with the rank of general. After the reorganisation of the governorate in the first half of July 1917, von Weber was replaced by reserve General Heinrich Count Clam-Martinic. The governorate was centred in the Montenegrin capital Cetinje.

Plans for the Balkans and the Near East

Just as pre-war Serbia had been part of an extensive zone designated for the infiltration of Central European imperialism towards the Near East, so occupied Serbia and the Balkans as a whole became part of the wartime and long-term post-war economic policies of Germany and Austria-Hungary. The successful outcome of Army Group Mackensen's offensive in the autumn of 1915 made it increasingly evident that the occupiers had new and significant economic plans for the future, with the Balkans and Near East opening up as a unique economic space—one that already had the role of supplementary economic space for the wartime economy.[26]

The territories to the southeast of Central Europe had traditionally been objects of aspiration for Germany and Austria-Hungary in their search for spheres of interest. Thus in the World War they grew greatly in importance. The two Central Powers were, after all, surrounded in the west by France and Britain, in the east by Russia and in the south by Italy, which had decided to enter the war. They tried to find economic relief by strengthening trade relations with Scandinavia, the Netherlands and Switzerland, but the southeast was of particular importance. Their infiltration in that direction was opposed by Serbia and Montenegro, but Turkey had been their ally from the very start of the war, first covertly and then from late October 1914 overtly. Bulgaria, for its part, had been neutral but markedly favourable towards Germany and Austria-Hungary, and it had later joined them as an ally. In and, to a certain extent, through Turkey and Bulgaria, the Central Powers were able to acquire raw materials necessary for their war effort, but those materials were in increasingly short supply. However, before the collapse of the

Serbian—and Montenegrin—defences, there had been the problem of transport to and from Turkey and Bulgaria. That problem had been exacerbated by Romania which, citing its neutrality, had placed ever greater obstacles in the way of transport across its territory.

But the earlier rivalry between Germany and Austria-Hungary over the Balkans and the Near East sharpened with every day that passed during the infiltration of the German, Austro-Hungarian and Bulgarian armies into Serbia. Vienna and Budapest considered the Balkans, especially the territories of the Serbian state bordering on the Monarchy, as within their sphere of interest. On 1 November 1915 Tisza reminded the Ministry of Foreign Affairs: 'Germany enjoys far greater advantages from the possession of foreign territories [in France, Belgium and Russia] than we do, and it could agree to this small and poor region that lies in our vicinity politically and economically [Serbia] being under our administration rather than being exploited for German ends.'[27] In this belief the Austro-Hungarian Foreign Ministry based its stand *vis-à-vis* the Germans on the assumption that Serbia 'lies in our direct sphere of interest', and on 7 November sought from its chief of general staff that this stand should be conveyed resolutely to the German general staff. It also ordered on 18 November that the Ambassador in Berlin should expressly and persistently defend this stand in his dealings with the German government.[28]

In line with the pre-war conviction that the Balkan peninsula offered the German economy considerable opportunities, and following the routes that its capital had already opened up, Germany tried to secure for itself most of the natural resources of the Balkans including those in Serbia, both for the duration of the war and subsequently. However, its authorities had to pay lip-service at least to the demands of the Monarchy's representatives. Nonetheless, German leaders agreed among themselves not to give in to Austro-Hungarian demands concerning the Balkans, and the chief of the general staff wrote to the German Foreign Minister saying that in his view Austria-Hungary had no right whatever to declare that 'the Imperial-Royal sphere of interest started west of the agreed upon border [with Bulgaria].' The Foreign Minister replied that he agreed completely.[29] German diplomats, consular representatives, military commanders and prominent publicists therefore acted as if they themselves were businessmen. The German naval attaché in Sofia reported that German deputies devoted 'far greater attention to each German tradesman ... than to the momentous issues of war and politics.'[30] On 28 October 1915 the chief of staff of the Mackensen Army Group wrote that he was dealing with so many questions involving copper and the export of wheat from Serbia that he felt himself to be more like a merchant than a general.[31] What was happening in the Near East only served to confirm what an Austro-Hungarian military envoy had written on 4 February 1915: 'In any case we have to understand that the Germans will want to consider the whole of Turkey as exclusively their own sphere of interest and will try to exclude us as rivals as far as possible.'[32] The Deutsch-Orientalische Handelsgesellschaft (German-Oriental Trade Society), a new association for business with Balkan and Near Eastern countries (possibly the sixth of its kind), was set up in Germany in November. In the second half of January 1916 Gustav Stresemann, a leading figure in German heavy industry, went on a study tour through the Balkans to Constantinople. Summing up his impressions and fearing that unscrupulous acts could threaten German plans to exploit the region, he informed the Under Secretary of State for Foreign Affairs that Germany was dealing with Turkey and Bulgaria as if they were 'conquered colonies'.[33]

As the German, Austro-Hungarian and Bulgarian armies went deeper into Serbia, it became the hub of rivalry over the whole Balkan and Near Eastern region. This was evident as the attacking troops were seen to be a means for the individual countries to achieve specific economic objectives. The German 11th Army acted as if it were an extension of the German economy, taking over mines, the most important factories and the main transport routes and removing agricultural produce. All Germany's military authorities, from the Prussian Minister of War to the military commands on the ground, were exerting great pressure on the Bulgarian authorities to cede to them all major economic facilities lying within those Serbian territories that had been promised to Bulgaria in the agreement of 6 September 1915. The Monarchy saw clearly what was happening, and on 27 December the Foreign Ministry in Vienna wrote to its Ambassador in Berlin:

> The German military leadership is taking such economic advantage of the territories it has occupied in the Russian part of Poland and in Serbia that it is causing not only an increase in poverty, but also the permanent economic

impoverishment of the population.... German commands are committing ruthless economic acts in Serbia. They are exploiting the country's resources without consideration for the needs of the people or their future, and they are doing so almost exclusively to meet German requirements. They are requisitioning huge quantities of livestock, wheat, flour, wine, salt and paraffin. They have even set up improvised slaughterhouses for pigs and are sending their produce to Germany. Not only has hunger reared its head here, but the population has also become seriously impoverished.[34]

In a series of notes the Austria-Hungarian embassy in Berlin placed all the key issues on the agenda: Austro-Hungarian occupation administration should be introduced in the territories not promised to Bulgaria (21 November); as soon as the occupation authorities started functioning, the German military authorities should cede to Austria-Hungary 'all railway lines' they held, and pending issues with Bulgaria should be resolved directly by Vienna with Sofia (24 November); the Majdanpek, Rudna Glava and Bor mines should be yielded to the Monarchy (1 December); Austro-Hungarian military authorities should take over the Smederevo-Niš railway line that was in German hands and the Skopje-Mitrovica railway line that was in Bulgarian hands (12 December); and the Bulgarian government should state that if the German government did not object, it was ready to reach agreement with Austria-Hungary on the Bor and Majdanpek mines (24 December).[35] Little attention was paid to this in Berlin.

Still, the authorities in both Germany and Austria-Hungary were aware that some kind of agreement had to be reached. On several occasions that autumn Austro-Hungarian economic experts and officials repeated that their country's task in the southeast was 'unattainable without Germany's participation in our economic sphere of influence in the Balkans', and they suggested an agreement.[36] Leading German military circles and experts in the ministries were also aware that Austro-Hungarian demands could not be totally ignored, and in the first half of December they agreed internally that of the mines at least Majdanpek should be ceded to Austria-Hungary for exploitation. But the Germans were actually trying to take as much for themselves as they could before sitting down to negotiate, and therefore postponed dialogue till the beginning of 1916. However, they were putting pressure on Bulgaria to obtain everything they wanted from it, since that, in the judgement of the Prussian Ministry of War, would give German negotiators 'weight' when they met Austro-Hungarian representatives. Entering into only preliminary dialogue with Austria-Hungary, they took advantage of their own financing of Bulgaria's participation in the war, of their greater readiness than Austria-Hungary's to agree to increased Bulgarian designs on Serbian territory, and the fact that their troops held those very territories that had been promised to Bulgaria, where the railways and mines they wanted were located.

On 24 December 1915 the German government responded with only one note to the first four of the five Austro-Hungarian notes. In it Germany agreed to Austria-Hungary and Bulgaria organising occupation administration in Serbian territory. However, Serbia represented for Germany a 'supply and transit territory', and Germany therefore sought free passage through it and the right to use its raw materials and food. It further sought that the railway running through the Morava-Vardar valleys, the town of Kragujevac with its armaments factory and the rail link to it, and the Bor mine should remain in the hands of the German military authorities. It ceded Majdanpek to Austria-Hungary, and the question of the Rudna Glava mine was left to be resolved later. The Bulgarian Plakalnica mine was offered for joint administration, with the stipulation that the ore mined should be shared between Austria-Hungary and Germany. Meanwhile the German general staff put the following basic demands to their Bulgarian counterparts:

> The use of ores already being exploited or yet to be discovered, over the entire territory [of Serbia] that has been ceded to Bulgarian military administration is the right of the German military authorities. The Bulgarian military leadership should undertake to support and assist with all means the German administration [of the mines] and its bodies. However, this is not a precedent that will extend into peacetime; it will be used only for military purposes for the duration of war.[37]

That agreement referred to regions in the valley of the Morava and the Južna Morava rivers and eastern Serbia, including the mines in the Bor basin, the Vardar river valley and much of Kosovo.[38]

On 10 December 1915 the Bulgarian military leadership agreed to the German demands, and on 20 December it confirmed that agreement. At its session of 17 December the Bulgarian government also agreed in principle that Germany's demands should be accepted, and finally, on 29 December, the German and Bulgarian supreme commands concluded a military convention on the German right to use the economic resources of the Bulgarian zone of occupied Serbia. The question of the use of railways was also resolved in early January 1916: these mainly went over to the administration of the German Seventh Military Railway Authority, in which Austria-Hungary had its own officer plenipotentiary. The Niš-Skopje-Veles-Gevgelija railway line was entrusted to a separate Bulgarian authority, with the stipulation that the latter was subordinate to the German Seventh Authority. As for the Kosovska Mitrovica-Skopje railway line, the part from Kosovska Mitrovica to Priština went to the Austro-Hungarian military authorities, and the past from Priština to Skopje to the Bulgarian authorities.[39]

The agreement was followed by an exchange of views in Vienna on 7 and 8 January 1916, conducted at the level of the German and Austro-Hungarian war ministries by high-ranking officials and not ministers, which meant that the points agreed upon were valid only for the duration of the war. The two sides consented to replace the provisional agreement concluded between Germany and Austria-Hungary on 27 November 1915 with a new accord signed on 8 January.[40] Although 'purchase of raw materials in Turkey and Bulgaria' was given priority, with the stipulation that they should be 'primarily for the military needs of the two sides', the new agreement encompassed many key issues that were still unresolved. The basic objective of the agreement was expressed as follows: 'The raw materials are to be secured ... that can be obtained in Bulgaria and Turkey in order to cover the military requirements of the two sides ..., and the eastern market is to be organised by excluding trade speculation and avoiding mutual rivalry.... Due to the transport difficulties encountered in the East ..., the means of transport there should be made available for the dispatch of raw materials to meet urgent military requirements.' It was specified that the new agreement encompassed 'all raw materials that serve military purposes or could do so in the future.'

The Balkan-Near East region was divided in such a way that the commissioning and organisation of work would be taken over in Turkey by the Prussian Ministry of Labour and in Bulgaria by the Austro-Hungarian Joint Ministry of War, with the stipulation that those two institutions should cooperate. A prominent role was given to the Deutsch-Orientalische Handelsgesellschaft, whose founders—the Deutsche Bank and the Deutsch-Orientbank—were to agree to Austrian and Hungarian banks selected by the Austrian and Hungarian finance ministries taking part in financing transactions. The Deutsch-Orientalische Handelsgesellschaft was granted a profit of 3% on the total price of the commodities, plus all interest and storage and insurance costs. One short article in the agreement referred to Serbia: 'The above-mentioned principles shall be implemented analogically with respect to Serbia. The details shall be settled when the provisions to be concluded by the two supreme commands are known.'[41]

With the basic document there was a separate 'agreement on metals', the second section of which provided for the following:

Plakalnica in Bulgaria and Bor in Serbia shall be in German hands, but one third of the production in Bor and one half of the production in Plakalnica shall be supplied to Austria-Hungary.... In the case of the Bor mine, Austria-Hungary will bear one third and Germany two thirds of the total costs of operating the mine, the workers' wages and production and transport costs, whereas in the case of Plakalnica the costs shall be divided equally between the two countries.... All metals and smelting products from the Balkans may be used for the military purposes of the two countries.

It was further envisaged that future profits from smelting in the two mines would be used to cover German expenses resulting from the use of its own metal to supply Bulgaria and Turkey with ammunition. It was therefore envisaged that a subsequent calculation would determine how much of the metal produced would actually go to Austria-Hungary (which in any case could not obtain less than a quarter of Plakalnica's production and a fifth of Bor's production). It was evidently tacitly confirmed that Majdanpek would go to Austria-Hungary, as stated in the German note of 24 December 1915.[42]

The operative centre of the Deutsch-Orientalische Handelsgesellschaft was in Constantinople, but its headquarters were in Bremen. The Deutsche Bank and the Deutsch-Orientbank, which appeared as founders of the Deutsch-Orientalische Handelsgesellschaft, were actually only representatives of large merchant houses from Bremen and Hamburg that had been forced to seek opportunities for large-scale business in the Near East owing to the war and the British blockade.[43]

The agreement reached in Vienna was aimed at reducing the rivalry between Germany and Austria-Hungary concerning the acquisition of raw materials in the Balkans and the Near East. It was therefore envisaged that the Deutsch-Orientalische Handelsgesellshaft would be transformed from a purely German enterprise into a mixed one with German and Austro-Hungarian capital. However, it was first decided in the Monarchy not to entrust cooperation with the Deutsch-Orientalische Handelsgesellschaft to banks, but rather to the Austrian Kriegsrohstoff-Gesellschaft and the Hungarian Die Vereinigung der Rohstoff Zentrale der Länder der Heiligen Ungarischen Krönen. These were two private capital associations headed by political, civilian or military institutions that had been established in the Monarchy in the autumn of 1914 with the object of raising money for the war effort; they did not enter the Deutsch-Orientalische Handelsgesellschaft as co-founders but to 'undertake and carry out obligations agreed upon on 8 January 1916', that is to say the purchase of raw materials in 'Turkey, Bulgaria and possibly Serbia'. That was how the Deutsch-Österreich-Ungarische Einkaufs-Vereinigung—shortened to Dövung—came about. Dövung continued to be organised in the same way as the Deutsch-Orientalische Handelsgesellschaft, being headed by a board consisting of two representatives of the Deutsch-Orientalische Handelsgesellschaft and one representative each of the Austrian and Hungarian partners. The contract covering the creation of Dövung was signed in two places and on two dates: Vienna on 5 February 1916 and Berlin on 10 May 1916.[44] A 'supplementary contract' was soon drawn up, and signed on 11 May 1916 in Berlin; this was the Vienna text with some details altered and the stipulation added that business transactions were entrusted to Dövung instead of the Deutsch-Orientalische Handelsgesellschaft. A separate 'agreement on metals' was again added, noting that 'the changes of 11 May 1916 correspondingly refer to metals', but repeating the provisions concerning Plakalnica and Bor agreed in Vienna.[45]

The agreement on resolving problems arising from rivalry was based on the division of spheres of interest, with the Balkans being considered as a mainly Austro-Hungarian sphere and the Near East a mainly German one. However, it was done in such a way that the two geographical regions were considered as one entity in which the greater quantities of raw materials belonged to Germany, as did the lion's share of the profit from the mines in Serbia and Bulgaria. That was the basis for the contract concluded by Germany with Bulgaria on 5 May 1916, whereby Germany was granted exploitation of the Bor mine for the duration of the war and for nine months after its conclusion. A contract containing the same provisions concerning the coal mines in eastern Serbia and the valley of the Južna Morava was concluded on 17 August. The issue of French and Belgian ownership was simply overlooked, as was the fact that Serbia was still actively engaged in the war.

Although Germany and Austria-Hungary, with this non-political agreement, eliminated some friction between them for the duration of the war, economic rivalry remained. The Deutsche Bank and the Deutsch-Orientbank were traditionally headed by concerns that conducted business in Turkey, while the Direktion der Discontogesellschaft headed a group of financiers interested in the Balkans' natural resources. The interest of German capital in exploiting the entire area was evident particularly in the creation of new companies. Before the outbreak of war there had been three major companies of that type, but another four were created in 1915, including the Deutsch-Orientalische Handelsgesellschaft, and another five in 1916: Deutscher Levante-Verband, Dresdner Orient- und Übersee-Gesellschaft m.b.H., Mitteleuropäische Handelsvereinigung, Industrie-Propagandestelle für den Orient, and Deutsch-Türkische Handelsgesellschaft.[46]

The competition from the Monarchy was considerably weaker. To make his country a stronger rival to Germany, Emperor Karl encouraged the creation of an Oriental Department for Turkey and Bulgaria within the Joint Ministry of War, and on 25 June 1917 it was officially set up as a separate department for military and economic matters. Among the Monarchy's economic institutions that had dealings with German capital, the first was the Österreichische Orient- und Übersee-Gesellschaft. The largest Austrian bankers also created an Orientgruppe, a consortium made up of the Wiener-Kreditanstalt as 'the leading member' and the Wiener Bankverein, the Pester Ungarische Commerzialbank and the Ungarische Allgemeine

Kreditbank. Individual banks in the Monarchy also came to be channelled in the same direction, and the Hypothec Bank set up the guideline: 'Our sphere of interest is to be extended to the Balkans.' Moreover, at meetings of its sections on 25 June 1917 the Viennese Chamber of Trade and Crafts set out requirements that had to be met to boost the Monarchy's economic activities in the Near East.[47]

It was along these lines that capital flowed not only into the occupied regions of Serbia but also into Bulgaria. Back in December 1915, the Pester Ungarische Commerzialbank had lodged a request with political and military authorities in the Monarchy for a renewal of the activity of the Banka Andrejevic i Ko A.D. in Belgrade, which had been its branch since 1906 but had been forced to close down on the outbreak of war. The Banka Andrejevic i Ko actually re-opened at the beginning of 1916.[48] In January that year the Wiener Bankverein lodged a request with the Austro-Hungarian Ministry of Finance to open a branch in Belgrade, pointing out that it was endeavouring to 'serve the interests of the homeland' by 'expanding the Monarchy's economic impact beyond its borders'.[49] In 1916 the Wiener Kreditanstalt, the Wiener Bankverein, the Rothschildbank of Vienna and the Pester Ungarische Commerzialbank managed to turn the Balkanska Banka in Sofia into their stronghold within the framework of their Balkan and Near East ambitions. For its part the Wiener Kreditanstalt took advantage of Allied links with Bulgaria to ensure that its capital flowed into the sugar factory in Sofia and to use the occupation of Serbia to take over the sugar factory in Belgrade. Moreover, in 1917 the Wiener Kreditanstalt of Vienna, working with the Pester Ungarische Commerzialbank, managed to turn the General Bulgarian Bank, which it had owned since 1906, into its own foothold. In mid-1917, with the aim of making use of the economic potential there, many attempts were made by banks from Vienna and Budapest to set up their own companies in Bulgaria, also encompassing the annexed territories of Serbia. They wished to conduct 'trade and industrial business' and mortgage operations and build railways, ports, factories, docks etc.[50]

However, the result of all this effort was relatively small because of Germany's economic and political superiority.[51] In the summer of 1917 the Deutsche Bank opened a branch in Sofia to expand Germany's economic position further and, as Austro-Hungarian representatives accurately assessed, to offer sharp competition to the Austro-Hungarian Orientgruppe, while at the same time 'ensuring political advantage for the German government'.[52]

The nature and extent of German capital's interest in an expanded Bulgaria was demonstrated by the rapid increase in the number of associations specialising in economic links. As early as 1915, when the political rapprochement between Germany and Bulgaria was already well advanced, three such 'wartime associations' were created in Germany: the Deutsch-Bulgarische Gesellschaft in Munich, the Hamburger Vereinigung der Freunde Bulgariens in Hamburg and the Deutsch-Bulgarischer Kulturverein in Sofia. The Deutsch-bulgarischer Verein was founded in Berlin on 30 November 1914 and registered on 11 January 1915. These bodies were aimed at promoting Germany's 'cultural and economic rapprochement' with Bulgaria, as well as fostering the development of 'trade relations between Bulgaria and Germany'. However, the most important body of this kind was not founded until mid-1916: this was the Institut für den Wirtschaftsverkehr mit Bulgarien, established by the elite Zentralverband Deutscher Industrieller, Bund der Industriellen and Bund der Landwirte under the patronage of King Ferdinand of Bulgaria. At the same time the Deutsch-bulgarische Gesellschaft was formed in Berlin with the objective of 'promoting overall spiritual and economic relations between Germany and Bulgaria'; though chaired by the Duke of Schleswig-Holstein, it was actually run by Gustav Stresemann.[53] However, Germany's strongest infiltration into the Bulgarian economy came about through the Direktion der Discontogesellschaft, which had gathered a powerful consortium of banks and some industrial firms. It was also a creditor of the Bulgarian state.[54]

Kaiser Wilhelm II described Germany's task in Bulgaria thus: 'prepare a prompt economic infiltration into Bulgaria for the postwar period too.'[55] Germany and Austria-Hungary were in fact trying to turn Bulgaria into a political and economic advance-post for their lasting hegemony in the Balkans. Leading figures in German politics and finance were thereby evolving a thesis on 'the complementary natures' of the German and Bulgarian economies. In an internal memo the head of the department for trade policy in the German Foreign Ministry wrote: 'Bulgaria is an agrarian country.... It must therefore import industrial products and will be happy to take German commodities. On the other hand, Germany has, partly or completely, to import such products as Bulgaria possesses.... Germany can help [Bulgaria] with capital and material for the construction of railways and factories.'[56] While the war was in progress the Germans were trying in particular to secure for themselves the exploitation of the parts of Serbia under Bulgarian occupation. In January 1916 they concluded a contract with the Bulgarians covering the purchase of agricultural products, which gave them the right to the 'exclusive exploitation of the stage zone region, including market gardening, particularly in the districts of Požarevac, Ćuprija and Zaječar.'[57] New contracts for the purchase of agricultural produce were concluded on 15 October 1916 and then on 26 January, 8 May and October 1917.[58] Through Bulgarian mediation Germany took over all the railway lines in eastern Serbia in the autumn of 1916 and, on 9 November, it appropriated the Niš–Sofia line, an important section of the main communications route to and from the Orient. The Germans also wanted economic benefit from the territories occupied by Austria-Hungary, and to that end they opened a consulate in Belgrade in March 1916.

Carrying out the Vienna and Berlin agreements on the division of spheres of influence caused considerable friction between the two sides. This sometimes related to the part of Serbia under Bulgarian occupation. In the summer of 1916 a sharp dispute erupted over the right to purchase raw materials in 'the northern part under Bulgarian occupation administration', and this was followed by a dispute over chromium ore from the Macedonian Orašje mine.[59] In the spring of 1916, an internal memo from the department for trade policy in the German Foreign Ministry stated: 'It is a matter of great difficulty that Austria-Hungary sees the Balkans as its own economic domain, from which if possible Germany should be excluded.'[60] However, Germany did not wish to spoil relations and therefore sometimes acceded to the wishes of the Monarchy. On 29 July 1916, the Dresden-based Deutsch-Orientalische Handelsgesellschaft drew the government's attention to the need for caution where the interests of allied countries were concerned, while the Direktion der Discontogesellschaft regularly included Austrian and Hungarian banks from the Orientgruppe in its consortia, as with the creation of a finance group under the name of the 'Bulgarian National Mining

Society' for the exploitation of the Bulgarian Pernik and Bobovdol mines.[61]

At the end of January 1916, the Budapest-based Pester Ungarische Commerzialbank, together with the Deutsch-Orientalische Handelsgesellschaft raised the issue of opening a branch of the Opstebugarska Banka in Niš and Skopje, taking advantage of the fact that the Bulgarian bank was already in the hands of the Budapest-based bank (Niš and Skopje were occupied towns but still towns in Serbia from the point of view of international law). For a time Bulgaria managed to thwart such a move, and its supreme command prevented the implementation of the idea, replying that such a thing could only be done 'after demobilisation has been completed', that is after a victorious end to the war.[62] The Budapest bank tried again in the autumn of 1917, when it also sought the support of the Foreign Ministry in Vienna and mentioned that it wished 'to open a branch first in Niš, and then in other towns on [Serbian] territory under Bulgarian occupation.'[63] In parallel to this, a rival group made up of the Wiener Bankverein (the leading member), Creditanstalt für Handel und Gewerbe, Ungarische Allgemeine Bank and Rothschildbank took similar steps using their Sofia branch of the Balkanska Banka.[64]

The leading figures in the group behind the Balkanska Banka explained their request for the 'immediate opening of a branch in Skopje' by saying that such a branch would 'serve as a basis for the Monarchy's economic infiltration into Bulgaria.'[65] The Pester Ungarische Commerzialbank justified its request with the claim that it had 'been acting as an institution that had opened up paths for the economic expansion of our Monarchy for over thirty years' and had constantly 'gladly put itself at the service of the country's foreign policy'.[66] However the Narodna Banka in Sofia opened a branch in Skopje immediately after occupation administration had been set up at the beginning of 1916, while the Skopska Trgovinska Banka was set up late in 1917 with Bulgarian capital and with the 'indubitable aim of achieving political goals besides serving business interests'— this was the judgement of the Austro-Hungarian representatives. In their desire to preserve the economic exploitation of Macedonia for themselves the Bulgarians were evidently putting up the best possible resistance.[67]

It was just at this time that, because of the belief that Macedonian land was very rich, Skopje, its largest town, came to be the focus of interest of Central European capital. As a consequence German, Austrian and Hungarian banks, with the full support of their diplomatic, consular and military services in Sofia and Skopje, invested great efforts in strengthening their positions there. The first success was recorded by the Direktion der Discontogesellschaft, probably thanks to its financing of the Bulgarian government. Through its Kreditna Banka branch in Sofia, it managed to overcome Bulgarian resistance and to open a branch in Skopje. The branch opened at the beginning of January 1918, and it had the full support of the 11th Army Command, even to the extent of using military couriers and telephone and telegraph links for business purposes. Representatives of the Monarchy saw the move as a warning sign that something should be done. A consular representative in Skopje immediately warned Vienna that there must be 'an acceleration of the creation of a branch' of the Sofia-based Balkanska Banka, which was financed by a group led by the Wiener Bankverein, in order not to 'allow ourselves to be gradually suppressed'. The representative further warned that the branch in Skopje should be provided with the same help and support as the German military authorities were already providing to the rival Kreditna Banka branch.[68] However, it was not until July 1918 that, through the General Bulgarian Bank, Austro-Hungarian capital managed to open a branch in Skopje, and it was estimated that if the greatest possible military and political support were not provided by Austria-Hungary the branch would find itself in a state of 'extremely difficult and unequal rivalry with the Skopje branch of the Kreditna Banka (Discontogesellschaft)'.[69] Further economic rivalry between Germany and Austria-Hungary, in which Bulgaria participated as much as it could, was waged over the acquisition of the rights to long-term exploitation of the mineral resources in Serbian territory under Bulgarian occupation.

The longer the war lasted, the more persistent Germany was in its endeavours to secure the Balkans' economic resources for itself by using Bulgaria. In late April 1917 the German general staff, which in reality had already taken over the country's political life, emphasised 'the special importance of taking Serbian mineral resources into our hands'. It was added that Germany had to 'make up the shortage of various metals and raw materials, of copper, manganese and chromium ores, and of machine oil for future wars.' Moreover, as

Bulgaria 'had German weapons to thank' for having conquered the territories it wanted, those territories could not be handed over to Bulgaria 'on a permanent basis without something in return', including 'yielding unreservedly the mineral resources' to be found there.[70] In parallel to this, Germany demanded that Austria-Hungary should simply yield the mineral resources. After 'summit talks' with Austria-Hungary on war aims conducted in Kreuznach on 17 and 18 April 1917, Germany succeeded in including the following in the final document: 'Germany wants the Monarchy to give it a free hand in the agreed exploitation of the mineral resources in New Bulgaria [virtually meaning the occupied territories of Serbia at that time]. Germany sees this as an integral element in the mutual adjustment of common conditions for a [future] peace.'[71] In so doing Germany was particularly trying to secure for itself the exploitation of the Bor mine, which was the general aim of all the ministries involved. Mutually rival groups of banks led by the Direktion der Discontogesellschaft and Mansfeldsche Kupferschieferbauende Gewerkschaften insisted on this especially.[72]

When the Bulgarian Prime Minister Radoslavov visited Germany, this demand was put to him by the German government (8 June 1917) and the general staff (13 June). Radoslavov consented, not only because the German side threatened to dispute Bulgarian territorial aspirations, but because it also raised the issue of Bulgaria's enormous war debts to German banks and its further supply of German war material.[73] Negotiations through diplomatic channels followed, and in the spring of 1918 the first specific agreements, which were about the Bor mine, were reached.[74] According to these agreements, Bor was to belong to a joint-stock company to be founded and financed by a consortium of mainly German but also Austrian and Hungarian banks, with the symbolic participation of Bulgarian capital. That consortium was made up of the following German banks: the Berlin-based *Direktion der Discontogesellschaft* (leader of the consortium), Dresdner Bank, Bank S. Bleichröder, Handels Disconto Bank, Nationalbank für Deutschland; the Cologne-based Bank S. Oppenheim, Abraham Schaffhausen Bankverein, Bank A. Loevy; the Hamburg-based Norddeutsche Bank, Bank Max M. Warburg, Unionbank, Bank Bernst und Söhne, Bank Gebrüder Schröder; the Frankfurt-based, Dreyfussbank, Metalbank, Metalürgische Gesellschaft; and the Eissleben-based Mansfeldsche Kupferschieferbauende Gewerkschaften. The Austrian group comprised: the Vienna-based Creditanstalt für Handel und Gewerbe, Wiener Bank; the Budapest-based Pester Ungarische Handelsbank, Ungarische Allgemeine Kreditbank. The Bulgarian group comprised the Sofia-based Kreditna Banka, Balkanska Banka and General Bulgarian Bank.[75]

Germany had numerical superiority in this consortium with sixteen banks and firms out of the total of twenty-four, while Austria had five and Bulgaria three. Moreover, it accounted for 75% of the capital and Austria-Hungary for 25%. The Sofia-based Balkanska Banka and General Bulgarian Bank were in the hands of Austrian banks and accounted for an insignificant amount, while the Sofia-based Kreditna Banka was a branch of the Direktion der Discontogesellschaft, which also participated through its Abraham Schaffhausen Bankverein, and Norddeutsche Bank. Bank S. Bleichröder had been a weaker partner for a long time. In line with the percentage of capital invested, Germany had the right to 75% of the overall production of the mine in Bor. It is interesting to note that the same concern, with the sole exception of the Mansfeldsche Kupferschieferbauende Gewerkschaften, obtained the right to exploitation of the other minerals in territories under Bulgarian occupation.

Germany and Austria-Hungary showed equal interest—and rivalry—in taking over Balkan railway lines on a permanent basis, particularly those running through the Velika Morava and Vardar valleys. The Germans did not want to let go of the railway lines over which they had control for the duration of the war; on that government, military circles and big capital were in total agreement. The largest German banks, including the Direktion der Discontogesellschaft, Deutsche Bank, Nationalbank für Deutschland, Bank S. Bleichröder and Berliner Handelsgesellschaft, sought the right to run those railway lines.[76] The military leadership saw the solution for the future as lying 'exclusively in the creation of a German-Bulgarian company with 75% German participation.'[77] For its part the Foreign Ministry considered all German economic objectives in the Balkans as being vitally linked to the issue of railway transport, stating that for the post-war period Germany also wished to obtain from the Bulgarian government

...the right to exploit the mineral resources in Bulgaria-Serbia [!]. The professional exploitation of already existing and future mines is feasible only if the administration of the railways and the construction of new lines serve the needs of the mining industry. The issue of the railways is therefore inseparable from that of mines, which is why railway administration should be handed over to a German-Bulgarian company under German control.⁷⁸

For its part, however, the Austro-Hungarian leadership was looking for a way to take the main Balkan railways out of German hands. It was in favour of reaching some kind of agreement that would still bring it some profit, which was needed because of the weakness of its economy and, therefore, of its banks.⁷⁹ Hence a plan came about for the creation of an international company for administering the Belgrade-Niš-Ristovac railway line, with the stipulation that it could also obtain the right to run other railways in Serbia. It was planned to create the company with German, Austrian, Hungarian and Bulgarian capital, while the greater part of the shares, the majority of the board and the general direction would be in the hands of Austrian and Hungarian financial institutions headed by the Vienna-based Creditanstalt für Handel und Gewerbe. Agreement was supposed to be reached before the conclusion of a peace treaty, with the stipulation that Austria-Hungary and Bulgaria had to do their utmost in the peace negotiations to ensure the acceptance of the idea. Felix Somary, an eminent financial expert and businessman, was thought to be behind the idea, and when he visited Sofia, probably in May 1917, he put it to Prime Minister Radoslavov, who responded favourably. The Austro-Hungarian embassy in Berlin officially put the proposal to the German government in a note of 31 May and also called on Count Czernin to gather Austrian, Hungarian, German and Bulgarian representatives for an initial 'expert exchange of opinion'.⁸⁰ The German Foreign Ministry did not respond officially till 8 July, when it sent a note, saying: 'In its present form, the project is somewhat contrary to the intentions of the German government *vis-à-vis* Serbian territories promised to Bulgaria', and it left no room for doubt that Germany would keep a tight hold on the railways.⁸¹

Soon the Nationalbank für Deutschland, together with the Bank S. Bleichröder (probably with the Direktion der Discontogesellschaft behind them), expressed interest in taking over all Balkan railways. On 17 and 26 July 1917, the Nationalbank für Deutschland submitted a proposal to the Foreign Ministry in Berlin that had been elaborated by its director Hjalmar Schacht; that proposal was in the spirit of Germany's long-term goals, and was accepted by the German government.[82] According to the director's plan, the Nationalbank für Deutschland advocated the creation of a German-Austro-Hungarian joint stock company to run the railways, with the proviso that 'German influence must be decisive', because 'powerful military, political and economic influence over the entire territory will be of ever greater importance for Germany in the future.' The bank therefore considered that the entire Belgrade-Salonika railway line should be taken over, since it represented an 'international railway line of exceptional importance for Balkan politics as a whole': a company should be founded to run that 'true backbone of the Balkan railway system' and try to 'control it in such a way that we hold all the main railway routes' in the Balkan peninsula. This also meant the right to build a line from Bitola to the Adriatic. Schacht's plan not only comprised railway lines within the Bulgarian and Austro-Hungarian zones of occupation in Serbia, but also extended to Greek and Albanian territory.

However, although negotiations were conducted on several occasions and their foreign ministries exchanged a large number of memoranda, Germany and Austria-Hungary had such different priorities that right up to the end of the war they could not reach agreement on railways either in Serbia or in the rest of the Balkans.

Violence and oppression

The occupation authorities had a dual task in Serbia; first they had to keep a firm hold on the occupied territories and make the greatest possible use of Serbia's natural resources for their war economies, and secondly they needed to work out plans for the permanent acquisition of the territories, thus ensuring their political and economic advantage. For these reasons the occupation authorities took draconian steps to control political life. Further, they did their utmost to stifle the population's national awareness and were ruthless in their exploitation of economic resources.

It quickly became evident that the Bulgarian occupation authorities intended to conduct a ruthless denationalisation programme as quickly and systematically as possible.[83] On the heels of the army came first civil servants and then teachers who, together with the armed forces, were to lay the groundwork for implementation of a Bulgarianisation programme. The denationalisation measures targeted mainly Serbs, but they also affected members of other nationalities—Albanians, Turks, Greeks and Jews—who lived in greater or lesser numbers in the occupied territories.[84] On 20 February 1916 a certain Colonel von Lustig, an Austro-Hungarian liaison officer attached to the headquarters of the German 11th Army, wrote a confidential report to his supreme command:

> The Bulgarians are certainly making use of their occupation of eastern Serbia and Macedonia. They have been ruthless and brutal in introducing their new administration.... Bulgarianisation takes two basic directions; the destruction of the upper and middle classes (the intelligentsia) of the domestic population, and the enforced introduction of the Bulgarian language.[85]

One of the first measures undertaken was the mass deportation of adult males. On 14 December 1916, the Governor General ordered that 'all men between the ages of 18 and 50 who have served in the Serbian army, all officers, former teachers, priests, journalists, former deputies, military functionaries and all suspect persons' should be arrested and interned.[86] However, in the first months, under the guise of deportation, mass executions took place. Men were arrested and allegedly sent to Bulgaria, but they were in fact executed. Colonel von Lustig reported:

> It is known that most of the Serbian intelligentsia, i.e. functionaries, teachers, priests and others, withdrew with what was left of the Serbian army, but a certain number of them have gradually started to return for psychological or material reasons. Here, in occupied territory, it is virtually impossible to find either them or those who did not flee; they have 'gone to Sofia', as the new Bulgarian saying goes. These men were handed over to Bulgarian patrols (usually *comitadji*) as suspects without any proper judicial procedure, with the order that they should be 'taken to Sofia'. The patrols actually return the next day without them. Whether they are taken 20 or 200 kilometres, it is all the same. The patrols pick up spades, disappear into the mountains and quickly return, but without the prisoners. Bulgarian officers do not even try to conceal the executions, they boast about them.[87]

At the end of 1918, just after the war, an international commission of inquiry established that at least 100 Serbian priests had been killed in this way in the regions around Niš, Surdulica and Zaječar.[88]

According to another inquiry, in the district of Vranje alone around 3,500 men, including 500 intellectuals, were killed in the first six months of occupation. Most of the men 'sent to Sofia' were taken to Surdulica and killed there, the most brutal methods often being used; it is calculated that, in the first months of occupation, between 2,000 and 3,000 men were killed there. The Bulgarian head of the district of Vranje described those men as 'killers, thieves and butchers' who had committed such crimes that 'at least ten years will be needed to mend their evil'.[89] Colonel von Lustig reported that the evil did not end with the men being 'sent to Sofia', but the victims' relatives and heirs also suffered.[90]

A new 'Law on Property' was proclaimed confiscating the movable and immovable property of people who were not in the same place as their property when Bulgarian troops entered; it was also confiscated from those who had it in different locations and simply could not be in more than one place at a time. Colonel von Lustig remarked: 'Thanks to such measures, there is the systematic impoverishment of the more prosperous among the population, and that is a goal in itself.'[91]

Although in the spring of 1916 the brutality and terror started to wane a little, oppressive measures did not end. One aspect of oppression that was constantly present was the deportation of all undesirable persons. In mid-September the Austro-Hungarian consul in Niš reported to Baron Burian that 'mass internment by Bulgaria was not in evidence.' He added that the male civilian population was nonetheless ceaselessly being sent to Bulgaria, but such measures were carried out 'quietly and unobserved, usually at night'.[92] As time went by, these measures, as well as violence in general, were being perpetrated more and more against the working class too. The decision to conduct a census for recruitment purposes of all men aged between eighteen and fifty was not made purely for military reasons; its real purpose was evidently denationalisation by means of recruitment into the Bulgarian army.

From the very beginning the use of Serb names and inscriptions as well as the written and spoken Serbian language were banned. According to Colonel von Lustig, 'Just a week or two after Niš had been taken, there was no Serbian inscription to be seen in the streets or on the shops. The surnames Petrović, Marković, Živković etc. had in one fell swoop become Petrov, Markov and Zekov [Živkov?].'[93] It was further ordered that all textbooks and other teaching material in Serbian should be confiscated by 15 February 1916. Another injunction passed in May 1916 ordered the 'confiscation of all Serbian books, pictures and maps in public institutions, bookshops and private houses'. Trade in Bulgarian books was permitted, as well as in 'books and printed matter in other foreign languages, with the exception of Serbian'. Circulars were sent to occupation officials exhorting that 'correspondence in Serbian is absolutely banned.' One circular forbade the use of certain Serbian words.

Churches too were not spared. First they were desecrated, for example by using them as cowsheds. Later Bulgarian priests were brought in. Bulgarian icons replaced Serbian ones, and the faces of Serbian saints in frescoes were scratched out. The celebration of Serbian patron saints' days (*slava*) was banned, and infants could only be baptised with Bulgarian names. Serbian folk attire was forbidden, particularly the *šajkaca* cap.[94]

At the end of July 1916 the Austro-Hungarian consul in Niš reported to his superiors that the Bulgarians were using 'few cultural means' in their denationalisation programme, and that 'with the exception of the introduction of schooling in Bulgarian, there have been no other such innovations.'[95] Some primary schools were opened soon after the occupation and in the spring of 1916 they were functioning, but teaching was exclusively in Bulgarian, and Serbian children received Bulgarian names. The only subject taught with any seriousness was the Bulgarian language, while all other teaching boiled down to propaganda aimed at making the children consider themselves Bulgarians. At school festivities, children were encouraged to declare that they were pleased to have 'had their Bulgarian nationality restored'. More and more measures were introduced in the course of 1916 to influence the younger generations. From the autumn of 1916 and during 1917 new primary schools were opened, as were high schools in some towns. Teaching was also in Bulgarian and totally channelled towards Bulgarian propaganda, while attendance was compulsory for Serb children. Books printed in Bulgarian were distributed among the population free of charge, and documentary films about 'the Bulgarian Pomoravlje [Morava valley]' were shown in schools in Niš. A number of Bulgarian university professors, ethnologists, historians and geographers were assigned the task of elaborating the basic principles of Bulgarianisation by finding and selecting the necessary facts.

In June 1917 the *Moravski Glas*, the organ of the occupation authorities, started to appear in Niš. Bulgarian officers had the last word over editorial matters, and the newspaper office quickly developed into a propaganda headquarters; somewhat later its activists also founded the *Moravsko Društvo* association for the promotion of culture and art. This association, for example, recruited young people under the age of twenty to perform *tambura* concerts, and a *tambura* orchestra was soon set up, about which the Austro-Hungarian vice-consul Haas commented: 'Under the influence of certain young police agents, who became members of this association for that very purpose, the orchestra was gradually turned into an organised body numbering over fifty young "New Bulgarians" in the service of the political police and propaganda.'[96] Haas added that a number of 'young people who just wanted to have a good time' and 'had nothing at all to do with politics' had been recruited. However, by joining the orchestra these youngsters 'gained certain freedoms and privileges, such as the right to be outdoors at night.' As time went by, the *Moravsko Društvo* started becoming involved in economic activities, and its activists founded a trade association. Association members were granted the monopoly of imports of various commodities from abroad, on condition that they declared themselves Bulgarians.

A Morava People's Education Committee was set up in Sofia to monitor overall propaganda activity. One method of denationalisation was releasing prisoners, returning deportees and pardoning those who had been condemned to death if they and their families declared themselves to be Bulgarian. The authorities made great efforts to compel people to sign various petitions declaring themselves members of the Bulgarian nation. These petitions were sent to King Ferdinand, Prime Minister Radoslavov and the Bulgarian authorities generally.[97]

The occupation authorities in the Macedonia area also tried to impose Bulgarianisation by force, sometimes using methods that people from outside considered ridiculous. Colonel von Lustig found it laughable, for example, that the mosque minaret and the

Orthodox church bell tower in Skopje were 'painted from top to bottom in red, green and white',[98] the Bulgarian national colours. The new authorities sought to impose their propaganda through the press, publications, public lectures, schools and societies promoting culture. Thus they wished to create a new political and ideological situation both in Macedonia and in Kosovo, where their attacks, both physical and spiritual, targeted Serbs, Turks and Albanians alike. The conduct of the authorities in Kosovo was seen by the Austro-Hungarian supreme command as follows: 'As is the case throughout Macedonia, the basic principle is that the land must become purely Bulgarian, even at the cost of transforming it into a Bulgarian desert.' Hence efforts were made 'to achieve Bulgarianisation by fire and by sword'.[99]

Unlike the state of affairs in Serbia proper, it would seem that in Macedonia the Serbs were the easiest people to deal with because they were deeply disturbed and dejected.[100] Judging from Austro-Hungarian sources, Bulgarians simply dispatched Serbs from Macedonia to internment in Bulgaria or moved them north to the river Morava area. Austro-Hungarian Serb citizens in Macedonia (who numbered a few score) were ordered to leave. A report reached the Austro-Hungarian command saying: 'Serbs already seem harmless. It appears that broad strata of the people can really become quickly assimilated, while the intelligentsia have been destroyed or deported and interned in Bulgaria or the Morava area.'[101] Albanians and Turks caused far greater problems as they put up tough resistance, to which the authorities responded with violent oppression. Albanians, for example, were forced into slave labour; one eyewitness said they were starved so that they resembled skeletons and just dropped dead while they were working.[102]

The fundamental principle of the Austro-Hungarian occupation authorities was that Serbia should be destroyed and Montenegro won over for the Monarchy. Therefore they tried both to crush the people's political self-awareness and to introduce disorder and division among the population of the occupied countries on a national and religious basis. While determining the principles of the Monarchy's rule in Serbia, Burian wrote of the need for a 'cruel regime to crush Serbdom and destroy its strength for as long as possible'.[103]

On 15 March 1916 General Conrad gave instructions to Governor Count Salis-Seewis: 'Focus all your relentless energy on the good of the war and the armed forces', adding that he should 'crush any rebellion and implement the broadest possible exploitation forcefully and with ruthless severity.' Conrad emphasised that Serbia was necessary to Austria-Hungary 'both economically and because of its population who should be used to serve our future objectives' (probably for the trialist reorganisation of the Monarchy). On the same day Conrad described to Burian the principles that were guiding the military authorities:

> At the start of the offensive [against the Serbs in October 1915], the supreme command expressly ordered the army to exploit the occupied districts ruthlessly. The Military Governorate is now using draconian severity to disarm the population and make the country safe, as well as to exploit Serbia's material resources to their utmost and without any consideration for the population. If this is borne in mind, then it is not a sign of inconsistency but a sign of wisdom that the Military Governorate General is trying to thwart open or passive resistance by implementing a corresponding procedure towards the population, that is by showing the country's economic productivity, which is vital to us for our economy, as an increase in the living standard [of the population] and by organising neglected education in this sense.[104]

On several occasions Count Tisza too advocated 'the maintenance of order' and 'the exploitation of the country's economic strength' with an unsparing occupation administration. He called for 'industrial and other plants and facilities to be taken over in the occupied districts with the utmost severity.'[105] Governor General von Remen acquiesced in all this. For example, when it became known on 30 August 1916 that Romania had entered the war, there were stirrings of rebellion among the population, and he ordered his district commanders that 'peace and security must … be ensured with the severest possible measures (taking and shooting hostages, burning houses etc.).'[106]

Austria-Hungary's propaganda portrayed its administration in Serbia and Montenegro as 'civilising'. However, when one of the first representatives of the Belgrade Governorate published an article in 1917 titled 'Promotion of Culture in an Enemy Country', the German consul hastened to inform the Chancellor in Berlin that 'the claim that Austro-Hungarian military authorities were offering an occupied country great cultural achievements was an entirely empty one.' He added: 'There can be no question whatever that the

Serbian side will later express appreciation of what our ally has done here.'[107] According to the consul, 'the population are not being treated sufficiently expertly and justly,' and 'many of the authorities' measures are marked by police harassment.'[108]

As soon as they entered the country, the occupation forces banned all existing forms of public life and dispersed all professional, cultural and sports organisations and associations. They further started mass internment, took a large number of hostages, and were merciless in their search for hidden weapons. The authorities gave no specific reason for the mass internment beyond the preservation in principle of 'military security'.[109] The Military Governorate in Belgrade formulated this in the following way: 'Internment is primarily a military security measure. Internment for other reasons is possible only in exceptional cases.... Essentially the aims of internment are not punitive; it is a pre-emptive measure to be taken as and when the general military situation requires it.'[110] Such a vague definition of internment enabled the authorities simply to intern anyone. The actual aim in Serbia was the removal of all remaining males aged between seventeen and fifty-five, as well as all those who could possibly agitate against the Monarchy or lead any possible disorder, regardless of their age. Anyone who had actually violated the rules of the occupying Governorate in any respect was not interned but handed over to the military authorities, the police or the courts, often to be executed on the spot or publicly hanged. Many people were executed as hostages as a result of resistance by others.

Internment continued throughout the three years of occupation. People were interned individually, in small groups and in large groups, but in fact it occurred in four main waves.[111] The first took place during and soon after the entry of Austro-Hungarian troops into Serbia at the end of the autumn of 1915, when between 20,000 and 25,000 people were interned. The second large wave occurred after Romania's entry into the war, or, to be more precise, at the end of the summer and in the early autumn of 1916. The arrest, pending deportation, was then ordered of male town-dwellers aged between seventeen and fifty who were capable of military service, all former Serbian soldiers throughout the Governorate who had avoided imprisonment or internment, and all politically suspect individuals, be they town- or country-dwellers, men or women, and regardless of age. This measure also included all men of Romanian nationality capable of bearing arms. The arrest and internment were then specifically ordered of all persons in Serbia who were members not only of the Black Hand, Narodna Odbrana and the Yugoslav Club, but also of all kinds of associations such as even the Pobratimstvo football club and the Kolo Srpske Brace and Kolo Srpskih Sestara charity associations, and all Masons regardless of which lodges they belonged to. That order also extended to permanent editorial staff of all former political and humorous magazines. The campaign of arrests was sudden and violent, and the German consul reported to Berlin that patrols were literally picking people up off the streets of Belgrade.[112] By the end of September around 8,500 people had been arrested and sent to camps outside Serbia, and by the time the wave ended at the beginning of November the figure had reached 16,500. Most of those arrested were interned outside the Governorate, while some were sent to places in the occupation zone. The third wave of arrests came in the spring of 1917, after the uprising in Toplica, and included *comitadji* who had responded to a call promising amnesty in the case of surrender. It also included those suspected of helping *comitadji*. The fourth and smallest wave took place when the Entente Allies broke through the Salonika front in the autumn of 1918.

The internment camps in the Monarchy were located in Aschach, Heinrichsgrien, Arad, Keczkemet, Drosendorf, Nezider, Vac, Cegled, Nagymegyer and Boldagaszon.[113] Moreover, the Austro-Hungarian authorities handed over to the Bulgarians some high-ranking church dignitaries, who spent the war interned in Bulgaria. Internees also included many women and children under the age of seventeen, which in mid-April 1917 prompted the papal nuncio in Vienna to ask Czernin why children aged between ten and fifteen had been brought from Serbia for internment in the Monarchy. The internees were badly fed and suffered mistreatment and violence from their guards; they spent their time working on the land or in industrial plants. Those interned in Serbia, who seem to have been exclusively peasants, were divided into work brigades, 250 to 300 strong, and forced to work in the fields or in workshops. From time to time the brigades were supplemented with people who had been released from camps in the Monarchy to work in the Governorate. For example, in the summer of 1917 a commission sent 2,927 persons from eleven camps in the Monarchy to join work brigades, and another 1,254 'trained persons' (probably artisans) were sent to do work for which they were qualified.

It is clear that the severity of the occupation authorities' regime was designed to destroy national culture. This process had began with the theft of items of cultural value at the time of military operations. It is difficult to determine exactly what was stolen and removed from the country at that time. In November 1915 a German lieutenant took the Prizren manuscript of Emperor Dušan's Code of Laws; this invaluable work was only rediscovered in Germany in 1933 and returned to Belgrade in 1935.[114] The treasures of the Dečani, Ravanica, Manasija and other monasteries were plundered, as were museums and libraries in Belgrade. The Austro-Hungarian authorities confiscated books from public libraries that dealt with Serbian history and relations between Serbia and the Monarchy, and banned them from public circulation. In an endeavour to quell the cultural unity of Serbs, books by Jovan Jovanović Zmaj and Branko Radičević were also banned, simply because they were Serb poets from the Habsburg Empire. The occupation authorities took particular interest in the official material of Serbian government institutions, especially Foreign Ministry documents. They also focused on writings by the leading parties and political figures, and a special commission was set up to find such material, examine it and send it to Vienna. In 1916 academics and teams of experts started to arrive in Serbia to carry out research in institutions of culture and in the interior of the country.

The official Governorate mouthpiece was a propaganda-based newspaper titled *Beogradske Novosti*, which had a supplement called *Avala* that dealt with matters concerning cultural activities. All previous Serbian newspapers had been closed down and banned. Newspapers arrived from the Yugoslav regions of the Monarchy, but they created problems as the Governorate feared strengthening the sense of Serb community and were vigilant about the content of those papers. In the spring of 1917, for example, the *Hrvatska Riječ* was banned for a time because the authorities in Belgrade considered its content unsuitable owing to its Yugoslav nature. The *Glas Srba, Hrvata i Slovenaca* was also banned for the same reason.

Particular attention was devoted to education. The fundamental objective of education was, as Kerchnawe wrote after the war, to ensure that children 'were brought up and educated under our control.'[115] The goal was, as Burian and Conrad agreed in the spring of 1916, 'primarily through schools' to obtain 'an insight into the soul of the people' and 'the possibility of influencing it.' Conrad himself reported that the people should be educated from an early age 'firstly in the spirit of strict discipline and respect for order.'[116] In August 1918, a few months before the fall of Austria-Hungary, it was estimated that opening schools was 'an exceptionally valuable measure from a political viewpoint', because it was through schools that many young people would be placed 'under constant supervision and discipline'.[117]

A large number of primary and secondary Serbian, Albanian and Muslim schools were opened in the period from the beginning of 1916 to mid-1918.[118] On 10 February 1916 the first primary school was opened in Belgrade, to be followed by other schools in the interior of the country during the spring. At the end of March 1917 there were altogether 125 primary schools, ninety-two of which were for Serbs and four for Albanians, while there were twenty-seven Muslim primary schools and one Muslim secondary school. A *real* (practical) high school, a high school for girls and a trade academy were opened in Belgrade, while six-year high schools were opened in Šabac, Valjevo and Užice and eight-year high schools in Kragujevac and Kruševac. Secondary schools were attended by about 4,000 full-time and 3,000 part-time pupils. However, the university was closed for the duration of the occupation.[119]

Teaching was geared totally to politics, and Serbian Cyrillic script was banned from the schoolroom; children were taught to use the Latin script. Cyrillic was allowed to remain only in religious instruction for Orthodox pupils. Insistence was placed on textbooks being printed in Latin script, but with the shortage of paper and other materials it was difficult to reproduce the teaching materials in use in the part of the Monarchy where Serbo-Croatian was used. Not till August 1918 was permission sought for the use of textbooks printed in Cyrillic that were in use in Vojvodina. By then, however, the occupation administration was drawing to an end.

The teaching of German and Hungarian was compulsory in secondary schools, equal importance being attached to each; of other foreign languages, only French was taught as an alternative to Latin and geometry.[120] Teaching as a whole glorified the Habsburgs and their state, and in Muslim religious schools, besides teaching of the Koran, there was also a special secular course designed by the military commanders. Teaching of the Orthodox faith was limited to prayers, and even that teaching was subject to the rules laid down by the highest religious institutions of the Austro-Hungarian army. While Count Salis-Seewis was Governor, the teaching staff in the schools were mainly Austro-Hungarian non-commissioned officers, two female teachers in primary schools being the only exception. Except for the teaching of history and literature, more and more civilian teachers were from the local population. Some teachers were also brought from Austria-Hungary.

Political and economic circumstances

Only to a certain extent did the occupying forces seek the support of the small number of pro-Austrian Serb supporters of the Obrenović dynasty; to avoid appearing to accede to the wishes of any Serbian political element, however pro-Habsburg it may have been, they would not give such people any political authority.

During the great famine at the end of the winter of 1916 Count Salis-Seewis formed a committee of local people, but it was resolutely stressed that 'any kind of old politics must be excluded from its work.'[121] There were, in fact, two views concerning the use of local Serbs. One idea, favoured by the military leadership, was described by General Conrad: 'The peasant and merchant strata must progress under us, while the politically active, the so-called intelligentsia—former ministers, functionaries, lawyers, teachers and priests—should not be supported but rather eliminated. That is to say their return [from exile] must be prevented with the greatest determination for as long as possible.'[122] In fact, it was necessary to raise the standard of those strata whose agricultural assets could be useful to the Monarchy, while at the same time suppressing national and state awareness. Conrad's concept that the greater part of Serbia should be annexed was obviously involved here. The second view, favoured by the Hungarian leadership, considered that only when necessary should reliance be placed on the old, pro-Austrian Obrenović era politicians, while as a matter of principle all Serbs should be kept as far away from politics as possible—and in poverty.

Soon after entering Serbia, the occupying forces set up the Belgrade Municipal Committee, which was reorganised and expanded in March 1916 when Vojislav Veljković, a leading liberal and former finance minister, was appointed its chairman.[123] The Committee's members were prominent supporters of the Monarchy, but Count Salis-Seewis considered that it 'should not deal with important issues'. Moreover, it was under the district command, and its activities were monitored by both a special civilian commissioner and a military adviser.[124] However, when Baron von Remen was appointed Governor the Committee ceased to be important. In the further construction of the administrative system in Belgrade and elsewhere, the occupying forces recruited local people and gave them everyday jobs. Certain individuals were recruited to carry out intelligence tasks.

The attitude of the occupying forces to all those who agreed to cooperate with them, as well as to prominent supporters of the Monarchy since the time of the Obrenović dynasty, ensured that they were placed in powerless and frequently humiliating positions. They were constantly reminded that they were members of the subjugated population of a defeated state. When, for example, in mid-January 1916 the former Serbian Prime Minister Jovan Avakumović came to Count Salis-Seewis with the proposal that they should jointly issue a call to the population for law and order, the occupation authorities became infuriated that a visitor could even think that 'his name could stand beside the name of an Austrian general who represents His Imperial and Royal Apostolic Majesty.' Avakumović was immediately arrested and interned. And when, at the beginning of April 1916, a certain Milivoje Spasojević criticised the occupation authorities at a session of the Belgrade Municipal Committee, the civilian commissioner bellowed furiously at him. Spasojević left the session and then resigned from the Committee, and his internment was immediately demanded. The Committee chairman Veljković also had difficulties over a statement he made suggesting that the military authorities supported his Committee, which in the Governorate administration was interpreted to mean that in Veljkovic's view the Committee had 'the leading role'. This attitude deteriorated even more under Baron von Remen, and in the early autumn of 1916 the pro-Austrian professors Živojin Perić and Jovan

B. Jovanović sent this complaint to Vienna. 'We are of the opinion that the present military regime should have greater regard for the leaders and members of the Conservative Party; if that is not the case, there will be no justifiable grounds for its existence and it will break up. What is the sense of a party that declares itself pro-Austrian if Austria-Hungary, when in full power, ignores it?'[125]

In line with the Monarchy's basic strategy of introducing new divisions among Balkan nations as well as exploiting old ones, the occupation authorities endeavoured to show that their intentions towards the Albanian nation and the Muslim population as a whole were friendly; so besides granting them certain economic privileges and tax reductions, they tried to find allies in that part of the population to help them in their administration. In Kosovo the occupiers quickly came into contact both with people who had earlier fled to Albania and with Albanian beys, and in the Sandžak they contacted those who before 1908 had been Turkish officers and their helpers.[126] The most significant person to place himself at their disposal in Kosovo was Hasan Priština, while a former Turkish gendarmerie officer, Dervish Bey, was the occupiers' most prominent collaborator in the districts of Novi Pazar and Prijepolje, as well as the district of Plevlja which was in the Governorate of Montenegro. It was with much display and propaganda that special commissions to recruit volunteers were set up, civilian commissioner Thallóczy playing a major role. Hasan Priština and Dervish Bey were particularly active in the recruitment campaign, and 8,000 people came forward in the Governorate as a whole.[127] Some of the volunteers were attached to the Bosnian-Herzegovinan gendarmerie forces, and some to the 14th Corps of the Turkish Imperial Army fighting on the Galician front, while a considerable number of Albanian volunteers entered the service of the Austro-Hungarian district command in Kosovska Mitrovica, where they became members of pursuit units, each of between twenty and thirty men. Dervish Bey became commander of a separate volunteer battalion formed at the beginning of 1917 and had four companies of 100 men each. The company officers were former Turkish officers and non-commissioned officers, and commands were given in Turkish. At first the rules of service and tactics were Turkish, but they later became those of Austria-Hungary, while the officers and men swore allegiance to the Imperial-Royal

Governor in Belgrade. Most of the men in the battalion were Albanians.

However, there was resistance to the occupiers among the Albanians, and a commander in Kosovska Mitrovica said that there would be no peace in Kosovo until some of the leaders were publicly hanged. Armed companies of Albanians also appeared in the Belgrade and Skopje Governorates, where they had several clashes with the occupying gendarmerie and army. However, these armed companies were usually more intent on pillage than on achieving political ends.

The occupation authorities did nothing to prevent the population from dying of hunger. Indeed, when they had entered the war-torn country they encountered many who simply lacked the means to support life.[128] Reports from the late autumn of 1915 tell of destitution that threatened to become catastrophic. On Governor Salis-Seewis' appointment in early January 1916, in his first reports to the supreme command he saw fit to press for 'urgent assistance'. The news of the famine raging in Serbia quickly spread throughout the world, and American, Swiss and Dutch charity organisations offered assistance. Baron Burian himself wrote in official acts that 'Serbia is faced with imminent famine and death', and 'the maintenance of supplies is becoming dangerous.' However, the second half of March came, and neither Burian nor any other official had decided to send assistance. Food shortages had by then reached the level of a famine, and when a decision was finally taken, it was only to send 'the minimum of resources for survival' by limiting consignments to 'the most important foods, mainly maize and salt', which meant 150,000 'reduced daily portions and 3,650 tonnes of seeds for sowing maize and oats'. By the time that small amount of assistance arrived the famine was six months old. It is impossible to determine how many people died of hunger, but the numbers were certainly large.

By the late spring of 1916 the state of affairs was no longer so critical, but hunger was still widespread. In early July 1917 the Governorate's intelligence service reported that there were still food shortages and many anonymous threatening letters—one, addressed to General von Remen, bore witness to 'food supply difficulties among the domestic population, particularly in Belgrade.' The International Red Cross established that up to 1 September 1917 over 8,000 people had died of hunger in Serbia.[129] But despite that, a high-ranking occupation official complained in July 1917 of the bad quality of the threshing machines manufactured in Hungary. That was quoted as the reason for the small quantities of wheat being sent from Serbia to Austria-Hungary.[130]

For the entire occupation period food was rationed in towns, and ration books were introduced. To give just a few examples, every adult was initially entitled to 400 grams of bread daily and every child to 200 grams. In October 1916 that quantity was reduced for adults to 320 grams. In January 1918 children in Belgrade aged between five and thirteen were entitled to 80 grams of meat a day and 30 grams of lard a week, while persons older than thirteen had a daily ration of 120 grams of meat and a weekly ration of 60 grams of lard. However, because three days a week were non-meat days, each adult was actually entitled to 70 grams of meat a day. The state of affairs in the villages was somewhat better, but large-scale requisitioning and high taxation kept the rural population in short supply.

For Austria-Hungary the territory of the Military Governorate General of Serbia was merely land subjected to ruthless economic exploitation. In the period immediately after the entry of occupation troops there was large-scale pillaging. The following three years of occupation were geared to achieving the greatest possible economic profit.[131] Military authorities, in alliance with Austro-Hungarian capital, took over the management of all production forces and branches of the economy.

On 22 June 1916 the Governorate administration artificially transformed the previous temporary devaluation of the dinar into a permanent one, thus reducing the value of Serbia's currency by 50% against the crown.[132] This devaluation brought up prices in the Governorate, which in turn led to a further deterioration in living conditions. However, it also gave rise to financial and monetary disarray, for what actually happened was that the real value of the dinar remained higher than that of the crown, with 100 dinars being obtained for 102 crowns in the Governorate. However, in Niš, which was the centre of the Bulgarian occupation zone, 100 dinars were being exchanged in November 1917 for as many as 140 crowns. Nor did the redenomination of the Serbian currency, which was performed as part of the devaluation measures, yield the desired results, as only 38 million out of the calculated 150 million dinars on the territory of the Governorate were actually redenominated. A German expert, well versed in Serbia's financial circumstances having spent over thirty years in the country, explained the situation in the *Frankfürter Zeitung*:

> It was quickly learned that the National Bank [of Serbia] had actually transferred gold reserves to the value of 60 million francs to a safe place in Greece and that around 200 million francs had been remitted to the Serbian government from surpluses at the Banque de France in Paris. In that way the 300 million banknotes in circulation were actually covered by 260 million francs in gold. Hence the Serbian currency was in demand again, and it was being purchased at an exchange rate that was growing daily above the stipulated parity. Speculation was rife as the Austrian currency was falling in value at the same time.[133]

The occupying authorities enforced a large number of other measures. For example, in line with a decree issued in Belgrade on 4 May 1916, they took over the largest industrial companies, trading houses and banks, and the military authorities appointed new managers from the ranks of Austrian and Hungarian business leaders.[134] In the spring of that year a monopoly was introduced on a number of consumer products, with for example the Ungarsiche Bank und Handels Aktien Gesellschaft having the monopoly on cigarette paper, tobacco, salt and matches, and the Pester Ungarische Commerzialbank on methylated spirits. Zagreb branches of the Hungarian banks were responsible for these transactions. A decree also opened up the Governorate market to Austro-Hungarian merchants, while the Monarchy's market was now closed to all Serbian goods. A new tariff system was introduced for that purpose in late 1915 and supplemented in the first half of 1916. The few Serbian surplus goods for sale in the Monarchy and neutral countries were initially appropriated by an improvised military Central Goods Depot, but, according to an order of 25 March 1916, the import and export of a large number of commodities were banned even through that channel. In May the ban was slackened somewhat, and for 1 June slightly freer trade was permitted, but still under the strict supervision of the Central Goods Trade Office, another military institution. Such an import and export policy only served to increase shortages among the population. A report submitted in January 1918 by the Governorate authorities on the performance of the Central Goods Trade

Office stated: 'This month there have also been considerable shortages of paraffin and matches, two monopoly commodities. The approved contingents arrive only partly from Austria and not at all from Hungary. The consequence of this is black-marketeering and fantastically high prices. There is also a severe shortage of salt.'[135] A citizen of Belgrade who was a child during the occupation recalled: 'In normal circumstances the word black-market signifies criminal activity. However, during the period of occupation it signified the struggle to survive.'[136]

War, epidemics, exile, mass internment—all made manpower a grave problem. And that in turn threatened to frustrate the intention to exploit the occupied territories to the limit. The citizen of Belgrade mentioned above wrote of seven- or eight-year-old boys being at that time 'the man of the house'.[137] To solve the problem of low productivity, Austro-Hungarians had recourse to coercive measures.[138] They introduced forced labour according to which men had to work a specific number of days in the week under the orders of the military commanders. They even had to provide their own tools, livestock and carts to perform the jobs assigned to them. Hard labour was also meted out by the police to those who had committed minor misdemeanours such as 'dealing in politics' (which meant they had discussed politics) or frequenting taverns. Manpower was also provided by 'labour groups' comprising 2-3,000 internees. When extra manpower was needed prisoners of war from Entente countries who worked in camps throughout the Governorate were set to work alongside internees. To achieve the greatest possible degree of exploitation, a bureaucratic machinery was set up comprising experts, retired officers and those physically unfit for active war service, under the management of the group in charge of economic matters in the Governorate's administration. There were a number of officials in each district command who were in charge of such matters. Consequently the already ailing economy was further encumbered by the occupiers' excessively large bureaucracy. To maintain that bureaucratic machinery and, at the same time, provide surpluses to send to the Monarchy, the population was subjected to confiscation, requisition, high taxation etc.[139]

A Military Mining Administration formed in early 1916 was in charge of mine exploitation.[140] The Austro-Hungarian authorities exploited all the mines in their zone as well as at Majdanpek, which was under Bulgarian occupation. These mines contained antimony, lead, copper and coal of various types. Large-scale geological exploration was also under way, since the Monarchy believed that it would continue to exploit the mineral resources after the war.[141]

All types of cereals (particularly wheat), fruit and vegetables were requisitioned in large quantities. By the end of October 1917, for example, 80,780 tonnes of cereals had been collected, including 69,310 tonnes of wheat and rye. Moreover, livestock was also requisitioned mercilessly. According to data from the Austro-Hungarian supreme command, by mid-May 1917 around 170,000 head of cattle, 190,000 sheep and 50,000 pigs had been transported from Serbia to the Monarchy alone. And that did not include the livestock confiscated for use in the Governorate. The Austro-Hungarians estimated that Serbia 'contributed the most from among all the occupied territories'; this means that to satisfy the needs of Austria-Hungary's war economy, the most was removed from Serbia. In October 1917, 2,398 calves, 13,327 sheep and 1,159 pigs were commandeered, while in July 1918 it had been planned to collect 5,449 calves, 6,995 sheep and 5,000 pigs, but as many as 10,305 calves and 9,730 sheep were actually collected (the number of pigs was less—2,938).[142]

Bulgaria's attempt to denationalise the territories it had occupied yielded results that were reported ironically by vice-consul Haas a few days after Bulgarian capitulation in the autumn of 1918: 'The "liberated Bulgarians of Pomoravlje" are truly rejoicing at the departure of their "liberators".'[143] On hearing that Bulgarian occupation had come to an end the civilians certainly breathed a huge sigh of relief. From the most brutal acts of terror to attempts to win the population over by means of granting privileges, all the measures used by the Bulgarians had had no effect whatsoever. A report submitted by the military governor general in Niš dated 20 November 1916 had stated: 'In this part of the former Serbia that today constitutes the Morava Military Inspection Area the majority of the population deems itself Serb' or 'It is pure Serb, or considers itself as such.' An analysis of the national situation from district to district, which was given in the report, only served to corroborate this view. In the case of Vranje and its environs, the report went on: 'It would be naïve to believe that the population of Vranje is for the present Bulgarian or could soon become assimilated as such.' In the case of Pirot and its environs, 'The inhabitants of the district ... feel themselves to be true Serbs.... They are patiently awaiting the establishment of a Serb kingdom.' As for Niš and its environs, 'According to statistics of May this year, 170,000 of the inhabitants are Serbs, thirty-one are Bulgarians, and the remainder are of other nationalities.'[144]

In a report on the failure of the Bulgarianisation programme in education policy Austro-Hungarian representatives in Niš had spoken almost prophetically. Serb pupils, the report said, had been compelled at some kind of school festivity in July 1916 to say how happy they were to be Bulgarians again. But things worked out rather differently from the way the Bulgarians had expected, because the children's parents had wept on seeing what was being done to their children.[145] On another occasion, on Saturday 16 February 1918, a 'propaganda film show' was laid on for the pupils of a high school in Niš, during which 'different landscapes of Bulgarian Pomoravlje' were shown. The director then addressed the children using 'customary phrases', saying that the Morava area had always been Bulgarian and 'now had to stay Bulgarian'. According to the report he added that the pupils had to bear in mind that their parents had always been Bulgarian and would now, after liberation, remain so. One boy then shouted out, 'Our ancestors have always been Serb and they will always remain that way.' A commotion ensued, and the children all shouted 'Long live Serbia!' The director demanded the names of the children involved, but no one would tell him. An investigation was carried out the next day, but nothing more was found out. When the director tried to lecture the children on politics again, there was a frank discussion during which the children declared that to ask them to say they felt Bulgarian was asking the impossible. The father of one of them was a Serb officer, another was in a Bulgarian jail, a third had been shot by the Bulgarians when they took Niš... The director did not know how to respond to such arguments, so he had recourse to the customary Bulgarian *ultima ratio*, warning the children that they were putting their families at risk of internment. The discussion ended on that note. The next report drew the following conclusion:

> This case casts light on the constant claims made in the press that the entire population, and especially young people, welcome and glorify the Bul-

garian liberators. Just like these children, the whole population is well aware what nationality it is, although the people do not demonstrate it so openly.... In practice this is not a question of historical hair-splitting but of the actual conviction of the population, as can be clearly seen in the example of the children.

The results of all other denationalisation measures clearly showed Bulgaria's allies that Bulgarianisation was having little success. In a report of 26 August 1917 Otto Count Czernin, the Austro-Hungarian envoy to Sofia, told his brother Ottokar that Bulgarian claims should be doubted because 'the population of the Pirot district ..., with the exception of a few older people here and there, feel themselves totally Serb.' He added that confidential intelligence had been obtained that the inhabitants of Niš felt 'extremely bitter towards Bulgarians', and 'hardly anyone reads the *Moravski Glas*, the Bulgarian newspaper launched for propaganda purposes'. He went on: 'Only certain citizens or merchants can be described as being Bulgarian, and they only wish to take advantage of the present circumstances,' emphasising that the local population did not take Bulgarian designs on Niš and other places seriously. In January 1918 Haas, the Vice-Consul, reported that, despite the pressure on them, some inhabitants of Zaječar and Brza Palanka were refusing to sign statements declaring themselves Bulgarian. He added that in Niš the local authorities themselves were expecting conflict as a result of the order to collect signatures, because 'the largest and most influential families, mostly there engaged in commerce, are already indicating that they will not sign' such a statement, believing that they would ruin their future if they took part in any anti-Serb manifestation. Haas further noted that some merchants were 'already declaring themselves ill in order to have a ready excuse for not taking part in such a manifestation.' Strabanov, the mayor of Niš who had been brought from Sofia, himself believed that statements of Bulgarian nationality could not be forced from the inhabitants of the city, and that the occupation authorities would only create problems for themselves if they insisted on such a step. In January 1918 it was reported to Vienna that everyone in Niš was convinced the Bulgarian occupation was a mere 'short provisional period' and that the Serbs would return. Moreover, contrary to the claims in the Bulgarian press, 'the people firmly believed that Niš would once again belong to Serbia.' On 8 August 1918 it was further reported that in Niš 'Bulgarians have not yet succeeded' in obtaining from the people even a formal declaration stating that they felt Bulgarian, although there had been numerous attempts to do so.

Things were not going well for the occupiers in the Military Inspection Area of Macedonia either, as was demonstrated by the need for the constantly increasing Bulgarianisation propaganda, which had already taken on the character and proportions of psychological terror. The Austro-Hungarian consul in Skopje wittily remarked: 'The basic concept being used is summed up in the word "great". Bulgaria's great history, the greatness of Bulgaria's ancient empire, the great Bulgarian army, the great Bulgarian culture etc.— that is what virtually all public addresses consist of and there can be no deviation from it or the police become involved.'[146] The forms of propaganda also multiplied with the introduction of concerts with Bulgarian themes, public readings, public festivities etc. By providing a number of reductions and privileges, the Bulgarians also sought to win over the wealthier strata of society.

The reality was that the population's resistance to Bulgarianisation was constantly felt, and the desire for the creation of an independent Macedonia was also evident. However, owing to the strict military regime, such aspirations could not assume even political form, not to mention armed activity. News of such aspirations started to pour in, and the Austro-Hungarian command's military intelligence drew the following conclusion: 'Many Macedonians are in favour of political separatism; they do not want unification with Bulgaria.'[147] Such news caused uncertainty both in the Austro-Hungarian legation in Sofia and among leading figures in the Monarchy, and it was decided in the autumn of 1917 to send Consul Vrbanić, a Bulgarian speaker, on a month's secret fact-finding mission. Vrbanić, evidently highly in favour of official Bulgarian policy in Macedonia, did not find any political independence movement, but his report still contained a number of interesting details:

Macedonians who have never actually been under Bulgarian rule (with the exception of the ancient emperors) cannot simply look to the past. They have to accept new, contemporary circumstances, which are certainly not of the best. Their dialect differs from the one spoken in Bulgaria, and that is not an insignificant matter.... The country's assimilation will not run smoothly of itself; it requires time, and the desire for secession will continue for a lengthy period. Bulgarians themselves admit to that, realising that there is still a great deal of hard work to be done in Macedonia in all respects, including the national issue.... It will also be necessary to increase the population's prosperity. In the next thirty to forty years, Bulgaria will be totally engaged in Macedonia's material and cultural construction.[148]

Studying the state of affairs that had ensued in December 1917 with the news that the Bolshevik government was prepared to get out of the war, Governorate intelligence in Serbia assessed that if the view prevailed that a puppet state should be created on that territory, the Monarchy could rely only on older persons, or rather those persons on whom it had been able to rely from the beginning.[149] The Governor, General von Remen, reported that 'pro-Austrian progressists and liberals' were hoping to come to power if they assisted in 'the creation of new relations towards the Monarchy,' and therefore remained loyal.[150] This was actually an extremely narrow circle of people advanced in age and without influence in the country. In mid-March 1918 the German consul also reported to his superiors on the subject, saying: 'only a small group, mainly liberal leaders, no longer expect anything from the Entente.'[151] Moreover, it can be concluded from historical sources of Austro-Hungarian origin that the already narrow circle of Monarchy supporters had diminished as liberal leaders had become disappointed and were conducting themselves with ever greater and detachment.

In mid-March 1916 Count Szechenyi was able to conclude with accuracy 'on the basis of intelligence from various quarters' that it was 'fallacious to think that the Serb nation considers it has already been defeated and finally overcome,' as a huge number of inhabitants still hoped for some kind of 'help from outside,' i.e. from the Entente, and from its government and army in exile.[152] Summing up all his impressions, Szechenyi said that the feelings of Serbs could have been described as 'fear of Germans, indescribable hatred of Bulgarians, and hatred and contempt for us.'[153] In a report of September 1917, the Governorate administration claimed that the population was 'counting on the return of Serb authorities despite the success of our arms.'[154]

The people were secretly singing a song. Its words were perhaps naïve, but their meaning was far-reaching, full of determination and hope: 'The Serb dinar is greater than the Austrian crown/Serbs are pushing forward from Salonika town.' Moreover, the Governorate authorities were constantly reporting that 'whatever is contrary to our wishes suits the Serbs,' since they had hopes for 'a better tomorrow.'[155] The German consul reported that 'one should not count on quick and easy success' in Serbia. He also said it was indisputable that Austrians and Hungarians alike were hated by Serbs, but what was far worse was that Serbs did not fear them.[156] All research shows that in March 1917 the words of one Austro-Hungarian reporter were true of the entire occupation: 'The fanatical hope of an independent Serbia is alive among the great majority of inhabitants.'[157]

6
ARMED RESISTANCE

From the population's opposition, their refusal to surrender, their bitter feelings and their hopes—in short, from their desire for freedom—an armed resistance movement was born. It is difficult to determine exactly when and how it arose: probably spontaneously at the time when the defence of Serbia was collapsing. It happened in both Serbia and Montenegro when the occupiers were seeking out army stragglers and soldiers who had decided not to withdraw through Albania, and removing them to prison camps. At first these men hid in and around dwellings, but in the spring they took to the woods. In the general chaos of occupation and the change in authorities, bandit groups were also formed which not only robbed the native population but struck at the occupiers as well. The poverty and hunger throughout the country aggravated the situation.

It was probably at about the same time that certain patriots started to organise armed resistance. The first noticeable manifestations of this in the occupied military governorates in the Balkans took place in Montenegro, immediately after the introduction of occupation rule,[1] the first indication being the killing of a gendarme. But apart from this a number of people were working in secret on preparations for an uprising; one of the main plotters was Brigadier Radomir Vešović, who established links with many prominent individuals, amassed weapons and collected resources. Many distinguished figures believed that 'the abject people should not be exposed to inevitable defeat,' and that it would be wise to await the moment when Allied troops were closer 'for us to rise up too and strike the Austrians.' Vešović disagreed, evidently prompted by the desire to compensate for what had been lost by the act of capitulation, and through armed struggle to assure for Montenegro the best possible position when peace was finally restored. From this viewpoint it can be seen that he was opposed to unification with Serbia, a stand that was later to separate him from the armed resistance movement. Still, the occupiers learned of the uprising plan and in mid-July started to arrest prominent Montenegrins. Vešović too was apprehended, but he managed to escape by killing an officer of the guard that had arrested him.

This incident became known throughout Montenegro, and many other distinguished figures took to the woods and mountains to avoid capture. Groups (*chete*) of guerrillas (*comitadji*) thus assembled at a number of places. Captain Milinko Vlahović from Rovce and his brother Toško founded one such group of twenty men in the region of Kolašin, as did Jovan Radović, a teacher, and Miljan Drljević, a lawyer, both from Morača.[2] Having calculated that such a struggle was virtually impossible in Montenegro, Vlahović and his men set off for Serbia in September, intending to join the Russian forces in Romania. However, many *comitadji* groups remained in Montenegro, and from August 1916, when the occupation authorities set out after them, with the particular aim of capturing or killing Vešović, they fought on many occasions.[3] Such intermittent fighting continued throughout the war.

However, Vlahović and the men with him did not have to travel as far as Romania to take part in serious fighting. What the Germans called guerrilla warfare was already rife in Serbia,[4] since those unwilling to be reconciled to occupation had already taken up arms. The villages and woods were swarming with armed men, and infiltrators in the towns were spreading the message that the Serb state would rise again and encouraging their compatriots to keep their weapons. In the summer of 1916 in Brus, according to Austro-Hungarian documents, 'an organisation was discovered plotting a coup d'état.'[5] The plot was fomented by Sibin Jeličić, a prosperous citizen, whom the authorities accused of inciting the people to 'conceal weapons and explosives for a future uprising'. Jeličić and seven of his fellow-plotters were hanged. The authorities were also hard on the heels of another conspirator, the twenty-four-year-old Kosta Vojinović, a reservist second lieutenant in the Serbian army, who owing to wounds had not been able to withdraw with the army and had stayed with his father in Kosovska Mitrovica. In his diary Kosta Vojinović wrote: 'I have managed to convince the Serb people that Serbia is not lost; it will continue to exist, far larger in the future, and everyone must safeguard their weapons as we shall have great need of them later. I have convened prominent persons to secret places and explained that to them.'[6] There are indications that Vojinović had been in contact with Jeličić, but unlike Jeličić he managed to escape in time and seek refuge in the mountains, where he was soon joined by about fifty armed men. This can be considered the start of large-scale armed resistance in Serbia.

In the meantime, General von Remen's oppressive measures in the Belgrade Governorate in the summer of 1916 were pouring oil onto the flames, while Governor Kutinchev's acts in the Niš Governorate were causing great animosity. In addition, rumours were circulating through the Bulgarian occupation zone that the Bulgarians intended to mobilise Serbs into their army, and as a result many young Serbs took to the woods. On 2 September the German consul in Belgrade informed Berlin that the Serb population was 'drawing fresh hope' from Romania's entry into the war, adding that their eagerness could not be ignored since it was 'being expressed quite overtly'. The consul also noted that a certain Orthodox priest in the environs of Belgrade had been advocating resistance in his sermons and had consequently been hanged by the authorities.[7] Another priest, Dragoljub Glišić, had been put on trial for the same reason.[8] The greatest problems for the authorities seem to have been created in the district of Kragujevac. Reports from the occupation intelligence service noted that Romania's entry into the war had been received with 'great exhilaration' in that district, and had 'left a powerful impression' in Kragujevac itself, where 'the very same day a large number of Serb women, most of whom were in mourning, had gone out on to the streets and walked around carrying red umbrellas', something that had never happened before. Moreover, in all Serb homes 'candles were lit before icons of family patron saints.'[9]

It soon became clear that something was brewing in the environs of Kragujevac. More and more people, mainly military returnees, were gathering in the woods and forests, and although many had no weapons, some bore arms, even the occasional machine-gun.[10] The occupiers believed that such activity had been provoked by 'dangerous individual elements' who were inciting the people with reports that the Serbian and Romanian armies were closing in. On 11 September the Austro-Hungarian local occupation command sought reinforcements, and an entire regiment was sent from Belgrade. The German consul reported that 'an uprising near Kragujevac had been thwarted,' involving as many as 2,000 Serbs.[11] After the war, Kerchnawe wrote that the reports of Romania's declaration of war had led to 'the formation of armed groups and risings in the southern parts of the Kragujevac district'. The authorities sent a squadron of dragoons and three infantry battalions, but they were only able to find 'primitive and deserted peasant trenches on the edges of the forests'.[12] All the indications are that a spontaneous movement suddenly arose and equally suddenly vanished with the approach of large-scale enemy forces. Many men were later executed in a number of municipalities, and houses and property were burnt down.[13]

On 16 September the Austro-Hungarian consul in the Bulgarian Governorate centred in Niš wrote that 'Serb troops were arriving on the scene in various ways.'[14] The authorities also learned of armed guerrilla groups in the Mount Kopaonik area of the Austro-Hungarian Governorate, and some time in September a gendarmerie detachment heading into Gomirje encountered Kosta Vojinović's group, and fighting ensued. Vojinović's men withdrew, it was reported, 'with losses on both sides'.[15] Although there was no organised, systematic uprising, the mood of the people was ripe for rebellion. The Austro-Hungarian consul in Niš described their frame of mind when he said that 'in their hallucinations they see liberating Serb troops emerging over the horizon, not only from Romania.'[16]

Without government knowledge the Serbian supreme command tried to prepare for an uprising in the Morava valley in late September 1916, but it was actually to take place somewhat later. To that end Lieutenant Kosta Milovanović-Pećanac was sent by plane from the Salonika front to the village of Mehane southwest of Niš, where he immediately contacted *comitadji* guerrilla groups, many of whom had already rallied.[17] Pećanac's assignment was limited in scope. The logics of the resistance movement required constant armed opposition to the enemy as long as occupation continued, which presupposed the eventuality of an uprising whenever a favourable moment occurred. But Pećanac's arrival was actually most closely aimed at ensuring support for an intended Allied offensive from the Salonika front. He had written orders restricting his assignment to the organisation of activity only when it was 'clear that the Bulgarians were withdrawing'. He was charged first with locating 'our conscripts' in the district of Toplica and the valley of the Južna Morava river, and then with 'notifying them of our impending arrival' and organising them 'for Chetnik action'. Thus his mission was only to disseminate information that help was on the way. He also had to ensure that the Bulgarian occupation authorities should learn nothing of his existence, to prevent them from taking 'repressive measures against the population'. Pećanac was also given the task of destroying the railway line and bridges 'to paralyse enemy transport.'[18]

Therefore the aim of Kosta Pećanac's mission was not to organise an uprising; he was only to contact conscripts and concentrate diversionary activity on lines of communications, exclusively in the area under Bulgarian occupation and within the strip of territory containing the railway. Moreover, any activity was to depend totally on the success of the Allied offensive, which meant that nothing should be done until Serb troops entered Skopje. Although his mission was not to inflame the population's urge to resist, or to promote the incipient armed resistance, his arrival in fact had that effect. The news that an officer of the army in exile had arrived, tasked with making preparations for the country's imminent liberation, in itself had the effect of strengthening fighting morale. Pećanac even seems to have become a leading figure for the resistance, to judge by his actions and his achievements in the last months of 1916; he did raise morale to a certain extent, probably because he brought news of the impending arrival of the Serbian army from the south. He did in fact order Kosta Vojinović to attack an Austro-Hungarian supply train, and the two of them signed a proclamation to the people calling for a 'people's uprising': 'after a year of slavery the moment has come for liberation from the German-Bulgarian yoke, as our valiant warriors are heading towards us.'[19] This proclamation had doubtlessly been drafted in preparation for the time when the Serbian supreme command planned that an uprising should take place, but it was distributed in advance to guerrilla group leaders who immediately made it known among the population.

So it is no wonder that in the period from October 1916 to February 1917 Serbs fought battle after battle with the occupying forces in the valley of the Južna Morava, on Mount Kopaonik and in Kosovo. There was also fighting in other parts of Serbia, without any intervention by Pećanac or Vojinović. An Austro-Hungarian report from January 1917 summed up this phase of armed resistance:

> During the autumn of last year, two regions where banditry and guerrilla warfare were rife were perceived in the military administration territory in Serbia. While banditry and the burning of peasants' houses occurred in the district of Užice, guerrilla warfare in the border areas of the Kruševac and Kuršumlija districts (the latter within the Bulgarian administration zone) has assumed the form of a systematically organised insurrectionist movement.[20]

A later Bulgarian report described the situation more vaguely:

> In that period, the movement assumed the forms…of a movement with political and military objectives. Typical of that period was propaganda by word of mouth, and through terror and influence. It was also a period when uprising was organised throughout the entire region.… Spirits were noticeably rising, and hopes growing.… Large-scale, organised groups of men appeared led by former Serb officers, teachers and priests, as did some audacious agitators, and there were skirmishes between troops and Serb guerrillas.[21]

The fighting spirit against the enemy was far greater on Mount Kopaonik than elsewhere. Both Kosta Vojinović and Kosta Pećanac had set up their headquarters there, as had many other guerrilla leaders. Captain Vlahović's group of fighters had arrived there on their way from Montenegro to Romania, and had not moved on; Milan Dečanski, a former *comitadji*, arrived from Banat, and Ramadan Nezirović, an Albanian from Priština, joined them. But rivalry soon arose between Kosta Vojinović and Kosta Pećanac, although Vojinović recognised Pećanac's seniority and Pećanac recognised Vojinović as a close second in seniority. But while Pećanac's leadership had come from the orders and authority of the supreme command, Vojinović had developed his qualities as a leader naturally without outside influence, within the movement itself. Hence he wanted immediate action, and to spread fear and agitation among the enemy. However, Pećanac had been ordered to wait until preparations were complete, so while he was preparing for future action, Vojinović was urging unremitting struggle and was at the forefront setting a personal example. In such a situation a degree of conflict was inevitable.[22]

In the meantime increased caution was being forced on the occupying troops. On 15 December 1916 a nine-man patrol of Austro-Hungarian gendarmes was attacked near Blaževo, and only one man escaped with his life.[23] The Austro-Hungarian authorities connected the incident to the disappearance of a four-man patrol in mid-November, and in cooperation with Bulgarian forces organised the largest-ever anti-guerrilla campaign that lasted from 30 December 1916 to 4 January 1917. Houses and woods were searched, weapons confiscated, many citizens were arrested and interrogated, over fifty houses were burnt to the ground, and in Brus and elsewhere about thirty men thought or merely suspected of being *comitadji* were executed on the spot. The bodies of twelve gendarmes killed in November and December were unearthed. Kosta Vojinović and his insurrectionists were not found, but the authorities were satisfied, considering: 'We can certainly hope, given the severity of the punishments meted out, that peace has been restored to the area of Blaževo for a long time. Therefore no special measures against guerrillas are needed here for the present.'

But the authorities soon realised that 'young men were taking refuge in the mountains and the woods'.[24] Consequently, since the campaign over the New Year period the 'little war' (*Klein Krieg*) on the territory of occupied Serbia had entered a phase that was to last for nearly two years of brutal and cruel fighting. Kosta Pećanac tried to participate as little as possible, while Kosta Vojinović devoted his life to it. In order to present their fight against the guerrillas as morally justifiable and therefore make it easier, while at the same time frightening the population and members of the guerrilla groups alike, the occupiers simply proclaimed the guerrilla combatants to be bandits. Under the headline 'Serb Banditry', the *Beogradske Novosti* of 13 February 1917 reported that the authorities had carried out a campaign against 'gangs of bandits' that had been a total success. Having read the article, the German consul in Belgrade reported to his superiors in Berlin: 'The entire Chetnik (guerrilla) movement has been presented as one of banditry, and there has been no mention whatever of political machinations.'[25]

Large-scale campaigns and arrests followed, in the course of which reliable intelligence about Chetnik activity was obtained. On 11 January 1917 the commander of the Mitrovica district informed Governor von Remen: 'From the statements of those captured we have the impression that what is involved is a large-scale rebel movement.'[26] Twenty-four Albanian gendarmes were sent to the Mitrovica district to track down and apprehend rebel leaders. Near Slatina they encountered a group of Serb guerrillas and discovered the proclamation of October 1916 by Pećanac and Vojinović in the village home of one of their prisoners. This development seemed so important that on 15 January 1917 the German consul telegraphed the German Chancellor:

> The entire movement seems to have been organised from Bitola [which the Entente had been holding since November 1916]. This is proved by letters that have been discovered.... The leaders are four former Serb officers each with around 150 men as a standing force. Partly through coercion they have started recruiting in the villages, sometimes even taking boys under the age of sixteen. After recruitment they are trained in groups, and then sent away with orders to gather at specific locations at the start of the uprising. The number of men and boys assembled and trained in this way is estimated at between 400 and 600. Action seems to be planned for next spring.... A reliable agent of mine...believes that we should reckon with the population attempting an uprising.[27]

The commander at Kosovska Mitrovica also sounded the alarm in a report dated 11 January: 'If we do not manage to stifle attempts at an uprising now, we will have to reckon with an incomparably more powerful *comitadji* movement in the spring.'[28] The repressive measures were harshest in the district of Kosovska Mitrovica. Around 100 suspects were detained, and in Kosovska Mitrovica in early February forty-seven men were accused of being *comitadji* 'who had infiltrated from Blaževo'. Twenty-nine of them were sentenced to death and eleven to terms of imprisonment 'because they were under twenty years of age', while seven were submitted to 'regular judicial procedures'. Of the twenty-nine men sentenced to death, thirteen had their sentences commuted immediately and three just before execution was due to take place, and thirteen were actually executed. The sentences commuted were to terms of between five and twenty years' imprisonment.[29]

Uprising

Despite the occupiers' attempts at suppression, the areas of Toplica, the Južna Morava valley and Kopaonik remained centres of rebel activity. Because of Bulgaria's denationalisation policy and its brutal and slipshod administration, the zone under its occupation was more unstable than the Austro-Hungarian zone. The activities of the population in February 1917 were slipping out of the control of the Bulgarian administration authorities and even of the *comitadji* leaders. Reports that the Bulgarians intended to recruit Serbs into their army proved true, and recruitment commissions arrived to register conscripts. The potential conscripts, appalled at the idea of being recruited into a foreign army, took to the hills and the woods *en masse*, joining the many who had already taken refuge there. Faced with such a situation, the authorities put pressure on the families involved in order to force the fugitives to return and register with the conscription commissions. Tensions on both sides reached fever pitch.

Seeing how matters were progressing, guerrilla leaders met secretly near the village of Obilić near Leskovac on 21 February 1917, their deliberations lasting for two days.[30] There were around 300 *comitadji* there, including prominent leaders such as Kosta Pećanac, Kosta Vojinović and Milinko Vlahović, but once again there were disagreements and a vote had to be taken on whether to launch an uprising or not. Pećanac and his adjutant Miljan Drljević were 'against', and everyone else was 'for'. It was also decided that the uprising should start in the first half of March, with the stipulation that they should wait for an order from Kosta Pećanac. A proclamation was also prepared calling for a 'general uprising'. 'Military recruits, both with and without weapons', should answer the call, those too old or unfit to bear arms should maintain order within insurrectionist territory, and the actual day and place of the general uprising and place would be determined when the time was ripe.

However, when the Serb military and guerrilla leaders set off to carry out their assigned tasks on 22 February, they found themselves in the midst of an uprising that had begun without them. How this happened remains unclear,[31] but it is certain that when Kosta Vojinović declared an uprising in Kuršumlija on 28 February, it was already well under way. Some men probably started shooting to protect themselves and their families, while elsewhere Bulgarian gendarmes shot first to intimidate or punish the population. Pećanac later complained that 'sporadic fighting with the enemy had begun'[32] without any order from him on 23 February. Shooting took place in several places in Toplica on that day, and in numerous locations the next day armed citizens, or organised *comitadji*, simply encountered Bulgarian patrols or units, and whoever was able to fire the first shot did so. Total chaos descended, and no one at first had any idea that they were in the midst of a large-scale uprising. An inspection in Niš on 24 February reported 'armed Serb guerrillas' in the regions of Prokuplje, Kuršumlija and Lebane southwest of Niš and Leskovac, who were evidently 'linked to an organisation' in the Austro-Hungarian Governorate.[33] On 25 February the Bulgarian governor in Niš informed his counterpart in Belgrade that agitation was growing visibly in the Prokuplje-Kuršumlija-Lebane sector and was 'swaying the peasant population in a hostile sense against our authorities'; there had recently been cases of 'insubordination on the part of the population'. Kutinchev indicated 'impending rigorous moves to destroy the guerrilla groups', and called on the Austro-Hungarian authorities to prevent crossings into Bulgarian-administered territory by deploying more frontier forces.[34] However, the Austro-Hungarian military attaché in Sofia reported that 'the activities of armed Serb guerrillas in the Prokuplje-Kuršumlija-Lebane area' had assumed 'frightening proportions', and 'a virtual uprising' was involved.

Comitadji and guerrilla group leaders became involved in the uprising—some intentionally while others were simply dragged in. The guerrilla leader Milinko Vlahović had ordered that 'everyone should be armed and ready' for an uprising that was to start on 11 March. However, early in the morning of 24 February his company unexpectedly encountered a strong Bulgarian infantry unit and in the ensuing fight inflicted serious losses on it. It was reported in the Belgrade Governorate that the Bulgarian infantry had been 'assailed by several hundred *comitadji*' and after a 'tough and bloody clash' had been put to flight with the loss of twenty men.[35] Vlahović, for his part, informed Pećanac that on 24 February he had caught up with a Bulgarian unit and 'killed around twenty of them'.[36] Other spontaneous clashes occurred in that day, but it seems that Milinko Vlahović won the first major victory in an uprising he did not even know was happening; he only joined battle that day routinely as a *comitadji*.

On 24 February a Bulgarian document came into the hands of Pećanac stating that, because of the frantic agitation recruitment had caused among the population, the Niš Governorate was ordering a temporary halt to it. He and Vojinović consequently agreed to cease hostilities for a few days. They then ordered the 'regional *comitadji* units' to pacify the situation,[37] but no one would heed them. The previous night around fifteen *comitadji*, under two previously less-known leaders, had clashed with a Bulgarian patrol, and given the universal sense of urgency felt by the population, this had aroused the whole area around Kuršumlija. Consequently these two leaders were suddenly joined by a large number of men who, in pursuit of a Bulgarian patrol, entered Kuršumlija itself and liberated it on 26 February. When Vojinović arrived there on the 28th, he found the town already in the hands of insurrectionists, and he helped to crush the last vestiges of resistance by the Albanian gendarmerie within the Bulgarian units. Without consulting Pećanac, he then ordered the entire population of Toplica to rise in a general insurrection,[38] and while all the guerrilla and *comitadji* leaders hastened to join the uprising, Kosta Pećanac was doing his atmost to prevent it.[39] But he himself was caught up in the tide of events: while heading for Kuršumlija, he clashed with and crushed two Bulgarian units, one on 28 February and the other on 1 March, and on his arrival in Kuršumlija on 1 March he was greeted as commander of the liberation movement. However, he told the population that the uprising was premature and warned that the momentary hour of freedom could well bode ill for the future. Yet even Pećanac realised there could be no going back. Thus the *comitadji* leaders became involved in the uprising without having been its immediate instigators, but they were virtually preordained to be its leaders thanks to their prestige and fighting ability, and because their *comitadji* units were the best combatants. Despite this, they still to some extent lagged behind initiatives put forward by the eager population. Pećanac and Vojinović received a written message from the leaders of six newly-formed units informing them that it had been decided at some kind of 'council of war' to attack Prokuplje, starting at dawn the next day.[40]

Meanwhile the occupying forces had finally started to grasp what was actually happening. On 3 March the Austro-Hungarian vice-consul in Kosovska Mitrovica reported: 'There are many signs that this is a large-scale, organised uprising against Bulgarian oppression.'[41] The German consul in Belgrade condensed the reports gathered up to 11 March, as follows: 'What is involved is a people's uprising in which all who can bear arms are participating, even old men and children, while the women are in charge of supplies.'[42] Estimates of the number of participants varied between 4,000 and 15,000. Many people took part who did not actually fight, but it is certain that there were around 4,000 actual combatants, the *comitadji* forming the strike force.

When the insurrectionists were less than 10 km. from Niš, the Bulgarian governor and the German commander of the 11th military-railway inspection called urgently for reinforcements. At two minutes to midnight on 3 March the Austro-Hungarian liaison officer at the Bulgarian supreme command telegraphed his general staff: 'Of the greatest urgency! The Bulgarian chief of general staff has announced that the situation around Niš is extremely grave. Insurgent Serbs are 9 km. from Niš.'[43] The following day the governor general in Belgrade stated that, according to intelligence obtained, the situation in the insurrectionist area southwest of Niš was 'highly dangerous'.[44] General von Remen ordered the commander of the forces deployed around Blace to march towards Prokuplje to relieve the insurrectionists' pressure on the Bulgarians'[45] but this produced no results. On 3 March an Austro-Hungarian reconnaissance patrol was destroyed, and then Vojinović's units attacked the main body of the Austro-Hungarian forces. Fighting was fierce and both sides suffered losses, but finally the Austro-Hungarians were forced to withdraw, and on 7 March the insurrectionists took Blace, driving the enemy across the Rasina river.[46]

The German consul in Belgrade described the extent of liberated territory, 'which the insurrectionists consider is still to be expanded', as

[stretching] basically to near the Morava in the east (which they have, however, already crossed both to the north and the south of Niš), to the Jastrebac mountain range in the north (including the most northerly slopes), to the Ibar valley in the west and to the line running approximately from Slatina on the Ibar (18 km. north of Mitrovica) to Vranje. To the east of the Morava insurrectionists have appeared in Vlasotince, east of Leskovac, in Knjaževac on the Timok, in Sokobanja and in Matejevac, not far from Niš, which is a sign that the population in the old Serb regions is also uneasy.[47]

Kuršumlija and Prokuplje were the centres of liberated territory, but other regions were liberated in the areas of Vlasotince and Sokobanja. Much of the population had taken to the woods, and the guerrilla units consisted mainly of local inhabitants.

In the meantime the enemy had assembled the dispersed units of the Morava military inspection district and brought in fighting troops from the Romanian, Italian and Salonika fronts. By 7 March the Bulgarians had concentrated fifteen-and-a-half battalions with twenty-two machine-guns and twenty-eight cannon.[48] Kutinchev had been replaced by Colonel Protogerov, a former Bulgarian *comitadji* leader, who had fought a guerrilla campaign in Macedonia. For his part General von Remen was assembling all the forces he could muster without endangering his own Governorate, and had requested that the Austro-Hungarian supreme command should send him as much assistance as possible. Out of a total of sixteen pursuit units, he sent twelve into the sector south of Kruševac, as well as a special mountain detachment. He further formed a new gendarmerie battalion comprising cadets at a field gendarmerie school in Belgrade and gendarmes from all districts. He also created a battalion for the protection of the railway lines in the Governorate, and sent this with the gendarmerie battalion to the borders of the areas held by the insurrectionists. The Austro-Hungarian supreme command allocated two battalions of the 102nd Infantry Regiment together with a hill battery from the Socha front, the 3rd border battalion, a Landsturm battalion, an armoured train and a gendarmerie battalion from Bosnia. With the exception of the Landsturm battalion, which remained inside the zone occupied by the Austro-Hungarians to safeguard communications, all these units were sent swiftly to Serbia towards liberated territory. The 102nd Infantry Regiment arrived in Kruševac on 10 March, and the armoured train the same day. Thus the concentration of Austro-Hungarian troops was complete.

At the time of the growing uprising, the Germans had a battalion of recruits and a battery near Vranje that had already been sent into action at the beginning of March. However, they were quickly brought to a halt, probably because they encountered fierce resistance; moreover, they could see Bulgarians withdrawing on all sides.[49] Hearing of the uprising, the German army command on the Salonika front, which was located in Skopje, sent a battalion quickly from the battlefront to the insurrectionist area. The battalion was first stationed in Niš and then probably had the task of securing the railway line. On 4 March the Austro-Hungarian military attaché in Sofia reported: 'This morning, the situation has improved because two German battalions are already on the spot.'[50] In addition another German company, which happened to be in Belgrade en route elsewhere, was tasked with accompanying railway transports between Smederevo and Niš.

Available data tell us that the three enemy armies, with the intention of crushing the uprising, possibly deployed around 30,000 men, of whom 25,000 to 26,000 were involved in operations. The Bulgarians began an attack on 8 March with five-and-a-half battalions, with strong artillery and air support. Albanian detachments in the service of the Bulgarians also took part. The insurrectionists were thus enclosed within a ring of steel. According to Kosta Pećanac, they numbered around 13,000 men armed with guns and mere cold steel, with perhaps eight machine-guns in working order. They had no cannon and insufficient ammunition; they were exhausted after three weeks of fighting; and no help was expected from any quarter.[51] The Austro-Hungarian attack started on 12 March from the Dubci-Zlatari sector. Faced with numerically far superior Bulgarian forces from the direction of Niš, Pećanac started to withdraw without a fight, acting as if his only wish was to save as many of his fighters as possible.[52] He was actually performing an unexpected manoeuvre by allowing the Bulgarians to advance and then fighting and defeating the Albanians to the south. He then set off for Prokuplje to order a halt to the resistance. He himself said that he ordered the insurrectionists and *comitadji* to 'break through the enemy front secretly, under cover of darkness, and then re-form in groups of about ten at the rear of the enemy.' They were then to 'hide in the greatest secrecy until they received further orders' near their villages. Contrary to Pećanac's orders, the two Vlahović brothers joined battle and withdrew step by step. When they could no longer maintain a front, they assumed the tactic of surprise guerrilla attacks with the remnants of their companies.[53]

But the Austro-Hungarian troops were facing Kosta Vojinović's detachments, whose orders were totally different from those given by Pećanac. 'Hold the positions around Blace even if you die in the attempt. Resist. Do not withdraw…'[54] After the war Pećanac paid tribute to his rival: 'Vojinović was at that time waging a desperate battle with the Austrians at the Jankova gorge, on Mount Kopaonik, and in Brus.' And the greatest victory of the entire uprising was won during Vojinović's fierce defensive operation. His orders and reports of 14 March speak for themselves: 'My *comitadji* companies around Brus are striking the enemy at every step; their cannon and machine-guns are of no help to them. Forward, forward in the name of God. You have nothing to fear!' That same day Pećanac reported: 'The enemy has been totally defeated on Mramor; they fell like flies. There were even officers.' On 18 March the German consul reported: 'A Serb company, which the Austro-Hungarian commander had believed to be in front of him, suddenly emerged at his rear, killing one officer and fifty-three soldiers, with 120 reported missing.'[55]

Military reports state that on 14 March an Austro-Hungarian detachment of some 630 men, which had been reinforced with two cannon and around 170 men, had suffered the loss of two officers and fifty soldiers killed, sixteen wounded, 126 missing and twenty-two sick. Moreover the detachment was withdrew in terror, and whole supply train consisting of twenty men, one doctor and twenty horses fell into insurrectionist hands. As of 14 March this was the most unsuccessful of the battles fought against Kosta Vojinović's guerrillas.[56]

According to figures issued later by Kerchnawe, the Austro-Hungarian forces lost three officers and seventy-eight men, while forty-eight were wounded and fifty-four reported missing (Kerchnawe insisted that they be counted among the dead).[57] A report dated 1 April 1917 stated that, according to available figures, Austro-Hungarian troops had lost three officers and seventy soldiers, had 120 other casualties and had fifty persons reported missing.[58] Given the losses suffered in the battle on 14 March and other fighting, that number could be even higher. Bulgarian losses are not known.

While Vojinović was attacking enthusiastically, Pećanac was warning his fighters to hide out in the woods and mountains. Vlahović was reaching the limit of his strength; there was no ammunition for those who wanted to fight. Consequently the Bulgarian troops took Prokuplje on 14 March, and the Austro-Hungarian 102nd Regiment entered Kuršumlija on 16 March. Fighting continued, but there were fewer and less fierce clashes. It was only on 24 March that the Austro-Hungarian command decided the uprising had finally been suppressed and ordered its troops out of the Bulgarian occupation zone. On 25 March the Bulgarian command declared an end to operations.

The occupation authorities seem to have been very successful in concealing what was happening, and it was not until the uprising had been stifled that the first sketchy reports reached Allied commands. However it was notable that in early March the Serbian legation in The Hague made an appeal to the world speaking of the terror being perpetrated in occupied Serbia. Although there was mention of the killings and internment taking place there, nothing was mentioned of the uprising. Mention was also made of the execution of Sibin Jeličić, nine months previously—so perhaps the Serbian government had learnt something of what was happening and was trying to heighten awareness by using the facts it had at its disposal.[59]

The insurrectionists were not supported, at least not in a planned way, in other parts of occupied Serbia, except in the eastern districts of Vlasotince, Sokobanja, Knjaževac and Zaječar, and there was no general uprising there. The population in Niš regarded the events with great sympathy, but the Bulgarians precluded active support by interning about fifty of the town's most prominent citizens and then bringing in powerful reinforcements. Little was known in Belgrade about developments in the south of the country, but the situation in the Austro-Hungarian Governorate could hardly be described as peaceful. A gendarmerie patrol engaged a group of Serb guerrillas in Mačva; the gendarmerie in Kruševac clashed with a guerrilla leader, who managed to escape into the woods; the authorities performing pre-emptive searches in the district of Kragujevac discovered a large cache of weapons and executed thirty men on the spot.[60] There was also considerable activity around the small town of Rekovac.[61]

The day after the start of the counterattack, the Bulgarian Prime Minister Vasil Radoslavov explained to Otto Count Czernin that the reason for the uprising had been Bulgarian leniency, and that henceforth there would be no dilemma over whether the 'ruthless obliteration of the Serb element' was justified. On 9 March Czernin informed his foreign minister, who was also his brother, that there had actually been no 'leniency' towards Serbs, adding that bloodshed would certainly follow 'the like of which has not been seen in our times'. He underlined in his report of 10 March that the Serb uprising was 'certainly a consequence not of any leniency on the part of the Bulgarian regime, but rather of Bulgarian carelessness and recklessness'.[62]

Bulgarian reprisals were merciless. They started in the areas around the railway lines, where no uprising had actually taken place. The troops burned down villages, interned men and forced women and children out of their homes. As they entered insurrectionist areas, their acts of brutality multiplied. On the second day of the offensive, the Austro-Hungarian consul in Niš reported: 'The Bulgarians are destroying everywhere in insurrectionist territory.' On 28 March Baron Kun reported: 'According to the latest reports, many insurrectionists have died.'[63]

It seems clear that the occupying troops did not wish to take prisoners. A report tells us that a certain Major Farkas captured about 100 insurrectionists and peasants and executed them, claiming that all were *comitadji*. An Austro-Hungarian report noted: 'Of the insurrectionists, who according to the latest estimates could have numbered between 5,000 and 6,000, barely half have survived. Besides those who fell in battle, our troops have executed 600 of them, and the Bulgarians have certainly executed twice that number.' Austro-Hungarian reports from the summer of 1917 mention the figure of 20,000 people killed, which is also the number established by an international commission set up after the war. Although the occupying forces suppressed the uprising, they did little to break the backbone of resistance.

According to Kosta Pećanac, nearly 2,600 fighters remained hidden in the mountains and woods, including all the leaders of the armed struggle.[64] Baron Kun knew this and had complained on 21 March: 'We have not yet managed to capture or kill one single guerrilla leader.' On the day when operations were halted he felt the same:

> It is true that, as a result of military operations in the insurrectionist region, it can be claimed that the uprising has been suppressed. However, the burning of villages and the capture and execution of hundreds of *comitadji* … cannot really be considered a satisfactory result, as all the rebel leaders,

such as Kosta Vojinović, Kosta Pećanac and Vlahović, have succeeded in evading us and finding shelter.⁶⁵

It had, in fact, been a spontaneous people's uprising that had not been directly provoked by *comitadji* groups. Furthermore, it was the only uprising against enemy occupation during the whole of the First World War.⁶⁶

The uprising had been suppressed, but there was no peace in the hilly terrain of the insurrectionist region. The occupying forces, momentarily victorious, continued to create havoc in the mountains, shooting people and burning villages.⁶⁷ A report from the Austro-Hungarian Governorate issued on 30 March describes the state of affairs in the wake of the uprising: 'Shooting between patrols and individual *comitadji* are daily occurrences. We have burnt down several villages.' The commander of a gendarmerie battalion reported: 'Kosta Vojinović and experienced *comitadji* will not surrender.' Consequently, the Bulgarian and Austro-Hungarian troops were still having to track down *comitadji* groups. However, the occupation authorities were also resorting to another method. On 28 March Colonel Protogerov declared an 'amnesty', and on 29 March General von Remen did the same. The two declarations, evidently synchronised, promised that those who surrendered by 10 April, with or without weapons, would not be executed but only interned. The deadline was later extended to 20 April, but the result was basically the same as when the uprising was suppressed, because the men who surrendered were just ordinary insurrectionists, not the more prominent *comitadji*, guerrilla and military leaders.

The collapse of the uprising inevitably led to serious crises within the resistance movement. Demoralisation took many forms. Profound uncertainty reigned in the region that had suffered the true horror of merciless reprisals. As leading *comitadji* had succeeded in avoiding reprisals, and had even fled to safety, the population started to feel disenchantment and even hostility towards them. Never before had the occupiers obtained so much intelligence on the *comitadji* and their movements as they did during April 1917. Some prominent peasants even joined in the hunt for them. Chaos and disorder emerged among the *comitadji*, and discipline, which had always been a problem, ceased to exist.

Detachments split up into companies, and companies into larger and smaller groups. Having lost the support of the population, the *comitadji* found obtaining refuge and food increasingly difficult. It had been a matter of principle (not always respected) that the guerrillas should pay for the food they obtained from peasants, but that code of honour disappeared almost completely. For this there were various reasons: some of the scattered guerrilla groups had no money; some had money but did not wish to pay; and some peasants, terrified of the occupying forces, did not want to sell food to the *comitadji*. Whatever the reasons, the guerrilla and *comitadji* groups started stealing from the population. The guerrillas then reacted to the population's weakening support by punishing them; without consulting their military leaders, they meted out their own peremptory justice, sometimes very harsh. The guerrilla leaders also started to quarrel among themselves, exchanging threats and even resorting to killing. What is more, the lives of those guerrilla leaders who had managed to keep some money were threatened both by their own men and by the population.

Pećanac, Vlahović and Radović hid during that period, but Vojinović absolutely refused to do so.[68] All the hue and cry in April was mainly about him and his company of men. Whenever he tried to find some respite, he would find himself surrounded by Bulgarian and Austro-Hungarian pursuers. His previously steadfast guerrilla leaders started to defy him, and the well-concealed Pećanac gave him the first sign that he was alive with a stream of insults and threats of punishment for supposed banditry. It was then rumoured that Pećanac had decided Vojinović should be killed. But the weather at that time was bad, with blizzards blowing on Mount Kopaonik. At the same time the enemy was also trying, by offering favourable conditions, to induce Vojinović to surrender,[69] but Vojinović resisted the offers and managed to keep a strong group of men around him at all times; they successfully withstood enemy pursuit, joining battle and then rapidly disengaging. He responded to Pećanac's insults in kind, and continued to endure the icy, wintry conditions. One could say that the crisis in the resistance movement manifested itself as Kosta Vojinović's personal drama, but his sheer persistence showed that the movement could not be crushed. As Kerchnawe wrote, Vojinović 'kept the occupying troops on their toes for a long time with his small groups of men.'[70]

At the same time, a certain Vojin Marjanović was extremely active in the Austro-Hungarian zone of occupation, operating with a group of about twenty men in the south-western part of the Austro-Hungarian Governorate. While search parties were hunting Vojinović, Marjanović and his men ambushed the pursuers, and on at least one occasion bore the brunt of an attack intended for Vojinović and his guerrillas. As the snow melted and the weather improved with the onset of spring, the forests and hills in the insurrectionist regions of both governorates came alive again. Towards the end of April Kosta Pećanac unexpectedly emerged again.[71] He was surprised at the high level of morale among the people of the southern regions, and more than 1,200 fighters, including several guerrilla leaders from the time of the uprising, responded to his call to gather at a specified rendezvous. Probably following the axiom that attack is the best form of defence, Pećanac selected a few hundred men on foot and around 100 men with horses and launched a surprise attack to the south. At dawn on 13 May he attacked the railway station at Ristovac, inflicting considerable casualties on the Bulgarians and Germans stationed there. He also destroyed an iron bridge over the Južna Morava, thus halting transport for some days on that important strategic line to the Salonika front.[72] A strong Bulgarian and German party set off in hot pursuit, and air support was also called in. Pećanac could not go unnoticed this time, and his detachment clashed with German units reinforced by Bulgarian troops. However, the main body of the *comitadji* forces managed to escape, but with the loss of over seventy men.

Kosta Pećanac then reduced his detachment to around 130 of his best fighters. Evidently using the tactic of surprise attack, they set off to the east,[73] and entered Bulgaria unnoticed. On 15 May, under the slogan 'fight fire with fire', he attacked Bosiljgrad, a border town then in Bulgaria. He set the town ablaze (reports recorded 100 houses being burnt and a large number damaged), and then returned to Serbia leaving in his wake the smoke of burnt dwellings and corpses. The Bulgarian army set off after him but to no avail. Pećanac had taken with him a thirteen-year-old Bulgarian boy, but soon released him with the message that Serbs 'do not kill Bulgarian children, as Bulgarians do Serb children, but every Bulgarian soldier and public functionary will be killed.' The impression this incident made on the Bulgarians is revealed by one of their military documents: 'There is absolutely nothing to guarantee that something similar will not happen again in a few days.' An Austro-Hungarian source described the great insecurity in the Bosiljgrad region, despite the fact that Ćustendil, the site of the Bulgarian supreme command, was only about 40 km. away. A member of the official Bulgarian commission that visited Bosiljgrad to investigate this incident told an Austro-Hungarian colonel that 'Serbs are doing [this] out of desperation, because as a rule the Bulgarian authorities forcibly deprive them of their money, their clothes, their linen, their livestock etc.'[74]

The greener the woods and the warmer the weather, the denser became the network of guerrillas. All the leaders had called on their men, and despite lingering animosity between Pećanac and Vojinović mutual links had been restored. The Bulgarians were then writing what their allies from the neighbouring governorate had concluded back in late March: 'None of their prominent leaders or organisers has yet been captured.' The following are excerpts from the occupiers' reports: 'peace has not been established in totality in the Bulgarian region on either side of the [Južna] Morava' (13 May 1917); '[there is] a renewal of the uprising in the Bulgarian occupation zone in Serbia' (20 May); 'the insurrectionist movement in the Bulgarian occupation zone has revived [but] compared with the movement in March, which was organised, we are today faced with scattered manoeuvre groups' (23 May); 'the entire current situation shows that one can expect the eruption of a new uprising' (30 May).[75] Nor was there peace beyond the Mount Kopaonik-Toplica sector. Major and minor incidents occurred throughout the northwestern district of Šabac; the gendarmerie was compelled to take up arms sixteen times and to kill six men in July 1917.[76] There was also fighting east of the Morava. Occupiers' documents for July stated that 'gangs mainly of bandits are operating in the districts of Negotin, Požarevac, Zaječar and Ćuprija and in areas of the Niš district.' It was noted that the second half of July had seen their number increase. It was evident by then that they had 'acquired a marked revolutionary character'.[77]

The coming of spring also saw a build-up of the 'Little War' in Montenegro, where new groups of guerrilla combatants (*comitadji*) had sprung up in several places.[78] Among them were Russians who had escaped from imprisonment, and as time passed they included more deserters from the Austro-Hungarian army. Attempts were made to establish links with the *comitadji* in the regions of Mount Kopaonik, Toplica and Jablanica. One group of *comitadji* managed to reach Captain Milinko Vlahović on Mount Jastrebac. It returned to Montenegro with a message from Vlahović that guerrilla groups should be formed and then await the Allied offensive on the Salonika front. *Comitadji* from Serbia also sought contact with their fellow fighters in Montenegro; a group leader arrived in Montenegro in the late autumn of 1917 with orders from Kosta Pećanac that a *comitadji* movement should be organised. Meanwhile guerrilla warfare had of its own accord become widespread in Montenegro. Fighting was becoming more intense and bloody.

In the effort to prevent the spread of armed resistance, the occupation authorities tried to induce prominent figures to come over to their side. In September 1917 the Austro-Hungarian governor of Montenegro released General Janko Vukotić from internment, in the knowledge that he opposed the *comitadji* struggle and the hope that he would therefore work to halt the guerrilla movement in line with his own convictions. But Vukotić did not wish to serve the occupation authorities, and refused to take any side after being released from internment. However, with Brigadier Radomir Vešović it was a different matter altogether. When the Austro-Hungarian authorities did not succeed in neutralising him, they started sending him messages urging him to surrender, with the assurance that his life would be spared. Vešović had not actually participated in *comitadji* operations, although he had gone into hiding with different guerrilla groups. But it seems that he had tired of such a life, and he decided to accept the offer and on 1 January 1918 surrendered. He then undertook to campaign for a halt to *comitadji* warfare, in line with the wishes of the governor of Montenegro.

Vešović had previously wished to become involved in a rising to ensure that Montenegro would have a strong position *vis-à-vis* Serbia, while the movement spreading through Montenegro was actually aimed at unification.[79] Many guerrilla leaders, such as Obren Božović, were engaged in active operations and at the same time campaigning for unification and exalting Serbia's perseverance in the war. The Austro-Hungarian authorities were well aware of that tendency, and General Conrad wrote that the *comitadji* were fighting in the 'hope of a Greater Serbian state'. For that reason Vešović could not enjoy any great prestige among the population, and his services to the occupation forces only served to make him lose what remained of his reputation. Seeing he was of no use to them, the occupation authorities finally interned him near Graz.

The more fighting took place in occupied Serbia and Montenegro, the more the enemy hunted down the guerrillas: they exerted themselves to the utmost to locate the spots where they rested, determine their strength in numbers, identify their leaders, learn details of their methods, step up propaganda and expand their network of informers. They also regrouped their forces and created special units.[80] Consequently in the summer of 1917, drawing on their rich experience of previous guerrilla warfare throughout the Ottoman Empire, the Bulgarians introduced a significant innovation, by forming a number of *protivchete* (literally anti-*chete*—anti-guerrilla groups). The instructions for the organisation and activity of these detachments included the following: 'The tactics of *protivchete* are the same as those of *comitadji*'; '*protivchete* have the task of pursuing a specific group of *comitadji* for days, weeks and months until they destroy it … this principle has the force of law'; 'the strongest weapon of *protivchete* is surprise, and their greatest force lies in initiative'; 'it is important that the *protivchete* should conceal their movements'; 'each *protivchete* numbers between fifteen and twenty men.' The equipment of each *protivchete* member comprised a rifle with 100 rounds, a grenade and a small bandage kit, while food and overcoats were carried by horses. In the autumn of 1917 the Belgrade Governorate began to follow the Bulgarian example, but used special military or gendarmerie units.

Among the many battles fought throughout Serbia and Montenegro in the summer of 1917, the largest took place once again in the Mount Kopaonik-Mount Jastrebac region. This was in July when the Belgrade and Niš occupation commands embarked on a coordinated operation aimed at annihilating the guerrilla groups of Kosta Pećanac and Kosta Vojinović.[81] Albanians also took part. The main body of the enemy troops was concentrated in the Mount Jastrebac region. Once again Pećanac disappeared, but Vojinović went into battle. The left wing of the Austro-Hungarian units (a total force of four companies of the Pursuit Regiment, one company of

Bosnian-Herzegovinan gendarmerie and one company of the 'S' gendarmerie battalion) encountered unexpectedly strong resistance from Vojinović's fighters. A report noted that at 8 a.m. on 20 July two pursuit companies had fought an enemy that was well dug in and able to command covering fire.[82] Neighbouring Austro-Hungarian units were sent to this point, and a Bulgarian company operated to Vojinović's rear. However, Vojinović and his men fought successfully all day and then simply vanished under cover of darkness. According to Austro-Hungarian reports, the fighting lasted thirty hours. While withdrawing, Vojinović came upon a Bulgarian pursuit group on 24 July and, after striking at it, disappeared with his men into the woods.

It was during this operation that the first Bulgarian *protivchete* went into action, with the task of hunting down and capturing Vojinović, who in the meantime had reached Toplica. The southern wing of the Austro-Hungarian pursuit encountered a strong force commanded by Captain Milinko Vlahović, who escaped without suffering major losses. While the pursuit forces were operating, mainly without success, Vojin Marjanović went into action behind their backs, probably to relieve the pressure on Vojinović. Over a period of five days he managed to capture money collected in taxes from two municipal treasuries.[83] The German consul described what was happening:

> The [Austro-Hungarian] authorities have organised, under the slogan of "the last manoeuvre", large-scale pursuit of the guerrilla groups on Mount Jastrebac, but with minimal results and the loss of three dead and eighteen wounded. The audacity of the guerrilla leaders is such that they went to the rear of the pursuing troops and seized 10,000 crowns belonging to the authorities from a place near Kruševac.[84]

The Bulgarians were somewhat more successful, having managed to kill a guerrilla commander.

During all these months of large- and small-scale fighting, the armed resistance movement opened up a permanent battlefront, quite independent of all other fronts and without any links whatever to either an Allied command or the Serbian supreme command. It is known that Pećanac did send a messenger that summer to travel through Albania to the Italian part of the front and present a letter to the Serbian supreme command describing events and circumstances in occupied Serbia. However, the messenger was intercepted and captured by the enemy near Prizren.[85]

Kosta Vojinović then also made an attempt to contact the supreme command by letter,[86] requesting a stepping-up of propaganda activity and assistance in the form of money, trained *comitadji*, doctors and medical equipment. He was in fact asking for the wherewithal to strengthen the armed resistance movement. Explaining why he had decided to wage guerrilla warfare, Vojinović gave political reasons, in addition to the wave of terror inflicted by the occupiers: 'Our people have started to break down both materially and morally and to lose all hope that independence and freedom will ever return.' Even in the most difficult circumstances, he had also been inspired by the idea of organising *comitadji* operations through guerrilla activity, to prove to the people that Serbia had not fallen, that it would always be great, and that 'today the greatest empires are fighting for our just cause'. He said that the uprising in Toplica had been directed against Bulgarian attempts to recruit Serbs into their forces; the guerrilla leaders had participated in the revolt because they felt it their duty to 'obey the will of the people'.

Seven volunteers were entrusted with carrying the message. These volunteers split up, and only one group of three succeeded in penetrating the lines of the Salonika front and reaching the 4th Russian Regiment. Vojinović's letter reached the Serbian supreme command on 17 September 1917,[87] and in October it decided to send an officer into occupied territory at the earliest possible moment to 'inform Lieutenant Pećanac that he should halt any further activity'. The plan was that the envoy, Captain Jovan Ilić, would be taken in a French plane to the area of Toplica, where he was to set about finding Kosta Pećanac and Kosta Vojinović, and take over command from them and other officers. Ilić was also charged with limiting activity to 'cooperation with local guerrilla leaders there' and dealing with 'the clandestine organisation of guerrilla groups' in different areas. It was further stipulated that the Serbian supreme command would determine 'the moment when those groups should go into action' (which would certainly be 'at a time when our army reaches the area of Skopje, and our enemy is in full retreat'). They were the same orders Pećanac had already once received. The reason the supreme command gave for halting all guerrilla activity was its anxiety to spare innocent people suffering, but it also probably wanted to exclude the possibility of official Serbia losing control of the situation in occupied Serbia. Nor should one forget that a revolution was under way in Russia, and the conflict with Black Hand, which had traditionally been strongly supported by *comitadji*, was still fresh in the minds of the supreme command.[88]

However, a strong Bulgarian pursuit detachment was deployed near the site where the plane carrying Ilić landed, and Ilić and his pilot fell into their hands. Therefore the *comitadji* only heard that a plane had landed and its crew had been captured. Thus they still had no news from the supreme command, and were left to their own devices.

From the second half of the summer of 1917 the 'Little War' entered a highly complex phase. Fierce fighting covered an increasingly broad territory in the Austro-Hungarian occupation zone, and the activity of small guerrilla groups was also spreading in the Niš occupation zone.[89] The Austro-Hungarian consul in Niš reported that the guerrilla warfare taking place was marked by 'overall fragmentation into small and even minute groups'.[90] Some of the guerrilla groups were linked to centres in Toplica and on Mount Kopaonik, while others arose from autonomous, intermittent activity by the local population.[91] New leaders were appearing on all sides. Faced with these facts, the occupation authorities were determined to make the best possible use of their prime advantage— sheer force of numbers against small, isolated guerrilla groups.[92] The situation in Mačva was of particular concern. A typical report said: 'This district is more important than all others, and the most significant economically.' Mačva, being agriculturally rich, was the minimal objective of the Monarchy's conquests and of great importance for its war economy. The pursuit of guerrilla groups became a regular occurrence throughout the occupation zones. There were losses on both sides, but the guerrillas and the Serb population suffered most.

Officials in the Governorate of Serbia then presented the Austro-Hungarian supreme command with a new idea:

> It is becoming increasingly necessary to supply all district commands with small tracking or military pursuit detachments tasked exclusively with hunting down guerrilla groups. These detachments should be fashioned

upon *protivchete*. Their members should be capable of fighting as guerrillas and should consist mainly of men who have volunteered for such arduous duties and are capable of performing them. Moreover, the Pursuit Regiment and the gendarmerie battalion should remain at our disposal for the execution of large-scale tasks [...]. To organise such *protivchete* it is necessary for the supreme command to allocate to the Military General Governorate in Serbia a further 500 men capable of guerrilla warfare.[93]

Although the Monarchy was woefully lacking in men to fight in the main theatres of war, its supreme command agreed to the proposal and in October 1917 250 battle-hardened soldiers arrived in Serbia. However, the entire process lasted until the spring of 1918. From that time the Belgrade Governorate had twelve *protivchete*, each comprising one officer and forty soldiers. Special 'mobile patrols' were also set up to 'overpower guerrilla groups in association with the gendarmerie and make them harmless.'

Having constantly improved their strategies, the Bulgarians were in a position by the late summer and early autumn of 1917 to strike heavily at the resistance movement thanks to their organisation and tactics and the strength of their available forces. The Bulgarian command implemented the following tactical principles:

Every single guerrilla group that appears must be hunted down, and it is essential to find and destroy their hideouts; experience and overall activity to date have confirmed that the only ways to defeat and destroy *comitadji* are, first, to ensure rigorous, accurate and constant intelligence; secondly to find and totally destroy their hideouts, confiscate weapons [from the population] and intern *comitadji* family members; and thirdly to hunt down and destroy guerrilla groups with our *protivchete*, with the staunch cooperation of regular troops.[94]

Moreover, previously tried and tested methods continued to be used. The domestic population were terrorised, and the families of certain resistance leaders were mistreated, while at the same time favourable conditions were offered to *comitadji* who surrendered. Those who agreed to cooperate in hunting down their fellow guerrillas were promised freedom of movement and, if they joined Bulgarian *protivchete*, they were offered part of the bounty placed on the heads of certain guerrilla leaders. Bulgarian planes constantly flew over the insurrectionist region and dropped leaflets calling for surrender.

Nonetheless, military experts among the occupation authorities were accurate when they provided contradictory estimates of the state of affairs on the ground, such as the following: 'The Chetnik [Serb guerrilla] movement is fundamentally well-organised ... in the entire "Morava" region they are noticeably dropping out in considerable numbers.' In other words, the number of *comitadji* had greatly decreased.⁹⁵ It was true that, since the end of the summer, *comitadji* had felt a sense of hopelessness. Many of them had been roaming the woods and mountains for a year or more, and were worn out and disillusioned because nothing had happened on the distant southerly front. They were demoralised by what the occupation authorities were doing to their families and anguished by the thoughts of what another winter would bring. During the crisis in late March and April 1917 none of the even slightly prominent *comitadji* or insurrectionists had so much as given a thought to surrender, but it became a mass phenomenon during the autumn of that year, even encompassing movement leaders. Bulgarian reports indicate that in one month pursuits by the Niš Governorate resulted in one dead and fourteen wounded among their own men and forty-two *comitadji* killed in action, fifty-eight executed (including people who had harboured them), ninety-seven prisoners and 190 men who had responded to the Bulgarian call for surrender. According to Austro-Hungarian reports: 'Since 1 September between five and ten *comitadji* have been surrendering to the Bulgarians daily.' On the other hand, 'five to twenty *comitadji* are being killed daily, and as many as fifty-four of them were killed on the twelfth of this month [September].'⁹⁶ As autumn drew in, Austro-Hungarian reports spoke regularly of more and more *comitadji* surrendering; according to one report, about 250 of them, including guerrilla leaders and prominent members, surrendered to the Bulgarians during September and October. Among those who surrendered, a certain number agreed, when promised a reward, to reveal who had sheltered guerrillas, where their hideouts were and hidden tracks leading to them, while some of them even took part in hunting down their former guerrilla leaders. Enemy headquarters estimated that by mid-November over 400 individuals who had either given refuge to *comitadji* or supplied them had surrendered. The parallel search for military matériel was also working out successfully.

The Bulgarians happily concluded that 'the Chetnik movement is on its last legs,' but added, in a contradictory statement, that 'the spirit of the malcontents has not been crushed.'[97] Over 'sixty clashes or exchanges of shots' were recorded in September and October, and the Bulgarians were always victorious. As a result of the increasingly accurate intelligence the Bulgarians were obtaining, the Serbs who were continuing the fight no longer had safe pathways or hideouts. Finally, on 2 November the guerrilla leader Toško Vlahović and his group of men were ambushed northwest of Kuršumlija and killed. As for Pećanac, he once again dispersed his men, secretly entered the Austro-Hungarian Governorate and remained hidden right up till mid-1918. Captain Vlahović and the guerrilla leader Radović also disappeared from sight and thus survived.

As he had done during the crisis in April, Kosta Vojinović went from battle to battle,[98] and according to his diary clashed with the Bulgarians on 28 August, on 21, 22, 28 and 29 September and on 5 and 6 October, always managing to escape the enemy despite losses. He made a habit of marching at the head of a strong group of guerrillas on a supply train, and was constantly visible to the enemy. Owing to the drop in the number of guerrillas and the death of so many of their leaders, he and his men were once again left to their own devices, and the leaders who remained had gone into hiding. Battle-weariness was felt even in that most elite unit of the resistance movement. In the first half of October, the Bulgarians made an enormous effort to seek out and destroy this most dangerous of the Serb guerrilla leaders; they organised a meticulous two-day search, and Austro-Hungarian commanders deployed strong forces where the two zones were contiguous and set up a dense network for mounting ambushes. Consequently, on 16 October Vojinović and some forty of his men finally fell into a well-laid trap. They found themselves surrounded by two companies of the Bulgarian 11th Infantry Regiment, one *protivchete* (which certainly included some former Serb *comitadji*) and one Austro-Hungarian machine-gun squad. Vojinović fought for the entire day, and when night fell, though wounded in the leg, he and some of his men escaped the encirclement, leaving behind eighteen dead, his entire supply train and his archives. According to uncertain data, three Bulgarians were killed and one wounded. Ottokar Count Czernin was immediately informed from Belgrade that the Bulgarians were on the track of Vojinović and had struck him a fearful blow a few days previously.[99] Vojinović's diary, dated 3 (16) October 1917, tells us: 'Surrounded by traitors and enemy soldiers, I fought, wounded, right up till nightfall.'[100]

Two to three weeks later, the enemy was once again in close pursuit of Vojinović. With a seeping wound and often needing the help of his fellow fighters to keep moving, he had to withdraw time and time again, frequently after fighting. In his diary he wrote: 'Many men were in pursuit. Chetniks that had surrendered to the enemy were particularly assiduous in their search. [...]. We fought for hours on end and then retreated [...]. My leg still cannot bear my weight [...]. I have been betrayed by prosperous peasants, while the poor have helped us and looked after me.'[101] He was finally surrounded near the village of Grgur in December 1917. He fought to the bitter end.[102] According to a reliable tradition, the enemy did not manage to kill Vojinović, and he died by his own hand. Baron Kun felt it necessary to write in a confidential report to his minister that 'it cannot be denied that Kosta Vojinović showed a certain nobility in the way he led his men.'[103] After the war, Hugo Kerchnawe wrote that Vojinović fought chivalrously and ordered his guerrillas not to commit any crimes, and to treat prisoners generously.[104]

But it was once again demonstrated that, although the guerrilla leaders made up the strike force of the resistance, resistance continued and persevered without them. Vojinović's death was a severe but not a fatal blow to armed resistance. And it was a fact that while the guerrilla leaders were alive and evading the enemy, the population had borne the brunt of the enemy's fury. Indeed, at times of crisis those leaders had been a burden upon the population; enemy propaganda had of course made use of this and tried to whip up popular enmity towards them. But the death of many prominent resistance leaders showed everyone that those very leaders had actually been martyrs to their cause. The name of Kosta Vojinović became legendary, and his death actually helped the battle to continue.

Meanwhile in Montenegro armed groups of guerrillas had not only multiplied but also gradually begun to act in such a way that, unlike in Serbia, they could be said to have gained the initiative and even gone over to a general offensive.[105] A condensed review of events elaborated by the operations department of the Austro-Hungarian supreme command on 18 February 1918 contains the following: 'Since the summer of 1917 there has been a significant increase in guerrilla warfare in Montenegro. Recently it has evolved in the district of Nikšić into an organised uprising that evidently also threatens the region of Herzegovina.'[106] In January 1918 Montenegrin guerrilla warfare expanded hugely throughout the country, and there was nowhere that the occupiers could feel safe. *Comitadji* were attacking more and more, seizing gendarmerie posts, and cutting all the communication lines of rural and even regional commands. They were even going over into Serbia and establishing links with guerrilla leaders on Mount Kopaonik and in Toplica. Neighbouring Herzegovina, a territory under Austro-Hungarian sovereignty, was also becoming more and more restless, and guerrilla groups were appearing and sometimes fighting in the areas around Bileće and Trebinje. Activity was particularly intense in the area around the frontier with Montenegro. On 24 October 1917 the commander of the Austro-Hungarian forces in Bosnia, Herzegovina and Dalmatia reported that small groups of guerrillas were roaming the area,[107] and in January 1918 the Monarchy's supreme command evidently feared that 'an organised uprising around Nikšić could spread into areas of Herzegovina.'[108] *Comitadji* operations and clashes also occurred in the coastal region and around Dubrovnik, also under Austro-Hungarian sovereignty.

Events once again repeated themselves. In mid-February 1918 Austro-Hungarian experts were only able to ascertain that rigorous anti-guerrilla action was 'continuing through armed struggle in Bulgarian Morava', although the Bulgarians had 'for some months been daily confiscating rifles and ammunition, capturing *comitadji*, and having *comitadji* and their leaders surrendering to them.' The conclusion was that the threat of rebellion, 'which is deeply entrenched in the people', was ever present. In short, Serbia was 'constantly prepared for an uprising'.[109] In addition to all the pursuits organised by their Governorate, there were constant reports of guerrilla groups, each numbering between ten and twenty men, operating in the southern and central regions of the Governorate. A report dated 27 March 1918 noted: 'Guerrilla warfare is extending to the northern regions, to the southerly area of the districts of Belgrade and Palanka, and to the northern areas of the districts of Gornji Milanovac and Kragujevac.... The guerrilla groups number up to twenty men.'[110] Also groups from Montenegro were attacking more and more frequently, simply seeking 'conflict with the gendarmerie'. On 1 May the Governorate intelligence service reported to Vienna that the available security forces were no longer strong enough to counter the *comitadji*.[111] There were no large-scale battles, but in all areas there were frequent small-scale clashes during which the occupying forces lost between one and six men; taken together, these losses were not insignificant. At the beginning of July Governor von Remen reported to his superiors on 'big losses in the units'.[112] However, there was little mention of the guerrilla leaders who had survived the events of 1917: they were well concealed and not active, but their very names brought fear to the hearts of the occupying forces.

The country's passive population continued to take the full impact of the enemy's reprisals. The mildest form of punishment was the imposition of a huge fine on villages where the inhabitants were even suspected of not reporting *comitadji* they believed to be in the vicinity. To prevent the diversionist burning of crops, General von Remen ordered on 25 July 1918 the introduction of a state of emergency that required execution on the spot for those directly involved in such sabotage. Besides, the collective responsibility of each individual municipality was also introduced, and from this time on, any municipality on whose territory such sabotage took place was held responsible. This embraced anyone working on the threshers, and all livestock not used for working purposes was confiscated from the municipality. If it was established that an inhabitant of a specific municipality had taken part in sabotage, the entire municipality was fined 50,000 crowns, and all men aged between sixteen and sixty were interned. The houses of the saboteurs and their collaborators were to be burnt down and, if it was considered necessary, so were all the rest.[113] Many hostages were executed and in some cases members of their families also. In July 1918 the Austro-Hungarian authorities executed both parents of two *comitadji* and the mother of one.[114]

Large-scale campaigns to clear the terrain of guerrillas multiplied in the area of Rekovac and Mount Juhor, and attempts were made by the so-called 'Orient Corps', which had been deployed in western Serbia in early May 1918, to locate them throughout the Governorate of Serbia.[115] Although these were originally troops that had been prepared to be sent as reinforcements to Turkey, they were now on the move between Belgrade and Mitrovica. Meanwhile a special detachment, comprising parts of that corps, the Pursuit Regiment and the 'S' gendarmerie battalion, searched the district of Kruševac to hunt down guerrillas and frighten the population. Many clashes took place, and almost all the new guerrilla leaders were killed.[116]

However, even this did not produce the results the enemy wanted. During the whole summer Governorate representatives in Belgrade kept informing Vienna that on the whole 'guerrilla warfare has grown.' Reports noted that at the beginning of August Serbia seemed in a 'state of general uprising'. On 23 September 1918, General von Remen wrote that guerrilla warfare in the whole Military Governorate of Serbia had been on the increase throughout August and September. 'Guerrilla warfare has become more aggressive and seemingly stronger with the participation of both the indigenous population and deserters,' he added. Other reports told of some Italians having joined the guerrillas after escaping from prison camps near Kragujevac, as well as some Hungarians interned near Kruševac. The governor general lamented: 'In the district of Belgrade, *comitadji* are fighting with a freedom that is incomprehensible. Acts of banditry are commonplace.'[117]

7

TOWARDS A YUGOSLAV STATE

The collapse of the Serbian and Montenegrin military front did not impede the growth of the Yugoslav movement; on the contrary, the movement expanded. On 20 March 1916 the Paris press had published a statement made by Ante Trumbić:

> The Austro-Germans deemed that by conquering Serbia they had removed the Yugoslav question from the agenda. But, what they actually did was inflate it and make the resolution of that issue even more urgent than it had been before.... Serbia's collapse did not eradicate that ideal, but only strengthened it. Misfortune has actually worked to unite the Yugoslavs.[1]

On 5 April 1916 Regent Alexander spoke in London about the realisation of the ideal 'for which we have striven for so many centuries', of unification 'into one homeland of all Serbs, Croats and Slovenes, which are one nation with the same traditions, the same language and the same aspirations', but a nation 'divided by misfortune'.[2] Although these were only verbal declarations, they still revealed the state of affairs at the time and defined the goals and the essence of the ongoing struggle. And this was despite considerable political differences.

The longer the war lasted, the more Serbia's fate became linked to that of the other Yugoslav peoples within the movement, and it was becoming almost impossible to separate Serbia and the Serbs from the Yugoslav movement as a whole. Hence awareness of ethnic kinship was playing an ever more important role. That awareness, expressed through the claim that Serbs, Croats and Slovenes were one nation, was based on the desire to escape from foreign rule, then embodied in the state idea of the Habsburg Empire and the aspirations of other powers such as Germany and Italy. However, the Yugoslav movement was showing signs of greater internal complexity than in

1914 and 1915, and programmes were beginning to appear that differed among themselves to a varying degrees. What they had in common was the concept of the territory that the Yugoslav state should encompass; the greatest differences lay in the concepts of internal political and state organisation. In 1916 and especially in 1917 the whole unification issue became more complicated, with serious differences emerging.

It was apparent that the number of unification factors involved had multiplied: Serbia had once again proved itself a force to be reckoned with on the battlefield; the Yugoslav Committee had further asserted itself as a factor of unification; and the Serbian government and the Yugoslav Committee had drawn up and published the basic principles of a common war objective. Official Montenegro did not support this programme, but the Montenegrin Committee did. Moreover, the population of the occupied areas of Serbia and Montenegro had retained the strong desire for freedom and demonstrated their espousal of this ideal through ceaseless armed resistance over a broad front. As for the situation in the Monarchy itself, a Yugoslav movement with autochthonous roots, while still seeking solutions within the framework of Habsburg rule, was developing and actually contributing to the Monarchy's internal crisis. Covert links between representatives of the movement in the Monarchy on the one hand and the Yugoslav Committee and the Serbian government on the other had revealed similarities despite the differences in the programmes proclaimed. Furthermore, the revolution in Russia had strengthened national and social-revolutionary trends in the weakened Monarchy, as well as in Germany. This weakened the Yugoslav programme's main enemies.

However, overall circumstances in 1917 and 1918 seemed to be against Yugoslav unification, which could only be achieved in its entirety if the Habsburg state were to collapse. At one point developments seemed to be heading in a direction that presupposed the perpetuation of the Monarchy. First of all, the Entente bloc did not officially wish to include the elimination of the Habsburg state in its war objectives. Then there was the weakening of Russia as a factor in the war, and then its withdrawal. Under the peace treaty concluded in Brest-Litovsk on 3 March 1918,[3] Germany, Austria-Hungary, Turkey and Bulgaria, negotiating from a position of strength, demanded extremely difficult terms for a peace settlement from revolutionary Russia. This had the effect of imperialist policy as a whole appearing momentarily successful. That in turn affected the Yugoslav movement because of its anti-imperialist character and because, according to the exact terms of the peace treaty, Austria-Hungary had ostensibly gained in strength. Finally, the war aims of Britain and the United States, which were made known early in 1918, explicitly included the perpetuation of the Habsburg state, while France and Britain, in secret talks on a separate peace with Austria-Hungary, had shown signs of readiness to accept it as a great power in the future too.

Serbia had retained its central position within the increasingly complex Yugoslav movement mainly as the result of its successful military comeback, but also partly because of its government's determination to adhere to the foreign policy programme set out in the autumn of 1914. The Serbian leadership wanted that central position, and used it in relation both to other important factors in the unification movement and to the Entente powers. Ideologically the essence of Serbia's Yugoslav programme lay in the concept of a 'nation with three names', as indeed did that of the other factors in the Yugoslav movement at that time. The confusion in terminology present in official Serbian documents of all kinds demonstrated that certain concepts remained unclear, and it is therefore difficult to draw accurate conclusions. Still, it is evident that 'Serbs-Croats-Slovenes' was being used more and more alongside the adjectival phrase 'Serb-Croat-Slovene', while 'Yugoslavs' and the adjective 'Yugoslav' were being used less often. 'Serbia' was being used as a synonym for Yugoslavia, as was 'Greater Serbia', though more rarely.

Serbia's Prime Minister Nikola Pašić considered that instances where other European states had been unified demonstrated that the name of the 'strongest part of the nation'[4] would always predominate. However, that was inaccurate: the Savoyards (Piedmontese) had agreed to be Italians; the Prussians to be Germans; the English to be British; and the Flemish and Walloons to be Belgians. Although there was no insistence on the use of 'Serbs', 'Yugoslavs' was avoided as much as possible, and 'Serbs-Croats-Slovenes' (or rather 'Serbo-Croats and Slovenes') predominated, which was taken as a compromise. This confusion revealed a divergence in political awareness between Serbia's separate historical tradition and its statehood. The former was manifested in Serb national awareness, and the latter by the need for the Serb sense of separateness, which had been built up over the passage of time, to be overcome in order not to impede the aspiration for Yugoslav unification.

The Serbian leadership upheld Serbia's right to a central position, arguing that nations that already had an independent state core should assemble around that core, i.e. 'that national liberation from German-Hungarian bondage will only be accomplished if Serbs, Croats and Slovenes unite with free Serbia, Romanians with Romania, Italians with Italy' (while other nations were to create new states: the Czechoslovaks Czechoslovakia, and the Poles Poland). To substantiate this, the key political explanation of the Yugoslav programme was based on the doctrine of Serbia's historical position and role. 'Lying between two worlds and two cultures', Serbia had, 'as a result of its geographical position', already achieved 'first-rate importance in the world struggle for domination'. Not only that 'in the Middle Ages ... it was the barrier against the Turkish onslaught on Central Europe for a hundred years, and now it is the barrier against the Germanic onslaught on the East.' Thus, according to this doctrine, the proof that Serbia should be supported in its efforts to create a powerful Yugoslav state around it lay in interpretations of national movements and rebellions in the nineteenth century ('in the struggle against Turks, Serbia embodied Christianity's battle against Islam'), as well as in interpretations of the basic political issue at that time: 'Would Germany really establish its superiority over the rest of the world? Would it continue to be able to march across Serbia to Constantinople and the Persian Gulf?' For Serbia 'has now become the symbol of the fight for freedom and the right of nations to self-determination in the face of power and conquest.'[5]

In the second half of the World War, fewer elements were participating in the Serbian state's decision-making process than ever before. Regent Alexander was at the front with the army, totally involved in war operations; the Independent Radicals and Liberals had walked out of the government; and division within the Radical Party had created a state of affairs where Pašić was in absolute control of the homogeneous Old Radical government and the Serbian Radical Party. Moreover, the Black Hand had been broken up and its influence greatly diminished. It should also be recalled that the island of Corfu had become the centre of the state where decisions were being made, but there was actually no real political life there. While Paris and Geneva were rife with political infighting among Serb politicians in exile, the government in Corfu was isolated from either disturbances or influence. With the support of the Regent at that time and with the full trust of the governments of the Allied Great Powers, the only thing with which Pašić had to concern himself was having agents pressurise Serb political circles scattered throughout Allied and neutral countries and having the police monitor political trends. As for the National Assembly, it was not convened for sixteen months, from its dissolution on 22 October 1916 until 25 February 1918. Consequently, it was possible for Serbia's war aim to be a Yugoslav programme as interpreted by one figure, Nikola Pašić, despite the fact that the programme had emerged as a result of historical movements.[6] Hence the differences between the Serbian government and the opposition in the Assembly frequently boiled down to the issue of whether Pašić should remain prime minister, while disagreements between official Serbia and the Yugoslav Committee were many-sided and centred on Pašić.

King Nicholas of Montenegro and his supporters were also waging a propaganda war against the Montenegrin Committee for National Unification. In the summer of 1918 they went as far as to threaten Radović and his followers with charges of high treason.[7] Regarding Serbia, King Nicholas was playing a waiting game. He did not enter publicly into any argument, and he told the Serbian chargé d'affaires that he was prepared to make sacrifices for unification. He proposed a union of Serbia and Montenegro with joint jurisdiction over military affairs, foreign affairs and finance, as previously envisaged in the 'real union'. At the same time, King Nicholas was endeavouring to become included in the Yugoslav Committee on his own account, and made it known that the liberation and unification 'of all Yugoslavs' had been the ideal of 'Montenegro's state and national programme for over five centuries'. He added that throughout his rule of nearly sixty years he had worked constantly to that end, stretching back to the cooperation he had established with 'Prince Mihailo and the great Croat Strossmayer'. He was acting in such a way in order to thwart unification between Serbia and Montenegro, but at the same time to avoid criticism that he was conducting a policy of separatism, which would at that time have been extremely dangerous for him politically as a ruler.[8]

The Montenegrin Committee for National Unification and its leader Andrija Radović were also extremely active, and moreover were more successful in their activities than the King and his government.[9] On 15 April 1917, in the first edition of its newspaper *Ujedinjenje*, the Montenegrin Committee published a declaration it had made on 27 March that year, stating that it was 'expressing the wishes and the centuries-old aspirations of the people of Montenegro'. The Committee, the declaration continued, was aware that the activities of Montenegro's official representatives were directed against the 'pledged ideals of that country' and sought that Montenegro should 'unite with Serbia and other Serb, Croat and Slovene countries into one independent state'. The declaration further stated that the 'division of the Serb nation' into two states and the separation of Montenegro from Serbia not only signified the abandonment of the centuries-old aspirations of Montenegrins, but were also actions that would only benefit the enemy. This was especially so since Montenegro, a small, poor country, could not survive alone. In the form of a pledge to Serbs, the Committee condemned King Nicholas for causing a division. It conducted itself *vis-à-vis* the Yugoslav Committee as a factor with a parallel task, albeit a more limited one, directed towards an objective that was 'essentially the same as that of the Yugoslav Committee, that is to say the unification of all Serbs, Croats and Slovenes into one state'. The Montenegrin Committee achieved good results, and was acknowledged by a broad circle of Montenegrins. However, it owed its expansion and acceptance to political, diplomatic and financial assistance from the Serbian government.

Pašić's government was conducting a determined policy towards King Nicholas, evidently in agreement with all other Serbian political factors. This policy was carried out in two stages.[10] In the first stage attempts were made to win the King over to the idea of the unification of Serbia and Montenegro during the war itself, and it was left to leading Montenegrin politicians to convince him of that. In the second stage, during which relations were not broken off and there was no overt public or official campaign against King Nicholas, attempts were made to achieve the diplomatic isolation of the King among the Entente powers, especially France. The Serbian government also fostered links with Montenegrins who had broken away from their government in the belief that unification should be achieved as soon as possible. Particular efforts were directed towards preventing the creation of a separate Montenegrin army abroad, and these efforts proved successful. Finally, during this stage, the Serbian government did not react to the Montenegrin government's belated official proposal of 1 July 1917 recommending that Serbia and Montenegro, as the two Serb states, should first reach agreement on their future relations. This was because it was believed that King Nicholas was trying to become an equal partner in his relations with Serbia once again.[11] Regarding the form of unification, it was considered that Montenegro should not have autonomy but, as formulated on 15 December 1916, its citizens should have 'absolutely the same rights' as the those of Serbia. The dynasty issue was to be resolved by guaranteeing members of the Petrović family the lifelong right to use their titles and the right to apanage, on the condition that they did not work against the Yugoslav state or its order.

Quite a different process was under way in Austria-Hungary.[12] Extreme anti-Serb policy and activity had not yielded the expected results, and this was because among the Serb population such a policy had not obliterated political awareness of unity with Serbs from Serbia; it had not eliminated the idea of a brotherhood of Yugoslavs, nor had it checked the growth of the Yugoslav movement. The longer the war continued, causing the Monarchy to groan under the burden of economic, social and political difficulties while at the same time exacting ever greater loss of life, the more the broad mass of the people felt the weight of the state on their own backs, and the more it saw the state as demanding suffering so that others, notably the Habsburgs, might profit. News arrived daily from distant fronts of husbands, sons, relatives and friends reported dead, wounded, missing or taken prisoner, while those anxiously waiting at home were faced with food shortages and even famine. Hence many people were more and more inclined to accept Yugoslav statehood as a key political idea that offered hope and was after all part of their historical heritage.

This was best seen in Bosnia and Herzegovina, where pressure on the Serbs was the strongest and where the authorities obstinately thwarted all attempts to create a legal framework for political activity.[13] The *Sabor* (Assembly) of Bosnia and Herzegovina, which had not actually met since the beginning of the war, was officially dissolved by an imperial decree of on February 1915, and Danilo Dimović, leader of the so-called loyal Serbs, was dismissed from the post of deputy speaker of the *Sabor* a few weeks later. At the same time, the persecution that had started in the summer of 1914 continued, only now in the form of a series of large-scale trials. These trials were a singular aspect of the conflict between the ongoing desire for independence through unification and the Habsburg Empire which defended the existing order. The Austro-Hungarian authorities were faced with the problem of young people's powerful national sentiments, although during the war they were able to use mobilisation as a weapon against such sentiments, and huge numbers of such youngsters were sent to the front line. Many young people were charged and put on trial; in Banjaluka in March 1915 twenty-seven high school pupils, three teachers and a number of ordinary citizens were tried on the charge of attempting to found student associations of a Yugoslav or pan-Slav nature. In May that same year in Sarajevo the same thing happened when eight pupils and two craftsmen, all from Mostar, were put on trial, while sixty-five pupils from Sarajevo were taken to court in Travnik in June, and the same fate befell forty pupils and three teachers from Tuzla in a court in Bihac. In Travnik a senior high school pupil, Todor Ilić, was sentenced to death, but the sentence was commuted. Most of the people accused and sentenced were Serbs, but there were also some Croats and Muslims. The largest such trial to take place, however, was in Banjaluka in the spring of 1916, and on that occasion the charges were mainly brought against adult or middle-aged men. A total of 159 Serbs, prominent figures in public life and on the cultural scene and including seven *Sabor* deputies, were put on trial. All were charged with high treason as propagators of the unification of Bosnia with Serbia.[14] On 22 April sixteen of those on trial were sentenced to death by hanging, and eighty-seven to prison terms of between three and twenty years; the death sentences had to be commuted because of protests from the international community, which was informed of these developments by influential figures in Bosnia (particularly Danilo Dimović, who had been the defence lawyer at the trial) and by Serb émigrés. Other trials passed death sentences, which were also commuted.

Danilo Dimović endeavoured to show loyalty to the Monarchy and its dynasty, but he also tried to protect his fellow countrymen from persecution and to maintain political links with the Croat-Serb Coalition in Zagreb. He fostered good political relations with certain Croatian political leaders in Bosnia and Herzegovina such as Josip Sunarić, a former *Sabor* deputy speaker, and Vjekoslav Jelavić, secretary of the Chamber of Commerce. In the winter of 1916–17 the authorities were looking with the greatest mistrust on the increasingly frequent meetings between leading Serb and Croat figures, and Muslim beys in the district of Travnik were provoking the authorities by associating with interned Serb priests. This was especially the case with a group led by Derviš-bey Miralem. Furthermore, Bosnian Franciscans were not in agreement with the extreme, pro-regime, anti-Serb policies of Josip Štadler, the Bishop of Vrhbosna.[15]

In Croatia the Croat-Serb Coalition was attempting to avoid politics as much as possible and thus ensure there would be no pretext for abolition of the constitutional state of affairs under which Serbs in Croatia were in an incomparably better position than in Bosnia and Herzegovina.[16] But for that there was a price to pay. The Coalition actually ended up supporting the Monarchy in the war, which is to say in the war against Serbia too. However, the most significant thing to emerge in Croatian political life was the growing belief in ethnic links among Yugoslavs. Both officially and publicly, the Coalition was in favour of grouping together Yugoslavs within the Hungarian part of the Monarchy, which was in line with the principle of dualism. It was in favour of the grouping of Croatia and Slavonia with Dalmatia and Bosnia-Herzegovina, which was in accordance with the aspirations of the government in Budapest. However, Starčević's Party of Right was manifesting the desire to abandon the dualist system and support the grouping of all Yugoslavs into a separate, third unit of the Monarchy, in line with the trialist aspirations of Austrian legitimists. In the given circumstances, there could be no mention, either officially or publicly, of any desire for unification with Serbia and Montenegro, and for the moment the representatives of the two main parties—the Croat-Serb Coalition and Starčević's Party of the Right—stressed their loyalty to the Habsburgs and the Monarchy.

Nonetheless, with the passing of time tendencies became more and more pro-Yugoslav. Of particular importance were initiatives encouraged by Slovene clerical and liberal circles. Although officially loyal to the Habsburgs, these circles contributed little by little to cracks starting to appear in the very foundations of the Monarchy. And they, in turn, led to the great problems that induced Emperor Karl I to state at a Crown Council on 30 May 1918 that 'the Yugoslav issue is of the greatest importance to the Monarchy,'[17] and the German ambassador to Vienna to inform Berlin in July 1918: 'The most dangerous place of dissension is Croatia. Until recently the many parties there were sharply divided from one another but they are now united in the aim of bringing together all Serbo-Croats into one state.'[18] On the other side, contrary to these pro-Yugoslav tendencies, were the two parties—those of Ivan Frank and Stjepan Radić—that were the weakest in the Croatian *Sabor* at that time.

When the news broke that Russia had withdrawn from the war, a group of pro-Austrians in occupied Serbia proposed to the Governorate representatives in Belgrade the convening of a 'constituent assembly' in the area under Austro-Hungarian control. Such an assembly, headed by loyalists of the Monarchy and under the aegis of the occupation authorities, would, they suggested, proclaim that the government in Corfu and the Karadjordjević dynasty had been overthrown, announce that the National Assembly had no jurisdiction on foreign soil, and form a pro-Austrian government with the task of immediately concluding a separate peace with Austria-Hungary.[19] This initiative, which was said to have come from Professor Živojin Perić, was first presented in detail by Professor Jovan B. Jovanović in a conversation with the head of the Belgrade Governorate's intelligence service that took place on 4 December 1917. However, a certain Stevan Ćurčić visited the Governorate representative that same day to repeat the proposal 'also on the part of the Liberal Party'. Vukašin Petrović, deputy to the Governor General, touched on the same subject around that time. This initiative was discussed right up to the middle of the spring of 1918 and reached as far as Emperor Karl and, of course, the minister Ottokar Count Czernin.

An even more obscure group emerged in Switzerland and contacted the Austro-Hungarian military intelligence and diplomatic service with similar plans.[20] The group seems to have been made up of a dozen men who had founded some kind of 'Association of Independent Serbs' in Geneva back in October 1917. Headed by Živan Moskovljević, a lawyer from Jagodina, the group made its views known in the *Srpski List* newspaper. Moskovljević even went so far as to address the Emperor with a lengthy petition (written by hand and in Cyrillic script), proposing that he should act 'ruthlessly towards the Serbian government'. In the petition Moskovljević called for the toppling of King Peter I, the ousting of Pašić's government, and the dissolution of the National Assembly, while the Association's main committee should 'take in hand all Serbia's state business and the Serbian nation' and conclude a separate peace with the Monarchy. The petition was read by Count Czernin. There were also attempts to form links between the group and one in occupied Serbia.[21] At the same time, a merchant named Milivoj Sjenicki was carrying out his own similar campaign, possibly unconnected with Moskovljević and his Association. A common factor among all these pro-Austrians was a programme in which a diminished Serbia, which would cede Macedonia to Bulgaria and retain the areas east of the Velika Morava river and the valley of the Južna Morava, would come under the rule of the Monarchy in a manner deemed fit by the Austro-Hungarian leadership. Besides that, Perić's group also suggested that a Habsburg archduke—the Emperor's brother Maximilian was mentioned—should be the ruler of Serbia. Moskovljević, for his part, proposed that the best solution would be for Serbia to 'enter into a confederation and [economic?] union with Austria-Hungary.' It was hoped that Austria-Hungary could also give Serbia access to the sea. It was mentioned in Moskovljević's group that such access could be achieved by uniting a diminished Serbia with Montenegro under King Nicholas and under the protection of the Habsburg Monarchy.

Although their feasibility was doubted from the beginning, such proposals conformed with Austro-Hungarian plans to achieve a victorious peace through diplomatic means, and consequently the authorities in Vienna did not reject them out of hand. Indeed, Emperor Karl himself showed interest in them.[22] However, officials in the Foreign Ministry, including Czernin, decided in the spring of

1918 that it was not possible to create 'seeds of pro-Austrian evolution' among Serbs, and that the men putting themselves forward did not have sufficient support among émigrés or in the country to oust Pašić's government, which had decided to continue with the war. All in all, it was decided that 'no serious importance should be attached' to this tendency.[23] They also had to take into account the political and international legal difficulties the Monarchy would encounter with Bulgaria if it accepted such proposals. Moreover, the Governorate authorities in Belgrade were also against such plans in principle, considering that no proposals from the Serbian side should be accepted because any eventual concessions made to Serbs should be given, or at least appear to be given, as the 'clemency of the victor towards the vanquished'.[24]

During the crisis months of late 1917 and early 1918, Vienna attempted to make use of groups around Prince Mirko and Jovan Plamenac in Montenegro to achieve permanent gains for the Monarchy by means of separate peace treaties.[25] Count Czernin himself made the most important move when he resorted to trickery and took advantage of the visit of the terminally ill Prince Mirko, who had come to Vienna for treatment. He met Prince Mirko on 31 December 1917.[26] Here it must be recalled that Czernin had informed the Emperor that he had done 'all a man could do' to achieve a separate peace with Serbia and 'looked sceptically' upon the possibility of achieving that aim because the government in Corfu did not wish to negotiate. But what he told Prince Mirko was that Serbia was offering peace to the Monarchy and, in return for its readiness to cede territory to Bulgaria and Austria-Hungary, it had sought a 'union' with Montenegro. He further threatened that the Monarchy would accept Serbia's offer unless Montenegro decided 'to conclude a peace with us as quickly as possible under conditions set by us.' Prince Mirko took Czernin's words seriously, but in Montenegro he received support from only a few people, while most refused to cooperate with him. In any case on 3 March 1918 he died.

Signs of community spirit

The working relations between the Serbian government and the Yugoslav Committee were not sufficiently close or sufficiently comprehensive to ensure complete coordination of activity.[27] Pašić's government was trying to maintain control of political activity while leaving the Committee to its own devices in the scope of the generally accepted programme. As a consequence Pašić found it necessary in the spring of 1917 to inform Trumbić that it was Serbia that was the 'bearer of our common political aspiration and its official representative before our Allies and the rest of the world', while paying tribute to the Yugoslav Committee for its 'patriotic work of enlightenment ... for the unification of all Serbs, Croats and Slovenes into one common Yugoslav state with Serbia.'[28] Essentially Pašić was placing the Yugoslav Committee in the framework of the policies he was conducting with regard to all émigrés from the Yugoslav lands of Austria-Hungary, according to which Serbia both supported and financially assisted those émigrés and expected them to help it as the main promoter of unification. The Serbian government had allocated considerable resources for this purpose and had set up a separate Yugoslav Department in the Foreign Ministry in Corfu to deal with such activities. According to incomplete reports, around 520,000 dinars were allocated to the Yugoslav Committee in 1916, around 1.2 million in 1917, and around 1.5 million in 1918.[29] The Committee had basically accepted Serbia as the leading player, and this continued until the spring of 1918. Trumbić had written to Supilo on 2 June 1917 that 'Croatia must unite with Serbia,' because 'without that there can be no national unity', that 'Serbia and its people have hundreds of shortcomings' but, despite that, it had to be admitted that 'not one of our countries is capable of being a bleeding Piedmont of our people such as it is.'[30]

The Yugoslav Committee was a complex body. Its members included politicians, of greater or lesser prominence, from the different Yugoslav lands in the Austro-Hungarian Monarchy, while Serbia was represented by Professor Pavle Popović[31] and, for a few months in the first half of 1917, by Stojan Protić, one of the most prominent representatives of the Old Radicals and a leading figure on the Serbian political scene. It can be said to have been a representative body, especially because a large number of proponents of the Yugoslav idea were still interned in the Monarchy. However, those were people with greatly differing political ideas, representatives of different provinces and with beliefs, concepts and interests born of the regions they came from. Besides, out of necessity, many of them were scattered throughout Western Europe, Russia and the Americas, which, in turn, reduced the Committee's flexibility and made reaching agreement on common programmes and activities difficult. To add to that, there were differences in the Committee itself, some of which were of great political importance. Nonetheless, in the second half of 1915 it was only Supilo who was at variance with the Serbian government or its policies, but later, before his death, he decided to cooperate with it again. Other members differed considerably in their concept of the Committee's autonomy with regard to the Serbian government.

Where the political programme was concerned, all Committee members, with the exception of Supilo in the period when he still vacillated, were certainly resolute in their support for the creation of Yugoslavia, but their visions of the future state differed. Some saw it as having a centralist and others a federal system; thus, for a lengthy period, the Committee itself could only present the most vague views. The question whether it was to be a federation or not arose in early 1917, whereupon Trumbić and those of like mind declared:

> The Yugoslav Committee has never come to any kind of conclusion concerning the future internal organisation of Yugoslav lands, and therefore it has not decided on a *federative* union of those lands. The Committee has created a programme calling for all Yugoslav lands in Austria-Hungary to be liberated from it and unified together with Serbia and Montenegro in a nation state. Everyone is entitled to have his own personal opinion concerning the principles of the organisation of our future Yugoslav unified state, but, as a member of the Committee, he may not campaign in favour of his opinion until the Committee has presented its stand on the subject. The issue of internal organisation is an extremely difficult and complex one, and therefore it is not advisable to act out of hand or without authorisation.[32]

Consequently, the most delicate internal issue was deferred.

As the number of Yugoslav émigrés grew with the influx of new refugees and new prisoners of war, and as developments in the war highlighted the right of nations to self-determination, Trumbić started to show greater autonomy in his views with regard to those of Pašić. The support given to the Committee by prominent British figures such as R.W. Seton-Watson and Henry Wickham Steed contributed greatly to this. Moreover, the spread of the Yugoslav idea among émigrés in America led to large donations from there, which gave the Yugoslav Committee the financial basis for such autonomy.[33] What is more, at one point the Committee was demonstrating a certain desire for independence: at a session on 23 March 1917 the five Committee members present decided to set up their own volunteer armed forces named the 'Yugoslav Legion'.[34]

In the spring of 1917 it was not certain how the war would end; everything looked much more complex and ambiguous than it had done in the previous two years. The warring states of both blocs were showing signs of exhaustion. The revolution in Russia had given rise to a powerful wave of democracy, and it was impossible to predict how that would affect the outcome of the war, although Russia had suddenly grown much weaker. Moreover, the United States had entered the war, but had not hitherto shown itself politically committed to Entente plans. On the other side, a covert exchange of opinion was taking place among the capitals of the warring countries in Europe in order to find possibilities for concluding peace. In addition to that, rumours were circulating that Italy and Bulgaria would gladly withdraw from the war if they could achieve separate peace agreements and some gains, which meant gains to the detriment of Austria-Hungary and Serbia. It was therefore necessary to clarify unresolved issues in the Yugoslav programme in order to step up activity and make it known that Yugoslavs were determined to win their own unified state despite a certain degree of confusion. Nikola Pašić expressed this determination by stating, first, that 'the Allies must be made to believe that unification is the desire of the entire nation and that we are one nation', and issues of internal organisation should 'be up to us'; and secondly, that 'the Serbian government and the Yugoslav Committee must reach agreement on basic internal organisation since it would hinder us if certain major issues were not clarified.'[35]

On 15 June 1917 a meeting between the Serbian government and the Yugoslav Committee got under way in Corfu, and deliberations continued till 27 July.[36] It was initially a working dialogue, but the nature of the gathering was to change quickly. First of all, the Serbian government found itself faced with a crisis on account of the death penalty passed on Colonel Dimitrijević, whereupon Ljubomir Davidović, Milorad Drašković and Vojislav Marinković had resigned from the government. They did, however, remain participants in the deliberations, as a result of which the deliberations became three-sided, between the Serbian government, the strongest Serbian opposition parties and the Yugoslav Committee. The Serbian government was represented by all its ministers and the speaker of the National Assembly, headed by Nikola Pašić. The Committee in London had designated Ante Trumbić, Hinko Hinković (both Croats), Bogumil Vošnjak (a Slovene) and Dušan Vasiljević (a Serb from Bosnia) to take part in the talks, and they had been joined by Franko Potočnjak and Dinko Trinajstić (Croats). These two did not actually have the mandate to take an active part—they had travelled to Corfu only for an 'exchange of opinion'—but as the talks progressed it became evident that they had assumed the right to conduct discussions on an equal footing and to make decisions. The meeting was thus transformed into negotiations on the finalisation of a document of extreme, far-reaching importance. The talks were not easy, and many differences of opinion arose, but goodwill prevailed, and the participants were aware that agreement had to be reached. Full agreement was finally accomplished, and a declaration was adopted which was signed by Nikola Pašić on behalf of the Serbian government and by Ante Trumbić on behalf of the Yugoslav Committee.

The document was dated 20 July 1917, and it has gone down in history as the Corfu Declaration.[37] It contained the following: the name of the future state was to be the Kingdom of Serbs, Croats and Slovenes; the new state of 'Serbs, Croats and Slovenes, known also under the name of Southern Slavs or Yugoslavs', was to be a sovereign state with integral territory and integral statehood; it was to be a 'constitutional, democratic and parliamentary monarchy', and its emblems were to be 'a national coat of arms, a national flag and a crown'. These emblems were to be made up of the 'existing separate emblems' of the three individual peoples, and they 'could also be used freely on all occasions'. 'All three national denominations' were to be equal and each of them could be used 'by anyone and on any occasion of public life and before all authorities.' Cyrillic and Latin script were also to be 'completely equal' and 'anyone could use either of them freely over the entire territory of the kingdom.' Moreover, the 'state and autonomous authorities' were to have the 'duty and the right' to use both scripts 'according to the wishes of the citizens'. 'Orthodox, Roman Catholic and Islamic confessions' were to be equal 'in the eyes of the state' and 'equal to one another', while the 'legislator' was 'obliged to ensure that confessional peace should be preserved and maintained'. It was also emphasised that all citizens were to be 'equal and have equal rights before the state and in the eyes of the law,' while the right to vote was 'equal and general'.

It was thus a vision of a centralist state founded on the principles of civic parliamentary democracy. Some of the points assumed the significance of a foreign policy programme in wartime; this was especially true of the ninth point, which stipulated that the unified state 'encompasses all the territory inhabited by our three-named nation in a compact and uninterrupted mass', which could not be diminished without 'violating the vital interests of the whole'. It was added that 'our nation seeks nothing that belongs to others', but wanted 'only what is its own,' for it wished 'to become liberated and united as a single entity.' This was why any partial resolution of national liberation and unification was excluded. It based its demands on the principle of 'free national self-determination', and this was why no part could be separated (without its consent). 'Our nation, as an indivisible entity, poses the question of its liberation from Austria-Hungary and its unification with Serbia and Montenegro into one state.'

The document was accepted by all members of the Yugoslav Committee that had not taken part in the Corfu deliberations.[38] Frano Supilo stated on 31 July 1917 that 'in its basic principles' the Corfu Declaration went in a positive sense beyond his own 'postulates'.[39] The Montenegrin Committee for National Unification examined the Corfu Declaration at a session in Paris on 11 August and then announced that, 'aware of its national duties' and 'finding that with this war Montenegro ends its role as a separate Serb state' and that it remained only 'to enter into the Kingdom of Serbs, Croats and Slovenes', it accepted the Corfu Declaration in its entirety 'in the conviction that it expresses the wishes of the Serb nation in Montenegro'.[40] On 18 August the Executive Committee of the Yugoslav National Council in the United States accepted the Declaration as an act of epochal importance.[41] Only the government of King Nicholas of Montenegro rejected the agreement reached in Corfu, and stated as much in a strongly worded communiqué.[42]

The revolution in Russia, meanwhile, had had a great effect on the Volunteer Corps.[43] Towards the end of March, lower-ranking officers proposed the setting up of military councils within the Volunteer Corps in line with 'Order No. 1', which was one of the first measures of the revolutionary authorities. The proposal was supported and encouraged by the revolutionary councils in the sectors of Odessa and Voznesensky, where the Corps was located. The Corps command first tried to resist the impact of revolutionary events and ideas on the military units, relying for this on part of the army and officer personnel, especially Serbs. It also sought and received assistance from the Serbian legation in Petrograd, the Serbian military envoy to the Russian supreme command, members of the Yugoslav Committee in Russia—Ante Mandić and Milivoje Jambrišak (Croats)—and the Serbian Government. However, because that demand could not be refused, especially when orders to that effect came from the Russian supreme command, on 18 April 1917 General Mihailo Živković introduced company, regiment and division councils and a corps assembly. However, it was clear that the intention was to use these bodies to exert the maximum influence on political trends and discipline in the units.

It was not by chance that changes affecting the Volunteer Corps in the Revolution started with the circulation of inaccurate rumours that Corps units had fired into crowds of revolutionaries to defend the regime of the Tsar. Opponents of a common Yugoslav army, including Croatian followers of Ivan Frank and Monarchy supporters among the volunteers, as well as German, Austro-Hungarian and to a certain extent Italian agents, were in fact the first to try to take advantage of the new revolutionary developments. Members of the Black Hand, including Srb, Simić, Gojković and Radoje Janković, also tried to make use of the new circumstances. However, the contradictions already existing in Corps units were far more to blame for what had started to happen.

The Revolution overturned existing relations and restrictions, thus enabling many suppressed problems to rise to the surface, especially those that existed in the Corps itself. One problem was that all prisoners of war had been accepted into the Corps without exception; the bad material conditions were another problem; and yet another was the excessively narrow base of political principles on which—despite advice to the contrary from General Živković—the Serbian government had formed those units and let them go into battle. The very name 'Serb Volunteer Corps' demonstrated the narrowness of the basic political principles, and this was aggravated by the use of exclusively Serbian emblems and the predominance of Serbian ideological values in moral and political training. On top of that, officers from Serbia itself enjoyed different rights from officers from the Yugoslav areas of the Monarchy, and it was only after a warning from General Živković that Pašić's government finally opted for broader political principles. General Živković did, however, warn that the basic political principles should be changed in order to preserve the Corps' raison d'être and prevent all Croats and Slovenes from withdrawing from it. He further proposed that regiments should be called 'Serb', 'Croat' or 'Slovene' depending on the ethnic majority of officers they contained.[44]

At a session on 6 April 1917, the Serbian Government agreed to the name being changed to the 'Volunteer Corps of Serbs, Croats and Slovenes', and to all officers from Yugoslav areas being equal in all respects to officers from Serbia if they so desired and if they personally submitted a request for acceptance 'as a subject' (which should be understood as taking account of the international legal aspect of this issue). It also conceded that regiments could be named 'Croat' or 'Slovene'. The following explanation was given of the names used: 'The denomination Yugoslavs shall not be used officially because Bulgarians, who are Yugoslavs too, are not with us.'[45] It would seem that Bulgarians served here merely as a pretext, and what was most important was that the Serbian authorities, and primarily Nikola Pašić, were endeavouring to retain the names 'Serbs' and 'Serbia'. Finally, the Government insisted on the principle of 'volunteerism', and ordered that those who wished to leave the ranks of the volunteers should not be detained but handed over to the Russian authorities who had taken them prisoner. Jambrišak also agreed to this proposal.

The complexity of the state of affairs is demonstrated by the fact that these basic principles inflamed those very men who had been guided to become volunteers by the ideal of unity regardless of all differences. This was despite the fact that the Government had tried to suggest that the new clarifications were satisfactory since they retained the necessary national denominations. However, a large number of officers left the Volunteer Corps for the very reason that the word 'Yugoslav' was avoided, whereas they had been fighting out of Yugoslav convictions. One assembly in Odessa proclaimed:

> Our national-political ideal has been and will remain the Yugoslav ideal, i.e. the unification of all Serbs, Croats and Slovenes in one completely free and independent state—Yugoslavia, a state founded on the principles of democracy and the total equality of all three nationalities.... It is for this reason that we reject 'Greater Serbia', just as we reject 'Greater Croatia' and 'Greater Slovenia', as criminal concepts.... Our ideal is therefore federal Yugoslavia.... The Russian Revolution and the victory of Russian democracy...signify a new era in the history of mankind...and that is why the Russian Revolution cannot remain only Russian.... We wish to contribute so far as much as we are able to the victory of our ideals in the ranks of the Russian revolutionary army.[46]

Numbers dwindled in the Corps at this time; some men pulled out in an organised manner, within the 'dissident movement', and joined the Russian army, then the revolutionary army. Others, however simply deserted from their units. The process lasted from spring to summer 1917. According to data supplied by General Živković, the Corps numbered 36,609 men in February, of whom 981 were officers, and 19,334 in June, of whom 640 were officers.[47] Many of the men who had left the Corps returned to it later.

Disagreement occurred between the Russian and Serbian governments as to whether volunteer units should be sent to the Romanian front or brought out of Russia and sent as assistance to the Serbian army.[48] General Živković was in favour of leaving Russia and of the units later being reinforced with volunteers from America and dispatched to the front as a separate military formation. After many contradictory orders, the 2nd division of the Volunteer Corps was evacuated via Archangel, where it boarded British ships and set sail on 20 and 21 September. The 1st brigade of the Corps 1st division also set sail from Archangel to travel round Europe to the Salonika front, where it arrived in December 1917 and early January 1918. Around 5,000 men of the 2nd brigade had been in Russia when the October Revolution occurred, and they were evacuated through Siberia to the Far Eastern ocean port of Dairen. There they boarded British ships on 23 February 1918 and sailed round Asia to the Salonika front, reaching it in late March.

Consequently, in the first months of 1918 a considerable number of Yugoslav volunteer forces arrived on the Salonika front,[49] including combatants from all the Yugoslav peoples and all the Yugoslav provinces of the Monarchy, as well as from Serbia and Montenegro.[50] Over 4,000 volunteers arrived from America, and 12,500 from Russia. The Yugoslav Committee was particularly insistent on a volunteer formation being created, and Trumbić evidently wished to resolve the politically important issue of the name of such a volunteer formation by offering a compromise. In a letter of 7 January 1918 he suggested to Regent Alexander that it should be called the 'Yugoslav division of Serb, Croat and Slovene volunteers'. Alexander replied that it would be called the 'Yugoslav division'.[51] In order to equip the new division, the Vardar division was split up[52] and the Macedonians from it joined the Yugoslav division in February 1918 and became part of the 2nd Army in April 1918. It numbered around 10,000 officers and men.

Revolutionaries, most of them Serbs, were among the most significant Yugoslavs to remain in Russia.[53] As early as the spring of 1917 a considerable number of them had become closely connected to leftist tendencies in the Russian Revolution. The newspaper *Revolucija* was then published as the 'gazette of the Yugoslav communist group at the Russian Communist Party'. As from mid-summer 1917, the *Jugoslavija* newspaper voiced the opinions of those who wanted to be 'true revolutionaries' and sought 'freedom not only for one class but for the entire nation', and 'not only for our nation but for all nations'. The military committees created in April 1917, particularly those in 'dissident units', were mainly of left-wing commitment, and the Serb Strike Battalion, which was formed in the summer of 1917 and quickly changed its name to the Yugoslav Strike Battalion and then the Yugoslav Revolutionary Detachment, was also leftist in orientation. The various committees were soon to set up the Yugoslav Revolutionary Council, at first numbering nearly 20,000 men. With the October Revolution came the separation of the Bolshevik wing, many representatives of which took part in the civil war as Red Army combatants and commanders. Serb members of the Red Army passed a resolution in Saratov in August 1918 stressing the firm determination to fight 'with all internal and foreign enemies that would act against the Soviet authorities'.

Separate linkages

The earlier mentioned links in Austria-Hungary between Slovene and Croat politicians in 1915 were to multiply in the following years and become transformed into a campaign for Croat-Slovene unity. However, it was also a campaign that allowed for the inclusion of Serb political forces. The campaign became particularly prominent when Emperor Karl came to the throne in 1916.[54] It was headed by Slovene clericalists and young Liberals, Croatian followers of Starčević, leading Dalmatian figures and Serb deputies from Dalmatia in the Austrian Parliament. And it was when the Austrian Parliament was reconvened that the campaign achieved its first major result. What actually happened was that on 29 May 1917, the day before the first session of Parliament, a common Yugoslav Club was created, and the next day Anton Korošec, a Slovene, read out a declaration at the first official Parliament session. The declaration stated that Yugoslav Club deputies would participate in parliamentary deliberations by supporting, 'with all their might' and on the basis of the 'national principle and Croatian state law', the demand 'of their united nation' for the 'unification of all Monarchy lands inhabited by Slovenes, Croats and Serbs' into 'an autonomous state body, free from the domination of other nations and built on a democratic basis'. The state body, he added, would be 'under the sceptre of the Habsburg-Lorraine dynasty'.[55] The declaration was signed by Yugoslav Club members.[56] It is not yet clear why two Serb deputies did not sign the declaration.

That document, known as the May Declaration, was a compromise between diverse objectives—those of the Yugoslav Club and those of Starčević's Party of the Right, which was not directly represented in Vienna because Croatia belonged to the Hungarian part of the Monarchy. However, it had been reached with the Party of the Right's agreement, and it was on account of that Party that 'Croatian state law' was quoted. The May Declaration was a result of the independent evolution of the Yugoslav movement on the territory of the Monarchy itself. It represented a programme that reflected the strongest political civic tendencies in Slovenia and Dalmatia, as well as the strongest purely Croatian tendency in the *banovina* of Croatia. Although that course of events had been under way for over a year and was directed at aims contrary to those championed by Serbia, Montenegro and the Yugoslav Committee, it still opted for a unification programme within the Habsburg state and was nonetheless historically significant because it was directed against the dualist foundations of the Monarchy, i.e. against the inequality of its nations. The significance of the Declaration did not lie in its contents, but in the process to which it belonged. It therefore depended on further developments in that process, which in turn depended on the battles being fought in the war, and mainly the battle being waged by the proponents of the Yugoslav programme within the Allied bloc. Objectively the May Declaration was located in a far broader historical process than the one from which it stemmed.

The May Declaration resounded throughout the Yugoslav provinces of the Monarchy, which was split up into a number of separate administrative areas. The first to respond was Starčević's Party of the Right in Croatia, as a consequence of that party's lengthy pro-Yugoslav cooperation with the Slovene clericalists Krek and Korošec. The head of Starčević's deputies in the Croatian Assembly (*Sabor*), Ante Pavelić (not to be confused with the future Croatian Ustaše leader of the same name) made a statement on 5 June in which he emphasised that the right of each nation to self-determination had to be 'the core of the ultimate organisation of international relations after this war,' underlining that it was vital to 'reorganise the Habsburg Monarchy on the basis of the full equality of its nations' and in a 'democratic spirit'. He added that Starčević's Party was in favour of 'the national unity of Croats, Slovenes and Serbs,' and that it 'called particularly on Serbs who were citizens of the Kingdom of Croatia…to work with Croats and Slovenes to unify the entire Slav south of the Habsburg Monarchy.'[57]

Headed by Bishop Anton Jeglić of Ljubljana, Slovene right-wing clericalists also agreed to the May Declaration.[58] Announcements of support from Croatians in Bosnia and Herzegovina and from Franciscans in Herzegovina also arrived in great number.[59] In January 1918 students at the University of Zagreb called, in the name of the single 'Slovene-Croat-Serb nation, divided into several states', for state unification and freedom on a broad democratic basis.[60] Deputies of the Istria Assembly (*Sabor*), led by Matko Laginja and Vjekoslav Spinčić, representatives in the Vienna Parliament, also declared their support.⁶¹ The Serb People's Radical Party in Vojvodina, among others, stated that Croats, Slovenes and Serbs were one nation with three names, 'whose lives made it necessary to live together'.⁶²

The conduct of the Croat-Serb Coalition, especially that of the Serb side, was understandable as a manoeuvre to ensure that the Hungarian leadership continued to provide some sort of protection for Serbs on the one hand, and to prevent involvement in anything that could lead to direct conflict with Serbia's foreign policy programme on the other. The Coalition must have known that extreme Austrian forces, headed by the supreme command, used trialism as a means to rid themselves of dualism in order to ensure the predomination of Austria, or rather Austrian Germans, in the Monarchy; and those forces were both striving to destroy Serbia and Montenegro and calling for repressive measures against the Serb population in the Monarchy. The Coalition's conduct was, therefore, dictated by circumstances. It did not wish to hinder the 'Declaration Movement' but did not wish to join it either. The Coalition further considered it best to keep the unification movement within the framework of the state system and political forces and thus make use of the Hungarian wish to attach Dalmatia, Bosnia and Herzegovina to their part of the Habsburg state, in order to gather part of the Yugoslav population into one entity.

However, the belief prevailed among some Coalition leaders that the time was ripe to change tactics. Consequently, Srdjan Budisavljević and Valerijan Pribićević withdrew from the Coalition in July 1917 to form their own separate political group.⁶³ At a Croatian *Sabor* session on 13 July, Budisavljević read out a statement in which he stressed that it was the 'resolute demand of the Monarchy's entire Slav south, on the basis of the national principle, historical rights and the right of nations to self-determination, that all lands of the Monarchy inhabited by Slovenes, Croats and Serbs should unite into a totally autonomous, independent body.' Budisavljević and Pribićević were evidently in agreement with the May Declaration and supported it, but they radicalised its demands by omitting from their programme the idea that the Yugoslav solution should be realised under the 'sceptre of the Habsburg-Lorraine dynasty'. The two

Coalition dissidents were joined in the autumn of 1917 by others, including Ivan Krstelj and Mate Drinković, two leading Croatian figures from Dalmatia, and they later launched a newspaper called *Glas Slovenaca, Hrvata i Srba*. This was actually the political group that long remained the most radical within the broader 'Declaration Movement'. Together with leading figures from Starčević's Party, representatives of that group made a statement on 3 December 1917 in support of the Bolshevik Declaration of Peace, once again underlining that the people they represented demanded the conclusion of a 'democratic peace' which would 'guarantee the total freedom of state, cultural and economic life and progress for all nations, and therefore also the single nation of Croats, Serbs and Slovenes'. The statement made the clearest demand hitherto for an independent, i.e. totally sovereign state.

Serb politicians from Bosnia and Herzegovina also joined the broad movement that had arisen in the wake of the May Declaration. They came from all Bosnian and Herzegovinan political groups with the exception of that headed by Bishop Štadler and that represented by the leading Muslim figures Arnautović and Bašagić. The followings of these two groups soon began to decrease under the influence of the 'Declaration Movement'.[64] It would seem that Danilo Dimović played a prominent role in all this; he had participated in the talks in Zagreb back in July 1915, and, during the foundation of the Yugoslav Club, he had not only worked to that end in Vienna, but had also done all he could to include leading Bosnian and Herzegovinan figures in the Club. He had then invited Sunarić, Arnautović and Bašagić to go to Vienna and take part in the creation of the Yugoslav movement, but only Sunarić had accepted the invitation. It was also thanks to Dimović that the Club decided to channel its political work towards Bosnia and Herzegovina to the same extent as towards Croatia. It was for that reason that Korošec, at the invitation of Dimović and Sunarić, visited Bosnia in the capacity of president of the Yugoslav Club. He was highly active politically during his visit there.

The May Declaration provoked a broad political process. It was not the announcements of support from civic political groups that lent the 'Declaration Movement' true significance, but rather the fact that the entire campaign had fallen onto already prepared ground. National, social and political dissatisfaction was growing from month to month. There was, in fact, an intensification of the 'internal' front in the Habsburg Empire, which was all the more important since it formed part of the broader national and social trends leading the Monarchy to the brink of collapse. From then on two separate, albeit connected, issues were on the historical agenda. The first issue was whether Serbia would be among the victors at the end of the war, and the second was whether internal processes would cause Austria-Hungary to collapse. Serbia's victory in the war and the collapse of the Monarchy were, therefore, separate requirements for the realisation of the Yugoslav programme.

The causes of such trends were to be found primarily in the Monarchy's disastrous economic circumstances. Already weak and obsolete, the economy was at the very edge of ruin as a result of its enormous war expenses. In December 1917 Franjo Markić, a socialist who had fled abroad, described the situation in Bosnia and Herzegovina in the most grim terms, saying that people were 'collapsing from hunger and dying', and that the poor were 'even eating the bark of trees'. Local authorities in the mining town of Breza claimed that miners' wages were 'far below the minimum necessary for keeping body and soul together.'[65] What was happening was that protest was rooted in social and national causes. Nameless poets from among the ranks of the people spoke of these circumstances in an inexperienced but highly effective manner. The police in Zagreb found the following handwritten words, signed by 'Slav revolutionaries' on a notice board:

We fear not the gallows, Wilhelm./We fear not janissaries, Charles./A million of us have already fallen./A million have fallen for you./Another million of us will die [...]/To rid ourselves of your tyranny.

In January 1918, a sign was posted uniting the otherwise split movement, saying: 'Long live Trumbić and Supilo,/Long live Trešić and Vojnović,/Long live Pašić and Korošec!'[66]

There were more and more men who no longer wanted to fight under the black and yellow standard of Austria-Hungary. Throughout the Yugoslav lands the woods were filling with fugitives from the military. The Croatian-Slavonian command complained in early

1918 that it did not have enough men to capture all the fugitives, although the gendarmerie had arrested 20,000 persons in 1917. The command stressed: 'It has been noted that the population at large is helping deserters by providing them with food and shelter and informing them of search parties in their vicinity.'[67] The impact of Habsburg propaganda and ideology was diminishing day by day. The population was espousing new value systems—national, social and social-revolutionary. The fugitives in the woods—'green cadres'— formed, in fact, a spontaneous movement of a revolutionary nature.

There was also a revival of social democracy,[68] and the authorities were compelled to allow it on to the political scene to alleviate the political pressure within the population, which became particularly strong with the news of the revolution in Russia.[69] New socialist mouthpieces sprang up throughout the Yugoslav regions of the Monarchy in the summer of 1917. *Sloboda* was published in Croatia, to be replaced at the end of the year by *Pravda*, while the *Glas Slobode* came out in Bosnia and Herzegovina. Trade union and strike movements started up in the industrial centres of Croatia. The authorities were, in fact, living in fear of the impact not only of ideas from Russia, but also of the activities of Karl Liebknecht and his followers. In Bosnia and Herzegovina they hailed the intentions of Bishop Štadler to prevent the strengthening of social democracy with the help of Catholic ideology and organisation. The *Sloboda* newspaper was therefore banned in Croatia in December 1917.

Wartime political problems

The publicly declared programmes of the British and US governments had an unsettling effect on the Yugoslav political émigrés, provoking strife among leading Yugoslav figures and an intensification of foreign policy activity. Serbia's opposition parties joined together and on 14 January 1918 sought the earliest possible convening of the National Assembly in order to call the Government to account.[70] Because the Government had already decided to convene the Assembly for internal political reasons,[71] it seems that Pašić also considered that relations with the opposition had reached a point where it was necessary to have recourse to the Assembly again. When the Assembly finally met on 25 February, once again in Corfu despite opposition efforts to have the session held in France, Pašić proposed the creation of a coalition government, but stipulated that he should continue to be prime minister and the Old Radicals should continue to comprise the leadership. As he was the person the opposition actually wanted to topple, they managed, by means of obstruction, to prevent the election of the government candidate Djordje Bračinac to the position of Assembly speaker, and the government resigned on 27 February. Parties then started vying for the post of prime minister, but it became evident that the opposition did not have the strength to oust Pašić. Regent Alexander supported him and gave him the mandate to create 'if possible a coalition cabinet, but, if that proved impossible, a homogeneous one'.

After a month of unsuccessful negotiations, Pašić formed a cabinet of Old Radicals on 27 March in which all the former ministers retained their posts. That put an end to the government crisis, but tensions remained till June. Differences centred on the existence, or non-existence, of a quorum for decision-making in the Assembly. Citing extraordinary circumstances, the Government was calculating the quorum according to the number of deputies in exile, while the opposition was demanding adherence to the letter of the constitution and calculating the quorum according to the total number of seats, i.e. also including the deputies who had remained in Serbia.[72] The opposition concentrated the political battle with the Government on the foreign policy issue, but it soon became clear that the opposition had not only no other programme to offer besides the Yugoslav programme, but no other concept within that programme either. The Assembly finally ended in June without any decision having been made, and Pašić and the Old Radicals remained in power.

A number of opponents of Pašić and the Old Radicals were in exile, but not part of the Assembly opposition, and their views concerning the organisation of the future Yugoslav state differed greatly from those officially held. Many prominent individuals disagreed with Pašić's political ideas and challenged the way in which he conducted politics. The most eminent among these was Professor Jovan Cvijić.[73] It is not known why Cvijić was such a bitter adversary of Pašić, although it is clear that his idea of Yugoslavia was more idealistic and that Pašić's ideas, such as the 'Serb nation with three names', must have greatly irritated him. There were also calls for a federal republic, perhaps under the name of the Unified Yugoslav State, the members of which would be Serbia and Montenegro each within its pre-war borders, Bosnia and Herzegovina, the *banovina* of Croatia, Dalmatia, Slovenia and Backa with Banat.

Serbia's war aim, however, remained the same as that laid down in the second half of 1914, whereby its territorial programme had become more specific and detailed. Just as the Austro-Hungarian attack had had the effect of finally bringing about a territorial programme, so Bulgaria's attack caused an enlargement of such a programme. The issue of Albania's fate during the war allowed the possibility of expansion in that direction to be included in the programme. A more detailed border project was elaborated in Corfu in the second half of 1916 within the scope of the war aim and territorial programme adopted earlier. That project was submitted to Serbia's diplomatic representatives in foreign countries on 2 February 1917, but not as a document to be presented to Allied governments;[74] it was in a memorandum of 31 March 1918 that Serbia's foreign policy programme was officially presented to the Allied Great Powers,[75] and according to its terms 'our minimum demands' encompassed the territory extending from the border with Greece, as determined in the Bucharest peace treaty of 10 August 1913, to the River Maroš, Mount Mecsek, and hills north of Klagenfurt and Villach, that is from (but not including) Lom Palanka, along the River Struma up to (and including) Gorica. The lack of absolute clarity indirectly indicates readiness to yield Trieste and Pula with their surrounding areas to Italy in the west, to seek Scutari in the southwest, and to encompass the area up to but not including Szeged and Baja in the north. The line running down the centre of eastern Banat was retained from the programme elaborated in 1914, leaving on the Yugoslav side the belt of land including Anina, Resita and the territory stretching 40–50 km. east of Temešvar (Timişoara). The lines drawn in northern Banat remained the same as they had been in the 1914 plan, while demands were reduced to a certain extent in northern Bačka, with the border running to the north of Subotica and south of Baja. The rest of the border up to north-western Styria stayed the same as previously, which meant that Prekomurje still remained outside it. Further west, the minimum borderline stipulated in 1914 was retained, which also applied to the territories west of Villach. Towards Italy, the former demand for Gradisca was abandoned, while the possibility remained for negotiations with Italy on the subject of western Istria. The provisions concerning Trieste indicate that it was to be ceded to Italy.

The border projects combined, first and foremost, the national principle and, secondly and additionally, the strategic principle. Certain details reveal a lack of ethnic knowledge (in the far north and particularly in the northwest). Furthermore, the impact was felt of political ambitions as contained in the more recent tradition of both Serbian and Montenegrin foreign policy (in relation to Albania and Bulgaria), and the principle of punishing the aggressor (Bulgaria) was adopted. With respect to Italy, it was evident that its status as a large Allied power was always borne in mind; its aspirations could not be accepted but certain concessions were nonetheless sought through a 'special agreement' (not an agreement between Serbia and Italy or between Serbia and the Entente, but 'between representatives of Italy and representatives of Yugoslavs' who, legally speaking, were citizens of Austria-Hungary).[76]

The programme was explicitly filled into the Entente's general war aims, with the application of liberal Western ideas, especially those stemming from US President Wilson, but the essence of the provisions was the desire to ensure lasting peace. The fundamental aim was to dismantle Austria-Hungary, since allegedly 'its nations do not wish to remain in it' and its historical sense lay in 'serving the drive of German power and culture towards the East'. Furthermore, 'there will be no peace, nor there can be, for as long as the Habsburg Monarchy survives.' The provisions further concluded:

The new state of affairs that will be created by giving nationalities their freedom and the right to self-determination will be considerably more conducive to the maintenance of lasting peace, as it will be supported by the new states that have been founded on the principles of the rights and freedom of nations (the Yugoslav state with 12 million inhabitants, Hungary with 10 million, Czechoslovakia with 10 million, unified Romanians with 12 million, and the German Kingdom made up of Germans and the lands of Upper and Lower Austria, Tyrol and Salzburg with about 10 million). As a result of this ... Germanism will lose strength; it will lose around 40 million people of non-German nations who now live in Austria-Hungary and serve German policy. Germany will thus be cut off from the east ... with Poland, Czechoslovakia and the Yugoslav state, which all together will number 46 million inhabitants who will wish to defend their survival and prevent a German drive to the East. German power will thus be weakened and limited to its own nation.

A study of Serbia's project for the Yugoslav borders reveals that it can be divided into two parts. One part comprised demands *vis-à-vis* Bulgaria, the unification of Vojvodina, the assumed desire for unification with Montenegro and plans concerning northern Albania, with the stipulation that those territories should enter into Serbia and, with Serbia, into Yugoslavia. The unification of Serbia and Montenegro was thus constantly regarded as a separate issue and exclusively the affair of those two states; a foreign policy duel with Romania was accepted on account of Banat, based on the rights of Serbs and the strategic interests of Serbia (which was accompanied by a separate study); the eastern border was considered to be an issue involving only Serbia and Bulgaria; and, finally, northern Albania was taken as an issue of interest to Serbia, alone or unified with Montenegro. The rest of the programme resembled a separate part of the territorial project. It was not, however, the intention to present one smaller and one larger project, but rather two parts of the same programme.

In January 1918 the Serbian government, the Yugoslav Committee and Yugoslav associations and organisations in exile were highly active in two directions. Attempts were made, on the one hand, to convince the Russian Bolshevik government that the creation of a Yugoslav state was in line with the revolutionary programme, and on the other hand to assure the British and US governments that their war programme aspiring to preserve Austria-Hungary was misconceived. There followed a series of confidential talks, public meetings, appeals and protests on the part of the Yugoslav Society in Paris, the Yugoslav Society in Petrograd, Serb university professors and the General Organisation of United Serb-Croat-Slovene Academic Youth in Switzerland.

It was while all this activity was taking place that the Serbian side first deliberately mentioned Yugoslav Club activity in the Monarchy and the increasingly widespread movement provoked by the May Declaration. A statement made by the student youth organisation in Switzerland on 22 January 1918 contained the following: 'Yugoslav deputies in the Vienna Parliament and the Croatian Sabor are constantly and unanimously demanding the unification of their nation into one independent state.'[77] Moreover, an official letter addressed by the Socialist Committee to the Conference of Allied Countries' Labour Parties in Nottingham, England, on 24 January stated that proof of the determination of the Yugoslav people to be free and independent lay in the 30,000 people who had been shot or hanged or had died in Austro-Hungarian prisons in the course of the war, in addition to the statements by Yugoslav deputies in the Austrian Parliament, and resolutions of all civic and socialist parties.[78] These public proclamations were preceded by the use of the same proof in a note from the Serbian Legation in London to the British Government on 23 January.[79] The annex to that note stated: 'Parliamentary representatives of our nation in Austria-Hungary have recently voted against war credits.... These representatives officially called in the Parliament in Vienna for the unification of all Serbs, Croats and Slovenes in an independent state.... These same ideas are to be found in the declarations made by all Sabor parties in Zagreb.' Added to this were statements by Korošec, Laginja and Ribarž.

The idea of 'peace without annexation', which was highlighted by the Russian Revolution, became at that time a frequently cited slogan not only at public events but also at secret meetings of politicians (even German ones). For the Yugoslav movement the slogan also signified the possibility of challenging past annexations—or, to be precise, the Austro-Hungarian annexation of Bosnia and Herzegovina. A resolution from a Yugoslav gathering in Geneva on 5 January contained the following sentence: 'We cannot imagine Russian democracy being able to forget the annexations of past years.'[80] Pašić evidently wanted to take advantage of that possibility and to this end employed Serbs from Bosnia and Herzegovina. Nikola Stojanović, a Yugoslav Committee member, sent a letter to Lloyd George, the British prime minister, reminding him that the annexation had been a 'terrible violation of international law'.[81] In association with Milan Srškić, Stojanović also drew up a document entitled 'Bosnian-Herzegovinan revolutionaries to Russian revolutionaries' and sent it to the Bolshevik Council of People's Commissars, which it urged to work to ensure that the two provinces should not remain 'under Austro-Hungarian aggressors and militarists'.[82] The document was forwarded to the Bolshevik leadership. Moves by the Serbian Government itself clearly demonstrated that the issue of Bosnia and Herzegovina was to be raised: this occurred in a note of 17 January, though incorporated into the Yugoslav programme as a whole.[83] On 22 January Pašić instructed the envoy in Washington to induce US authorities to take steps to make the act of annexation of Bosnia and Herzegovina null and void.[84] However, this instruction was seen in some Serbian diplomatic circles and in the Yugoslav movement as an indication that in a time of crisis Prime Minister Pašić would not insist on the Yugoslav programme as a whole, and perhaps had only a 'minimal programme' in mind.[85]

Two contradictory facts are evident here. First, there is no sign of any renunciation of the Yugoslav programme in its entirety in Serbia's official documents or in moves made at that time; and secondly, Pašić was indeed particularly interested in Bosnia and Herzegovina at this time and laid special emphasis on the issue on several occasions. Reasonable interpretations indicate that Pašić was truly continuing to defend the entire programme, but, at the same time, considering that minimum gains from the war should be ensured. But something quite different was probably also involved—something that became clear in the autumn of 1916. Pašić was actually trying to attach as many territories as possible to Serbia, to enter with these territories into the Yugoslav state (besides Bosnia and Herzegovina, these territories included Montenegro, Vojvodina and possible gains in Bulgaria and Albania).

In the spring of 1917, Serbian Social Democrats had renewed their political activities in exile under the influence of the revolution in Russia.[86] They were starting to consider convening a conference of members of that party in exile. Moreover, Vojislav Popović had undertaken to re-establish a Chamber of Workers, and he sent a petition to that effect to the Ministry of the Economy in Corfu. A Conference of Social Democrats was held in Marseilles from 23 to 25 April 1917, and two major decisions were made there. It was decided, first, 'to start fulfilling our duty towards the nation, the working class and socialism', and secondly 'to work for the establishment of a Chamber of Workers to protect our workers in France and...assist workers' families in Serbia and workers that have been taken prisoner.'[87] A start was made on the implementation of these two decisions, and the Chamber of Workers was re-established in July 1917 following a decision by the Minister of Justice. The Chamber's headquarters were in Paris, and Kosta Novaković was elected its secretary. In pursuit of the tasks stipulated at the Marseilles conference, the first assistance from the Chamber went to about 200 addresses in occupied Serbia. Besides, on 22 July 1917 a separate political committee of Serb Social Democrats was set up in France, and a sub-committee was established in late August for work with party members who were soldiers on the Salonika front. In the first half of 1918 the Committee inaugurated a newspaper called *Budućnost*.

The revolution in Russia had given rise to a large number of questions, doubts, differences and arguments, particularly after the Bolsheviks assumed power in early November 1917. As in the European Social Democratic movement as a whole, the basic issue discussed among the Serb Social Democrats was whether to support Bolshevik views and activities or not. On the other hand, the issue of whether or not the Entente could be expected to support the people's struggle for freedom was of particular importance for Serb Social Democrats, given their specific conditions. The committee and its newspaper *Budućnost* had accused the Central Powers of having provoked the war and being proponents of imperialism, and they naturally considered that they could expect support from the Entente in battles for national freedom. Dušan Popović, a leading Social Democrat figure who had emigrated with Triša Kaclerović from occupied Serbia in the summer of 1917,[88] exemplifies the complexity of the options facing Serb Social Democrats. In a letter sent to the committee in Paris in early August 1918,[89] he stated that Social Democracy had to be based on the hypothesis that 'this war was provoked by imperialistic motives on both sides and is being waged for imperialistic objectives on both sides.' It was, he said, 'a brutal capitalist war *par excellence*,' in which 'the ruling classes of large states on both sides are exploiting the slogan of the rights and the liberation of small and subjugated nations out of ... selfish interests.' Popović continued by hailing the revolution in Russia and stating that he saw it as 'the best guarantee for world peace at the earliest possible moment' and 'the embryo of the new International.'[90] It must further be noted that many Serbs were, actually, committed to Bolshevism.[91] Filip Filipović had translated the most important political and ideological document of that time, Lenin's *The State and Revolution*.⁹²

Moreover, the two émigré Social Democrat deputies did not take part in the National Assembly session in Corfu. Dragiša Lapčević had remained in occupied Serbia, and Triša Kaclerović, for his part, had been ignored by the government because of his participation in the Stockholm Conference. The Social Democratic Committee in Paris came out on several occasions in favour of a Balkan Federation, because it was seen as a way to prevent the Great Powers from realising their aggressive or hegemonic aspirations in South-Eastern Europe. The committee demanded the creation of conditions for free development of Balkan nations on the basis of respect for the principle of self-determination.⁹³ In a statement made public in February 1918, the committee also advocated that Macedonia should become a member of the Balkan Federation in its own right. The Paris group, in line with the stands adopted at the Conference in Marseilles in April 1917, gave priority to realisation of the Yugoslav programme. In August 1917 the committee had addressed a separate letter to French socialists, explaining that Serbs, Croats and Slovenes were one nation linked by a common language, common customs and traditions, and the desire for unity. In the crisis that unfolded in early 1918, the committee worked to prove that the war programmes of the Western Great Powers were not appropriate. But Dušan Popović objected to this letter being sent and stated in early 1918 that he considered 'a Balkan federation with Macedonia as an autonomous member' to be 'the only correct, good ... and possible solution,' with the proviso that the federation's realisation had to be the fruit of revolutionary activity on the part of socialists.⁹⁴

End of the War

As 1918 drew on, Austria-Hungary floundered more and more, exhausted by the efforts demanded of it by the war and weighed down by economic, social and political burdens. A general lack of organisation was also becoming evident.⁹⁵ At the same time, conditions in its Yugoslav provinces were becoming less stable by the hour, while guerrilla warfare was rife in the occupied areas of Serbia and Montenegro. In vain Germany mobilised its last forces to fight on the front in France, and in the summer of 1918 the Allied side finally took the initiative on the battlefield, and German troops started to withdraw. Revolution stood at the gates of the two Central European empires. And the Allies were preparing a decisive strike on the Salonika front. With General Petar Bojović commanding the 1st Army, Vojvoda Stepa Stepanović commanding the 2nd Army and Vojvoda Živojin Mišić as chief-of-staff in June 1918, the Serbian army was finally preparing to advance.[96]

And so it was that 8 a.m. on 14 September 1918 the general Allied offensive started on the Salonika front with fire from about 2,000 guns. At 5.30 the next morning the Serbian 2nd Army was the first to charge.[97] The Allies had around 628,000 men, 1,800 cannon and 200 aeroplanes, while the Bulgarian-German defence numbered around 626,000 men, 1,600 cannon and eighty aeroplanes over a 450-km. front. To compensate for the lack of strength for a large-scale offensive, General Franchet d'Espérey of France, as commander of the Allied forces, concentrated three times as many men, machine-guns and aeroplanes as the enemy and four times as many cannon on the 33-km. breakthrough front. The blow was tremendous, and the enemy could not regroup. This was the start of the final military act in South-East Europe, which played a vital part in bringing the war to an end that autumn. The Serbian 1st and 2nd armies represented the main strike and pursuit forces. They numbered 150,000 men, including the Yugoslav volunteer troops, alongside 180,000 French soldiers, half of whom were from the colonies, 135,000 Greeks, 120,000 British, 42,000 Italians and 1,000 Albanians under Esat Pasha.

The Bulgarians quickly faltered and concluded a truce at the end of September. However, the German and Austro-Hungarian leaders did all they could to hold back the Allied breakthrough and keep Serbia occupied. Immediately after Bulgaria's withdrawal from the war, the Foreign Ministry in Berlin stated: 'It is not politically necessary to evacuate Serbia.... We are far more concerned with preventing the Entente forces from directly endangering Hungary and with retaining the possibility of keeping hold of Romania.'[98] With the ending of Bulgarian administration, a German military governorate was created in Niš on 3 October.[99]

The German supreme command was also endeavouring to place obstacles in the way of Allied forces by sending as many units as it could to the Balkan front. The entire Bavarian Alpine corps, which had previously been sent as reinforcements to Serbia in the autumn of 1915, was dispatched from the Belgian front, demonstrating the extent of Germany's determination to halt the breakthrough.[100] The 53rd corps and the 219th infantry division were also brought to the front in the Balkans, later to be joined by the 217th and 224th infantry divisions, while a number of outstandingly competent officers were sent to undertake command and staff duties. On 6 October the commander of the 11th German Army gave the following orders:

> Serb troops, supported by the French, are continuing to penetrate northwards. They wish to drive German and Austro-Hungarian troops from Serbia. If they succeed in doing this, Serbs will then directly threaten the borders of the Austro-Hungarian Monarchy and thus weaken our ally's resistance. Every officer and soldier in the 11th Army must be made fully aware that here in Serbia we are defending the existence of the German Reich.[101]

Austria–Hungary was also doing its utmost. The 9th, 30th and 59th divisions, as well as the 4th cavalry division, were sent as reinforcements to the troops ready for battle in the Belgrade Governorate. The command of all Austro-Hungarian and German forces was unified for the Balkans as a whole, and General Hermann Baron Kövess was appointed commander-in-chief.[102] But all was in vain as the northerly drive was unstoppable. German bankers seem to have been the first to realise that things were bad, if not hopeless. On 2 October the Direktion der Discontogesellschaft informed the Economics Ministry in Berlin that it could not ensure continued exploitation at the mine in Bor, 'until the situation has become clear'.[103]

Lack of discipline was also starting to bite in the armies of the two empires. Bulgarians had already started uncontrolled pillaging in an effort to take as much as they could after the defeat. Vice-Consul Haas was a witness in Niš:

> Bulgarian officers are trying to remove everything they used here, even furniture from Serb homes. But they do not have the necessary means of transport. They requisitioned all oxen at the last minute, but the Germans confiscated the oxen in Niš. And then the Serb population became involved.... As soon as the draught animals had been driven away, Serbs started taking everything that had been loaded on to the carts from the Bulgarians, including even rifles.[104]

The Germans soon started looting too. German soldiers were 'ruthlessly plundering private property' in such a way and to such an extent that Baron Kun asked his superiors to order the German commands to provide 'unconditional protection for the buildings of the [Austro-Hungarian] legations and consulates in Belgrade', together with their furnishings.[105] Revolts also occurred among Monarchy troops. One Hungarian *Jäger* battalion that had been transferred from Ukraine refused to go to the front, publicly displayed Bolshevik slogans, and had to be disarmed by force.[106]

In the meantime the Allies were advancing rapidly. According to Order no. 89 of 14 October, Franchet d'Esperey congratulated all the units under his command, including

…the Serbian army, with its eyes trained on its homeland, inspired by untameable strength, and full of faith in its just cause, which is toppling fortifications in which the enemy had considered himself impregnable; surging through these fortifications, [the Serbian army] has in five days managed to cut him off from the Vardar valley and forced him to withdraw in defeat.[107]

Serb troops arrived in Skopje on 24 September, Vranje on 1 October, Niš on 11 October, Kruševac on 15 October, Čačak and Kragujevac on 25 October, and Požarevac on 28 October. On 1 November the commander of the Serbian 1st Army sent a telegram to his commander-in-chief, stating that 'the blessed capital, proud Belgrade, today joyfully … greeted its liberators, glorious soldiers of the First Army', and was awaiting the Regent 'with open arms' to 'unfurl the banner of the entire Yugoslav nation whose fame will be celebrated for many centuries, and generations will take pride in the superhuman struggle of their ancestors.' It was 'the sign of an imminent, splendid future for the Yugoslav empire', he said.[108]

News of the successful Allied offensive brought the population of the occupied area to its feet.[109] Konstantin Fotijades, who was with the French troops, recalled that 'the whole of Serbia is seething; it resembles an organism trying by every known means to rid itself of a poison.… Old men, women and children did not wait for us to approach before driving their persecutors away.… The guerrilla forces made our advance easier.'[110] Lieutenant-Colonel Otto Landfried, chief of staff of the German 11th Army at the beginning of the Entente offensive, said after the war that every attempt to regroup the forces of the Central Powers was made more difficult not only by the determined onslaught of the Allied army but also by actions of the insurgent population.[111] Paul Kirch, who was to replace Landfried, wrote after the war:

> Serb troops were pouring into their country from the south, French forces were marching north on the eastern wing over Bulgarian territory, enemy *comitadji* were active behind the lines of the 11th Army.... The people fought too. Serb guerrilla groups emerged throughout the country and attacked our units when they were resting or eating. They also attacked our rearguard and our supply trains on the march, and sabotaged the railways. We have sent special *Jäger* groups against them, but it would have been easier to find a needle in a haystack than to find those guerrilla groups in the mountain terrain they are familiar with. That was why these guerrilla groups were a real menace right up to the end of the fighting in Serbia.[112]

Deep unrest was being felt not only in Serbia and Montenegro but also in some parts of Austria-Hungary itself. Landfried wrote that 'the Yugoslav population of the border provinces' of the Monarchy 'has come under dangerous influences since the Serb victory.' Karl Dietrich,[113] for his part, wrote that 'the threat of revolution was casting its shadow' in these areas, while Paul Kirch wrote that 'an uprising occurred in areas north of the Danube in the wake of Serb successes.'[114]

On 13 October General Kövess issued a special order to his army group. Because of insurrectionist activity his units were to gather together all the population behind the front in a suitable place and keep them under guard, while every individual was 'obliged to be on maximum alert in all places and at all times' in order to protect 'troops and, of course, transports, trains, communications lines, telegraph lines, posts in remote places, and so on.' He further ordered that 'around two per cent of the male population should be taken as hostages, and kept with the troops on the march,' adding that it should be made known that these hostages were 'guaranteeing with their lives that there would be no enemy activity in their regions.'[115] Regardless of whether the subordinate commands wanted to implement these or other measures, little could be done because of the rapid advance of Serb and French troops.

Reports from the Balkans to the Austro-Hungarian government and the supreme command no longer mentioned individual guerrilla groups but spoke generally of an agitated state of affairs resembling an uprising. On 19 October the operations department of the Monarchy's supreme command drew up a report that contained the following:

> Guerrilla warfare has quickly expanded and grown in significance with the entry of Entente forces into Macedonia. After these forces had crossed the Skopje-Priština line, the *comitadji* movement became extremely active, particularly in the areas of Prizren and Priština in Serbia, and that activity spread rapidly first to the eastern areas of Montenegro and then throughout the whole of Montenegro. As our troops withdrew, guerrilla warfare also broke out in Albania. Montenegro and Sandžak are today in a state of total rebellion. In eastern Serbia guerrillas are making war alongside the Serbian army.... Besides this guerrilla warfare, the people are rebelling in certain areas.[116]

On 22 October the Austro-Hungarian supreme command reported to the government in Vienna that 'with the collapse of the Macedonian front there was an immediate revival of guerrilla warfare in Albania, Montenegro and Serbia, which strengthened rapidly as our forces withdrew. That is particularly discernible in Serbia, where the entire male population, as soon as the withdrawal of our troops allowed, took up arms and combined forces to liberate their homeland.'[117] On 20 October a report from the commander of the Serbian cavalry division in the 1st Army in central Serbia noted that 'our people are attacking the enemy rear and sabotaging railway lines.'[118] On 22 October Baron Kun reported:

> Guerrilla warfare has assumed such proportions that it has considerably obstructed supplies to the front and, what is most important, it has virtually cut off the transport of our goods from areas that the enemy have not yet occupied. We can take only one tenth of the fruit and, out of a record maize harvest assessed at between 400,000 and 500,000 tonnes, we can take only a small percentage.[119]

Much of the population were truly combining forces and supporting the Entente offensive. And the *comitadji* that remained at large went into action. Headed by Kosta Pećanac and the Montenegrins Milinko Vlahović and Jovan Radović, an increasingly large number of *comitadji* groups penetrated into Sandžak, the Ibar valley and Montenegro.[120] And in those regions insurrections exploded in their wake. Territories were liberated before the arrival of the Serb and

French troops, and the same was to happen in the regions of Mount Rudnik and Mount Cer.[121]

The Serbian high command used guerrilla warfare and encouraged it by sending small groups of soldiers—sometimes even *comitadji* who were in the Serbian army—behind enemy lines. But it has to be stressed that insurrectionist and *comitadji* activity evolved independently. For example, on 14 October the high command informed the commander of the 2nd Yugoslav Infantry Regiment: 'There is no information as to whether there are still enemy troops in Metohija. According to unconfirmed reports, our insurrectionists have entered Novi Pazar and Peć.... Maintain vigilance and march with caution.'[122] In fact Pećanac, Vlahović and Radović controlled these areas. However, the Serbian state leadership regarded what was happening outside the area under their supervision with misgivings, and these heightened when they heard that the *comitadji* were not always doing what was expected of them at any given moment. On 11 October, on hearing of disorderly conduct among the *comitadji*, Stojan Protić, then acting for the Prime Minister, who was visiting London and Paris, telegraphed personally from Corfu:

> We have had just about enough of the *comitadji*. Here they are again doing damage that could be very dangerous. We most rigorously demand that the high command should be required either not to use them at all or to place them under the strictest possible control.... Pećanac, a common and uncivilised man..., will certainly create a mess for us to deal with. Inform the Albanians and our population that all stolen livestock will either be returned or paid for by the state.[123]

Evidently some kind of livestock theft was the reason for the telegram.

Austro-Hungarian authority was simply evaporating in the Monarchy's Yugoslav provinces. The political forces that had come together within the 'Declaration Movement' created national councils, and these developed into new bodies of authority. The Croat-Serb Coalition was also taking part in the common front of Yugoslav forces.[124] On 19 October 1918 the central committee of the National Council of Slovenes, Croats and Serbs in Zagreb defined its basic concept as being 'the unification of our entire nation of Slovenes, Croats and Serbs over the whole of its ethnographic territory... regardless of any provincial or state borders within which they live today.' On 29 October the Croatian *Sabor* announced the severance of all Croatia's state and legal links with Austria-Hungary and proclaimed that it was 'entering into a common national sovereign state of Slovenes, Croats and Serbs in accordance with the modern principle of nationhood and on the basis of national unity.'[125] The National Council then addressed the Entente powers on 31 October informing them that 'on the territory of Southern Slavs that up to the present has been within the Austro-Hungarian Monarchy' there had been born the State of Slovenes, Croats and Serbs that proclaimed 'it is not at war with the Allied states' and 'is prepared to enter into a common state with Serbia and Montenegro.'[126] During the following days provincial governments for Slovenia, Dalmatia and Bosnia and Herzegovina were formed.

In the mean time Serb troops had reached the rivers Drina, Sava and Danube and thus liberated their homeland as a whole; Montenegro was liberated by insurrectionists, *comitadji* and Serb troops (including units of the Yugoslav division). The defeated states of the enemy bloc surrendered their arms one after the other to the Entente powers: Bulgaria on 28 September, Turkey on 30 October, Austria-Hungary on 3 November and Germany on 11 November. Social and national unrest further contributed to the final disintegration of the Habsburg Monarchy.

The general conditions were thus created for the birth of a Yugoslav state. The hitherto separate participants in the movement for the independence of the 'Slav south'[127] were then united by the need to create a quite new historical state of affairs in the Yugoslav provinces that had belonged to the Monarchy. Serbia's war effort and success, Montenegro's contribution to the war, the work of the Yugoslav Committee, and the achievements of spontaneous guerrilla warfare on occupied Serbian and Montenegrin territory had combined with the aspirations and activity of the 'Declaration Movement' and the Croat-Serb Coalition, not to mention the important contribution of 'green cadres', to topple the state apparatus of Austria-Hungary and destroy its power. And while Poland, Czechoslovakia, Hungary and Austria were arising in Central Europe, the word 'Yugoslavia' was becoming the most potent slogan in the southeast of the continent, as a result of historical aspirations spread over a long period of time.

While there is ample evidence that the desire for unification predominated and was expressed with great enthusiasm, this of course did not mean that unification was without its opponents. It meant rather that the opponents were in the minority and without power. The war diary of the Alpine Corps, which was withdrawing through Srem, contains the following, written on 4 November, the day after the Monarchy's capitulation: 'On the roads we are marching along, we are constantly encountering soldiers returning home with red, white and blue rosettes on their caps.'[128] Josip Smodlaka was later to recall that people were 'overwhelmed with the noble desire for freedom and the nation state that was coming into being,' and that 'they were full of joy even at funerals, because even death was less terrible now.' In Spit, he added, 'all the inhabitants, male and female, young and old, stood in the cold and windy streets to greet the first Serbian unit, behind which stretched a broad green river of greenery and flowers with which the people had bedecked their warriors.'[129]

However, there remained the question whether the Yugoslav movement would manage to overcome hostile foreign policy factors, prevent separatist forces (leaderless and demoralised as they were) from gathering strength, prevail over internal differences and attempts at disintegration. Italy had sent its troops to the eastern Adriatic coast with the evident intention of advancing further inland; Romania was threatening to give military support to demands for Banat up to the river Tisza; Austrian and Hungarian forces, though routed, were resisting the new authorities with all their might and endeavouring to prevent the regions of Medjumurje, Styria and Carinthia from uniting with the other Yugoslav lands. Rudderless in a sea of political events, the new state of Slovenes, Croats and Serbs was isolated and unrecognised internationally, with no armed forces or law enforcement bodies of its own.

An order issued on 31 October by the command of Vojvoda Bojović's Serbian 1st Army said Vojvoda Mišić had ordered that 'the soldiers should rest after the superhuman efforts they have endured.'[130] However, on 30 October General Franchet d'Esperey had ordered that at least small Serb units should be sent over the large frontier rivers to demonstrate to the world that Entente troops had entered Austro-Hungarian territory. The Serbian high command therefore issued orders to that effect on 31 October, and parts of the 1st Army crossed the Danube and Sava on 3 and 4 November.

Franchet d'Espérey then issued another order directing Serb troops to sever railway links between Turnu-Severin and Timişoara (Temešvar). Moreover, as Hungary, having declared independence, was dragging its feet about acknowledging the truce of 3 November, Serb troops were also ordered to penetrate as far as possible into southern Hungary. By the end of November the Serbian army had taken Timisoara and reached the line stretching westwards from the Maros river north of Subotica and north of Baja. But the movement of Serbian troop across the 1914 borders was not dictated only by Allied war requirements. Vojvoda Mišić's order of 3 November stated that the Yugoslav lands were proclaiming their independence, and all Austro-Hungarian troops therefore had to withdraw from them. Greater interest had to be shown in these lands, he emphasised, because 'it is our historic right and duty towards the population.' Pašić had, in fact, telegraphed Mišić from Paris on 2 November, saying that, as a truce was to be signed with the Monarchy, it was essential to 'enter as quickly as possible into Bosnia, Banat, Srem and other areas of Austria-Hungary.'[131]

However, certain major disagreements among the individual elements in the Yugoslav movement were then coming to light because of different views concerning unification. From 6 to 9 November there was a meeting in Geneva between the Serbian prime minister on the one hand and representatives of Serbian opposition parties, the Zagreb National Council and the Yugoslav Committee on the other.[132] The talks that took place were not easy, but it was agreed that Serbia and the State of Slovenes, Croats and Serbs should remain as they were and have their own governments, while a joint six-member ministry was to be formed, with Serbia and the National Council each assigning three ministers. This joint ministry was to synchronise certain matters, mainly foreign affairs, and to prepare for a constituent assembly that would decide on the internal organisation of the unified state.[133] In his memoirs Smodlaka recalls that 'the foundations were laid in Geneva for some kind of dualistic organisation of Yugoslavia,' but he added that 'the Geneva ministry was stillborn, and no one either in Zagreb or elsewhere wished to revive it.'[134] The form of organisation agreed upon in Geneva was not destined to be implemented, since it had opponents in Serbia (Pašić had agreed to it unwillingly) and in Split, and it was evident that at least one strong faction in Zagreb had rejected it.

The Geneva conference clearly demonstrated how difficult it was to overcome historical division. At the moment when circumstances allowed unification, the full extent of the polarisation within the Yugoslav movement became evident, with Serbia on one side and the movement in the south-eastern provinces of the Habsburg Empire on the other. The form of organisation agreed upon at the time was federalist, but it was, even so, a case of dualism. And dualism was a sign of an attempt to cling on to the past, while the unification movement was doing its utmost to create something historically new. The reduction of federalism to dualism, which was all too reminiscent of the dead Monarchy, gave rise to a proposal for a centralist concept. That concept, being new, appeared a better solution, even though it prepared the way for the issue of internal organisation to remain for ever unresolved. So much was clear, even at that early stage, because unification between Serbia and the movement in the former Austro-Hungarian provinces was achieved with mutual consent to avoid the denomination of a 'Yugoslav' and 'Yugoslavia'; in other words, a solution was sought on the basis of the compound denomination 'Serb-Croat-Slovene' state. The problem which remained was how to establish relations between the existing separate entities and the desired new common community.

The Geneva conference provoked profound mutual distrust and the first great disappointments. The reaction among Serbia's representatives was reflected in the words of Stojan Protić: 'It is a monstrosity of a ministry, the like of which has never existed.' Serbia did not deserve such treatment, he said, adding: 'It is something that never happens to people who truly want national unity.' Pašić himself used no less telling words when he explained why he had agreed to the decisions in Geneva:

I too find this very difficult; never in my life—and there have been moments when I have been close to death—have I felt worse than I did when it was being decided whether our three-named nation would be united or whether, after all the sacrifices and magnificent achievements that have taken place, it would remain non-unified.... Unexpected difficulties have now arisen stemming from the motives and views of our brothers, who have long been under foreign influence and have unintentionally and unknowingly assumed some of our enemies' views.

Protić even reached the following conclusions: 'It is evident that our brothers from former Austria-Hungary have been materially liberated thanks to rivers of Serb and Allied blood, but they have not been liberated spiritually. Their ideology remains Austro-Hungarian.'[135]

There remained—once again—the word 'brothers' as the last ideological and psychological stronghold of the community. This was why Protić naturally wanted to verify the extent to which the views put forward in Geneva by Korošec, Trumbić and Žerjav were actually representative of other members of the Yugoslav movement in the former Monarchy. Such verification was particularly necessary because in the meantime he had heard a different standpoint from Ante Tresić-Pavičić in Corfu. And as for Serbia's leading figures being so emotionally affected by what was said in Geneva, the real reasons for that can be ascertained by reading between the lines of the messages they exchanged at the time. First, they all considered a dualist solution unacceptable. Members of the Serbian Government, led by Protić, rejected such a solution in principle, and were probably supported in this by Regent Alexander and the military leadership, perhaps mainly members of the White Hand. Pašić, on the other hand, considered this a temporary arrangement. Second, Protić's claim that it was 'quite unacceptable for ministers to swear an oath to anyone except our King, who is our common King' can be understood as resolute unwillingness to leave unresolved the issue of the ruling family in the new state, bearing in mind that nothing had been said in Geneva about agreeing to the Karadjordjević dynasty. The conviction evidently therefore reigned that Serbia should have the first say in matters of unification, and hence in the future new state too, and this, just as much as the proposal for dualism, demonstrated the extent to which separate views were entrenched to the detriment of a common commitment.

The population of the Yugoslav areas was at this time also calling on the Serbian army to protect its national territory and maintain law and order there.[136] On 4 November, a delegation of the National Council of Bosnia and Herzegovina transmitted a request to Vojvoda Stepanović for Serbian troops to enter its territory, whereupon units of the 2nd Army arrived in Sarajevo on 6 November. Envoys from Zemun, Pančevo and Osijek also arrived in Belgrade on 5 November with a request for military assistance. The National Council in Zagreb, in line with its previous decision to request Allied troops, sent a delegation to Serbia on 5 November, which arrived in Belgrade on 8 November. And, at the same time, Serb prisoners of war who had returned home from camps in Austria and Germany were in some places assuming the role that was actually expected of their comrades in the battle units. The Slovenian government detained a transport of these returnees in Ljubljana and created a special detachment under the command of the Serb Lieutenant Colonel Stevan Švabić. Upon a request from the National Council in Zagreb, Švabić placed some of these men under the command of Lieutenant Colonel Borisav Subotić and sent them to Zagreb. Moreover, on receiving a report that Italian forces were heading for Vrhnika and Ljubljana, the Slovenian government asked Švabić to halt the Italians and inform them that, in the name of the Entente, 'the Serbian army has occupied the area of Ljubljana', and that he would find it 'extremely unpleasant' if he were 'forced to have recourse to arms'. The Italian troops then halted their advance in the sector. According to a request from the National Council, a Serb battalion reached Zagreb on 14 November and entered Rijeka the next day. However, deceived by promises made by the commander of the Italian forces that had sailed into Rijeka, they soon left the port; but they remained in the sector and actually prevented the Italians from penetrating further inland.[137]

In parallel to this, the *de facto* unification of the states of Serbia and Montenegro with the Yugoslav lands of former Austria-Hungary was beginning. It was already clear that there were substantial differences of opinion over how such unification should take place and, especially, over the form of organisation the state would assume. Political disagreements also began to erupt. However, what was most important was that the Yugoslav movement was being realised within a state, and therefore all the differences and disagreements became an internal Yugoslav matter, as had been stipulated back in the autumn of 1914. Towards the end of November 1918 there was a series of proclamations of unification.[138] On 25 November in Novi Sad, the Great National Assembly proclaimed the unification of Srem, Banat and Bačka with Serbia. In Montenegro, supporters of the Montenegrin Committee were leading the way, and on 26 November the Great National Assembly proclaimed unification with Serbia in Podgorica, which meant the expulsion of the reigning

Petrović dynasty. It was also expected that unification with Serbia would be announced in Bosnia and Herzegovina, while many towns and districts—Banjaluka, Bihać, Zvornik, Prijedor, Bijeljina, Gacko, Jajce and others—independently proclaimed unification without recourse to the National Council in Sarajevo. In Zagreb the National Council decided on 25 November to unite 'the entire uninterrupted Yugoslav region of the former Austro-Hungarian Monarchy into a single state' with Serbia and Montenegro, and a delegation was sent to Belgrade for the 'united Kingdom of Serbs, Croats and Slovenes' to be declared on 1 December 1918.

The new Kingdom was first recognised by small states. Norway recognised it on 26 January 1919, followed by Greece towards the end of February, and Switzerland in early March.[139] The United States was the exception among the Great Powers in that it gave its recognition as early as 7 February. At the Peace Conference, which started in Paris on 18 February, Yugoslav representatives persistently and even demonstratively called themselves the 'Delegation of the Kingdom of Serbs, Croats and Slovenes', which indeed they were, but the conference bodies constantly addressed them as delegates of Serbia. It was not till the end of May that the Conference General Secretariat started referring to them in its documents as the 'Serb-Croat-Slovene' delegation. Britain gave its official recognition on 1 June, and France on 5 June. The issue was only really resolved when the name 'State of Serbs, Croats and Slovenes' was introduced into the peace treaty with Germany, and that treaty was then signed at Versailles on 28 June. Thereby Germany indirectly—and the other signatory countries directly—recognised the Yugoslav state. This was done by Austria in the peace treaty of St-Germain on 10 September, Bulgaria in the peace treaty of Neuilly on 27 November 1919, and Hungary in the peace treaty of Trianon on 4 June 1920. These three treaties also contained solutions for the northern and eastern borders, while the southern borders remained those that Serbia had had in 1914. The issue of the western border was resolved subsequently in a bilateral treaty with Italy at Rapallo on 12 November 1920. With the new borders, considerable sections of almost all the Yugoslav peoples remained in two or more neighbouring states (proportionally, the percentage of Slovenes who remained outside the national border was especially large). On the other hand, groups of several non-Yugoslav peoples remained in the territory of the Kingdom of Serbs, Croats and Slovenes.

The Yugoslav state, as it was then created, encompassed an area of 247,500 square kilometres, and, according to the census carried out in January 1921, had nearly 12 million inhabitants (members of the Yugoslav peoples accounting for 82.9 per cent). Along with foreign policy consolidation, the issue of internal organisation, with its origins in national and regional circumstances, came to the fore, and proved to be an exceptionally big problem.[140]

BIBLIOGRAPHY

SERBIAN LANGUAGE SOURCES

Ambrožić, K., 1979, *Nadežda Petrović*, Belgrade.

Arsenijević, M., 'Preobražaji ambijenta i ljudi starog trkališta' in *Beograd u sećanjima 1900–1918*, Belgrade, 1977.

Avramovski, Ž., 'Opredeljenje Bugarske za Centralne sile u prvom svetskom ratu (1914–1915)' in Ž. Avramovski (ed.), *Jugoslovensko-bugarski odnosi u XX veku*, vol. 1, Belgrade, 1980.

———, 'Bugarske pretenzije na aneksiju delova Kosova u prvom svetskom ratu (1915–1916)' in Ž. Avramovski (ed.), *Jugoslovensko-bugarski odnosi u XX veku*, vol. 2, Belgrade, 1982.

Bataković, D., 'Sukob vojnih i civilnih vlasti u Srbiji u proleće 1914', *Istorijski Časopis* (hereafter: *IČ*), 29–30 (1982–3).

Belić, A., 1915, *Srbija i južnoslovensko pitanje*, Niš.

Bogdanov, V., F. Čulinović and M. Kostrenčić (eds), 1966, *Jugoslavenski odbor u Londonu*, Zagreb.

Boppe, A., 1918, *Sa srpskom vladom od Niša do Krfa*, Geneva.

Budisavljević, S., 1958, *Stvaranje Države Srba, Hrvata i Slovenaca*, Zagreb.

Čizmić, I., 1974, *Jugoslavenski iseljenički pokret u SAD i stvaranje jugoslavenske države*, Zagreb.

Ćorović, V., 1920, *Crna knjiga*, Belgrade.

Dedijer, V., 'Putevi ujedinjenja i borba za socijalnu revoluciju' in I. Božić, S. Ćirković, M. Ekmečić and V. Dedijer, *Istorija Jugoslavije*, Belgrade, 1972.

———, 1978, *Sarajevo 1914*, 1–2, Belgrade.

Derok, J.V., 1940, *Toplički ustanak i oružani otpor u okupiranoj otadžbini 1916–1919*, Belgrade.

Dimitrijević, S., 1982, *Socijalistički radnički pokret u Srbiji*, Belgrade.

Dinaricus, 1915, *Jedinstvo Jugoslovena*, Niš.

Diplomatičeski dokumenti, Sofia, 1920.

Djokić, R., 'Na krvavom Vardaru' in R. Kašanin and J. Mitrović (eds), *Dobrovoljci u ratovima 1912–1918*, Belgrade, 1971.

Djoković, M., 'Deca pod okupacijom 1915–1918' in *Beograd u sećanjima 1900–1918*, Belgrade, 1977.

Djordjević, D., 'Austrougarski okupacioni režim u Srbiji i njegov slom 1918' in *Naučni skup u povodu 50-godišnjice raspada Austro-Ugarske Monarhije i stvaranja jugoslavenske države*, Zagreb, 1969.

——, 'U senci Austro-Ugarske' in *Istorija srpskog naroda*, VI–1, Belgrade, 1983.

Djurić, A., 1938, *Ka pobedi*, Belgrade.

Djurisić, M., 'Neki ekonomski i politički problemi Srbije u ratnoj 1914. godini', *Vojnoistorijskig Glasnik* (hereafter: *VIG*), 4 (1964).

Dokumenti o spoljnoj politici Kraljevine Srbije [*Dokumenti Srbije*], prepared by V. Dedijer and Ž. Anić, Belgrade, 1980.

Glišić Dragomir, Ratni period 1914–1918, Exhibition Catalogue, Belgrade, 1983, diaries I and II.

'Dvomesečni ratni doživljaj Drag.[utina] Markovića' in *Arhiva Istorijskog instituta Srbije u Beogradu*, Ostavština Stanoja Stanojevića.

Ekmečić, M., 'Stavovi Nikole Pašića prema američkim planovima pretvaranja Austro-Ugarske u federativnu državu' in *Naučni skup u povodu 50-godišnjice raspada Austro-Ugarske Monarhije i stvaranja jugoslavenske države*, Zagreb, 1969.

——, 1973, *Ratni ciljevi Srbije 1914*, Belgrade.

Fellner, F., 'Die "Mission Hoyos"' in V. Čubrilović (ed.), *Velike sile i Srbija pred prvi svetski rat*, Belgrade, 1976.

Gledović, B., B. Ratković, M. Djurišić, M. Grabovac and P. Opačić (eds), 1975, *Prvi svetski rat—Srbija i Crna Gora*, Cetinje.

Hrabak, B., 'Učešće stanovništva Srbije u proterivanju okupatora oktobra 1918', *Istorijski glasnik*, 3–4 (1958).

——, 'Albanija od julske krize do proleća 1916. godine na osnovu ruske diplomatske gradje (II)', *Obeležja*, 6 (1963).

——, 'Suparništvo izmedju srpskih delegata i propagatora i zvanične Crne Gore oko oslobodjenja i regrutovanja interniranih bivših dobrovoljaca na Liparima i Korzici 1916–1918', *Istorijski glasnik*, 1–4 (1964).

——, 'Borba izmedju crnogorskog dvora i srpske vlade oko crnogorske vojske i oko dobrovoljaca 1916–1918', *Istorija XX veka*, 6 (1964).

——, 'Elaborat srpskog Ministarstva inostranih dela o pripremama srpske okupacije severne Albanije 1915 godine', *Vjetar i arkivit te Kosoves*, 2–3 (1966–7).

——, 'Jugoslovenski sovjeti u Rusiji i Ukrajini 1919–1921', *Tokovi revolucije*, 2 (1967).

——, 'Delatnost pripadnika organizacije "Ujedinjenje ili smrt" za vreme prvog svetskog rata', *Naša prošlost*, 6 (1971–2).

——, 1980, *Jugosloveni zarobljenici u Italiji i njihovo dobrovoljačko pitanje 1915–1918*, Novi Sad.

Hrabak, B. and K. Džambazovski, 'Srpski socijaldemokrati na Solunskom frontu, u Solunu i na Krfu 1916–1918', *Istorijski glasnik*, 1–4 (1961).
Hrabak, B. and D. Janković, 1969, *Srbija 1918. Politika i napori Srbije u ratnoj 1918. godini*, Belgrade.
Ibrovac, M., 'Srpski djaci u francuskim školama za vreme prvog svetskog rata' in *Enciklopedija Jugoslavije*, vol. 3, Zagreb, 1958.
Istorija srpskog naroda, VI–1, Belgrade, 1983.
Istorija srpskog naroda, VI–2, Belgrade, 1983.
Jakovljević, M., 1923, *Iz rata i emigracije*, Subotica.
Janković, D., 'O radu srpske vlade za vreme prvog svetskog rata' in B. Krizman and B. Hrabak (eds), *Zapisnici sa sednica Delegacija Kraljevine SHS na mirovnoj konferenciji u Parizu 1919–1920*, Belgrade, 1960.
———, 'O posleratnim radovima na istoriji stvaranja jugoslovenske države 1918', *Jugoslovenski Istorijski Časopis* (hereafter: *JIČ*), 2 (1962).
———, 'Ženevska konferencija o stvaranju jugoslovenske zajednice 1918. godine', *Istorija XX veka*, 5 (1963).
———, 'Narodna skupština Srbije za vreme prvog svetskog rata i pitanje njenog kvoruma' in *Anali Pravnog fakulteta u Beogradu*, vol. 14, Belgrade, 1966.
———, 'Radovi o stvaranju jugoslovenske države objavljeni izmedju dva svetska rata', *JIČ*, 3–4 (1966).
———, 1967, *Jugoslovensko pitanje i Krfska deklaracija 1917. godine*, Belgrade.
———, 'Niška deklaracija', *Istorija XX veka*, 10 (1969).
———, 1973, *Srbija i jugoslovensko pitanje 1914–1915. godine*, Belgrade.
———, '"Veliki" i "mali" ratni program Nikole Pašića (1914–1918)', *Anali Pravnog fakulteta u Beogradu*, 2 (1973).
———, 'Radovi o jugoslovenskom pitanju u prvom svetskom ratu objavljevi poslednie decenije (1965–1974)', *JIČ*, 3–4 (1974).
———, 'Profesor Pavle Popović i jugoslovensko pitanje u prvom svetskom ratu', *Letopis Matice srpske*, September 1975.
———, 'Glavni faktori u procesu stvaranja Jugoslavije 1918. godine', *Naučni pregled*, 9 (1981).
Janković, D. and B. Krizman (eds), 1964, *Gradja o stvaranju jugoslovenske države* (1. 1–20. 12. 1918), Belgrade.
Jovanović, Lj., 'Pobuna u Toplici i Jablanici' in *Toplička spomenica*, Belgrade, 1934.
Jovanović, S., 1962, *Moji savremenici*, Windsor.
Kapidžić, H., 'Beogradski arhivi i Muzeji—ratni plijen austrougarskog okupatora za vrijeme prvog svjetskog rata', *Godišnjak istorijskog društva Bosne i Hercegovine*, 10 (1949–50).
———, 'Austro-ugarska politika u Bosni i Hercegovini i jugoslovensko pitanje za vrijeme prvog svjetskog rata', *Godišnjak istorijskog društva Bosne i Hercegovine*, 9 (1958), Sarajevo.

Karabegović, I., 1973, *Radnički pokret Bosne i Hercegovine izmedju revolucionarne i reformističke orijentacije (1909–1929)*, Sarajevo.
Karolyi, M., 1982, *Vjera bez iluzija*, Zagreb.
Kovačev, V., 'Ideološke i političke borbe u radničkom pokretu Hrvatske i Slavonije 1917–1919', *Istorija radničkog pokreta*, 3 (1966).
Krizman, B., 'O putu grofa Stj. Tise po jugoslavenskim zemljama u septembru 1918', *Historijski zbornik*, 11–12 (1958–9).
———, 'Pitanje medjunarodnog priznanja jugoslovenske države', *Istorija XX veka*, 3 (1962).
———, 'Povjerljive veze izmedju Jugoslavenskog odbora i domaćih političara za I svjetskog rata', *Historijski zbornik*, 15 (1962).
———, 'Stjepan Radić i Hrvatska pučka stranka u prvom svjetskom ratu', *Časopis za suvremenu povijest*, 2 (1970).
———, 'Vanjskopolitički položaj Kraljevine SHS godine 1919', *Časopis za suvremenu povijest*, 1 (1970).
———, 'Hrvatske stranke prema ujedinjenju i stvaranju jugoslovenske države' in D. Janković, P. Morača, B. Petranović and T. Stojkov (eds), *Politički život Jugoslavije 1914–1945*, Belgrade, 1973.
———, 1975, *Vanjska politika jugoslovenske države 1918–1941*, Zagreb.
———, 1977, *Raspad Austro-Ugarske i stvaranje jugoslovenske države*, Zagreb.
Krizman, B. and B. Hrabak (eds), 1960, *Zapisnici sa sednica Delegacija Kraljevine SHS na mirovnoj konferenciji u Parizu 1919–1920*, Belgrade.
Lapčević, D., 1925, *Rat i srpska socijalna demokratija*, Belgrade.
———, 1926, *Okupacija*, Belgrade.
Lapčević, V.D., 'Neke pojedinosti o odlasku socijalista na konferenciju u Stokholm 1917', *Istorijski glasnik*, 1–2 (1980).
Lapčević, V. and T. Milenković (eds), 1979, *Prepiska srpskih socijalista u toku prvog svetskog rata*, Belgrade.
Lebl, A., 'Vojvodjanske gradjanske partije u svetlu zapisnika peštanskog parlamenta' in V. Čubrilović (ed.), *Jugoslovenski narodi pred prvi svetski rat*, Belgrade, 1967.
———, 1979, *Gradjanske partije u Vojvodini 1887–1918*, Novi Sad.
M.T., 1915, *Austro-Ugarska protiv svojih podanika*, Niš.
Mandić, V., 1919, *Bosna u lancima*, Sarajevo.
Marjanović, M., 1960, *Londonski ugovor iz godine 1915*, Zagreb.
Milić, D., 1970, *Strani kapital u rudarstvu Srbije do 1918*, Belgrade.
Milikić, D., 'Beograd pod okupacijom u prvom svetskom ratu', *Godišnjak Grada Beograda* (hereafter: *GGB*), 5 (1958).
Milojević, P., 'Kad sećanja ožive', *Beograd u sećanjima 1900–1918*, Belgrade, 1977.
Milosavljević, P., 'Srpski djaci bataljon u Žoziju 1916–1917', *Istorijski glasnik*, 4 (1964).

Mišić, Ž., 1984, *Moje uspomene*, Belgrade.

Mitrović, A., 'Pokret otpora u austrougarskom Guvernmanu u Srbiji 1916–1918' in *Kruševac kroz vekove*, Kruševac, 1972.

———, 'Stvaranje nemačke okupacione zone i austrougarske okupacione uprave u Srbiji (jesen 1915—proleće 1916)', *Istorijski glasnik*, 1–2 (1977).

———, 'Die Kriegsziele der Mittelmaechte und die Jugoslawienfrage 1914–1918' in A. Wandruszka, R.G. Plaschka and A.M. Drabek (eds), *Die Donaumonarchie und die sudslawische Frage von 1848 bis 1918*, Vienna, 1978.

———, 'Tajni ugovor izmedju Centralnih sila i Bugarske od 6 septembra 1915', *Medjunarodni problemi*, 3–4 (1978).

———, 'Nemačko-bugarski ugovor o Borskom rudniku od 5 maja 1916', *Istorijski glasnik*, 1–2 (1979).

———, 'The 1919–1920 Peace Conference in Paris and the Yugoslav State: An historical evolution' in D. Djordjević (ed), *The Creation of Yugoslavia 1914–1918*, Santa Barbara, 1980.

———, 1981, *Prodor na Balkan. Srbija u planovima Austro-Ugarske i Nemačke 1908–1918*, Belgrade.

———, 'Balkanski planovi birokratije Balhauzplaca tokom prvog svetskog rata (1914–1916)', *JIČ*, 1–4 (1981).

———, 'Boj na kopaoničkom prevoju Mramor 14 marta 1917', *Istorijski glasnik*, 1–2 (1982).

———, 'Bugarska u planovima Austro-Ugarske i Nemačke tokom aneksione krize' in Z. Avramovski (ed.), *Jugoslovensko-bugarski odnosi u XX veku*, vol. 2, Belgrade, 1982.

———, 'Sporazum Centralnih sila o podeli balkanskih i bliskoistočnih sirovina (agreement of 8 January 1916)', *Balcanica*, 13–14 (1982–3).

———, 'Nadrastanje poraza i podela' in *Istorija srpskog naroda*, VI–2, Belgrade, 1983.

———, 'Sučeljavanje sa srednjoevropskim imperijalizmom' in *Istorija srpskog naroda*, VI–2, Belgrade, 1983.

———, 'Berliner Handelsgesellschaft i Srbija', *Zbornik Filozofskog fakulteta*, vol. XV–1 (1985), Belgrade.

Mitrović, M., '*Jugoslovenska akademska omladina u Švajcarskoj*', master's thesis (University of Belgrade, 1977).

———, 'Istorijska gradja u Beogradu o temi: Jugoslovenski studenti u Švajcarskoj 1916–1918. godine', GGB, 24 (1977).

———, 'Organizacije jugoslovenskih studenata u Švajcarskoj 1917. godine', *IČ*, 27 (1980).

———, 'Jugoslovenski studenti u Švajcarskoj i ujedinjenje (1917–1918)', *Istorijski glasnik*, 1–2 (1981).

———, 'Opšta organizacija akademske omladine u Švajcarskoj 1918. i njena delatnost', *IČ*, 28 (1981).
Mondesire, P. de 1936, *Albanska Golgota*, Belgrade.
Nešković, B., 1953, *Istina o Solunskom procesu*, Belgrade.
Očak, I.D., 1967, *Jugosloveni u Oktobru*, Belgrade.
Opačić, P., 1980, *Solunska ofanziva 1918*, Belgrade.
———, 1984, *Srbija i Solunski front*, Belgrade.
Ostojić, U., 'Britanski istoričari u Srbiji 1914–1915', unpublished master's thesis upheld at the Faculty of Philosophy, University of Belgrade, 1980.
Ostojić-Fejić, U., 'Britanski istoričari i makedonsko pitanje 1914–1915', *Istorija XX veka*, 1 (1983).
———, 'Stav britanskih javnih i naučnih radnika prema ratnim naporima Srbije 1914–1915', *VIG*, 2 (1983).
Passek, Z., 'Bilješke sa sjednica jugoslavenske političke emigracije iz 1915. i 1916. godine', *Radovi Arhiva JAZU*, 1 (1972).
———, 'Prilog bibliografiji o Jugoslavenskom odboru u Londonu', *Radovi Arhiva JAZU*, 1 (1972).
———, 'Pisma Vladimira Čerine dru Anti Trumbicu iz 1915. i 1916. godine', *Radovi Arhiva JAZU*, 2 (1973).
———, 'Zapisnici sjednica Jugoslavenskog odbora u Londonu iz 1916. 1917. i 1918 godine', *Radovi Arhiva JAZU*, 2 (1973).
Paulova, M., 1925, *Jugoslavenski odbor*, Zagreb.
Pavlović, Ž., 1915, *Rat Srbije sa Austro-Ugarskom, Nemačkom i Bugarskom 1915*, Belgrade.
Pekić, P., 1939, *Povijest oslobodjenja Vojvodine*, Subotica.
Perović, M., 1973, *Toplički ustanak 1917*, Belgrade.
Petranović, B., 1981, *Istorija Jugoslavije*, Belgrade.
Pleterski, J., 1971, *Prva odločitev Slovencev za Jugoslavijo*, Ljubljana.
Popov, D., 'Srpska štampa u Ugarskoj u vreme prvog svetskog rata', *Zbornik za istoriju Matice srpske*, 26 (1982), Novi Sad.
Popović, C.Dj., 'Apisov poverljiv raport', *Pregled*, 7–8 (1964).
Popović, N., 1977, *Jugoslovenski dobrovoljci u Rusiji 1914–1918*, Belgrade.
———, 1977, *Odnosi Srbije i Rusije u prvom svetskom ratu*, Belgrade.
Radojević, V.J. and D.J. Milenković, 1967, *Propast srpskih regruta 1915*, Belgrade.
Rakić, L., 1984, *Radikalna stranka u Vojvodini 1902–1919*, Novi Sad.
Rakočević, N., 1969, *Crna Gora u prvom svetskom ratu 1914–1918*, Cetinje.
———, 'Pokret za ujedinjenje Crne Gore sa Srbijom medju interniranim Crnogorcima i kod komitskog pokreta u Crnoj Gori u periodu 1916–1918' in *Naučni skup u povodu 50-godišnjice raspada Austro-Ugarske Monarhije i stvaranja jugoslavenske države*, Zagreb, 1969.

Bibliography

———, 'Politička aktivnost knjaza Mirka Petrovića u toku austro-ugarske okupacije Crne Gore', *Istorijski zapisi*, 3–4 (1970).

———, 'Crna Gora i ujedinjenje' in *Politički život Jugoslavije*, Belgrade, 1973.

———, 1981, *Politički odnosi Crne Gore i Srbije 1903–1918*, Cetinje.

Redžić, E., 1977, *Austromarksizam i jugoslovensko pitanje*, Belgrade.

Reiss, R.A., 1916, *Kako su Austro-Madjari ratovali u Srbiji*, Odessa (published in English: R.A. Reiss, *How Austria-Hungary Waged War in Serbia*, n.d.).

———, 1918, *Odgovor na austrougarske optužbe protiv Srbije*, Corfu.

———, 1928, *Šta sam video i doživeo u velikim danima*, Belgrade.

Šepić, D., 1961, *Supilo diplomat*, Zagreb.

——— (ed.), 1967, *Pisma i memorandumi Frana Supila*, Belgrade.

———, 1970, *Italija, saveznici i jugoslovensko pitanje 1914–1918*, Zagreb.

———, 'Hrvatska politika i pitanje jugoslovenskog ujedinjenja 1914–1918' in *Društveni razvoj u Hrvatskoj od 16. do početka 20. stoljeća*, Zagreb, 1981.

Šišić, F., 1920, *Dokumenti o postanku Kraljevine Srba, Hrvata i Slovenaca*, Zagreb.

Skoko, S., 1984, *Vojvoda Radomir Putnik*, 1–2, Belgrade.

Skoko, S. and P. Opačić, 1984, *Vojvoda Stepa Stepanović*, 1–2, Belgrade.

Slijepčević, P., 'Bosna i Hercegovina u svetskom ratu' in *Napori Bosne i Hercegovine za oslobodjenje i ujedinjenje*, Sarajevo, 1929.

Srbija i Crna Gora—see Gledović, B.

Stanković, Dj., 1984, *Nikola Pašić, saveznici i stvaranje Jugoslavije*, Belgrade.

———, 1985, *Nikola Pašić i jugoslovensko pitanje*, vol. 1–2, Belgrade.

Stanojević, S., 1915, *Šta hoće Srbija*, Niš.

Stanojević, V., 1925, *Naše ratno sanitetsko iskustvo*, Belgrade.

Stojančević, V., 'Gubici u stanovništvu Srbije i Beograda pod austrougarskom okupacijom za vreme prvog svetskog rata 1914–1918', *GGB*, 21 (1974).

———, 'Srpski civilni internirci u Austro-Ugarskoj za vreme prvog svetskog rata', *IČ*, 22 (1975).

Stojanović, N., 1927, *Jugoslovenski odbor*, Zagreb.

Strugar, V., 1965, *Socijaldemokratija i stvaranje Jugoslavije*, Belgrade.

———, 'Srpska vojska u zaštiti jugoslovenskog prostora krajem 1918. godine' in N. Popović (ed.), *Stvaranje jugoslovenske države 1918*, Belgrade, 1983.

Tartalja, O., 1928, *Veleizdajnik*, Zagreb.

Terzić, V., D. Vujošević, I. Jovanović and U. Kostić (eds), 1954, *Operacije crnogorske vojske u prvom svetskom ratu*, Belgrade.

Tomac, P., 1973, *Prvi svetski rat 1914–1918*, Belgrade.

Trgovčević, Lj., 'Jovan Cvijić u prvom svetskom ratu', *IČ*, 22 (1975).

———, 'Dva dokumenta o školovanju srpske omladine 1917. godine', *Istorijski glasnik*, 1–2 (1983).
———, 1986, *Naučnici Srbije i stvaranje jugoslovenske drzave 1914–1920*, Belgrade.
Tripković, Dj., 'Francuska i evakuacija srpske vojske iz Albanije', unpublished master's thesis, Belgrade, 1980.
———, 'Francuska i evakuacija srpske vojske iz Albanije', *VIG*, 3 (1981), (abbreviated version of mentioned manuscript).
Učešće jugoslovenskih radnih ljudi u oktobarskoj revoluciji i gradjanskom ratu u SSSR, prepared by P. Damjanović and others, Belgrade, 1979.
Vekić, M., 'Strane medicinske misije u Srbiji 1914–1915', unpublished graduation thesis upheld at the Faculty of Philosophy of the University of Belgrade, 1981.
Vidmar, J.J., 'Prilozi gradji za povijest 1917–1918. s osobitim obzirom na razvoj radničkog pokreta i odjeke Oktobarske revolucije kod nas', *Arhivski vijesnik*, 1 (1958).
Veliki rat Srbije [VRS] (Serbia's Great War), vols 1–32, Belgrade, 1924–37.
Vučković, V., 'Diplomatska pozadina ujedinjenja Srbije i Crne Gore' *Revija za medjunarodno pravo*, 2 (1959).
———, 'Iz odnosa Srbije i Jugoslovenskog odbora' *IČ*, 12–13 (1961–2).
———, 'Unutrašnje krize Srbije i prvi svetski rat', *IČ*, 14–15 (1963–5), Belgrade.
Vujović, D., 1962, *Ujedinjenje Crne Gore i Srbije*, Titograd.
———, 'Crnogorski dobrovoljci iz SAD 1914–1915. godine', *VIG*, 1 (1965).
Zapisi dr Josipa Smodlake, Zagreb, 1972.
Zečević, M., 1973, *Slovenska ljudska stranka i jugoslovensko ujedinjenje 1917–1921*, Belgrade.
Zelenika, M., 1962, *Prvi svetski rat 1914*, Belgrade.
Živanović, M.Ž., 1955, *Pukovnik Apis—Solunski proces 1917. Prilog za proučavanje političke istorije Srbije od 1903–1918. god.*, Belgrade.
———, 'O evakuaciji srpske vojske iz Albanije i njenoj reorganizaciji na Krfu (1915–1916) prema francuskim dokumentima', *IČ*, 14–15 (1963–5).
Živojinović, D., 1980, *Vatikan, Srbija i stvaranje jugoslovenske države 1914–1918*, Belgrade.
Zorić, M., 'Danuncijeva "Ode alla nazione serba" i njezini prevodioci' in *Glas CCCXXV SANU, Odeljenje jezika i književnosti*, vol. 11, Belgrade, 1980.
Zweig, S., 1962, *Jučerašnji svet*, Novi Sad.
Zwitter, F., J. Šidak and V. Bogdanov, 1962, *Nacionalni problemi v habsburski Monarhiji*, Ljubljana.

NON-SERBIAN LANGUAGE SOURCES

Amtsblatt, Mitteilungen der k. u. k. Warenverkehrszentrale des MGGs in Serbien; Entwicklung und Taetigkeit der k. u. k. Warenverkehrszentrale des MGGs Serbiens im Jahre 1916, Belgrade, 1917.

Apollonia, U. (ed.), 1972, Der Futurismus, Cologne (reproduction)

Berghabn, V.R., 1973, Germany and the Approach of War in 1914, London.

Bihl, W., 1970, Oesterreich-Ungarn und die Friedensschluesse von Brest-Litovsk, Vienna.

Bittner, L. and H. Uebersberger (eds), 1930, Österreich-Ungarische Aussenpolitik von der bosnischen Krise 1908 bis zum Kriegsausbruch 1914, Vienna.

Bourbon, S. de, 1920, L'offre de paix séparée de l'Autriche, Paris.

Conrad von Hötzendorf, 1923, Aus meiner Dienstzeit 1906–1918, vol. 4, Vienna.

Conrad von Hötzendorf, G. Gräfin, 1935, Mein Leben mit Conrad von Hötzendorf, Leipzig.

Cvijić, J., 1918, La péninsule balkanique, Paris.

Die Frage des Finanzkapitals in der Osterreichisch-Ungarischen Monarchie 1900–1918, Bucharest, 1965.

Die neuen Wege der Weltwirtschaft—Der Südosten, Vienna, 1914.

Dietrich, K., 1925, Weltkriegsende an der mazedonischen Front, Berlin.

Documents relatifs aux violations des conventions de La Haye et du Droit international en général, commises de 1915 à 1918 par les Bulgares en Serbie occupée, 1–3, Paris, 1919; The Enemy in Serbia, Documents Relative to the Bulgarian Atrocities of 1915–1918, Paris, 1919.

Dragnich, A.N., 1974, Serbia, Nikola Pašić and Yugoslavia, New Brunswick.

Droz, J., 1973, Les causes de la Première Guerre Mondiale, Paris.

Dürrenberger, C., 'Serbiens finanzielle und wirtschaftliche Lage', Zeitung (Frankfurt), special edition no. 53, 23 February 1916.

Ekstein, M.G. and Z. Steiner, 'The Sarajevo Crisis' in F.H. Hinsley (ed.), British Foreign Policy under Sir Edward Grey, Cambridge, 1977.

Fischer, F., 1965, Weltmacht oder Niederlage, Frankfurt an Main.

———, 1969, Krieg der Illusionen, Düsseldorf.

———, 1971, Griff nach der Weltmacht, Düsseldorf.

———, 1977, Der Erste Weltkrieg und das deutsche Geschichtsbild, Düsseldorf.

———, 1979, Bundnis der Elliten, Düsseldorf.

———, 1983, Juli 1914: Wir sind nicht hineingeschlittert, Reinbek bei Hamburg.

Freud, Sigmund and Karl Abracham, 1965, Briefe 1907–1926, Frankfurt an Main.

Fuchs, A., 1978, Geistige Stromungen in Österreich 1867–1918, Vienna.

Funder, F., 1952, Vom gestern ins heute, Vienna.

Geiss, I., 1963, Julikrise und Kriegsausbruch 1914. Eine Dokumentensammlung, vol. 1, Hanover.

Bibliography

——, 'Die deutsche Politik gegenüber Serbien in der Julikrise 1914' in V. Čubrilović (ed.), *Velike sile i Srbija pred prvi svetski rat*, Belgrade, 1976.

——, 'Origins of the First World War' in H.W. Koch (ed.), *The Origins of the First World War*, London, 1977.

——, 1978, *Das Deutsche Reich und Vorgeschichte des Ersten Weltkrieges*, Munich.

Gesemann, G., 1935, *Die Flucht*, Munich.

Giesl, W., 1927, *Zwei Jahrzehnte im Nahen Osten*, Berlin.

Griesinger, [J.], 'Die kritische Tage in Serbien', *Berliner Monatshefte*, 9 (1930).

Gutsche, W., 1984, *Sarajevo 1914. Vom Attentat zum Weltkrieg*, Berlin.

Hallgarten, G.W.F., 1963, *Imperialismus vor 1914*, vols 1–2, Munich.

Hanak, P., (ed.), 1966, *Die nationale Frage in der Österreichisch-Ungarischen Monarchie 1900–1918*, Budapest.

Hantsch, H., 1963, *Leopold Graf Berchtold*, Graz.

Harden, M., 'An der Kolubara', *Zukunft*, 2 January 1915.

Haselsteiner, H., 'Die Affäre Putnik', *Österreichische Osthefte*, 16 (1974).

Hoyos, A., 1922, *Der deutsch-englische Gegensatz und sein Einfluss auf die Balkanpolitik Österreich-Ungarns*, Berlin.

Islamov, T.M., 'Aus der Geschichte der Beziehungen zwischen Österreich und Ungarn am Anfang des 20. Jahrhunderts' in F. Klein (ed.), *Österreich-Ungarn in der Weltpolitik 1900–1918*, Berlin, 1965.

Johann, E. (ed.), 1968, *Innenansicht eines Krieges*, Frankfurt an Main.

Kann, R.A., 1950, *The Multinational Empire*, vols 1–2, New York.

——, 1971, *Kaiser Franz Josef und der Ausbruch des Weltkrieges*, Vienna.

Kanner, H., 1926, *Der Schlussel zur Kriegsschuldfrage*, Munich.

Kautsky, K., M. Montgelas and W. Schucking (eds), 1922, *Die deutschen Dokumente zum Kriegsausbruch*, vols 1–2, Berlin.

Kerchnawe, H., 'Die Militärverwaltung in Serbien' in *Die Militärverwaltung in den von den österreich-ungarischen Truppen besetzten Gebieten*, Vienna, 1928.

——, 'Die Organisation der Truppen des Militärgeneralgouvernements Serbien und der Verlauf der Operationen im grossem' in *Militärwissenschaftliche und technische Mitteilungen*, Vienna, 1928.

Kirch, P., *Krieg und Verwaltung in Serbien und Mazedonien 1916–1918*, Stuttgart, 1928.

Kis, E.E., 1983, *Zapisi to Kis*, Novi Sad.

Klein, F. (ed.), 1965, *Österreich-Ungarn in der Weltpolitik 1900–1918*, Berlin.

—— (ed.), 1968, *Deutschland im Ersten Weltkrieg*, vol. 1, Berlin.

Koch, H.W. (ed.), 1977, *The Origins of the First World War*, London.

Komjáthy, M. (ed.), 1966, *Protokolle des Gemeinsamen Ministerrates der Österreichisch-Ungarischen Monarchie 1914–1918*, Budapest.

Krumeich, G., 1980, *Aufrustung und Innenpolitik in Frankreich vor dem Ersten Weltkrieg*, Wiesbaden.
Kutschbach, A., 1929, *Brandherd Europas*, Leipzig.
Landfried, O., 1923, *Der Endkampf in Mazedonien 1918 und seine Vorgeschichte*, Berlin.
Lepsius, J., A.M. Bartholdy and F. Thimme (eds), 1926, *Die Grosse Politik der Europäischen Kabinette 1871–1914*, vol. 38, Berlin.
Lutzow, H., 1971, *Im diplomatischen Dienst der k. und k. Monarchie*, Munich.
Maulik, W., 'Bandenbekämpfung' in *Militärwissenschaftliche und technische Mitteilungen*, 1929.
März, E., 1981, *Österreichische Bankpolitik in der Zeit der grossen Wende 1913–1923*, Vienna.
Meier-Welcker, H., 1967, *Seeckt*, Frankfurt an Main.
Medunarodnie otnosenia v epohu imperialisma, III, Moscow, 1935.
Mikusch, G., 1918, *Wirtschaftliche Beobachtungen in dem von Österreich-Ungarn besetzten Gebiete Serbiens*, Vienna.
Mitrović, A., 'Die Kriegsziele der Mittelmächte und die Jugoslawienfrage 1914–1918' in A. Wandruszka, R.G. Plaschka and A.M. Drabek (eds), *Die Donaumonarchie und die südslawische Frage von 1848 bis 1918*, Vienna, 1978.
———, 'The 1919–1920 Peace Conference in Paris and the Yugoslav State: An Historical Evolution' in D. Djordjević (ed.), *The Creation of Yugoslavia 1914–1918*, Santa Barbara, 1980.
Moulins, A., 1917, *L'université française et la jeunesse serbe*, Brussels.
Novaković, S., 1915, *Problèmes Yougo-Slaves*, Paris.
Orientierung ueber Ausfuhrverbote, hg. von *Warenverkehrzentrale*, Belgrade, 1916.
OUA—see Bittner, L. and H. Uebersberger (eds).
Paget, Lady, *With our Serbian Allies*, London, n.d.
Pisarev, J., 'Okkupacia Serbii. Avstro-Vengerii i borba serbskogo naroda za svoe osvoboždenie', *Sovetskoe slavianovedenie*, 4 (1965).
———, 1968, *Serbija i čer nogorija v pervoi mirovoi voine*, Moscow.
———, 1975, *Obrazovanie jugoslovenskogo gosudarstva*, Moscow.
Plaschka, R.G., H. Haselsteiner and A. Suppan, 1974, *Innere Front*, 1–2, Vienna.
Poidevin, R., 'Les intérêts financiers français et allemands en Serbie de 1895 à 1914', *Revue Historique*, 232 (1964).
———, 1969, *Les relations économiques et financiers entre la France et l'Allemagne de 1898 à 1914*, Paris.
Pribram, A.F., 1971, *Austrian Foreign Policy 1908–1918*, Vienna.
Rathmann, L., 1963, *Stossrichtung Nahost 1914–1918*, Berlin.
Redlich, J., 'Schicksalsjahre Österreichs 1908–1919' in F. Fellner (ed.), *Das politische Tagebuch*, vol. 1, Graz, 1953.
Reed, J., 1916, *The War in Eastern Europe*, London.

Reiss, R.A., *How Austria-Hungary Waged War in Serbia*, n.d.
———, 1919, *Les Austro-Hongrois en Serbie envahie*, Paris.
———, 1919, *Rapport sur les atrocités commises par les troupes austro-hongroises pendant la première invasion de la Serbie*, Paris.
Reiss, R.A. and A. Bonnassieux, 1919, *Requisitoire contre la Bulgarie*, Paris.
Schmid, G., 'Der Ballhausplatz 1848–1914', *Österreichische Osthefte*, 23 (1981).
Steed, H.W., 1924, *Through Thirty Years*, vol. 1, London.
Steiner, Z.S., 1977, *Britain and the Origins of the First World War*, London.
Stern, F., 1975, *The Failure of Illiberalism*, Chicago.
Sundhaussen, H., 1982, *Geschichte Jugoslawiens 1918–1980*, Stuttgart.
Suppan, A., 'Zur Frage eines österreichisch-ungarischen Imperialismus in Südosteuropa' in A. Wandruszka, R.G. Plaschka and A.M. Drabek (eds), *Die Donaumonarchie und die südslawische Frage von 1848 bis 1918*, Vienna, 1978.
Thobie, J., 1977, *Intérêts et impérialisme français dans l'Empire ottoman (1895–1914)*, Paris.
Turner, L.C., 1970, *The Origins of the First World War*, London.
Ubersberger, H., 1958, *Österreich zwischen Russland und Serbien*, Cologne.
von Pastor, L., 1950, *Tagebücher, Briefe, Erinnerungen*, edited by Wuhr, Heidelberg.
Wandruszka, A., R.G. Plaschka and A.M. Drabek (eds), 1978, *Die Donaumonarchie und die südslawische Frage von 1848 bis 1918*, Vienna.
Wandruszka, A. and P. Urbanitsch (eds), 1973–80, *Die Habsburgermonarchie 1848–1918*, vols 1–3, Vienna.
Wank, S., 'Aehrenthal's Programme for the Constitutional Transformation of the Habsburg Monarchy', *Slavonic and East European Review*, 41 (1963).
———, 'Varieties of Political Despair: Three exchanges between Aehrenthal and Goluchowski 1898–1906' in S.B. Winters and J. Held (eds), *Intellectual and Social Developments in the Habsburg Empire from Maria Teresa to World War I*, New York, 1975.
Wurthle, F., 1975, *Die Spur führt nach Belgrad*, Vienna.
———, 1978, *Dokumente zum Sarajevo-prozess*, Vienna.

ARCHIVES

(Abbreviations where used)

Archive of Serbian Academy of Sciences and Arts, Belgrade   A SANU-Belgrade

Arhiv Jugoslavije (Archive of Yugoslavia), Belgrade   A-SFRY-Belgrade

Military Archive, Belgrade   AVII-Belgrade

Bibliography

Auswärtiges Amt, Bonn — AA-Bonn
Archive of Serbia, Belgrade — AS-Belgrade
  Ministry of Education — ME
  Militärgeneralgouvernement — MGG
  Ministry of Internal Affairs — MID
  Political-Propaganda Department
    Of Foreign Ministry
Allgemeines Verwaltungsarchiv, Vienna — AVA-Vienna
Arhiv Bosne, Sarajevo
Bundesarchiv/Militärarchiv, Freiburg — BA/MA-Freiburg i B
Bundesarchiv, Koblenz — BA-Koblenz
Bayerische Hauptstaatsarchiv, Munich — BayHStA—Munich
  Ministerium des Aussern — MA
Bayerische Hauptstaatsarchiv/Kriegsarchiv, Munich — BayHStA/KA—Munich
Haus-, Hof- und Staatsarchiv, Vienna — HHStA-Vienna
  Politisches Archiv — PA
Kriegsarchiv, Vienna — KA-Vienna
Public Record Office, London — PRO-London
Sorbonne/Archives, Paris
Zentrales Staatsarchiv, Potsdam — ZstA/Potsdam

NOTES

Introduction

1. Dobrica Ćosić, *Into the Battle* (translated by Muriel Heppell) (New York, 1983), 11.
2. A rare exception is Dimitrije Djordjević (ed.), *The Creation of Yugoslavia 1914–1918* (Santa Barbara, 1980). Otherwise, the best general overview in English remains Michael Boro Petrovich, *A History of Modern Serbia 1804–1918*, 2 vols (New York and London, 1976), vol. 1, 612–63; but a useful supplement is Dragan Živojinović, 'Serbia and Montenegro: The Home Front 1914–1918' in Béla K. Király and Nándor F. Dreisziger (eds), *East Central European Society in World War 1* (New York, 1985), 239–59. For broader context see the recent essays in Dejan Djokić (ed.), *Yugoslavism: Histories of a Failed Idea 1918–1992* (London, 2003).
3. Ćosić, *Into the Battle*, 62.
4. See Wayne Vucinich, *Serbia between East and West: The Events of 1903–8* (New York, 1968).
5. Apart from the current work, Andrej Mitrović has assessed Serbia's perception of Austrian aggression more fully in *Prodor na Balkan. Srbija u planovima Austro-Ugarske i Nemačke 1908–1918* (Belgrade, 1981).
6. The standard works on Vienna's outlook are F.R. Bridge, *The Habsburg Monarchy among the Great Powers, 1815–1918* (Oxford, 1990) and Samuel R. Williamson, *Austria-Hungary and the Origins of the First World War* (London, 1991).
7. For the behaviour of Belgrade and Vienna during the July Crisis, see Mark Cornwall, 'Serbia' in Keith Wilson (ed.), *Decisions for War 1914* (London, 1995); and John Leslie, 'The Antecedents of Austria-Hungary's War Aims: Policies and Policy-Makers in Vienna and Budapest before and during 1914', in *Archiv und Forschung. Wiener Beiträge zur Geschichte der Neuzeit*, vol. 20 (Vienna, 1993).
8. Stevan K. Pavlowitch, *Serbia: The History behind the Name* (London, 2002), 94.
9. For instance, see one compilation for the general public about Serbia's 'Golgotha and Easter': Silvija Djurić and Vidosav Stevanović (eds), *Golgota i vaskrs Srbije 1915–1918* (Belgrade, 1986).
10. The words of the Serbian minister to Britain, Mateja Bošković, in his introduction to Gordon Gordon-Smith, *Through the Serbian Campaign: The Great Retreat of the Serbian Army* (London, 1916), x. A good study of the Austro-Serbian clash of 1914 is Rudolf Jeřábek, *Potiorek. General im Schatten von Sarajevo* (Graz, Vienna and Cologne, 1991).

11. Živojinović, 'Serbia and Montenegro: The Home Front', 247.
12. For research in English on this subject see the works of David MacKenzie: *Apis: The Congenial Conspirator* (New York, 1989) and *The 'Black Hand' on Trial: Salonika 1917* (New York, 1995).
13. A revisionist exception is the current research of Jovana Knežević, including a paper delivered at Trinity College Dublin in September 2005: 'Laughing through Occupation? Entertainment and Celebrations in Occupied Belgrade, 1915–1918'.
14. Notably through the research of the Lausanne professor R.A. Reiss: *Report upon the Atrocities committed by the Austro-Hungarian Army during the First Invasion of Serbia* (London, 1916); *The Kingdom of Serbia: Infringements of the Rules and Laws of War committed by the Austro-Bulgaro-Germans. Letters of a Criminologist on the Serbian Macedonian Front* (London, 1919).
15. Andrej Mitrović, *Ustaničke borbe u Srbiji 1915–1918* (Belgrade, 1987).
16. See Mark Cornwall, 'The Experience of Yugoslav Agitation in Austria-Hungary 1917–1918' in Hugh Cecil and Peter Liddle (eds), *Facing Armageddon: The First World War Experienced* (London, 1996), which draws upon recent Slovene research on the 'Declaration movement'. For Croatia see Mark Biondich, *Stjepan Radić, the Croat Peasant Party and the Politics of Mass Mobilization, 1904–1928* (Toronto, 2000). A new analysis of the mentality of Habsburg South Slav soldiers is contained in Mark Cornwall, *The Undermining of Austria-Hungary: The Battle for Hearts and Minds* (Basingstoke, 2000).
17. See for instance the British naval mission based around Belgrade, in Charles E.J. Fryer, *The Royal Navy on the Danube* (New York, 1988).
18. Monica Krippner, *The Quality of Mercy. Women at War. Serbia 1915–1918* (Newton Abbot, 1980). A vivid personal account is Mabel St Clair Stobart, *The Flaming Sword in Serbia and Elsewhere* (London, 1916).
19. Flora Sandes, *The Autobiography of a Woman Soldier: A Brief Record of Adventure with the Serbian Army, 1916–1919* (New York, 1926), 13. See also Sandes, *An English Woman-Sergeant in the Serbian Army* (London, 1916).
20. James Berry, F. May Dickinson Berry and W. Lyon Bease, *The Story of a Red Cross Unit in Serbia* (London, 1916), 127, 129, 146; Alice and Claude Askew, *The Stricken Land: Serbia as we saw it* (London, 1916), 76.
21. Askew, *This Stricken Land*, 354, 358.
22. For a stimulating new assessment of how Britons conceived the South Slav problem, see James Evans, 'The Creation of Yugoslavia: British Attitudes to Questions of South Slav Nationality, 1900–1921', unpubl. DPhil thesis, Oxford University, 2005.
23. Harry Hanak, *Great Britain and Austria-Hungary during the First World War: A Study in the Formation of Public Opinion* (Oxford, 1962), 65–74; Hugh Seton-Watson et al. (eds), *R.W. Seton-Watson and the Yugoslavs: Correspondence, 1906–1941*, 2 vols (London and Zagreb, 1976), I, 199–200, 215.
24. Hugh and Christopher Seton-Watson, *The Making of a New Europe: R.W. Seton-Watson and the Last Years of Austria-Hungary* (London, 1981), 165 note 14.
25. Apart from Seton-Watson's journal *The New Europe*, a comprehensive statement of Serbia's case was set out in A.H.E. Taylor, *The Future of the Southern*

Slavs (London, 1917). Taylor, a long-time Serb-enthusiast, wrote (318) that Greater Serbia's European role would be to 'act as a sort of spring buffer between East and West', absorbing political shocks that originated in either area.
26. Quoted in Seton-Watsons, *The Making of a New Europe*, 224.

Chapter 1 *July 1914*

1. V. Dedijer, 'Putevi ujedinjenja i borba za socijalnu revoluciju' in I. Božić, S. Ćirković, M. Ekmečić and V. Dedijer, *Istorija Jugoslavije*, Belgrade, 1972, facsimile of telegram on illustration no. 157; H. Hantsch, *Leopold Graf Berchtold*, Graz, 1963, 619–20; A. Mitrović, *Prodor na Balkan. Srbija u planovima Austro-Ugarske i Nemačke 1908–1918*, Belgrade, 1981, 19.
2. L. Bittner and H. Uebersberger (eds), *Österreich-Ungarische Aussenpolitik von der bosnischen Krise 1908 bis zum Kriegsausbruch 1914* (hereafter: *OUA*), vol. 8, Vienna, 1930, 770–1; compare Conrad von Hötzendorf, *Aus meiner Dienstzeit 1906–1918*, vol. 4, Vienna, 1923, 139.
3. F. Šišić, *Dokumenti o postanku Kraljevine Srba, Hrvata i Slovenaca*, Zagreb, 1920, 2–3.
4. *Ibid.*, 6–7.
5. F. Fellner, 'Die "Mission Hoyos"' in V. Čubrilović (ed.), *Velike sile i Srbija pred prvi svetski rat*, Belgrade, 1976, 387–410 (Hoyos's memoirs *Meine Mission nach Berlin* were published in the supplement to Fellner's study—411–18 of that compendium); A. Mitrović, *Prodor na Balkan*, 44–54, 189, 192; H. Hantsch, *Leopold Graf Berchtold*, 572.
6. *OUA*, vol. 8, 250–61; see H. Hantsch, *Leopold Graf Berchtold*, 567.
7. I. Geiss, *Julikrise und Kriegsausbruch 1914: Eine Dokumentensammlung*, vol. 1, Hanover, 1963, 86–8, 95–8.
8. F. Fischer, *Krieg der Illusionen*, Düsseldorf, 1969, 692; F. Klein (ed.), *Deutschland im Ersten Weltkrieg*, vol. 1, Berlin, 1968, 222–3.
9. HHStA-Vienna, Politisches Archiv [hereafter PA] I, Card 512, report No. 239 of 6 July 1914 (published in: *OUA*, vol. 8, 319–20).
10. F. Fischer, *Griff nach der Weltmacht*, Düsseldorf, 1971, 60–6; A. Mitrović, *Prodor na Balkan*, 48–54.
11. V. Dedijer, *Sarajevo 1914*, 1–2, Belgrade, 1978; F. Wurthle, *Dokumente zum Sarajevo-prozess*, Vienna, 1978; F. Wurthle, *Die Spur führt nach Belgrad*, Vienna, 1975 (the book is of interest in that the author tries at all costs to prove the Austro-Hungarian reasons for declaring war, and in doing so, he starts from positions created by propaganda); W. Gutsche, *Sarajevo 1914, Vom Attentat zum Weltkrieg*, Berlin, 1984.
12. *Ibid.*
13. *OUA*, vol. 8, 436–7.
14. *Dokumenti o spoljnoj politici Kraljevine Srbije* [hereafter *Dokumenti Srbije*], VII–2, prepared by V. Dedijer and Ž. Anić, Belgrade, 1980, 418.
15. This reconstruction of events was mainly based on material published in *Dokumenti Srbije* and *OUA*, vol. 8.
16. *Dokumenti Srbije*, 421.

17. *Ibid.*, 422–3, 429.
18. *Ibid.*, 430.
19. *Ibid.*, 430–1.
20. N. Rakočević, *Crna Gora u prvom svetskom ratu 1914–1918*, Cetinje, 1969, 23–6.
21. *Ibid.*, 23.
22. *OUA*, vol. 8, 210–12.
23. *Ibid.*, 218–20.
24. N. Popović, *Odnosi Srbije i Rusije u prvom svetskom ratu*, Belgrade, 1977, 45.
25. *OUA*, vol. 8, 219.
26. *Ibid.*, 231.
27. *Ibid.*, 232.
28. *Ibid.*, 218.
29. F. Fischer, *Griff*; F. Fischer, *Krieg*; F. Fischer, *Weltmacht oder Niederlage*, Frankfurt a. M., 1965; F. Fischer, *Der Erste Weltkrieg und das deutsche Geschichtsbild*, Düsseldorf, 1977; F. Fischer, *Bundnis der Eliten*, Düsseldorf, 1979; F. Fischer, *Juli 1914. Wir sind nicht hineingeschlittert*, Reinbek bei Hamburg, 1983; I. Geiss, *Das Deutsche Reich und Vorgeschichte des Ersten Weltkrieges*, Munich, 1978; J. Droz, *Les causes de la Première Guerre Mondiale*, Paris, 1973; L.C. Turner, *The Origins of the First World War*, London, 1970; V.R. Berghabn, *Germany and the Approach of War in 1914*, London, 1973; F. Stern, *The Failure of Illiberalism*, Chicago, 1975, 75–188. Of unique value on the subject of the Balkan peninsula in the period of imperialism is the classic work by G.W.F. Hallgarten, *Imperialismus vor 1914*, vol. 1–2, Munich, 1963. Only the causes of the Austro-Hungarian declaration of war are of interest here.
30. Conrad, *Aus meiner Dienstzeit*, 36.
31. R.A. Kann, *Kaiser Franz Josef und der Ausbruch des Weltkrieges*, Vienna, 1971; see H. Kanner, *Der Schlussel zur Kriegsschuldfrage*, Munich, 1926.
32. K. Kautsky, M. Montgelas and W. Schucking (eds), *Die deutschen Dokumente zum Kriegsausbruch*, vol. 1, Berlin, 1922, 10–11, note alongside document no. 7; see: A. Mitrović, *Prodor na Balkan*, 40–3.
33. A. Mitrović, *Prodor na Balkan*, 31–9.
34. BayHStA-Munich, Ministerium des Aussern [hereafter MA], no. 2481/2.
35. *OUA*, vol. 8, 248.
36. A. Mitrović, *Prodor na Balkan*, 30–54.
37. *Dokumenti Srbije*, 454–5, 462–4.
38. *Ibid.*, 465–6.
39. *Ibid.*, 465.
40. *Ibid.*, 435, 479.
41. *Ibid.*, 464.
42. S. Zweig, *Jucerašnji svet*, Novi Sad, 1962, 208–9.
43. J. Redlich, 'Schicksalsjahre Osterreichs 1908–1919' in F. Fellner (ed.), *Das politische Tagebuch*, vol. 1, Graz, 1953, 235.
44. A. Mitrović, *Prodor na Balkan*, 23–30.
45. *Dokumenti Srbije*, 482–4.
46. A. Mitrović, *Prodor na Balkan*, 23–30.
47. BayHStA-Munich, MA, No. 2481/2, report of 30 June 1914.

48. H.W. Steed, *Through Thirty Years*, vol. 1, London, 1924, 404–5.
49. BayHStA-Munich, MA, No. 2481/2, report of 3 July 1914.
50. BayHStA-Munich, MA, No. 2481/2, report of 4 July 1914.
51. H. Lutzow, *Im diplomatischen Dienst der k. und k. Monarchie*, Munich, 1971, 222–3.
52. A. Fucks, *Geistige Stromungen in Österreich 1867–1918*, Vienna, 1978, 270–1.
53. Sigmund Freud and Karl Abracham, *Briefe 1907–1926*, Frankfürt/Main, 1965, 180.
54. S. Zweig, *Jučerasnji svet*, 214–16, 221–7.
55. *Dokumenti Srbije*, 482–4.
56. J. Redlich, 'Schicksalsjahre Österreichs 1908–1919', 234–5.
57. L. von Pastor, *Tagebücher, Briefe, Erinnerungen*, edited by Wuhr, Heidelberg, 1950, 604.
58. *Dokumenti Srbije*, 482–6.
59. *Ibid.*, 465.
60. F. Funder, *Vom gestern ins heute*, Vienna, 1952; on the subject of Mandl's proposals of how to destroy Serbia in the autumn of 1915, see A. Mitrović, *Prodor na Balkan*, 305–6.
61. *Dokumenti Srbije*, 482.
62. H. Lutzow, *Im diplomatischen Dienst*, 223.
63. Conrad, *Aus meiner Dienstzeit*, vol. 4, 16–17.
64. *Ibid.*, vol. 2, 265; *Ibid.*, vol. 3, 257, 622; J. Redlich, 'Schicksalsjahre Österreichs 1908–1919', 164.
65. *Dokumenti Srbije*, VII–1, 595, 606.
66. G. Gräfin Conrad von Hötzendorf, *Mein Leben mit Conrad von Hötzendorf*, Leipzig, 1935, 113–14.
67. H. Hantsch, *Leopold Graf Berchtold*, 558.
68. V. Ćorović, *Crna knjiga*, Belgrade, 1920, 28–34. In research literature see: B. Krizman, 'Hrvatske stranke prema ujedinjenju i stvaranju jugoslovenske države' in D. Janković, P. Morača, B. Petranović and T. Stojkov (eds), *Politički život Jugoslavije 1914–1945*, Belgrade, 1973, 103–6; D. Janković, *Srbija i jugoslovensko pitanje 1914–1915. godine*, Belgrade, 1973, 359–61; V. Dedijer, 'Putevi ujedinjenja', 394–5; B. Krizman, 'Stjepan Radić i Hrvatska pučka stranka u prvom svjetskom ratu', *Časopis za suvremenu povijest*, 2 (1970), 99–108.
69. V. Mandić, *Bosna u lancima*, Sarajevo, 1919; V. Ćorović, *Crna knjiga*, 35–49; P. Slijepčević, 'Bosna i Hercegovina u svetskom ratu' in *Napori Bosne i Hercegovine za oslobodjenje i ujedinjenje*, Sarajevo, 1929, 221–2. In research literature, see D. Janković, *Srbija i jugoslovensko pitanje*, 432–3; M. Ekmečić, *Ratni ciljevi Srbije 1914*, Belgrade, 1973, 165.
70. W. Gutsche, *Sarajevo 1914*, 41.
71. *Ibid.*
72. V. Ćorović, *Crna knjiga*, 51. In research literature, see D. Janković, *Srbija i jugoslovensko pitanje*, 399; J. Pleterski, *Prva odločitev Slovencev za Jugoslavijo*, Ljubljana, 1971, 11.
73. D. Janković, *Srbija i jugoslovensko pitanje*, 361–4, 432–3; B. Krizman, 'Hrvatske stranke prema ujedinjenju', 103–6; J. Pleterski, *Prva odločitev Slovencev*, 11–16.
74. *Ibid.*; J. Pisarev, *Obrazovanie jugoslovenskogo gosudarstva*, Moscow, 1975, 69–72.

75. V. Strugar, *Socijaldemokratija i stvaranje Jugoslavije*, Belgrade, 1965, 68–9; E. Redžić, *Austromarksizam i jugoslovensko pitanje*, Belgrade, 1977, 225, 292; J. Pleterski, *Prva odločitev Slovencev*, 10, 14.
76. A. Mitrović, *Prodor na Balkan*, 180–1, 244–5, 426–7 (here also reference to international literature).
77. BayHStA-Munich, MA, No. 2481/2, report of 30 June 1914.
78. I. Geiss, *Julikrise*, 68.
79. V. Dedijer, *Sarajevo 1914*; M.Ž. Živanović, *Pukovnik Apis—Solunski proces 1917. Prilog za proučavanje političke istorije Srbije od 1903–1918. god.*, Belgrade, 1955; B. Nešković, *Istina o Solunskom procesu*, Belgrade, 1953, 258–83.
80. D. Djordjević, 'U senci Austro-Ugarske' in *Istorija srpskog naroda*, VI–1, Belgrade, 1983, 133–4; also in the same book, 144, 186 and 199.
81. V. Vučković, 'Unutrašnje krize Srbije i prvi svetski rat', *IČ*, 14–15 (1963–5), Belgrade, 1965; D. Bataković, 'Sukob vojnih i civilnih vlasti u Srbiji u prolece 1914', *IČ*, 29–30 (1982–3), 477–92. An interesting testimony has also been provided by S. Jovanović, *Moji savremenici*, Windsor, 1962, 199–202 and 420.
82. See correspondence between bodies in Belgrade on the one hand, and the Ministry of Military Affairs and authorities in the Drina frontier sector on the other, in the course of the spring and early summer of 1914 in *Dokumenti Srbije*, VI–1/2, and reports from Austro-Hungarian diplomatic personnel from Belgrade to *OUA* in the same period of time, vol. 8.
83. *Dokumenti Srbije*, VII–2, 363–5; compare also 290–1.
84. *Ibid.*, 290–1; compare report of the commander of the Drina division sector, 345.
85. M.Ž. Živanović, *Pukovnik Apis*, 556–8.
86. *Dokumenti Srbije*, VII–2, 337–8.
87. *Ibid.*, 343–4, 363–5, 415–16, 421–2.
88. *Ibid.*, 368; V. Dedijer, *Sarajevo 1914*.
89. *Dokumenti Srbije*, VII–2, 290–1, 337–8, 342–7, 369.
90. *Ibid.*, 339, 391–2.
91. V. Dedijer, *Sarajevo 1914*.
92. M.Ž. Živanović, *Pukovnik Apis*, 553–61.
93. V. Dedijer, *Sarajevo 1914*, 371–411.
94. See footnote 29.
95. A. Wandruszka and P. Urbanitsch (eds), *Die Habsburgermonarchie 1848–1918*, vol. 1–3, Vienna, 1973–80; R. Kann, *The Multinational Empire*, vols 1–2, New York, 1950; F. Klein (ed.), *Osterreich-Ungarn in der Weltpolitik 1900–1918*, Berlin, 1965; F. Zwitter, J. Šidak and V. Bogdanov, *Nacionalni problemi v habsburski Monarhiji*, Ljubljana, 1962; P. Hanak (ed.), *Die nationale Frage in der Österreichisch-Ungarischen Monarchie 1900–1918*, Budapest, 1966; *Die Frage des Finanzkapitals in der Österreichisch-Ungarischen Monarchie 1900–1918*, Bucharest, 1965; E. März, *Österreichische Bankpolitik in der Zeit der grossen Wende 1913–1923*, Vienna, 1981; A. Wandruszka, R.G. Plaschka and A.M. Drabek (eds), *Die Donaumonarchie und die südslawische Frage von 1848 bis 1918*, Vienna, 1978; A.F. Pribram, *Austrian Foreign Policy 1908–1918*, Vienna, 1971; H. Ubersberger, *Österreich zwischen Russland und Serbien*, Cologne, 1958.

96. T.M. Islamov, 'Aus der Geschichte der Beziehungen zwischen Österreich und Ungarn am Anfang des 20. Jahrhunderts' in F. Klein (ed.), *Österreich-Ungarn in der Weltpolitik 1900–1918*, Berlin, 1965, 120.
97. A. Mitrović, *Prodor na Balkan*, 61–4.
98. *Ibid.*, 66–94.
99. S. Wank, 'Aehrenthal's Programme for the Constitutional Transformation of the Habsburg Monarchy', *The Slavonic and East European Review*, 41 (1963), 513–36; S. Wank, 'Varieties of Political Despair: Three exchanges between Aehrenthal and Goluchowski 1898–1906' in S.B. Winters and J. Held (eds), *Intellectual and Social Developments in the Habsburg Empire from Maria Teresia to World War I*, New York, 1975, 203–39.
100. A. Hoyos, *Der deutsch-englische Gegensatz und sein Einfluss auf die Balkanpolitik Österreich-Ungarns*, Berlin, 1922, 41–6.
101. A. Mitrović, 'Bugarska u planovima Austro-Ugarske i Nemačke tokom aneksione krize' in Z. Avramovski (ed.), *Jugoslovensko-bugarski odnosi u XX veku*, vol. 2, Belgrade, 1982, 57–90; A. Mitrović, *Prodor na Balkan*, 68–78.
102. A. Mitrović, *Prodor na Balkan*, 61–174.
103. *Ibid.*
104. F. Fellner, 'Die "Mission Hoyos"'; G. Schmid, 'Der Ballhausplatz 1848–1914', *Österreichische Osthefte*, 23 (1981), 18–37.
105. A. Mitrović, *Prodor na Balkan*.
106. F. Fischer, *Weltmacht*; F. Fischer, *Juli 1914*.
107. See footnote 29; H.W. Koch (ed.), *The Origins of the First World War*, London, 1977.
108. A. Hoyos, *Der deutsch-englische Gegensatz*, 46.
109. This is shown by documents in I. Geiss, *Julikrise*.
110. F. Klein (ed.), *Deutschland im Ersten Weltkrieg*, vol. 1, 242.
111. Z.S. Steiner, *Britain and the Origins of the First World War*, London, 1977; G. Krumeich, *Aufrustung und Innenpolitik in Frankreich vor dem Ersten Weltkrieg*, Wiesbaden, 1980.
112. F. Fischer, *Krieg*, 704–24; I. Geiss, 'Origins of the First World War' in H.W. Koch (ed.), *The Origins of the First World War*, London, 1977, 36–78.
113. F. Fischer, *Weltmacht*, 51–60.
114. A. Mitrović, *Prodor na Balkan*, 178–9, 188–97.
115. M. Komjáthy (ed.), *Protokolle des Gemeinsamen Ministerrates der Österreichisch-Ungarischen Monarhie 1914–1918*, Budapest, 1966, 141–54.
116. A. Mitrović, *Prodor na Balkan*, 186–97.
117. N. Rakočević, *Crna Gora 1914–1918*, 29–46; N. Rakočević, *Politički odnosi Crne Gore i Srbije 1903–1918*, Cetinje, 1981, 229–30; A. Mitrović, *Prodor na Balkan*, 197.
118. I. Geiss, *Julikrise*, contains the instructions given by the foreign ministries in Vienna and Berlin to their officials in St Petersburg, Paris, London and Rome.
119. This method had already been used during preparations for the annexation of Bosnia and Herzegovina in 1908 (A. Mitrović, 'Bugarska u planovima', 62–4).
120. *Dokumenti Srbije*, VII–2, 463.
121. F. Fischer, *Krieg*, 682–738.

122. A. Mitrović, *Prodor na Balkan*, 95–182.
123. Ibid.
124. I. Geiss, *Julikrise*.
125. F. Fischer, *Krieg*, 695–6.
126. N. Rakočević, *Crna Gora 1914–1918*, 23–4; N. Rakočević, *Politički odnosi*, 229–30.
127. *Dokumenti Srbije*, VII–2, 432–3, 595–8.
128. The rank of Vojvoda is the highest in the Serbian Army, approximately equivalent to field-marshal.
129. Ibid.
130. Ibid., 571–2.
131. Ibid., 595–8.
132. *OUA*, vol. 8, 264, 273–4.
133. I. Geiss, *Julikrise*, 264, 273–4; *OUA*, vol. 8, 575. Merely to conceal complicity, the Austro-Hungarian Embassy in Berlin presented another note to the German Foreign Ministry in the morning of 24 June 1914, that is at the same time as it presented notes to other powers.
134. *Dokumenti Srbije*, VII–2, 628–31.
135. I. Geiss, *Julikrise*, 332, 334–5.
136. Ibid., 365.
137. BayHStA-Munich, MA, No. 97510, report of 29 July 1914.
138. V. Dedijer, 'Putevi ujedinjenja', 378.
139. *Dokumenti Srbije*, VII–2, 633.
140. Ibid., 635–7; N. Popović, *Odnosi Srbije i Rusije*, 45–6.
141. F. Klein (ed.), *Deutschland im Ersten Weltkrieg*, vol. 1, 246.
142. *Dokumenti Srbije*, VII–2, 641.
143. H. Hantsch, *Leopold Graf Berchtold*, 629–33; F. Fischer, *Krieg*, 699–704, 709–19, 724–9; M.G. Ekstein and Z. Steiner, 'The Sarajevo Crisis' in F.H. Hinsley (ed.), *British Foreign Policy under Sir Edward Grey*, Cambridge, 1977, 401–10. The essence of British policy lay in the conviction that Germany should not be allowed to beat France and that Britain would have to enter the war if that occurred. The Austro-Hungarian ambassador to London was right in his assessment that 'England is cold towards Russian interests', and Grey wrote that if 'the Monarchy could vanquish Serbia militarily and at the same time satisfy Russia then all is well and good.' But it was evident that this was impossible, i.e. France would have to enter the war because of Russia, and London tried to preserve peace with a compromise that meant Serbia would suffer major losses.
144. *Dokumenti Srbije*, VII–2, 650.
145. Ibid., 650–1.
146. Ibid., 641.
147. Ibid., 640–1.
148. W. Giesl, *Zwei Jahrzehnte im Nahen Osten*, Berlin, 1927, 268.
149. Ibid., 264–5.
150. Ibid., 319.
151. *Dokumenti Srbije*, VII–2, 655–8.

152. K. Kautsky, M. Montgelas and W. Schucking (eds), *Die deutschen Dokumente zum Kriegsausbruch*, vol. 2, 18–19. An insight into the response of diplomats in Belgrade is provided by the German envoy: 'After we had studied the Serbian response calmly and in detail the sole conviction that reigned in the circle of colleagues gathered with me was that Baron Giesl had departed too quickly. It seemed to us all that Serbia had gone very far in meeting the demands and that our Austrian colleague had not allowed himself sufficient time to examine the response presented to him. That was because we all considered that we would have needed more time, and we concluded that he had received instructions in advance simply to leave if the Ultimatum was not immediately accepted in totality. In the meantime the Serbian response was published and we were reinforced in our understanding of why Giesl had left.' [J.] Griesinger, 'Die kritischen tage in Serbien', *Berliner Monatshefte*, 9 (1930), 839–40.
153. I. Geiss, 'Die deutsche Politik gegenüber Serbien in der Julikrise 1914' in V. Čubrilović (ed.), *Velike sile i Srbija pred prvi svetski rat*, Belgrade, 1976, 57–80.
154. *Veliki rat Srbije* (Serbia's Great War) [hereafter: *VRS*], 1, Belgrade 1924–37, 14.
155. *Dokumenti Srbije*, VII–2, 689.
156. *Ibid.*, 690.
157. H. Hantsch, *Leopold Graf Berchtold*, 617–23.
158. AS-Belgrade, Fond Ministarstva inostranih dela [hereafter: MID], Političko odeljenje, file I/3, statement of Sibe Milačić of 7 August 1934. Also to be found is the statement made by I. Gerasimović on 4 August 1934, according to which the telegram containing the declaration of war was delivered to Pašić in 'Evropa' by Momčilo Jurišić, a Ministry clerk. Having read it, he said, Pašić had declared: 'That is what we expected,' see: V. Dedijer, 'Putevi ujedinjenja', 379.
159. A. Suppan, 'Zur Frage eines österreichisch-ungarischen Imperialismus in Südosteuropa' in A. Wandruszka *et al.* (eds), *Die Donaumonarchie*, 103.
160. E. Johann (ed.), *Innenansicht eines Krieges*, Frankfürt/Main, 1968, 19–21.
161. M. Karolyi, *Vjera bez iluzija*, Zagreb, 1982, 60.
162. [J.] Griesinger, 'Die kritischen tage in Serbien', 845–8.
163. HHStA-Vienna, PA I, K. 819, report from Sofia dated 8 August 1914.

Chapter 2 *The Yugoslav Programme*

1. BayHStA/KA-Munich, Kriegsministerium, vol. 1829/1, reports of 29 and 30 July 1914. This was also reported by representatives of other German courts accredited to the Central Government in Berlin (W. Gutsche, *Sarajevo 1914*, 52).
2. V. Terzić, D. Vujošević, I. Jovanović and U. Kostić (eds), *Operacije crnogorske vojske u prvom svetskom ratu*, Belgrade, 1954, 76–8; N. Rakočević, *Crna Gora 1914–1918*, 38–41.
3. HHStA-Vienna, PA I, K. 871.
4. V. Terzić *et al.*, *Operacije crnogorske vojske*, 76–8; N. Rakočević, *Crna Gora 1914–1918*, 38–41; HHStA-Vienna, PA I, K. 497, Kriegserklarungen (it is written

here that Montenegro declared war against Austria-Hungary on 7 August 1914).
5. See *Istorija srpskog naroda*, VI–1, Belgrade, 1983, 7–207; A. Wandruszka and P. Urbanitsch (eds), *Die Habsburgermonarchie 1848–1918*, vol. 3, 734–74, and also 626–733, 801–38; *Die neuen Wege der Weltwirtschaft—Der Südosten*, Vienna, 1914, 60–75.
6. AA-Bonn, Oxfort, S. 574, Serbien 4, vol. 11, report from Belgrade of 3 August 1914.
7. A. Mitrović, 'Berliner Handelsgesellschaft i Srbija', *Zbornik Filozofskog fakulteta*, vol. XV–1 (1985), Belgrade.
8. R. Poidevin, 'Les intérêts financiers français et allemands en Serbie de 1895 à 1914', *Revue Historique*, 232 (1964), 49–66; R. Poidevin, *Les relations économiques et financières entre la France et l'Allemagne de 1898 à 1914*, Paris, 1969, 146–8, 322–40, 573–5, 680–3, 794–5. Compare J. Thobie, *Intérêts et impérialisme français dans l'Empire ottoman (1895–1914)*, Paris, 1977.
9. A-SFRY-Belgrade, no. 80–4–673–82.
10. *Ibid.*
11. *Ibid.*
12. D. Janković, 'Niška deklaracija', *Istorija XX veka*, 10 (1969), 25–6.
13. A-SFRY-Belgrade, no. 80–4–673–82.
14. M. Ekmečić, *Ratni ciljevi Srbije 1914*, 416.
15. *Ibid.*
16. Much information is to be found in a group of narrative sources: V. Ćorović, *Crna knjiga*, 52–133, 162–72; O. Tartalja, *Veleizdajnik*, Zagreb, 1928, 75–87; P. Slijepčević, 'Bosna i Hercegovina u Svetskom Ratu', 222–3; S. Budisavljević, *Stvaranje države Srba, Hrvata i Slovenaca*, Zagreb, 1958, 11–24; *Zapisi dr Josipa Smodlake*, Zagreb, 1972, 49–50; P. Pekić, *Povijest oslobodjenja Vojvodine*, Subotica, 1939, 55–64.
17. Research literature: N. Kapidžić, 'Austro-Ugarska politika u Bosni i Hercegovini i jugoslovensko pitanje za vrijeme prvog svjetskog rata', *Godišnjak istorijskog društva Bosne i Hercegovine*, 9 (1958), Sarajevo, 10–17; D. Janković, *Srbija i jugoslovensko pitanje*, 367–8, 399–403, 407–8, 413–15, 433–5, 439–41; M. Ekmečić, *Ratni ciljevi Srbije 1914*, 163–80; J. Pleterski, *Prva odločitev Slovencev*, 20–5; A. Lebl, *Gradjanske partije u Vojvodini 1887–1918*, Novi Sad, 1979, 124; D. Popov, 'Srpska štampa u Ugarskoj u vreme prvog svetskog rata', *Zbornik za istoriju Matice srpske*, 26 (1982), Novi Sad, 149–58; L. Rakić, *Radikalna stranka u Vojvodini 1902–1919*, Novi Sad, 1984, 165–79.
18. See footnotes 16 and 17.
19. *Ibid.*
20. *Ibid.*
21. J. Pleterski, *Prva odločitev Slovencev*, 20–5.
22. V. Dedijer, 'Putevi ujedinjenja', 383–4; B. Gledović, B. Ratković, M. Djurišić, M. Grabovac and P. Opačić (eds), *Prvi svetski rat - Srbija i Crna Gora* [hereafter: *Srbija i Crna Gora*], Cetinje, 1975, 47–9, 54–6; *VRS*, 1. 19–24.
23. F. Fellner, 'Die "Mission Hoyos"', 411.

24. D. Živojinović, *Vatikan, Srbija i stvaranje jugoslovenske države 1914–1918*, Belgrade, 1980.
25. *VRS*, vol. for year 1914; P. Tomac, *Prvi svetski rat 1914–1918*, Belgrade, 1973, 65–76, 120–9, 156–66; M. Zelenika, *Prvi svetski rat 1914*, Belgrade, 1962; *Srbija i Crna Gora*, 47–172; V. Terzić et al., *Operacije crnogorske vojske*, 101–237.
26. N. Rakočević, *Politicki odnosi*, 230–4.
27. *VRS*, 1, 254.
28. *Ibid.*, 269.
29. E.E. Kiš, *Zapisi to Kiš*, Novi Sad, 1983, 53–61.
30. See footnote 25.
31. *Ibid.*
32. *Ibid.*
33. In connection with this issue, interesting testimony on the Major Allied Powers is contained in a report from the British Ambassador in Petrograd that was dispatched to Sir Edward Grey on 12 November 1914. He stated that Sazonov had been informed that the head of the Serbian supreme command had notified his Prime Minister that the time had come for starting negotiations with Austria. Pašić had replied that he would resign immediately if such a step were taken. If the Serbs had to withdraw, Sazonov would call on the Entente Powers to guarantee Serbia's interests, the Ambassador added. Grey noted in his report that it would be a good idea for the Allies to send Serbia some encouragement at this time of crisis. (PRO-London, FO, no. 1903).
34. See footnote 25.
35. HHStA-Vienna, PA I, K. 789, copy.
36. *Ibid.*
37. A. Mitrović, *Prodor na Balkan*, 215–16.
38. *Diplomaticeski dokumenti*, Sofia, 1920, 296–7.
39. PRO-London, FO, no. 1. 803.
40. *VRS*, 7, 277.
41. *Ibid.*, 278.
42. E.E. Kiš, *Zapisi to Kiš*, 208–21.
43. HHStA-Vienna, PA I, K. 789, copy.
44. P. Milojević, 'Kad sećanja ožive' in *Beograd u sećanjima 1900–1918*, Belgrade, 1977, 201–4.
45. *VRS*, 7, 387.
46. *Ibid.*, 298.
47. M. Harden, 'An der Kolubara', *Zukunft*, 2 January 1915, 9–28; A. Mitrović, *Prodor na Balkan*, 214–17.
48. R.A. Reiss, *Rapport sur les atrocités commises par les troupes austro-hongroises pendant la première invasion de la Serbie*, Paris, 1919.
49. *VRS*, 1, 266–7.
50. *Ibid.*, 268.
51. *Ibid.*, 268–9.
52. *Ibid.*, 281–2.
53. Conrad, *Aus meiner Dienstzeit*, vol. 4, 346.
54. KA-Vienna, Op. Abt. No. 2312, report of 12 September 1914.

55. HHStA-Vienna, PA I, K. 982, report of 13 August 1914.
56. *Ibid.*, several reports.
57. *Ibid.*
58. See footnotes 16 and 17.
59. Arhiv Bosne—Sarajevo, O-P, 24, no. 729.
60. *Ibid.*, no. 723.
61. See footnotes 16 and 17.
62. *Ibid.*
63. F. Wurthle, *Dokumente zum Sarajevo-prozess.*
64. See footnotes 16 and 17.
65. A. Lebl, 'Vojvodjanske gradjanske partije u svetlu zapisnika peštanskog parlamenta' in V. Čubrilović (ed.), *Jugoslovenski narodi pred prvi svetski rat*, Belgrade, 1967, 477–8.
66. See footnotes 16 and 17.
67. HHStA-Vienna, PA I, K. 974, exchange of letters between Austro-Hungarian chief of general staff and Foreign Minister on 19 and 28 March 1916.
68. E. Redžić, *Austromarksizam i jugoslovensko pitanje*, 229–30, 292–4, 358–9; I. Karabegović, *Radnički pokret Bosne i Hercegovine izmedju revolucionarne i reformističke orijentacije (1909–1929)*, Sarajevo, 1973, 74–8; J. Pleterski, *Prva odločitev Slovencev,* 10–11, 14–15, 30.
69. M. Paulova, *Jugoslavenski odbor*, Zagreb, 1925; V. Bogdanov, F. Čulinović and M. Kostrenčić (eds), *Jugoslavenski odbor u Londonu*, Zagreb, 1966; D. Šepić, *Supilo diplomat*, Zagreb, 1961, 11–14; D. Janković, *Srbija i jugoslovensko pitanje*, 445–67.
70. *Pisma i memorandumi Frana Supila*, 47–8.
71. D. Janković, *Srbija i jugoslovensko pitanje*, 333–43.
72. A-SFRY-Belgrade, no. 80–4–256.
73. N. Popović, *Jugoslovenski dobrovoljci u Rusiji 1914–1918*, Belgrade, 1977, 12.
74. J. Pisarev, *Serbija i Černogorija v pervoi mirovoi voine*, Moscow, 1968, 64–6.
75. See footnote 72.
76. N. Popović, *Jugoslovenski dobrovoljci*, 3.
77. *Ibid.*, 4.
78. *Ibid.*, 3–18.
79. R. Djokić, 'Na krvavom Vardaru' in R. Kašanin and J. Mitrović (eds), *Dobrovoljci u ratovima 1912–1918*, Belgrade, 1971, 57.
80. N. Popović, *Jugoslovenski dobrovoljci*, 18–19.
81. *Ibid.*, 18–19.
82. *Ibid*, 2.
83. D. Janković, *Srbija i jugoslovensko pitanje*, 335–8.
84. J. Reed, *The War in Eastern Europe*, London, 1916, 42–3.
85. N. Popović, *Odnosi Srbije i Rusije*, 279–81; B. Krizman and B. Hrabak (eds), *Zapisnici sa sednica Delegacija Kraljevine SHS na mirovnoj konferenciji u Parizu 1919–1920*, Belgrade, 1960, 82–3.
86. N. Popović, *Jugoslovenski dobrovoljci*, 1.
87. I. Čizmić, *Jugoslavenski iseljenički pokret u SAD i stvaranje jugoslavenske države*, Zagreb, 1974, 79–83.

88. D. Janković, *Srbija i jugoslovensko pitanje*, 337.
89. P. Slijepčević, 'Bosna i Hercegovina u Svetskom Ratu', 244–5; D. Vujović, 'Crnogorski dobrovoljci iz SAD 1914–1915. godine', *VIG*, 1 (1965), 53–65.
90. Z. Passek, 'Bilješke sa sjednica jugoslavenske političke emigracije iz 1915. i 1916. godine', *Radovi Arhiva JAZU*, 1 (1972), 77.
91. F. Fellner, 'Die "Mission Hoyos"'.
92. *OUA*, vol. 8, 852.
93. *Ibid.*, 507.
94. *VRS*, 1, 14, 17.
95. F. Šišić, *Dokumenti*, 5–6, 8–9, 10–11.
96. M. Ekmečić, *Ratni ciljevi Srbije 1914*, 84.
97. F. Šišić, *Dokumenti*, 5–6.
98. *Ibid.*, 2–3.
99. A-SFRY-Belgrade, no. 80–4–573, note by J.M. Jovanović of 16 (29) August 1914; and no. 80–4–147, telegram of 21 September (4 October) 1914.
100. *Ibid.*, no. 80–4–673–82.
101. Dinaricus, *Jedinstvo Jugoslovena*, Niš, 1915, 2.
102. A SANU-Belgrade, no. 13887/1.
103. A-SFRY-Belgrade, no. 80–4–573.
104. *Ibid.*, no. 80–4–441.
105. *Ibid.*, no. 80–4–677.
106. *Ibid.*, no. 80–4–677–9.
107. M. Ekmečić, *Ratni ciljevi Srbije 1914*, 89.
108. A-SFRY-Belgrade, no. 80–4–673–82.
109. M. Ekmečić, *Ratni ciljevi Srbije 1914*, 87.
110. A-SFRY-Belgrade, no. 80–4–441; see: N. Popović, *Odnosi Srbije i Rusije*, 139–260.
111. Dinaricus, *Jedinstvo Jugoslovena*, 12–13.
112. A. Belić, *Srbija i južnoslovensko pitanje*, Niš, 1915, 70.
113. S. Novakovitch, *Problèmes Yougo-Slaves*, Paris, 1915, 28–9, 31.
114. *Diplomaticeski dokumenti*, 266–7.
115. *Ibid.*, report from Belgrade.
116. Lj. Trgovčević, *Naučnici Srbije i stvaranje jugoslovenske države 1914–1920*, Belgrade, 1986.
117. A-SFRY-Belgrade, no. 80–4–574, conclusions of agreement reached in Niš on 14 (27) October 1914; A SANU-Belgrade, No. 13887/1, letter from B. Marković to Lj. Stojanović of 17 (30) October 1914; N. Stojanović, *Jugoslovenski odbor*, Zagreb, 1927, 10–11.
118. *Ibid.*, no. 80–4–574.
119. A SANU-Belgrade, No. 13887/1.
120. A-SFRY-Belgrade, no. 80–4–574.
121. A SANU-Belgrade, No. 13887/1.
122. A-SFRY-Belgrade, no. 80–4–574.
123. A SANU-Belgrade, No. 13887/1.

124. V. Vučković, 'Diplomatska pozadina ujedinjenja Srbije i Crne Gore' *Revija za medjunarodno pravo*, 2 (1959), 227–58.
125. N. Rakočević, *Politički odnosi*, 197–215.
126. *Ibid*. On 25 February 1914 the German minister to Cetinje sent a report that ran as follows: 'On the basis of my confidential relations with the King, I am able to assert that His Majesty is not at the moment in the least inclined to allow the fusion of Serbia and Montenegro. When the King spoke of joint activity by the two countries in his address from the throne, he did so—as he had informed me previously—only to thwart the opposition that is demanding fusion. The great majority in the Skupština do want nothing to do with any kind of fusion. The Serbian minister, Mr Gavrilović, refrains from any agitation and restricts himself to following the course of events carefully. The King now ... is not even considering abandoning his throne. His Majesty has spoken with me for many hours in recent days about confidential issues here and confirmed that he holds the future of his dynasty dear.' J. Lepsius, A.M. Bartholdy and F. Thimme (eds), *Die Grosse Politik der Europäischen Kabinette 1871–1914*, vol. 38, Berlin, 1926, 328–9.
127. *Dokumenti Srbije*, VII–1, 152.
128. These two letters were published in N. Rakočević, *Politički odnosi*, 293–5.
129. V. Vučković, 'Iz odnosa Srbije i Jugoslovenskog odbora' *IČ*, 12–13 (1961–2), 345–85.
130. A-SFRY-Belgrade, no. 80–4–574.
131. A SANU-Belgrade, No. 13887/1.
132. *Ibid*.
133. F. Šišić, *Dokumenti*, 10; compare: D. Janković, *Srbija i jugoslovensko pitanje*, 468–80; M. Ekmečić, *Ratni ciljevi Srbije 1914*, 116.
134. V. Vučković, 'Diplomatska pozadina', 238.
135. A-SFRY-Belgrade, Legacy of J.M. Jovanović, vol. 56; on the map in the annex of Dinaricus, *Jedinstvo Jugoslovena*; and on the map attached to the report of the Russian Envoy in Niš on 26 January 1915, which was published in *Meždunarodnie otnosenia v epohu imperializma*, III, Moscow, 1935, 111–14.
136. A-SFRY-Belgrade, no. 80–4–677.
137. D. Šepić (ed.), *Pisma i memorandumi Frana Supila*, Belgrade, 1967, 3–4, 7, 9, 11, 13, 17; see: D. Šepić, *Supilo diplomat*, 25.
138. D. Janković, *Srbija i jugoslovensko pitanje*, 464–7.

Chapter 3 *Serbia Suffers*

1. J. Reed, *The War in Eastern Europe*, 35, 73, 90–8.
2. *Srbija i Crna Gora*, 143.
3. A VII-Belgrade, signatory 3, k. 470, sv. 2, no. 7; these data were officially presented at the Peace Conference, see B. Krizman and B. Hrabak (eds), *Zapisnici*, 371.
4. HHStA-Vienna, PA I, K. 789, copy.
5. KA-Vienna, Op. Abt. no. 9848, not dated; see: S. Skoko and P. Opačić, *Vojvoda Stepa Stepanović*, 1–2, Belgrade, 1984; S. Skoko, *Vojvoda Radomir Putnik*, 1–2,

Belgrade, 1984; H. Haselsteiner, 'Die Affäre Putnik', *Österreichische Osthefte*, 16 (1974), 238–44 (on the subject of Putnik's arrest on 25 and 26 July 1914 in Budapest, see also the unused act of Emperor Franz Joseph of 28 July 1914 and General Conrad's notes in KA-Vienna, Op. Abt. No. 53); Ž. Mišić, *Moje uspomene*, Belgrade, 1984.
6. BA/MA-Freiburg i B., no. 247/26, dated 10 September 1915.
7. KA-Vienna, Op. Abt. no. 9848.
8. D. Janković, *Srbija i jugoslovensko pitanje*, 223–50. Albin Kutschbach's reports provide plentiful specific data on circumstances and events in Serbia; originals of those reports: AA-Bonn, collection of copies: HHStA-Vienna, PA I, K. 789.
9. R.A. Reiss, *Kako su Austro-Madjari ratovali u Srbiji*, Odessa, 1916 (published in English as *How Austria-Hungary Waged War in Serbia*, n.d.); R.A. Reiss, *Odgovor na austrougarske optužbe protiv Srbije*, Corfu, 1918; French translation Paris, 1919.
10. U. Ostojić, 'Britanski istoričari u Srbiji 1914–1915', unpublished Master's thesis upheld at the Faculty of Philosophy, University of Belgrade, 1980.
11. U. Ostojić-Fejić, 'Stav britanskih javnih i naučnih radnika prema ratnim naporima Srbije 1914–1915', *VIG*, 2 (1983), 253–65; U. Ostojić-Fejić, 'Britanski istoričari i makedonsko pitanje 1914–1915', *Istorija XX veka*, 1 (1983), 117–25.
12. U. Apollonia (ed.), *Der Futurismus*, Cologne, 1972, 238–9 (reproduction); we analysed the original at an exhibition of Futurism in the Royal Academy of Arts in London in 1973.
13. M. Zorić, 'Danuncijeva "Ode alla nazione serba" i njezini prevodioci' in *Glas CCCXXV SANU, Odeljenje jezika i knjizevnosti*, vol. 11, Belgrade, 1980, 81–153.
14. M. Arsenijević, 'Preobražaji ambijenta i ljudi starog trkališta' in *Beograd u sećanjima 1900–1918*, Belgrade, 1977, 109.
15. J. Reed, *The War in Eastern Europe*, 49.
16. HHStA-Vienna, PA I, K. 789, report of 10 March 1915.
17. *Ibid.*
18. *Ibid.*
19. *Ibid.*
20. *Ibid.*
21. B. Krizman and B. Hrabak (eds), *Zapisnici*, 82–3.
22. N. Popović, *Odnosi Srbije i Rusije*, 279–81.
23. AA-Bonn, Oxfort, S. 1086, Weltkrieg 545-Anlage 11, Nachrichten aus Serbien.
24. *VRS*, 1, 271–2.
25. A SFRY-Belgrade, No. 80–4–256–8.
26. J. Pisarev, *Serbija i Černogorija*, 96–102; D. Janković, *Srbija i jugoslovensko pitanje*, 223–50; M. Djurišić, 'Neki ekonomski i politicki problemi Srbije u ratnoj 1914. godini', *VIG*, 4 (1964), 3–37.
27. A SFRY-Belgrade, no. 80–4–256–8.
28. J. Reed, *The War in Eastern Europe*, 87.
29. A SFRY-Belgrade, no. 80–4–246–58.
30. *Ibid.*

31. *VRS*, 8, 65.
32. Ž. Pavlović, *Rat Srbije sa Austro-Ugarskom, Nemačkom i Bugarskom 1915*, Belgrade, 1915, 3.
33. J. Reed, *The War in Eastern Europe*, 87.
34. See footnote 26; N. Popović, *Odnosi Srbije i Rusije*, 123–4.
35. *Ibid.*
36. A survey of economic circumstances by a representative of the Swedish Ministry of Trade after a lengthy stay in Serbia came into Austro-Hungarian hands: 'The price of flour rocketed and had increased by 100 per cent on the third day of the war (from 25 to 50 para per kilo). The largest mill owner in Serbia certainly contributed to that increase as he did not put all his huge stocks of wheat and milled products on to the market.' The sugar industry 'whose importance was growing year by year' understandably had a very bad year, and the Belgrade sugar plant could not operate since it was in a war zone and its warehouses had been destroyed. 'The remaining industry partly functioned and partly ceased production.... The breweries in Niš and Jagodina ... do not have raw materials.' 'The iron industry has totally ceased production. The largest iron plant in Serbia in Belgrade was completely destroyed at the beginning of the war.... Most mines have halted production.' Bor (producing copper and silver) had to close its plant owing to a shortage of coke, while the coal mines had no rolling stock. 'The country's monetary circumstances are desperate, although the state still has sufficient resources to wage war.' The price of a kilo of butter jumped from 3.5 to 8 dinars, a kilo of the best cheese from 4 to 11 dinars, potatoes from 0.15 to 0.35 dinars, flour from 0.25 to 0.90 dinars, sugar from 1.10 to 4.50 dinars, beans from 0.10 to 0.45 dinars, veal from 1.10 to 1.70 dinars; the price of eggs rose from 0.04 to 0.15 dinars each and a litre of milk from 0.25 to 0.60 dinars. 'Due to the ceaseless shelling from monitors on the Sava, ... much of value in Belgrade has been destroyed; mention should first be made of the customs warehouses where commodities to the value of 80 million francs were destroyed in a fire. Only textile works and the railways are functioning, but exclusively for military purposes.' (HHStA-Vienna, F. 34, K. 70, addendum to act from Salonika of 18 June 1915)
37. D. Janković, *Srbija i jugoslovensko pitanje*, 240–2.
38. HHStA-Vienna, PA I, K. 789.
39. HHStA-Vienna, F. 34, K. 70.
40. PRO-London, FO 371, no. 2252.
41. *Ibid.*
42. R.A. Reiss, *Šta sam video i doživeo u velikim danima*, Belgrade, 1928, 47–51.
43. J. Pisarev, *Serbija i Černogorija*, 103–4.
44. K. Ambrožić, *Nadežda Petrović*, Belgrade, 1979, 101.
45. J. Reed, *The War in Eastern Europe*, 104.
46. R.A. Reiss, *Šta sam video i doživeo u velikim danima*, 47–51.
47. The Serbian military put the number of dead in battle, from wounds received or from illness in the first eight months of 1915, at 56,842 (A VII-Belgrade, signatory 3, k. 470, sv. 2. No. 7).
48. J. Reed, *The War in Eastern Europe*, 95.

49. *VRS*, 8, 76.
50. V. Stanojević, *Naše ratno sanitetsko iskustvo*, Belgrade, 1925, 329–37; *Srbija i Crna Gora*, 174; M. Vekić, 'Strane medicinske misije u Srbiji 1914–1915', unpublished graduation thesis upheld at the Faculty of Philosophy of the University of Belgrade, 1981; N. Popović, *Odnosi Srbije i Rusije*, 131–3. Albin Kutschbach's reports are rich sources of information on this issue.
51. Lady Paget, *With our Serbian Allies*, London, n.d.
52. See footnote 51. Kutschbach's reports also contain a great deal of useful information.
53. *Ibid*.
54. A. Kutschbach, *Brandherd Europas*, Leipzig, 1929, 185–6.
55. G. Gesemann, *Die Flucht*, Munich, 1935, 12–25.
56. J. Reed, *The War in Eastern Europe*, 101.
57. Dj. Stanković, *Nikola Pašić i jugoslovensko pitanje*, vol. 1–2, Belgrade, 1985, 190.
58. HHStA-Vienna, PA I, K. 789, report of 15 January 1915.
59. HHStA-Vienna, PA I, K. 789, report of 6 March 1915.
60. J. Pisarev, *Serbija i Černogorija*, 104–13; D. Janković, *Srbija i jugoslovensko pitanje*, 248, 300–25.
61. *Diplomatičeski dokumenti*, 289.
62. D. Janković, *Srbija i jugoslovensko pitanje*, 325–30.
63. *VRS*, 8, 25, 27.
64. A SANU-Belgrade, No. 11437, D. Milutinović, *Moje komandovanje Albanskim trupama* (manuscript).
65. *Diplomaticeski dokumenti*, 289.
66. According to German sources in 1915 and Austro-Hungarian sources in 1917, Austrian sympathisers from Serbia were telling German agents in 1915 that a separate peace should be concluded.
67. E. Redžić, *Austromarksizam i jugoslovensko pitanje*, 414–26; D. Janković, *Srbija i jugoslovensko pitanje*, 300–25. See: D. Lapčević, *Rat i srpska socijalna demokratija*, Belgrade, 1925.
68. V. Lapčević and T. Milenković (eds), *Prepiska srpskih socijalista u toku prvog svetskog rata*, Belgrade, 1979, 27–9.
69. D. Janković, *Srbija i jugoslovensko pitanje*, 301–2.
70. PRO-London, FO 371, no. 2262, Chirol's report on his stay in the Balkans.
71. U. Ostojić, *Britanski istoričari u Srbiji 1914–1915*, 44 (in manuscript).
72. J. Reed, *The War in Eastern Europe*, 54.
73. See footnote 60.
74. M. Marjanović, *Londonski ugovor iz godine 1915*, Zagreb, 1960; D. Šepić, *Italija, saveznici i jugoslovensko pitanje 1914–1918*, Zagreb, 1970; M. Ekmečić, *Ratni ciljevi Srbije 1914*, 281–371.
75. N. Popović, *Odnosi Srbije i Rusije*, 140–82; M. Ekmečić, *Ratni ciljevi Srbije 1914*, 219–80; D. Janković, *Srbija i jugoslovensko pitanje*, 98–133.
76. A. Mitrović, 'Tajni ugovor izmedju Centralnih sila i Bugarske od 6 septembra 1915', *Medjunarodni problemi*, 3–4 (1978), 47–65.
77. See footnotes 75 and 76.

78. Dj. Stanković, *Nikola Pašić, Saveznici i stvaranje Jugoslavije*, Belgrade, 1984, 226.
79. J. Reed, *The War in Eastern Europe*, 55–6.
80. PRO-London, FO 371, No. 2262, Chirol's report on his stay in the Balkans.
81. PRO-London, FO 371, No. 2262, report of 6 May 1915.
82. A. Mitrović, *Prodor na Balkan*, 215–300; see also material in AA-Bonn, Oxfort, S. 1029–30, Weltkrieg; S. 1086, Weltkrieg 545-Anhang 11; S. 1087, Weltkrieg 11 geheim.
83. *Ibid.*
84. *Ibid.*
85. *Ibid.*
86. A. Kutschbach, *Brandherd Europas*, 189–96.
87. AA-Bonn, Oxfort, S. 1030, Weltkrieg 149, report from Niš of 20 September 1925.
88. A. Mitrović, *Prodor na Balkan*, 269–78.
89. Dj. Stanković, *Nikola Pašić*, 74–6.
90. *VRS*, 8, 25, 27.
91. *OUA*, vol. 8, 610.
92. *Ibid.*, 598–9.
93. AA-Bonn, Oxfort, S. 1149, GHQ 17, vol. 1–2, strictly confidential report of 9 August 1914.
94. *OUA*, vol. 8, 598–9.
95. A. Mitrović, *Prodor na Balkan*, 95–130.
96. *OUA*, vol. 8, 387, 391, 465–6, 506–7.
97. HHStA-Vienna, PA I, K. 512.
98. AA-Bonn, Oxfort, S. 1149, GHQ 17, vol. 1–2.
99. *Ibid.*
100. Ž. Avramovski, 'Opredeljenje Bugarske za Centralne sile u prvom svetskom ratu (1914–1915)' in Ž. Avramovski (ed.), *Jugoslovensko-bugarski odnosi u XX veku*, vol. 1, Belgrade, 1980, 61–97.
101. AA-Bonn, Oxfort, S. 96, Deutschland 128 No. 8 geheim, vol. 1, reports from Sofia of 1 and 4 August 1914.
102. AA-Bonn, Oxfort, S. 96, Deutschland 128 No. 8 geheim, vol. 1.
103. *Ibid.*, report from Sofia of 6 August 1914.
104. See footnote 91.
105. HHStA-Vienna, PA I, K. 820, reports from Sofia of 19, 21 and 22 October, instructions to Embassy in Berlin of 20 October and to Legation in Sofia of 21 October, as well as a telephone message from Berlin of 21 October 1914.
106. AA-Bonn, Oxfort, S. 1149, GHQ 17, vol. 1–2, Ministry of Foreign Affairs— to the Supreme General Staff, 27 October 1914.
107. AA-Bonn, Oxfort, S. 1149, GHQ 17, vol. 17, Supreme General Staff— Ministry of Foreign Affairs, 4 November 1914.
108. AA-Bonn, Oxfort, S. 1149, GHQ 17, vol. 1–2, 6 November 1914.
109. AA-Bonn, Oxfort, S. 237, Bulgarien 14, vol. 19, report from Sofia of 22 October 1914.
110. *Ibid.*
111. See M. Ekmečić, *Ratni ciljevi Srbije 1914*, 258–63.

112. Judging by the report of 11 March 1915 from the German Minister to Sofia, members of medical missions in Serbia that had come to Sofia had confirmed the news that 'indescribable misery' reigned among Serbs owing to disease, that 1,000 people were dying of spotted typhus every day ('150–160 soldiers and civilians every day' in Niš), that the 'Serbian Army was no longer capable of putting up resistance', and the population was 'worn out with war and desperation'. (AA-Bonn, S. 1083, Weltkrieg 1914 geheim, vol. 11)
113. *VRS*, 8, 90–1.
114. *Ibid.*, 91–2, 93–4.
115. *Ibid.*, 94.
116. HHStA-Vienna, PA I, K. 936 and *OUA*, vol. 8, 660, 710–11, 729, 789, 837–8, 852, 872–4.
117. HHStA-Vienna, PA I, K. 936, correspondence between Vienna and Durrës or Skadar, exchange of communiqués between Ministry of Foreign Affairs and Supreme Command, reports from Herceg-Novi and Budva.
118. M. Ekmečić, *Ratni ciljevi Srbije 1914*, 381. The Austro-Hungarian Minister to Durrës also spent some time in Herceg-Novi; he sent the following telegrams to Vienna: 'Consul General Krall, Hasan Priština and Isa Boljetinac today set off for Herceg-Novi to conduct talks.' (Herceg-Novi, 29 July 1914); 'Hasan Beg Priština and Isa Boljetinac returned from Herzeg-Novi yesterday' (Durrës, 31 July 1914). The content of the correspondence shows indisputably that it was concerned agreement on fomenting an uprising in Serbia (HHStA-Vienna, PA I, K. 936).
119. HHStA-Vienna, PA I, K. 936 and *OUA*, vol. 8, 598–9.
120. HHStA-Vienna, PA I, K. 936 and *OUA*, vol. 8, 598–9, 712–16, 745–6, 874–6, 956–7.
121. HHStA-Vienna, PA I, K. 936.
122. *Ibid.*, communiqué from military intelligence service of 10 August 1914.
123. *Ibid.*, and K. 982; See: M. Ekmečić, *Ratni ciljevi Srbije 1914*, 259–62.
124. HHStA-Vienna, PA I, K. 982.
125. *Ibid.*
126. *Ibid.*, report from Scutari of 8 January 1915.
127. *Ibid.*, report from Scutari of 27 April 1915.
128. *Ibid.*, instructions of 18 May 1915.
129. *Ibid.*, reports from Scutari of 12–16 and 19 February 1915.
130. *Ibid.*, Ministry of Foreign Affairs—Supreme Command, 15 February 1915.
131. KA-Vienna, Op. Abt. No. 7234, reply of Supreme Command of 16 February 1915.
132. HHStA-Vienna, PA I, K. 982, report from Constantinople of 25 February 1915; HHStA-Vienna, PA I, K. 936, report from Scutari of 18 October 1914; B. Hrabak, 'Albanija od julske krize do proleća 1916. godine na osnovu ruske diplomatske gradje (II)', *Obelezja*, 6 (1963), 133.
133. *VRS*, 1, several documents; M. Ekmečić, *Ratni ciljevi Srbije 1914*, 380–1; A SANU-Belgrade, No. 9870, Srpsko-talijanski odnosi.
134. M. Ekmečić, *Ratni ciljevi Srbije 1914*, 382–93; D. Janković, *Srbija i jugoslovensko pitanje*, 163–77.

135. A chronicle of Serbian foreign policy moves towards Italy on account of Albania is provided in a document in A SANU-Belgrade, no. 9870; compare with B. Hrabak, 'Elaborat srpskog Ministarstva inostranih dela o pripremama srpske okupacije severne Albanije 1915 godine', *Vjetar i arkivit te Kosoves,* 2–3 (1966–7), 9–35.
136. *VRS,* 8, 42–3.
137. A SANU-Belgrade, No. 9870, 15–16.
138. HHStA-Vienna, PA I, K. 789, report from Niš of 17 February 1915.
139. *Ibid.*
140. *VRS,* 8, 117.
141. *Ibid.,* 163.
142. A SANU-Belgrade, No. 11473, D. Milutinović, *Moje komandovanje Albanskim trupama* (manuscript), 29.
143. D. Janković, *Srbija i jugoslovensko pitanje,* 175–7; A SANU-Belgrade, No. 11473; D. Milutinović, *Moje komandovanje Albanskim trupama,* 10–21.
144. A. Mitrović, 'Balkanski planovi birokratije Balhauzplaca tokom prvog svetskog rata (1914–1916)', *JIČ,* 1–4 (1981), 139–67.
145. S. Stanojević, *Šta hoce Srbija,* Niš, 1915, 26.
146. *Ibid.*
147. A. Belić, *Srbija,* 95.
148. S. Novakovitch, *Problèmes Yougo-Slaves,* 27–8.
149. A. Belić, *Srbija,* 97.
150. S. Stanojević, *Šta hoce Srbija,* 27.
151. M. T., *Austro-Ugarska protiv svojih podanika,* Niš, 1915. There were few different opinions, see D. Janković, *Srbija i jugoslovensko pitanje,* 331.
152. N. Rakočević, *Crna Gora 1914–1918,* 54–83; N. Rakočević, *Politički odnosi,* 236–51; D. Vujović, *Ujedinjenje Crne Gore i Srbije,* Titograd, 1962, 147–63; J. Pisarev, *Serbija i Černogorija,* 90–5; D. Janković, *Srbija i jugoslovensko pitanje,* 147–63; M. Ekmečić, *Ratni ciljevi Srbije 1914,* 405–22.
153. *Ibid.*
154. *Ibid.*
155. *Ibid.*
156. Abroad, Prince Danilo looked into the possibility of Montenegro concluding a separate peace (on the subject of his activity in November 1915 see V. Vučković, 'Diplomatska pozadina', 239–44). The news that Cetinje wanted peace (even in the name of Serbia!) reached Vienna via intelligence centres in Sofia, and King Nicholas's daughters were mentioned, particularly Ksenija, who was alleged to be working on her father's instructions, and, as intermediary, the Dutch Baron Kruyff who acted on Prince Danilo's behalf in November (KA-Vienna, Op. Abt. vol. 551, several documents). The German Minister in Athens reported on 31 August 1915 that Danilo had requested the Greek king to mediate to the best of his ability in Berlin and Vienna to ensure that, on conclusion of peace, Montenegro would be treated mildly because 'the Montenegrin royal family has found itself in the war against its will.' Prince Danilo is said to have 'spoken particularly sharply against Russia.' (AA-Bonn, Oxfort, S. 1030, Weltkrieg 142)

157. See footnote 154.
158. *Ibid.*
159. At the end of 1915, Pašić wrote: 'Serbia is willing, and has given proof of its willingness, to give the Montenegrin dynasty the greatest possible material security and to preserve its prestige for all time, but under the condition that the unity of the Serb nation be secured at least in a real union. The issue of borders between Serbia and Montenegro should be considered an internal Serbian issue.' (M. Ekmečić, *Ratni ciljevi Srbije 1914*, 407).
160. See: Z. Passek, 'Bilješke sa sjednica, 47–85; Z. Passek, 'Zapisnici sjednica Jugoslavenskog odbora u Londonu iz 1916. 1917. i 1918 godine', *Radovi Arhiva JAZU*, 2 (1973), 5–70; also: Z. Passek, 'Pisma Vladimira Čerine dru Anti Trumbicu iz 1915. i 1916. godine', *Radovi Arhiva JAZU*, 2 (1973), 71–85.
161. F. Šišić, *Dokumenti*, 12–14.
162. *Ibid.*, 15–17; D. Janković, *Srbija i jugoslovensko pitanje*, 493–502.
163. F. Šišić, *Dokumenti*, 20–2.
164. D. Janković, 'Radovi o stvaranju jugoslovenske države objavljeni izmedju dva svetska rata', *JIČ*, 3–4 (1966), 79–103; D. Janković, 'O posleratnim radovima na istoriji stvaranja jugoslovenske države 1918', *JIČ*, 2 (1962), 68–87; D. Janković, 'Radovi o jugoslovenskom pitanju u prvom svetskom ratu objavljevi posledje decenije (1965–1974)', *JIČ*, 3–4 (1974), 95–122; Z. Passek, 'Prilog bibliografiji o Jugoslavenskom odboru u Londonu', *Radovi Arhiva JAZU*, 1 (1972), 33–45.
165. Dj. Stanković, *Nikola Pašić*, 228–33.
166. D. Šepić, *Supilo diplomat*, 140.
167. M. Ekmečić, *Ratni ciljevi Srbije 1914*, 219–80; D. Janković, *Srbija i jugoslovensko pitanje*, 98–133; N. Popović, *Odnosi Srbije i Rusije*, 140–82.
168. J. Pleterski, *Prva odločitev Slovencev*, 33–75.
169. *Srbija i Crna Gora*, 173–232; P. Tomac, *Prvi svetski rat*, 271–306. A. Mitrović, *Prodor na Balkan*, 257–300; Ž. Pavlović, *Rat Srbije sa Austro-Ugarskom*.
170. *VRS*, 9, 50.
171. *Ibid.*, 102–3.
172. See footnote 171.
173. *Ibid.*
174. D. Lapčević, *Okupacija*, Belgrade, 1926, 32, 35.
175. *VRS*, 11, 18.
176. HHStA-Vienna, PA I, K. 973, several documents. See: J. Pisarev, *Serbija i Černogorija*, 150.
177. HHStA-Vienna, PA I, K. 973, minutes and notes on meeting.
178. B. Krizman and B. Hrabak (eds), *Zapisnici*, 174.
179. See footnote 171.
180. A. Boppe, *Sa srpskom vladom od Niša do Krfa*, Geneva, 1918, 38.
181. Dj. Tripković, 'Francuska i evakuacija srpske vojske iz Albanije', unpublished of master's thesis, Belgrade, 1980, 17.
182. *VRS*, 13, 75.
183. Ž. Pavlović, *Rat Srbije sa Austro-Ugarskom*, 835, footnote 88.
184. *VRS*, 13, 116–18, 119–20, 128–9, 136–8.

185. Ibid., 136.
186. Ibid., 150; compare Ž. Pavlović, *Rat Srbije sa Austro-Ugarskom*, 845, footnote 95: 'This is Vojvoda Mišić's wish for a separate peace, which is in line with a conversation he had with me in Kruševac on 11 (24) October 1915 around 10 o'clock. I informed Vojvoda Putnik of that conversation immediately, and he informed Prime Minister Pašić.'
187. *VRS*, 13, 116–17.
188. Ibid., 136.
189. See: manuscript 'Dvomesečni ratni doživljaj Drag.[utina] Markovića' in *Arhiva Istorijskog instituta Srbije u Beogradu*, Ostavstina Stanoja Stanojevića.

Chapter 4 *On Foreign Soil*

1. A. Boppe, *Sa srpskom vladom od Niša do Krfa*, 73.
2. *VRS*, 13, 40.
3. *Srbija i Crna Gora*, 229; V.J. Radojević and D.J. Milenković, *Propast srpskih regruta 1915*, Belgrade, 1967, 181; P. Tomac, *Prvi svetski rat*, 304–5; D. Janković, 'O radu srpske vlade za vreme prvog svetskog rata' in B. Krizman and B. Hrabak (eds), *Zapisnici sa sednica Delegacija Kraljevine SHS mirovnoj konferenciji u Parizu 1919–1920*, Belgrade, 1960, 27; P. Opačić, *Solunska ofanziva 1918*, Belgrade, 1980, 16. It appears from the military material that was submitted to the Peace Conference that the losses in the fighting in the autumn of 1915 and during the withdrawal through Albania amounted to 150,000 dead and 77,278 missing, which are numbered among the dead (A VII-Belgrade, signatory 3, k. 470, sv. 2, No. 7). However, sources also speak of the collapse of the troops. On 10 December 1915 Jurišić-Sturm reported as follows: 'The state of the troops' morale is very low.... As soon as we had crossed the Sitnica River, patrols, guards and entire squads started to flee and to surrender' (*VRS*, 13, 253). On 21 December, Mišić transmitted a report of the Drina Division II that in the course of the previous day and night 'another 863 soldiers had fled from the 6th regiment ... and that regiment has virtually ceased to exist.' (*VRS*, 13, 362) It seems that most of the 'missing' stayed in Serbia, that is they returned home, and the occupying forces later interned tens of thousands of men from among those ranks. However, a constant and proportionally very strong movement of armed resistance in the occupied territory also emerged from those ranks.
4. *VRS*, 13, 331–4, 359, 368–9.
5. Ibid., 400.
6. *Srbija i Crna Gora*, 231–2; Dj. Tripković, 'Francuska i evakuacija'.
7. A. Boppe, *Sa srpskom vladom od Niša do Krfa*, 73–4.
8. *VRS*, 13, 388.
9. Ibid., 400.
10. Ibid., 402.
11. Ibid., 388.
12. A. Boppe, *Sa srpskom vladom od Niša do Krfa*, 73–4.

13. *VRS*, 14, 100.
14. *Ibid.*, 112.
15. *Srbija i Crna Gora*, 232.
16. P. de Mondesire, *Albanska Golgota*, Belgrade, 1936.
17. Dj. Tripković, 'Francuska i evakuacija srpske vojske iz Albanije', *VIG*, 3 (1981), 205–6 (abbreviated version of above mentioned manuscript).
18. V. Terzić et al., *Operacije crnogorske vojske*, 418–535; *Srbija i Crna Gora*, 253–70; N. Rakočević, *Crna Gora 1914–1918*, 121–98.
19. *Ibid.*
20. *Ibid.*
21. N. Rakočević, *Crna Gora 1914–1918*, 121–98.
22. A. Mitrović, 'Sučeljavanje sa srednjoevropskim imperijalizmom' in *Istorija srpskog naroda*, VI–2, Belgrade, 1983, 104.
23. N. Rakočević, *Crna Gora 1914–1918*, 121–98.
24. *Ibid.*
25. KA-Vienna, Op. Abt. No. 20674.
26. *Srbija i Crna Gora*, 233–6; P. Tomac, *Prvi svetski rat*, 311–13; M.Ž. Živanović, 'O evakuaciji srpske vojske iz Albanije i njenoj reorganizaciji na Krfu (1915–1916) prema francuskim dokumentima', *IČ*, 14–15 (1963–5), 231–307; N. Popović, *Odnosi Srbije i Rusije*, 106–11; Dj. Tripković, 'Francuska i evakuacija', 82–120.
27. Dj. Tripković, 'Francuska i evakuacija', 82–3; Popović, *Odnosi Srbije i Rusije*, 108–9.
28. N. Popović, *Odnosi Srbije i Rusije*, 108.
29. See footnote 27. The French Minister wrote in his memoirs: 'Death was rampant in those huge numbers of people. There were bones up to Medua, the corpses of horses, filth, in the midst of which there lay prostrate soldiers struggling to stay alive.' (A. Boppe, *Sa srpskom vladom od Niša do Krfa*, 106–10)
30. Dj. Tripković, 'Francuska i evakuacija', 85–7, 94–5.
31. The French Minister wrote the following testimony: 'When it was heard at dawn on 15 January in Medua that the *Città di Catania* had sailed that night with the government and Allied envoys on board, the crowds were first surprised, then indignant, and soon angry. On the crowded lighters …, in the tents filled with those sick with fever, by the fires around which they were huddled, people's deputies, officials, citizens… lamented their abandonment…. Those poor, desperate people were ready to believe even the worst rumours: the government had fled with the state treasury! The government had fled, abandoning both the army and the people! Everyone knew that Mr Pašić and his colleagues had to leave earlier in order to conclude an agreement with the allied governments and accelerate salvation measures, but everyone was saying that the ministers were only looking to save themselves.' (A. Boppe, *Sa srpskom vladom od Niša do Krfa*, 106–10)
32. See footnote 26.
33. The figures on the number of evacuees vary; it would seem that around 170,000 people were then evacuated, 150,000 of whom were soldiers.

34. P. de Mondesire, *Albanska Golgota*, 61; M.Ž. Živanović, 'O evakuaciji'.
35. *Ibid.*, 87.
36. M.Ž. Živanović, 'O evakuaciji', 293.
37. P. de Mondesire, *Albanska Golgota*, 68, 84.
38. *Ibid.*, 69–70; P. Tomac, *Prvi svetski rat*, 392–4; *Srbija i Crna Gora*, 298–9.
39. N. Popović, *Odnosi Srbije i Rusije*, 310–23; Dj. Stanković, *Nikola Pašić*, 236–51.
40. See footnote 38.
41. P. Opačić, *Solunska ofanziva*, 16–20; N. Popović, *Odnosi Srbije i Rusije*, 267–73.
42. *Ibid.*, 17–18; P. Tomac, *Prvi svetski rat*, 294–5, 396–9; *Srbija i Crna Gora*, 303–4.
43. P. Tomac, *Prvi svetski rat*, 399–404; *Srbija i Crna Gora*, 310–22.
44. *Ibid.*
45. Dragomir Glišić, *Ratni period 1914–1918*, Exhibition Catalogue, Belgrade, 1983, diaries I and II.
46. Dj. Stanković, *Nikola Pašić*, 504–7.
47. N. Popović, *Jugoslovenski dobrovoljci*, vii–xiv; D. Vujović, *Ujedinjenje Crne Gore i Srbije*, 202; N. Rakočević, *Politički odnosi*, 277–81.
48. N. Popović, *Odnosi Srbije i Rusije*, 279–305, 389–425; N. Popović, *Jugoslovenski dobrovoljci*, vi–vii (as in the documents in the corresponding passages).
49. A. Djurić, *Ka pobedi*, Belgrade, 1938, 5.
50. See footnote 48.
51. N. Popović, *Odnosi Srbije i Rusije*, 299–302.
52. B. Krizman and B. Hrabak (eds), *Zapisnici*, 345.
53. AS-Belgrade, Ministry of Education [hereafter ME] Paris, 4 (17) August 1916.
54. M. Ibrovac, 'Srpski djaci u francuskim školama za vreme provog svetskog rata' in *Enciklopedija Jugoslavije*, vol. 3, Zagreb, 1958; P. Milosavljević, 'Srpski djački bataljon u Žoziju 1916–1917', *Istorijski glasnik*, 4 (1964), 129–64; Dj. Tripković, 'Francuska i evakuacija', 119–20; A. Moulins, *L'université française et la jeunesse serbe*, Brussels, 1917. The basic material for this subject is in AS-Belgrade, ME Paris, 1916–18.
55. A. Moulins, *L'université française et la jeunesse serbe*, 13–14; Dj. Tripković, 'Francuska i evakuacija', 119–20.
56. A. Moulins, *L'université française et la jeunesse serbe*, 67–9.
57. Dj. Tripković, 'Francuska i evakuacija', 119–20.
58. Sorbonne/Archives-Paris, 324 Yugoslavia, 26 February 1917; see Lj. Trgovčević, 'Dva dokumenta o skolovanju srpske omladine 1917. godine', *Istorijski glasnik*, 1–2 (1983), 99–107.
59. A. Moulins, *L'université française et la jeunesse serbe*, 114–17.
60. AS-Belgrade, ME Paris 1916, 1 (14) August 1916.
61. See: P. Milosavljević, 'Srpski djački bataljon u Žoziju 1916–1917'.
62. AS-Belgrade, Political-Propaganda Department of Foreign Ministry, F. 1, Ministry of Education—Legation in Paris 18 (31) August 1916.
63. B. Krizman and B. Hrabak (eds), *Zapisnici*, 336.
64. Sorbonne/Archives-Paris, 324 Yugoslavia, 26 February 1917.
65. AS-Belgrade, ME Paris 1918, 15 (28) June 1918.

66. B. Krizman and B. Hrabak (eds), *Zapisnici*, 367. The Department of Education at the Serbian Legation in Paris (which was set up to work with schoolchildren and students in exile), sent, according to the act of 12 (25) January 1917, a group of matriculants from Nice to French universities; it determined a monthly scholarship of 135 French francs for twenty-six of them, 85 francs for five of them (they each received a further 50 francs from the municipality of the university in which they were enrolled), and 70 francs for one, with the stipulation that all but one of them were also allowed of 5 francs monthly each for books (AS-Belgrade, ME Paris 1917).
67. AS-Belgrade, ME Paris 1917, 8 (21) August 1917; AS-Belgrade, ME Paris 1918, 31 December 1917 (13 January 1918).
68. AS-Belgrade, ME Paris 1918, 10 April 1918 (it seems to have been dated according to the new calendar).
69. PRO-London, FO 371, no. 2894; see Lj. Trgovčević, 'Dva dokumenta'.
70. AS-Belgrade, ME Paris 1918, 4 (17) February 1918.
71. M. Jakovljević, *Iz rata i emigracije*, Subotica, 1923, 43.
72. AS-Belgrade, ME Paris 1916, 20 October (2 November) 1916.
73. *Ibid.*
74. M. Mitrović, 'Jugoslovenska akademska omladina u Švajcarskoj', master's thesis (University of Belgrade, 1977); M. Mitrović, 'Istorijska gradja u Beogradu o temi: Jugoslovenski studenti u Švajcarskoj 1916–1918. godine', *Godišnjak grada Beograda*, 24 (1977), 241–51; M. Mitrović, 'Organizacije jugoslovenskih studenata u Švajcarskoj 1917. godine', *IČ*, 27 (1980), 209–32; M. Mitrović, 'Jugoslovenski studenti u Švajcarskoj i ujedinjenje (1917–1918)', *Istorijski glasnik*, 1–2 (1981), 127–38; M. Mitrović, 'Opšta organizacija akademske omladine u Švajcarskoj 1918. i njena delatnost', *IČ*, 28 (1981), 137–54.
75. M. Mitrović, 'Jugoslovenska akademska omladina u Švajcarskoj', 22–5 (in manuscript).
76. Lj. Trgovčević, *Školovanje Srpske omladine u emigraciji 1916–1918*, IČ (1995), 95–113.
77. AS-Belgrade, ME Paris 1917, N. Vulić, 12 (25) December 1917.
78. AS-Belgrade, ME Paris 1918, S. Urošević, 27 January (9 February) 1918.
79. Lj. Trgovčević, 'Jovan Cvijić u prvom svetskom ratu', *IČ*, 22 (1975), 173–231.
80. *Ibid.*, 190–2.
81. J. Cvijić, *La péninsule balkanique*, Paris, 1918.
82. D. Janković, *Jugoslovensko pitanje i Krfska deklaracija 1917. godine*, Belgrade, 1967, 106–12, 131–42, 383–97; D. Vujović, *Ujedinjenje Crne Gore i Srbije*, 157–282; N. Rakočević, *Politički odnosi*, 262–81.
83. D. Janković, 'Narodna skupština Srbije za vreme prvog svetskog rata i pitanje njenog kvoruma' in *Anali Pravnog fakulteta u Beogradu*, vol. 14, Belgrade, 1966, 329–35.
84. *Ibid.*
85. *Ibid.*
86. B. Nešković, *Istina o Solunskom procesu*; M. Ž. Živanović, *Pukovnik Apis*; V. Dedijer, *Sarajevo 1914*, vol. 2, 197–209; B. Hrabak, 'Delatnost pripadnika organiza-

cije "Ujedinjenje ili smrt" za vreme prvog svetskog rata', *Naša prošlost*, 6 (1971–2), 5–19; V. Vučković, 'Unutrašnje krize Srbije', 203–22; D. Janković, *Jugoslovensko pitanje i Krfska deklaracija*, 67–73; A.N. Dragnich, *Serbia, Nikola Pašić and Yugoslavia*, New Brunswick, 1974, 81–5; S. Jovanović, 'Apis' in S. Jovanović, *Moji savremenici*, Windsor, 1962, 399–459; C.Dj. Popović, 'Apisov poverljiv raport', *Pregled*, 7–8 (1964), 81–95.
87. *Ibid.*
88. *Ibid.*
89. For more details on this see S. Jovanović, 'Apis' in S. Jovanović, *Moji savremenici*.
90. Of particular interest on this subject is B. Hrabak, 'Delatnost pripadnika organizacije'.
91. On this subject see particularly V. Dedijer, *Sarajevo 1914*.
92. Having arrived in Geneva in November 1918, Anton Korošec asked Božidar Marković if the Black Hand had really wanted agreement with Austria-Hungary (B. Krizman, *Raspad Austro-Ugarske i stvaranje jugoslovenske države*, Zagreb, 1977, 164).
93. According to testimony from a participant in the Battle for Kajmakcalan, Vojin Petrović (Vojvoda Vuk) was killed by a Bulgarian soldier when the Bulgarians had already withdrawn and Popović was binding his wounded arm. (R. Djokić, 'Na krvavom Vardaru', 61).
94. S. Jovanović, 'Apis' in S. Jovanović, *Moji savremenici*.
95. See footnote 86; see: N. Rakočević, *Politički odnosi*, 263.
96. S. Dimitrijević, *Socijalistički radnički pokret u Srbiji*, Belgrade, 1982.
97. *Ibid.*, 225–313; V. Strugar, *Socijaldemokratija*, 27–66; E. Redžić, *Austromarksizam i jugoslovensko pitanje*, 409–30. See: V. Lapčević and T. Milenković (eds), *Prepiska srpskih socijalista*.
98. B. Hrabak and K. Džambazovski, 'Srpski socijaldemokrati na Solunskom frontu, u Solunu i na Krfu 1916–1918', *Istorijski glasnik*, 1–4 (1961), 152–8.
99. V. Lapčević and T. Milenković (eds), *Prepiska srpskih socijalista*, 103–4.
100. D. Vujović, *Ujedinjenje Crne Gore i Srbije*, 157–229; N. Rakočević, *Politički odnosi*, 256–84.
101. The literature indicates 'some claims' that Regent Alexander put a halt to his enmity towards Pašić in autumn 1916 on the condition that Prime Minister Pašić should try to remove King Nicholas and Colonel Dragutin Dimitrijević Apis, both of whom Alexander considered his enemies (N. Rakočević, *Politički odnosi*, 263).
102. D. Vujović, *Ujedinjenje Crne Gore i Srbije*, 180–205; B. Hrabak, 'Borba izmedju crnogorskog dvora i srpske vlade oko crnogorske vojske i oko dobrovoljaca 1916–1918', *Istorija XX veka*, 6 (1964), 69–212; B. Hrabak, 'Suparništvo izmedju srpskih delegata i propagatora i zvanične Crne Gore oko oslobodjenja i regrutovanja interniranih bivših dobrovoljaca na Liparima i Korzici 1916–1918', *Istorijski glasnik*, 1–4 (1964), 147–86.
103. N. Rakočević, *Politički odnosi*, 257–8; See footnote 5.
104. *Ibid.*, 258–62, 268–9.
105. *Ibid.*, 269.

Chapter 5 Occupation

1. A. Mitrović, *Prodor na Balkan*, 257–339; A. Mitrović, 'Stvaranje nemačke okupacione zone i austrougarske okupacione uprave u Srbiji (jesen 1915— prolece 1916)', *Istorijski glasnik*, 1–2 (1977), 9–10.
2. A. Mitrović, *Prodor na Balkan*, 307–8, 333–4.
3. HHStA-Vienna, PA I, K. 499, op. no. 18400.
4. HHStA-Vienna, PA I, K. 499, op. no. 18557.
5. KA-Vienna, Archiv Conrads, B, vol. 7.
6. HHStA-Vienna, PA I, K. 497.
7. *Ibid.*, see also Tisza's memorandum of 30 December 1915 (K. 499).
8. *Ibid.*
9. *Ibid.*
10. A. Mitrović, *Prodor na Balkan*, 314–17.
11. HHStA-Vienna, PA I, K. 499, No. 5892.
12. M. Komjáthy (ed.), *Protokolle*, 352–81.
13. A. Mitrović, *Prodor na Balkan*.
14. HHStA-Vienna, PA I, K. 864.
15. *Ibid.* 503.
16. A. Mitrović, *Prodor na Balkan*, 394–405, 417–20. See S. de Bourbon, *L'offre de paix séparée de l'Autriche*, Paris, 1920, 40–1, 55.
17. A. Mitrović, *Prodor na Balkan*, 317–23.
18. A. Mitrović, 'Stvaranje nemačke okupacione zone', 26–8.
19. A. Mitrović, *Prodor na Balkan*, 323–33.
20. A. Mitrović, 'Stvaranje nemačke okupacione zone', 7–37.
21. Ž. Avramovski, 'Bugarske pretenzije na aneksiju delova Kosova u prvom svetskom ratu (1915–1916)' in Ž. Avramovski (ed.), *Jugoslovensko-bugarski odnosi u XX veku*, vol. 2, Belgrade, 1982, 110–51.
22. A. Mitrović, 'Stvaranje nemačke okupacione zone', 31–3.
23. *Ibid.*, 29–31.
24. D. Djordjević, 'Austrougarski okupacioni režim u Srbiji i njegov slom 1918' in *Naučni skup u povodu 50-godisnjice raspada Austro-Ugarske Monarhije i stvaranja jugoslavenske države*, Zagreb, 1969, 205–66; J. Pisarev, 'Okkupacia Serbii. Avstro-Vengerii i borba serbskogo naroda za svoe osvoboždenie', *Sovetskoe slavianovedenie*, 4 (1965), 28–39. Two high-ranking officers of the occupation armies also wrote on occupied Serbia after the War: H. Kerchnawe, 'Die Militärverwaltung in Serbien' in *Die Militärverwaltung in den von den österreich-ungarischen Truppen besetzten Gebieten*, Vienna, 1928, 63–269, and P. Kirch, *Krieg und Verwaltung in Serbien und Mazedonien 1916–1918*, Stuttgart, 1928.
25. N. Rakočević, *Crna Gora 1914–1918*, 199–233.
26. A. Mitrović, 'Die Kriegsziele der Mittelmächte und die Jugoslawienfrage 1914–1918' in A. Wandruszka *et al.* (eds), *Die Donaumonarchie*, 137–70.
27. HHStA-Vienna, PA I, K. 973.
28. *Ibid.*
29. AA-Bonn, Oxfort, S. 1134, GHQ 2, vol. 1, 3 March 1916.
30. BA/MA-Freiburg i B., RM 3 v. 2949, report from Sofia dated 16 October 1915.

31. H. Meier-Welcker, *Seeckt*, Frankfurt am Main, 1967, 68.
32. KA-Vienna, Archiv Conrads, B, vol. 7.
33. AA-Bonn, Kent II, S. 232, Nachlass Stresemann, vol. 158.
34. HHStA-Vienna, PA I, K. 973.
35. A. Mitrović, 'Nemačko-bugarski ugovor o Borskom rudniku od 5 maja 1916', *Istorijski glasnik*, 1–2 (1979), 34–9.
36. Allgemeines Verwaltungsarhiv-Vienna, Handelsministerium-Sektion IV, 18 October 1915.
37. A. Mitrović, 'Nemačko-bugarski ugovor', 38.
38. P. Kirch, *Krieg und Verwaltung*.
39. A. Mitrović, 'Nemačko-bugarski ugovor', 36–9.
40. A. Mitrović, 'Sporazum Centralnih sila o podeli balkanskih i bliskoistočnih sirovina (agreement of 8 January 1916)', *Balcanica*, 13–14 (1982–3), 233–53.
41. BayHStA/KA-Munich, vol. 183.
42. *Ibid.*
43. *Ibid.*
44. *Ibid.*
45. *Ibid.*
46. L. Rathmann, *Stossrichtung Nahost 1914–1918*, Berlin, 1963.
47. A. Mitrović, 'Sporazum Centralnih sila', 245–51.
48. HHStA-Vienna, F. 23, K. 70, several documents.
49. *Ibid.*
50. HHStA-Vienna, F. 23, K. 64, several documents.
51. Something of those efforts on the part of Viennese and Budapest banks has been analysed in E. März, *Österreichische Bankpolitik*, 232–9.
52. HHStA-Vienna, F. 23, K. 64, a strictly confidential act added to a report from Sofia dated 10 September 1917.
53. A. Mitrović, 'Sporazum Centralnih sila', 246–9.
54. On the role of the Direktion der Discontogesellschaft, see details in A. Mitrović, *Prodor na Balkan*.
55. AA-Bonn, Oxfort, S. 250, Bulgarien 24 geheim, o. vol., report of a German Foreign Ministry representative in the Kaiser's retinue of 25 June 1916.
56. ZstA-Potsdam, Reichskanzlei, No. 2458/2.
57. P. Kirch, *Krieg und Verwaltung*, 25–30.
58. *Ibid.*
59. KA-Vienna, Kriegsministerium, Praes. 51–9/4–2/1916; there was a dispute over the Rudna Glava mine in the summer of 1917 (AA-Bonn, Oxfort, S. 1145, GHQ 5, vol. 3).
60. ZStA-Potsdam, Reichskanzlei, No. 2458/2.
61. E. März, *Österreichische Bankpolitik*, 233–4.
62. HHStA-Vienna, F. 23, K. 64, several documents, particularly a report from Sofia of 20 May and a bank memo of 26 May 1916.
63. HHStA-Vienna, F. 23, K. 64, bank memo of 22 November 1917.
64. HHStA-Vienna, F. 23, K. 64, Balkanska Banka memo also of 22 November 1917.
65. HHStA-Vienna, F. 23, K. 64.

66. HHStA-Vienna, F. 23, K. 470, memo from December 1915. As an example of service to foreign policy, the branch mentioned was founded in Belgrade before the war (Banka Andrejevic i Ko); it opened a branch in Niš and intended to open a branch in Skopje too, although it suffered annual losses of 40,000 francs in an unequal contest with French capital (Franco-Serb Bank).
67. HHStA-Vienna, F. 23, K. 64, report from Skopje of 20 October 1917.
68. HHStA-Vienna, F. 23, K. 64, report from Skopje of 17 January 1918.
69. HHStA-Vienna, F. 23, K. 64, memo and report from Skopje of 6 February and 21 July, as well as a report from Sofia of 25 July 1918.
70. AA-Bonn, Oxfort, S. 1135, GHQ 5, vol. 2, memo from General Erich Ludendorf to the Foreign Minister dated 26 August 1917.
71. AA-Bonn, Oxfort, S. 1096, Weltkrieg 15 geheim, vol. 3, text of agreement of 18 May 1917.
72. A. Mitrović, 'Nemačko-bugarski ugovor', 27–55.
73. AA-Bonn, Oxfort, S. 97, Deutschland 128 No. 8 geheim, vol. 19, material prepared for meeting with Radoslavov and text of conclusions; AA-Bonn, Oxfort, S. 1135, GHQ 5, vol. 3, memo of 14 June 1917.
74. A. Mitrović, 'Nemačko-bugarski ugovor', 45–8.
75. ZStA-Potsdam, Reichswirtschaftsministerium, No. 902, memos from Direktion der Discontogesellschaft of 26 March and 22 May.
76. BA-Koblenz, R. 85, memo of Ministry of Foreign Affairs sent to the Supreme Command on 23 June 1917.
77. AA-Bonn, Oxfort, S. 1094, Weltkrieg 14d, vol. 1, from Supreme Command to Ministry of Foreign Affairs, 5 June 1917.
78. AA-Bonn, Oxfort, S. 1094, Weltkrieg 14d, vol. 1, a memo from the Foreign Ministry to the Austro-Hungarian embassy dated 8 July 1917.
79. A. Mitrović, *Prodor na Balkan*, 389–90.
80. BA-Koblenz, R. 85, No. 88.
81. AA-Bonn, Oxfort, S. 1094, Weltkrieg 14d, vol. 1.
82. BA-Koblenz, R. 85, No. 88.
83. Bulgarian material has been used here, with just one exception: M. Perović, *Toplički ustanak 1917*, Belgrade, 1973. However, the material from the archives of Bulgaria's allies in the war, Austria-Hungary and Germany, contains important testimony, for they have: a) part of Bulgarian material, that is to say official letters from the Bulgarian Government and the Bulgarian occupation authorities in Serbia to Austro-Hungarian and German bodies; b) reports from various Austro-Hungarian and German services (diplomatic-consular, military, intelligence, economic, propaganda and cultural).
84. M. Perović, *Toplički ustanak*, 28–56.
85. HHStA-Vienna, PA I, K. 976, supplement to a letter from the Supreme Command to the Foreign Ministry dated 26 February 1916.
86. M. Perović, *Toplički ustanak*, 48.
87. HHStA-Vienna, PA I, K. 976.
88. *Documents relatifs aux violations des conventions de La Haye et du Droit international en général, commises de 1915–1918 par les Bulgares en Serbie occupée*, 1–3, Paris, 1919. *The Enemy in Serbia, Documents Relative to the Bulgarian Atrocities of*

1915–1918, Paris, 1919; R.A. Reiss and A. Bonnassieux, *Requisitoire contre la Bulgarie*, Paris, 1919.
89. M. Perović, *Toplički ustanak*, 41, 313–26.
90. HHStA-Vienna, PA I, K. 976.
91. *Ibid.*
92. *Ibid.*, report from Niš dated 16 September 1916.
93. See footnote 86.
94. M. Perović, *Toplički ustanak*, 31–7, 299–308.
95. HHStA-Vienna, PA I, K. 976, report from Niš dated 22 July 1916.
96. HHStA-Vienna, PA I, K. 975, report from Niš dated 27 January 1918.
97. HHStA-Vienna, PA I, K. 976, reports from Niš dated 16 May, 11 July and 13 November 1917.
98. See footnote 86.
99. KA-Vienna Op. Abt. No. 40904, Baden 20 June 1917.
100. HHStA-Vienna, PA I, K. 976, 4 March 1917, No. 17500 (and the annexed telegram of 3 March 1917), telegrams Nos. 343/1 of 28 March 1917, 30 March 1917, No. 18193.
101. KA-Vienna, Op. Abt. No. 40904.
102. *Ibid.*; and several documents in: HHStA-Vienna, PA I, K. 976 and 977.
103. HHStA-Vienna, PA I, K. 974, correspondence between Burian, Tisza and Conrad in spring 1916 on desired policy in occupied Serbia.
104. *Ibid.*
105. *Ibid.*
106. D. Djordjević, 'Austrougarski okupacioni režim', 220–1.
107. AA-Bonn, Oxfort, S. 1094, Weltkrieg 14d, vol. 2, report of 7 August 1917.
108. AA-Bonn, Oxfort, S. 1094, Weltkrieg 14d, vol. 1, report of 10 July 1916.
109. V. Stojančević, 'Srpski civilni internirci u Austro-Ugarskoj za vreme prvog svetskog rata', *IČ*, 22 (1975), 149–71; V. Stojančević, 'Gubici u stanovništvu Srbije i Beograda pod austrougarskom okupacijom za vreme prvog svetskog rata 1914–1918', *GGB*, 21 (1974), 61–74.
110. HHStA-Vienna, PA I, K. 975, report from Belgrade of 27 September 1916 and a report by the Supreme Command of 21 July 1918.
111. AS-Belgrade, Militärgeneralgouvernement [hereafter MGG], VIII (richest group on this issue), in XVII and also in group V; of particular interest is the study of May 1917: VIII No. 1111.
112. AA-Bonn, Oxfort, S. 1094, Weltkrieg 14d, vol. 1, report of 2 September 1916.
113. In May 1917, there were the following numbers of internees: Nagymegyer 1,210, Bolgogaszon 3,024, Nezider 9,934, Arad 1,629, Heinrichsgrien 5,861, Czech Braunau 7,733, Aschach 6,355, Drosendorf 504, Oberhelabrun 12, Veickerschlag 12, Vac 334, Cegled 1,060, Keczkemet 71, and in other camps 1,620 persons (AS-Belgrade, MGG, VIII No. 1111).
114. AA-Bonn, Kent, II, S. 725; H. Kapidžić, 'Beogradski arhivi i Muzeji—ratni plijen austrougarskog okupatora za vrijeme prvog svjetskog rata', *Godišnjak istorijskog društva Bosne i Hercegovine*, 10 (1949–50), 345–63.
115. H. Kerchnawe, 'Die Militarverwaltung in Serbien', 224–33.

116. HHStA-Vienna, PA I, K. 974, Conrad's letters to Burian of February and March 1916.
117. *Ibid.*, report from Belgrade of 24 August 1918.
118. Besides the literature mentioned in footnote 25, see also HHStA-Vienna, PA I, K. 977, monthly reports.
119. *Ibid.*; and material in different groups in: AS-Belgrade, MGG.
120. See footnote 120.
121. *Ibid.*, reports from Foreign Ministry representatives in the Governorate General's command of March 1916.
122. *Ibid.*, letter from General Conrad to Baron Burian of 15 March 1916.
123. *Ibid.*, report from Belgrade of 18 March 1916.
124. D. Djordjević, 'Austrougarski okupacioni režim', 216–17; D. Milikić, 'Beograd pod okupacijom u prvom svetskom ratu', *GGB*, 5 (1958), 236–315.
125. HHStA-Vienna, PA I, K. 977.
126. H. Kerchnawe, 'Die Militärverwaltung in Serbien', 92–3.
127. Serbian soldiers of Muslim faith or Albanian nationality who had been taken prisoner also joined those units (AS-Belgrade, MGG, VIII No. 956).
128. D. Djordjević, 'Austrougarski okupacioni režim', 223–4.
129. J. Pisarev, 'Okkupacia Serbii', 33.
130. HHStA-Vienna, PA I, K. 977, Baron Kun, Foreign Ministry representative in the Governorate General command, in a report dated 22 July 1917.
131. See footnote 25.
132. Description of the economic situation is based on monthly reports collected in: HHStA-Vienna, PA I, K. 977, as well as *Amtsblatt, Mitteilungen der k. u. k. Warenverkehrszentrale des MGGs in Serbien; Entwicklung und Taetigkeit der k. u. k. Warenverkehrszentrale des MGGs Serbiens im Jahre 1916*, Belgrade, 1917; *Orientierung ueber Ausfuhrverbote, hg. von Warenverkehrzentrale*, Belgrade, 1916.
133. C. Dürrenberger, 'Serbiens finanzielle und wirtschaftliche Lage', *Zeitung* (Frankfurt), special edition no. 53, 23 February 1916.
134. See footnote 135 and material in: HHStA-Vienna, F. 23, K. 64–70.
135. HHStA-Vienna, PA I, K. 977, report for January 1918.
136. M. Djoković, 'Deca pod okupacijom 1915–1918' in *Beograd u sećanjima 1900–1918*, Belgrade, 1977, 217.
137. *Ibid.*, 214–15, 217.
138. H. Kerchnawe, 'Die Militärverwaltung in Serbien', 100–7.
139. See G. Mikusch, *Wirtschaftliche Beobachtungen in dem von Österreich-Ungarn besetzten Gebiete Serbiens*, Vienna, 1918.
140. D. Milić, *Strani kapital u rudarstvu Srbije do 1918*, Belgrade, 1970, 461–82.
141. A. Mitrović, *Prodor na Balkan*, 338–9.
142. On the subject of German economic exploitation, see P. Kirch, *Krieg und Verwaltung*; D. Milić, *Strani kapital*, 483–94.
143. HHStA-Vienna, PA I, K. 975, report from Niš dated 6 October 1918.
144. M. Perović, *Toplički ustanak*, 49, 55.
145. HHStA-Vienna, PA I, K. 976; contained here are reports by Kolruss, Haas and Otto Czernin, which are mentioned later.

146. HHStA-Vienna, PA I, K. 975, report from Skopje dated 9 July 1918.
147. HHStA-Vienna, PA I, K. 977, memo from Supreme Command to the Foreign Ministry dated 27 July 1917.
148. HHStA-Vienna, PA I, K. 976, Vrbanić's report dated 3 November 1917.
149. HHStA-Vienna, PA I, K. 977, report of 4 December 1917; compare report of 7 December.
150. *Ibid.*, report of 12 December 1917.
151. AA-Bonn, Oxfort, S. 579, Serbien 13 No. 2, vol. 6, report of 16 March 1918.
152. HHStA-Vienna, PA I, K. 977, report from Belgrade of 18 March 1916 (Until summer 1916 Count Szechenyi was Foreign Ministry representative in the Governorate General command, after which he was replaced by Baron Kun).
153. AS-Belgrade, MGG, VII No. 5.
154. HHStA-Vienna, PA I, K. 977, report for September 1917.
155. D. Djordjević, 'Austrougarski okupacioni režim', 224.
156. AA-Bonn, Oxfort, S. 1094, Weltkrieg 14d, vol. 1, report of 29 June 1916.
157. HHStA-Vienna, PA I, K. 977, report for March 1917.

Chapter 6 *Armed Resistance*

1. N. Rakočević, *Crna Gora 1914–1918*, 296–318.
2. *Ibid.*, 307, 373.
3. *Ibid.*, 378–80.
4. J.V. Derok, *Toplički ustanak i oružani otpor u okupiranoj otadžbini 1916–1919*, Belgrade, 1940; A. Mitrović, 'Pokret otpora u austrougarskom Guvernmanu u Srbiji 1916–1918' in *Kruševac kroz vekove*, Kruševac, 1972, 183–99.
5. HHStA-Vienna, PA I, K. 975, several documents, and K. 796, report of Governorate in Serbia dated 15 January 1917.
6. M. Perović, *Toplički ustanak*, 84–5. Quotations from Vojinović's diary have been taken from Perović's book, with the exception of those for the final months of 1917, for which period two leaves (four pages) of the original have been referenced (as will be correspondingly specified).
7. AA-Bonn, Oxfort, S. 1094, Weltkrieg 14d, vol. 1.
8. AS-Belgrade, MGG, XVII No. 30.
9. *Ibid.*
10. AS-Belgrade, MGG, XVII No. 33.
11. See footnote 7.
12. H. Kerchnawe, 'Die Militärverwaltung in Serbien', 255–6.
13. AS-Belgrade, MGG, XVII No. 33; it is stated here that fourteen houses were burnt down, twenty-three men executed, and 760 fugitives apprehended.
14. HHStA-Vienna, PA I, K. 976: report from Niš of 16 September 1916.
15. M. Perović, *Toplički ustanak*, 86; compare J.V. Derok, *Toplički*, 14.
16. See footnote 14.
17. J.V. Derok, *Toplički*, 7–9, 14–20; see: Pećanac's report of 19 December 1918 (1 January 1919) and Pećanac's testimony before the Commission of Inquiry in M. Perović, *Toplički ustanak*, 329–44, 345–56.
18. *Ibid.*, 60–1.

19. *Ibid.*, 88–9.
20. HHStA-Vienna, PA I, K. 977, report from Foreign Ministry representative in Governorate command dated 14 January 1917.
21. M. Perović, *Toplički ustanak*, 107.
22. HHStA-Vienna, PA I, K. 977, report from Belgrade from 14 and 15 January 1917.
23. *Ibid.*
24. H. Kerchnawe, 'Die Organisation der Truppen des Militärgeneralgouvernements Serbien und der Verlauf der Operationen im grossem' in *Militärwissenschaftlische und technische Mitteilungen*, Vienna, 1928, 29.
25. AA-Bonn, Oxfort, S. 1117, Weltkrieg 20e geheim, vol. 1, report of 14 February 1917.
26. HHStA-Vienna, PA I, K. 977.
27. *Ibid.*, report of 15 January 1917.
28. *Ibid.*
29. *Ibid.*
30. J.V. Derok, *Toplički*, 22–7; M. Perović, *Toplički ustanak*, 112–19, 125.
31. J.V. Derok, *Toplički*, 27–33; M. Perović, *Toplički ustanak*, 120–4.
32. M. Perović, *Toplički ustanak*, 333.
33. AA-Bonn, Oxfort, S. 1145, GHQ 37, vol. 1, report from German consul in Belgrade dated 25 February 1917.
34. HHStA-Vienna, PA I, K. 976.
35. HHStA-Vienna, PA I, K. 977, report from Niš of 3 March 1917; report from Belgrade dated 28 February 1917; AA-Bonn, Oxfort, S. 1117, Weltkrieg 20e geheim, report from Belgrade of March 1917 (without date of dispatch).
36. M. Perović, *Toplički ustanak*, 123.
37. *Ibid.*, 120–1; these are excerpts and quotations from Vojinović's diary.
38. J.V. Derok says that Vojinović ordered an uprising in Kuršumlija on 13 February, i.e. 26 February according to the new calendar (J.V. Derok, *Toplički*, 31), which seems to have been accepted by M. Perović (M. Perović, *Toplički ustanak*, 127). However, according to Vojinović's diary and a letter to Pećanac sent from Kuršumlija—(M. Perović, *Toplički ustanak*, 121, 126)—the date involved could only have been 15 February (28 February according to the new calendar) 1917.
39. M. Perović, *Toplički ustanak*, 332–4, 350–1.
40. J.V. Derok, *Toplički*, 32.
41. HHStA-Vienna, PA I, K. 976.
42. AA-Bonn, Oxfort, S. 1117, Weltkrieg 20e geheim, vol. 1.
43. KA-Vienna, Op. Abt. No. 775.
44. *Ibid.*
45. HHStA-Vienna, PA I, K. 976, report from Belgrade dated 4 March 1917.
46. H. Kerchnawe, 'Die Militärverwaltung in Serbien', 259–60; H. Kerchnawe, 'Die Organisation der Truppen', 186; J.V. Derok, *Toplički*, 52–3; M. Perović, *Toplički ustanak*, 167–8.
47. AA-Bonn, Oxfort, S. 1117, Weltkrieg 20e geheim, vol. 1, report dated 11 March 1917.

48. A. Mitrović, 'Boj na kopaoničkom prevoju Mramor 14 marta 1917', *Istorijski glasnik*, 1–2 (1982), 17–20.
49. *Ibid.*, 11, 17.
50. HHStA-Vienna, PA I, K. 976, report from legation in Sofia dated 4 March 1917.
51. J.V. Derok, *Toplički*, 64–72; M. Perović, *Toplički ustanak*, 185–98, 336–8, 352–3.
52. *Ibid.*
53. Milinko Vlahović wrote to Pećanac on 13 March 1917, saying: 'Insurrectionist fighting has stopped today, only guerrilla warfare continues. The enemy has taken the town of Lebane by concentrating on three sides and has committed terrible atrocities. But the main thing is not to give up. This minor change should not be allowed to deter us. It will have no effect on our general cause.' (M. Perović, *Toplički ustanak*, 196)
54. M. Perović, *Toplički ustanak*, 336, 363–7; compare H. Kerchnawe, 'Die Organisation der Truppen', 187.
55. A. Mitrović, 'Boj na kopaoničkom prevoju', 20–1.
56. *Ibid.*, 22–7.
57. H. Kerchnawe, 'Die Militärverwaltung in Serbien', 261.
58. HHStA-Vienna, PA I, K. 976, report of Foreign Ministry representative in Governorate command.
59. D. Janković, *Jugoslovensko pitanje i Krfska deklaracija*, 116, 179; HHStA-Vienna, PA I, K. 975, report from legation in The Hague dated 15 March 1917.
60. HHStA-Vienna, PA I, K. 977, report for March 1917; compare: National Museum of Kragujevac, AD-745, Proclamation (Kundmachung) of 28 March 1917.
61. A Foreign Ministry representative described the area around Rekovac in his report of 6 March as 'a point where guerrilla companies assemble.' (*Ibid.*)
62. HHStA-Vienna, PA I, K. 976.
63. HHStA-Vienna, PA I, K. 976 and 977, several reports from Niš and Belgrade in the course of March and April 1917.
64. M. Perović, *Toplički ustanak*, 336–7, 353.
65. HHStA-Vienna, PA I, K. 976.
66. Cases of the participation of citizens in the defence of Liège at the beginning of August 1914, the Easter Rising in Ireland in 1916 and the Arab Rebellion against the Ottoman are phenomena of another nature and importance.
67. HHStA-Vienna, PA I, K. 976; also, KA-Vienna, MGG/S. 1917.
68. M. Perović, *Toplički ustanak*, 220–49.
69. KA-Vienna, MGG/S 1917 (here is the original of Vojinović's letter to the Austro-Hungarian district commander in Kosovska Mitrovica dated 15 (28) April 1917, with a photograph attached showing Vojinović wearing the insignia of a *comitadji vojvoda*).
70. H. Kerchnawe, 'Die Organisation der Truppen', 189.
71. J.V. Derok, *Toplički*, 83–8; M. Perović, *Toplički ustanak*, 240–4, 338–9.
72. HHStA-Vienna, PA I, K. 976, report of Foreign Ministry representative dated 16 May 1917; AA-Bonn, Oxfort, S. 1117, Weltkrieg 20e geheim, vol. 1, report of German consul dated 16 May 1917. It follows from these and other reports

and documents submitted by the occupiers that the attack was carried out on 13 May, but in his post-war reports using the old calendar Pećanac gave the date as 1 May, that is 14 May according to the new calendar. After a careful study of available material, we have opted for 13 May (in *Istorija srpskog naroda*, VI–2, we adhered to Pećanac's testimony), but this date is still open to verification.
73. M. Perović, *Toplički ustanak*, 242–4, 338–9, 353–4.
74. HHStA-Vienna, PA I, K. 976, report of military envoys in Sofia dated 3 June 1917.
75. *Ibid.*, excerpts from various reports on *comitadji*.
76. HHStA-Vienna, PA I, K. 977, monthly reports.
77. M. Perović, *Toplički ustanak*, 260–2.
78. N. Rakočević, *Crna Gora 1914–1918*, 375–81.
79. N. Rakočević, 'Pokret za ujedinjenje Crne Gore sa Srbijom medju interniranim Crnogorcima i kod komitskog pokreta u Crnoj Gori u periodu 1916–1918' in *Naučni skup u povodu 50-godišnjice raspada Austro-Ugarske Monarhije i stvaranja jugoslavenske države*, Zagreb, 1969, 173–80.
80. W. Maulik, 'Bandenbekämpfung' in *Militärwissenschaftliche und technische Mitteilungen*, 1929, 189–94; H. Kerchnawe, 'Die Organisation der Truppen', 23–8; HHStA-Vienna, PA I, K. 976, Bulgarian 'Monthly report no. 1' of 10 July 1917.
81. HHStA-Vienna, PA I, K. 977, telegraph report from the Governorate to the Supreme Command Op. No. 951; H. Kerchnawe, 'Die Militärverwaltung in Serbien', 261–2; H. Kerchnawe, 'Die Organisation der Truppen', 188.
82. HHStA-Vienna, PA I, K. 977, Op. No. 951.
83. *Ibid.*
84. AA-Bonn, Oxfort, S. 1117, Weltkrieg 20e, vol. 1, 4 August 1917.
85. HHStA-Vienna, PA I, K. 977, von Remen's report of 17 July; the captured messenger gave his name as Anton Stanković.
86. J.V. Derok, *Toplički*, 88–97; M. Perović, *Toplički ustanak*, 273–7, 286–91, 339, 354.
87. *Ibid.*; see Lj. Jovanović, 'Pobuna u Toplici i Jablanici' in *Toplička spomenica*, Belgrade, 1934, 112–35.
88. *Ibid.*
89. HHStA-Vienna, PA I, K. 976, 'Monthly report No. 1' and von Remen's report of 31 August 1917.
90. *Ibid.*, 11 August 1917.
91. AS-Belgrade, MGG, VIII No. 899.
92. HHStA-Vienna, PA I, K. 976, several documents.
93. HHStA-Vienna, PA I, K. 976, Praes. No. 23594.
94. W. Maulik, 'Bandenbekämpfung', 193.
95. HHStA-Vienna, PA I, K. 976, reports from the consul in Niš of 5 and 13 November 1917; HHStA-Vienna, PA I, K. 977, Governorate report on the state of affairs of 16 September, and a report of the Military Inspection Zone in Niš of 28 September 1917.
96. HHStA-Vienna, PA I, K. 976, report from the consul in Niš dated 13 November 1917.

97. M. Perović, *Toplički ustanak*, 280–3, 339–40.
98. *Ibid.*, 284–6.
99. HHStA-Vienna, PA I, K. 977, 21 October 1917.
100. The original pages of Vojinović's dairy are privately owned, and I am grateful to Velibor Vukašnović for allowing me to see and use them.
101. *Ibid.*
102. KA-Vienna, MGG/S 1917, Op. No. 1483, 27 December 1917.
103. HHStA-Vienna, PA I, K. 977, 30 December 1917.
104. H. Kerchnawe, 'Die Militärverwaltung in Serbien', 262.
105. N. Rakočević, *Crna Gora 1914–1918*, 415–20.
106. HHStA-Vienna, PA I, K. 977, Op. No. 155.
107. KA-Vienna, Op. Abt. No. 46737.
108. KA-Vienna, Op. Abt. Nos 49401 and 49533.
109. HHStA-Vienna, PA I, K. 977, particularly Op. No. 155.
110. *Ibid.*, particularly the report of 16 March 1918.
111. *Ibid.*
112. *Ibid.*, report of 4 July 1918.
113. *Ibid.*, 'State of emergency on account of sabotage,' report from Foreign Ministry representative dated 31 July 1918.
114. *Ibid.*, von Remen's report of 2 August 1918.
115. *Ibid.*, telegraph report from the Military General Governorate to the Supreme Command Op. No. 508.
116. *Ibid.*, von Remen's report of 23 September 1918.
117. *Ibid.*

Chapter 7 *Towards a Yugoslav State*

1. F. Šišić, *Dokumenti*, 58–60.
2. *Ibid.*, 61–2.
3. From an abundance of literature on the peace treaty as a whole or its individual parts, the following are of particular interest: F. Fischer, *Griff*, 477–511, 627–74; W. Bihl, *Oesterreich-Ungarn und die Friedensschlüsse von Brest-Litovsk*, Vienna, 1970.
4. Dj. Stanković, *Nikola Pašić*, 575–82.
5. A note from the Serbian government to Allied governments dated 17 January and a 'Memorandum addressed to our Allies on the subject of our national demands' dated 31 March 1918 in D. Janković and B. Krizman (eds), *Gradja o stvaranju jugoslovenske države* (1. 1–20. 12. 1918), Belgrade, 1964, 34–41, 151–64; see M. Ekmečić, 'Stavovi Nikole Pašića prema američkim planovima pretvaranja Austro-Ugarske u federativnu državu' in *Naučni skup u povodu 50-godišnjice raspada Austro-Ugarske Monarhije i stvaranja jugoslavenske države*, Zagreb, 1969, 159–71.
6. In the 'Memorandum' of 31 March 1918 (see footnote 5), there is the parallel use of the names 'Serbs-Croats and Slovenes', 'Serbo-Croats and Slovenes' and 'Yugoslavs' (alongside 'Serbs and Croats' and 'Croats and Serbs'), as well as 'Slovene-Croatian-Serb-inhabited'; there is mention of the ethnic borders 'be-

tween Serbs and Romanians,' 'between Serbs-Croats and Hungarians' and 'between Slovenes and Italians'. The name 'Kingdom of Serbs, Croats and Slovenes' was used for the state, but the name 'Yugoslavia' was also used in the last section.
7. D. Vujović, *Ujedinjenje Crne Gore i Srbije*, 173–6.
8. *Ibid.*, 162–4, 170–1, 287–97; N. Rakočević, *Crna Gora 1914–1918*, 335–40; N. Rakočević, *Politički odnosi*, 257–8; N. Rakočević, 'Crna Gora i ujedinjenje' in *Politički život Jugoslavije*, Belgrade, 1973, 75–92.
9. D. Vujović, *Ujedinjenje Crne Gore i Srbije*, 173–6.
10. N. Rakočević, *Politički odnosi*, 262–8; B. Hrabak and D. Janković, *Srbija 1918. Politika i napori Srbije u ratnoj 1918. godini*, Belgrade, 1969, 94–101.
11. D. Vujović, *Ujedinjenje Crne Gore i Srbije*, 168–9.
12. D. Janković, *Jugoslovensko pitanje i Krfska deklaracija*, 117–31, 398–411; B. Krizman, 'Povjerljive veze izmedju Jugoslavenskog odbora i domaćih političara za I svjetskog rata', *Historijski zbornik*, 15 (1962), 217–29. Also J.J. Vidmar, 'Prilozi gradji za povijest 1917–1918. s osobitim obzirom na razvoj radničkog pokreta i odjeke Oktobarske revolucije kod nas', *Arhivski vijesnik*, 1 (1958), 11–173.
13. N. Kapidžić, 'Austro-Ugarska politika', 11–55; P. Slijepčević, 'Bosna i Hercegovina u Svetskom Ratu', 268–71; V. Ćorović, *Crna knjiga*, 7–23; S. Budisavljević, *Stvaranje države Srba*, 113–21; B. Krizman, 'O putu grofa Stj. Tise po jugoslavenskim zemljama u septembru 1918', *Historijski zbornik*, 11–12 (1958–9), 233–49.
14. KA-Vienna, Kommandirender General in Bosnien, Hercegovina und Dalmatien, Na. no. 2729 res: *Hochverrats- und Spionageprozesse* (I hereby express gratitude to Djordje Knežević who allowed me to study a copy of this material).
15. See footnote 13.
16. See footnote 12.
17. M. Komjáthy (ed.), *Protokolle*, 661.
18. AA-Bonn, Oxfort, S. 453, Oesterreich 70, vol. 53, 11 July 1918.
19. HHStA-Vienna, PA I, K. 963, 977 and 1087, several documents, and particularly reports from the head of the Governorate military intelligence service of 4 and 7 December 1917, 28 February, 11 March and 19 April 1918.
20. HHStA-Vienna, PA I, K. 963, several documents, and particularly reports from the Austro-Hungarian envoy in Berne of 22 February, 20 March, 5 April and 17 April 1918.
21. HHStA-Vienna, PA I, K. 963, report from Berne of 25 March 1918.
22. HHStA-Vienna, PA I, K. 1087, letter from Count Demblin of 23 March 1918.
23. HHStA-Vienna, PA I, K. 963 and 977, several documents, particularly drafts of the instructions from Count Czernin to Foreign Ministry representatives and to the Emperor, the Supreme Command, the Governorate in Serbia and to the envoy in Berne of 3 and 4 April 1918.
24. HHStA-Vienna, PA I, K. 963, Hugo Kerchnawe's note on the report of the head of the military intelligence service of 4 December 1917.
25. N. Rakočević, 'Politička aktivnost knjaza Mirka Petrovića u toku austrougarske okupacije Crne Gore', *Istorijski zapisi*, 3–4 (1970), 251–71.

26. A. Mitrović, 'Nadrastanje poraza i podela' in *Istorija srpskog naroda*, VI–2, Belgrade, 1983, 174–5, 239–40.
27. D. Janković, *Jugoslovensko pitanje i Krfska deklaracija*, 131–42; Dj. Stanković, *Nikola Pašić*, 363–450.
28. D. Janković, *Jugoslovensko pitanje i Krfska deklaracija*, 139.
29. Dj. Stanković, *Nikola Pašić*, 377–87.
30. D. Šepić, *Supilo diplomat*, 227–8.
31. D. Janković, 'Profesor Pavle Popović i jugoslovensko pitanje u prvom svetskom ratu', *Letopis Matice srpske*, September 1975, 219–33.
32. Z. Passek, 'Zapisnici sjednica Jugoslavenskog odbora', 25–6.
33. Dj. Stanković, *Nikola Pašić*, 327–76.
34. Z. Passek, 'Zapisnici sjednica Jugoslavenskog odbora', 36–7.
35. D. Janković, *Jugoslovensko pitanje i Krfska deklaracija*, 192.
36. *Ibid.*, 189–314.
37. F. Šišić, *Dokumenti*, 96–9.
38. D. Janković, *Jugoslovensko pitanje i Krfska deklaracija*, 294–8.
39. D. Šepić, *Supilo diplomat*, 239–41.
40. F. Šišić, *Dokumenti*, 100–1; D. Vujović, *Ujedinjenje Crne Gore i Srbije*, 234–5.
41. I. Čizmić, *Jugoslavenski iseljenički*, 135–6.
42. D. Vujović, *Ujedinjenje Crne Gore i Srbije*, 235.
43. N. Popović, *Odnosi Srbije i Rusije*, 389–425, 452–68.
44. *Ibid.*, 391–2.
45. B. Krizman and B. Hrabak (eds), *Zapisnici*, 394–5.
46. N. Popović, *Odnosi Srbije i Rusije*, 395–7.
47. *Ibid.*, 408–9.
48. See footnote 43.
49. B. Hrabak and D. Janković, *Srbija 1918*, 128–35; P. Opačić, *Solunska ofanziva*, 26, 74; N. Popović, *Jugoslovenski dobrovoljci*, 365–441.
50. B. Hrabak, *Jugosloveni zarobljenici u Italiji i njihovo dobrovoljačko pitanje 1915– 1918*, Novi Sad, 1980.
51. D. Janković and B. Krizman (eds), *Gradja o stvaranju jugoslovenske države*, 16–17, 35.
52. *Ibid*, 55–6.
53. I.D. Očak, *Jugosloveni u Oktobru*, Belgrade, 1967; *Učešće jugoslovenskih radnih ljudi u oktobarskoj revoluciji i gradjanskom ratu u SSSR*, prepared by P. Damjanović and others, Belgrade, 1979; B. Hrabak, 'Jugoslovenski sovjeti u Rusiji i Ukrajini 1919–1921', *Tokovi revolucije*, 2 (1967), 3–55.
54. J. Pleterski, *Prva odločitev Slovencev*, 96–145; *Zapisi dr Josipa Smodlake*, 51–5.
55. F. Šišić, *Dokumenti*, 94.
56. Their names are not contained in the text published by Šišić, and they are not mentioned in literature, although it is assumed that they signed the document. That issue would seem to require special investigation.
57. F. Šišić, *Dokumenti*, 94–6; B. Krizman, 'Hrvatske stranke prema ujedinjenju', 113.
58. J. Pleterski, *Prva odločitev Slovencev*, 129; F. Šišić, *Dokumenti*, 102–3.
59. F. Šišić, *Dokumenti*, 104–5, 107–8.

60. *Ibid.*, 114–15.
61. *Ibid.*, 116.
62. *Ibid.*, 116–17.
63. S. Budisavljević, *Stvaranje države Srba*, 32, 73–4.
64. N. Kapidžić, 'Austro-Ugarska politika', 24–31; M. Zečević, *Slovenska ljudska stranka i jugoslovensko ujedinjenje 1917–1921*, Belgrade, 1973, 43.
65. I. Karabegović, *Radnički pokret Bosne i Hercegovine*, 76, 95.
66. J.J. Vidmar, 'Prilozi gradji za povijest 1917–1918', 50.
67. *Ibid.*, 45–7.
68. V. Strugar, *Socijaldemokratija*, 71–93, 129–37, 185–7, 213–16; E. Redžić, *Austromarksizam i jugoslovensko pitanje*, 294–8, 358–66; I. Karabegović, *Radnički pokret Bosne i Hercegovine*, 79–94; V. Kovačev, 'Ideološke i političke borbe u radničkom pokretu Hrvatske i Slavonije 1917–1919', *Istorija radničkog pokreta*, 3 (1966), 7–59.
69. *Ibid.*
70. D. Janković, 'Narodna Skupština', 340–9.
71. B. Krizman and B. Hrabak (eds), *Zapisnici*, 468.
72. D. Janković, 'Narodna Skupština', 349–54.
73. Lj. Trgovčević, *Naucnici Srbije*, 218–223, 235–245.
74. Dj. Stanković, *Nikola Pašić*, 561–4.
75. D. Janković and B. Krizman (eds), *Gradja o stvaranju jugoslovenske države*, 151–64.
76. *Ibid.*, 37–41, 148–51, 151–64.
77. *Ibid.*, 47–8.
78. *Ibid.*, 52–3.
79. PRO-London, FO 371, no. 3149.
80. D. Janković and B. Krizman (eds), *Gradja o stvaranju jugoslovenske države*, 15.
81. *Ibid.*, 71; compare N. Stojanović, *Jugoslovenski odbor*, 55–60.
82. N. Popović, *Odnosi Srbije i Rusije*, 367, 444–5.
83. D. Janković and B. Krizman (eds), *Gradja o stvaranju jugoslovenske države*, 37–41.
84. *Ibid.*, 44–60.
85. Compare: D. Janković, '"Veliki" i "mali" ratni program Nikole Pašića (1914–1918)', *Anali Pravnog fakulteta u Beogradu*, 2 (1973), 151–67.
86. S. Dimitrijević, *Socijalistički*, 245–332.
87. B. Hrabak and K. Džambazovski, 'Srpski socijaldemokrati na Solunskom frontu', 154–5, 157, 174–80.
88. V.D. Lapčević, 'Neke pojedinosti o odlasku socijalista na konferenciju u Stokholm 1917', *Istorijski glasnik*, 1–2 (1980), 87–104.
89. B. Hrabak and D. Janković, *Srbija 1918*, 64–6.
90. S. Dimitrijević, *Socijalistički*, 274–84.
91. B. Hrabak and D. Janković, *Srbija 1918*, 66.
92. V. Strugar, *Socijaldemokratija*, 45–50; E. Redžić, *Austromarksizam i jugoslovensko pitanje*, 418–26.
93. *Ibid.*
94. V. Lapčević and T. Milenković (eds), *Prepiska srpskih socijalista*, 240–3.
95. R.G. Plaschka, H. Haselsteiner, A. Suppan, *Innere Front*, 1–2, Vienna, 1974.

96. P. Opačić, *Solunska ofanziva*, 56–163; P. Opačić, *Srbija i Solunski front*, Belgrade, 1984.
97. P. Opačić, *Solunska ofanziva*, 66–75, 101–11.
98. AA-Bonn, Oxfort, S. 1135, GHQ 5, vol. 7, from the Secretary of State for Foreign Affairs to representatives at the General Staff, 2 October 1918.
99. BayHStA/KA-Munich, Alpenkorps, vol 52.
100. BayHStA/KA-Munich, Alpenkorps, vol 2, Kriegstagebuch des Alpenkorps.
101. BayHStA/KA-Munich, Alpenkorps, vol 52, order of 6 October 1918.
102. HHStA-Vienna, PA I, K. 994; P. Kirch, *Krieg und Verwaltung*, 131.
103. ZStA-Potsdam, Reichwirtschaftsministerium, No. 903.
104. HHStA-Vienna, PA I, K. 975, report from Niš dated 6 October 1918.
105. HHStA-Vienna, PA I, K. 973, report from Belgrade of 17 October 1918.
106. HHStA-Vienna, PA I, K. 994, report from Belgrade of 20 October 1918.
107. *VRS*, 30, 6.
108. *Ibid.*, 662.
109. B. Hrabak, 'Učešće stanovništva Srbije u proterivanju okupatora oktobra 1918', *Istorijski glasnik*, 3–4 (1958), 25–50.
110. *Ibid.*, 26.
111. O. Landfried, *Der Endkampf in Mazedonien 1918 und seine Vorgeschichte*, Berlin, 1923, 33.
112. P. Kirch, *Krieg und Verwaltung*, 130–1, 139–41, 169.
113. K. Dietrich, *Weltkriegsende an der mazedonischen Front*, Berlin, 1925, 169.
114. BayHStA/KA-Munich, Alpenkorps, vol 2, Kriegstagebuch.
115. BayHStA/KA-Munich, Alpenkorps, vol 52.
116. HHStA-Vienna, PA I, K. 994.
117. In his memoirs General Dietrich says that 'Hussars were the last line of defence for eight days—surrounded on all sides by the hostile and well-armed population.' (K. Dietrich, *Weltkriegsende*, 153)
118. *VRS*, 30, 224; Serbian documents provide a great deal of data on the combined activity of the population (see B. Hrabak, 'Učešće stanovništva').
119. HHStA-Vienna, PA I, K. 977.
120. J.V. Derok, *Toplički*, 100–10; P. Opačić, *Solunska ofanziva*, 376–7; N. Rakočević, *Crna Gora 1914–1918*, 441–54.
121. *VRS*, 30, 5.
122. *Ibid.*, 2.
123. AS-Belgrade, MID, strictly confidential archive 1918.
124. B. Krizman, *Raspad Austro-Ugarske*; F. Šišić, *Dokumenti*, 189–219.
125. F. Šišić, *Dokumenti*, 189–210.
126. *Ibid.*, 216–7.
127. Compare: D. Janković, 'Glavni faktori u procesu stvaranja Jugoslavije 1918. godine', *Naučni pregled*, 9 (1981), 17–29.
128. BayHStA/KA-Munich, Alpenkorps, vol 2, Kriegstagebuch.
129. *Zapisi dr Josipa Smodlake*, 64–5.
130. B. Krizman, *Raspad Austro-Ugarske*, 183–221; P. Opačić, *Solunska ofanziva*, 388–401; B. Hrabak and D. Janković, *Srbija 1918*, 187–206.
131. D. Janković and B. Krizman (eds), *Gradja o stvaranju jugoslovenske države*, 456.

132. B. Krizman, *Raspad Austro-Ugarske*, 163–82; D. Janković, 'Ženevska konferencija o stvaranju jugoslovenske zajednice 1918. godine', *Istorija XX veka*, 5 (1963), 225–60.
133. D. Janković and B. Krizman (eds), *Gradja o stvaranju jugoslovenske države*, 523–5.
134. *Zapisi dr Josipa Smodlake*, 73.
135. AS–Belgrade, MID, strictly confidential archive 1918, Protić's telegrams dated 29 October (11 November) and 1 (14) November 1918 and Pašić's telegram dated 15 November 1918. In the second telegram Protić also wrote: 'We were not able to uphold our opinion that Serbia should represent our entire nation internationally until peace is concluded [...]. We nonetheless did well, in the given situation, to recognise the Yugoslav Council directly [...]. The hurried patching up that you unfortunately had to do in Geneva can do more harm than good [...]. We have reason to believe that there are many people in Zagreb who do not think like Trumbić does. [...] and in Corfu he had difficulty agreeing to even the general right to vote, and he is not in favour of a rapid and radical solution to the agrarian issue which is a point of cardinal importance in our nation's problems.' See D. Janković and B. Krizman (eds), *Gradja o stvaranju jugoslovenske države*, 553–5, 565–7, 574.
136. V. Strugar, 'Srpska vojska u zastiti jugoslovenskog prostora krajem 1918. godine' in N. Popović (ed.), *Stvaranje jugoslovenske drzave 1918*, Belgrade, 1983, 135–52.
137. B. Krizman, *Raspad Austro-Ugarske*, 183–221; P. Opačić, *Solunska ofanziva*, 388–401; B. Hrabak and D. Janković, *Srbija 1918*, 187–206.
138. See footnotes 149 and 150; N. Rakočević, *Politički odnosi*, 281–4; D. Vujović, *Ujedinjenje Crne Gore i Srbije*, 301–76; D. Šepić, 'Hrvatska politika i pitanje jugoslovenskog ujedinjenja 1914–1918' in *Društveni razvoj u Hrvatskoj od 16. do početka 20. stoljeća*, Zagreb, 1981, 400–5.
139. B. Krizman, 'Pitanje medjunarodnog priznanja jugoslovenske države', *Istorija XX veka*, 3 (1962), 345–86; B. Krizman, 'Vanjskopolitički položaj Kraljevine SHS godine 1919', *Časopis za suvremenu povijest*, 1 (1970), 23–60; A. Mitrović, 'The 1919–1920 Peace Conference in Paris and the Yugoslav State: An Historical Evolution' in D. Djordjević (ed.), *The Creation of Yugoslavia 1914–1918*, Santa Barbara, 1980, 207–17.
140. From amongst more recent literature on further historical developments, see B. Petranović, *Istorija Jugoslavije*, Belgrade, 1981; H. Sundhaussen, *Geschichte Jugoslawiens 1918–1980*, Stuttgart, 1982; B. Krizman, *Vanjska politika jugoslovenske države 1918–1941*, Zagreb, 1975.

INDEX

agriculture 56, 200, 206–7, 214–15, 235–6, 239
Albania, Albanians 114, 121–2, 128–35, 149–54, 157–60, 194–6, 201, 234–5, 255, 258, 306, 308, 313
Alexander, Regent 1–3, 24, 46, 51, 68, 106, 114, 119, 140, 160, 161, 162–3, 182–8, 278, 281, 283, 298, 305, 323
Apis, *see* Dimitrijević, Lt.-Col. Dragutin (Apis)
Arad 76, 78
arms supplies 30, 71, 128–9, 133
army (Serbian) 60, 68–73, 103–10, 111, 144–54, 158–69, 313–21, 323–4
arrests and detentions in Austria-Hungary 63–7, 74–8; in occupied Serbia and Montenegro 223, 228–9, 238
atrocities 73–8, 81, 104
Austria-Hungary: *passim*; anti-Serb actions 15–21, 63–7, 74–9, 284–6; diplomacy 3–4, 9–11, 28–51, 54–5, 85–6, 122–5; *see* arrests and detentions; atrocities; deportations; executions; resistance; trials

Balkan Peninsula, The 178–80
Balkan Wars (1912–13) 22, 31, 55, 67, 80, 123, 134
Banat 64, 78, 89, 306, 308, 320
Banjaluka 285
banks 107, 120, 210–21, 237
Belgrade 57, 70, 71, 72, 108, 129, 145, 177, 203, 228, 229, 233, 277, 315, 325
Belić, Aleksandar 90, 136–7
Berchtold, Count Leopold 10–11, 39, 40–1, 45, 54, 122, 129, 131

Bethman-Hollweg, Theobald von 3–4, 148
Bilinski, Leon von 10
Bitola 165, 252
Bizerta 152, 160, 161
Black Hand 23–6, 82, 114, 141, 162–3, 169, 182–8, 270, 282, 295
Bojović, General Petar 146, 162, 313, 320
Bolsheviks 115, 243, 298–9, 302, 308, 309–10
Boppe, Auguste 148, 153, 161
Bor mine 207–8, 218–19, 314
Bosiljgrad 264–5
Bosnia and Herzegovina 5–6, 18–21, 24, 25, 31, 49, 63, 65–6, 68, 71, 74–9, 80, 84, 139, 234, 275, 285, 300, 302, 303, 304, 309–10, 319, 323, 325
Briand, Aristide 154, 159
Brindisi 130, 157, 159
Britain 35, 45, 46, 47, 53, 62, 104, 111–12, 119, 161, 174, 280, 297, 309, 325
Budislavljević, Srdjan 65, 301
Bulgaria 60, 61, 85–6, 88–90, 99, 118–19, 121–8, 142–3, 144–7, 164–5, 193–5, 199–202, 204–26, 239–43, 247–75, 279, 296, 313, 319
Bulgarianisation programme 222–6, 240–3, 253
Burian, István Baron 131, 132, 148, 193–7, 198, 226–7, 231, 235

Čabrinović, Nedeljko 5, 26, 77
casualties of war 102, 152, 160–1, 165, 168, 261, 272
Catholic Church 15, 18, 20, 143–4, 286, 287, 300, 304

Cer, Mount 69, 73, 104, 318
Chamber of Workers 310–11
Chetniks, *see* guerrilla warfare
Chirol, Valentine 116, 119
Ciganović, Milan 5, 6, 23, 25–6, 44, 46, 50
clerical groups/movements 19, 20, 64, 68, 143–4, 300
comitadji 81–2, 125–30, 169, 229, 246–75, 317–19
Conrad von Hötzendorf, Baron 10, 16–17, 39, 158, 193–5, 201, 226–7, 231, 232
Constantine, King 120, 147, 154
Corfu 154, 158–65, 180–1, 282, 287, 304–5
Corfu Declaration (July 1917) 292–7
Croat-Serb Coalition 17, 65, 286–7, 301, 318–19
Croatia, Croats 16–21, 64–5, 75, 85, 87, 88, 91, 95, 143–4, 179, 286–7, 299–304, 318–26
currency 236–7
Cvijić, Professor Jovan (Dinaricus) 87, 89–90, 96–7, 136, 175, 178–80, 305–6
Czernin, Count Ottokar 197, 241, 260–1, 273, 287, 288, 289

Dalmatia 19, 64–5, 75, 76, 139, 144, 167, 275, 299, 319
Danilo, Prince 138, 139, 140
Danube 74, 109–10, 126, 144, 319
declaration of war 1–3, 51–2
Dervish Bey 234
deportations 75–8, 228–30
deserters 83, 150, 303–4
Deutsch-Orientalische Handelsgesellschaft 206, 210–12, 215
Dimitrijević, Lt-Col. Dragutin (Apis) 23–6, 114–15, 141, 162, 182–8, 292–3
Dimović, Danilo 66, 285, 286, 302
Direktion der Discontogesellschaft 212, 214–15, 217, 220, 314
Dobrudja 168–9
Dövung (Deutsch-Österreich-Ungarische Einkaufs-Vereinigung) 211

Drina 26, 68, 102, 126, 319
Dürenberger, Karl 120
Durrës 122, 128, 152, 158, 159

economic situation (Serbia) 107–10, 235–9
education 57, 78–9, 169–78, 230–2, 240–1
émigrés and exiles 80, 84, 99, 100, 141–2, 180, 282, 286, 291–2, 304
epidemics 110–13
Esat Pasha 114, 131, 133, 134, 152, 153, 313
executions and killings in Austria-Hungary 74–5; in occupied Serbia and Montenegro 73–4, 222–3, 228, 252, 261, 276

Falkenhayn, General Erich von 126
famine and hunger 232, 235–6, 303
Ferdinand, King 125, 201, 202
forced labour 238
France 24, 30, 34–9, 45, 53, 58, 62, 104, 112, 147, 154, 158, 159–64, 169–73, 280, 284, 310–11, 312, 313–16, 325
Franchet d'Esperey, General 313, 315, 320–1
Frank, Ivan 17, 21, 137, 287, 295
Franz Ferdinand, Archduke, assassination 3, 5–9, 12–16, 22–6, 33, 41–2, 44–6, 50, 63, 77, 186–7
Franz Joseph, Emperor 1–3, 10, 148, 157, 193
Fuad Bey 130, 133

Geneva 188, 288, 321–3
Germany 3–4, 22, 28, 32–41, 43, 47, 50–2, 53–5, 58, 62, 93–4, 115, 118, 119, 123, 144–8, 165, 186–7, 193, 198, 199, 229, 252, 257–8, 279, 312–16, 319; economic exploitation in occupied Serbia 201–2, 204–21
Giesl, Baron 38, 48–9
Greece 120, 147, 154, 177
Grey, Sir Edward 45

Index

guerrilla warfare 127–35, 245–77, 312, 315–18; *see also comitadji*

Halla, Karlo 128, 131–2
Herceg-Novi 128, 129–30
Herzegovina 157, 275; *see also* Bosnia and Herzegovina
Hinković, Hinko 79, 293
historic treasures, plunder of 230
Hoyos, Count Alexander 3–4, 11, 29–30, 33, 85
Hungary 13, 27–8, 29, 65, 77, 86, 194–6, 198, 202–3, 301, 321; *see also* Austria-Hungary

Ilić, Danilo 5, 26
Ilić, Capt. Jovan 269–70
Independent Radicals 87, 181, 281
industry 57, 213, 237
Istria 143–4, 301, 306
Italy 28, 43, 47, 48, 62, 88, 97, 99, 105, 118, 134, 135, 139, 152, 157, 167, 174, 180, 190–2, 306–7, 320, 324, 325

Janković, General Božidar 69, 139
Jedinstvo Jugoslovena 96–7
Jeličić, Sibin 246–7, 260
Jovanović, Jovan 6, 7–8, 11–12, 15, 38, 39, 42–3, 47, 60, 88, 100

Karl I, Emperor 287, 288, 299
Kerchnawe, Hugo 248, 259, 263, 274
Kolubara, battle of the 73, 104, 105
Kopaonik, Mount 248, 250, 252, 263, 265–7, 270, 275
Korošek, Anton 144, 299, 300
Kosovo 131, 133, 148, 201, 202, 206, 234, 250
Kosovska Mitrovica 202, 209, 234–5, 252, 255
Kövess, General Hermann Baron 314, 316
Kragujevac 5, 107, 247–8, 260
Krall, August von 128–9
Krek, Janez 144, 300
Kruševac 148, 257, 260, 277

Kun, Baron 261–2, 274, 315, 317
Kuršumlija 255, 257, 259, 273
Kutinchev, Governor 247, 254, 257
Kutschbach, Alvin 71, 72, 103, 105–6, 110, 114, 120–1, 134, 187

Liberal Party 20, 115, 281, 287
Ljubljana 19, 20, 75–6, 324
Lloyd George, David 309
London 137
Lovćen 155–6
Lustig, Colonel von 222–3, 225–6

Macedonia 60, 99, 118–19, 123–5, 127, 142–3, 200–2, 216–17, 225–6, 242–3, 312
Mackensen, Field Marshal August von 144–8, 201, 204, 206
Mačva 69, 108, 270
Majdanpek mine 207, 208, 210, 239
Marjanović, Vojin 263–4, 268
Marković, Professor Božidar 90, 91, 95
May Declaration (1917) 299–300
Medua 129, 152, 153, 158
Mehmedbašić, Muhamed 5, 37, 183
Mijušković, Lazar 156, 157, 191
military operations 68–74, 102–11, 144–61, 164–5, 168–9, 313–21, 323–4; *see also* resistance
mining 200, 202, 207–12, 215–16, 218–19, 238–9
Mišić, General Živojin 71, 73, 103, 149–50, 162, 163, 313, 320, 321
Moltke, Count Helmuth von 33, 53
Mondesire, General Pierron de 154, 160
Montenegrin Committee for National Unification 282, 283, 294
Montenegro 2, 8–9, 37, 48, 51, 54, 68, 84, 85, 104, 139, 147, 154–8, 162, 163, 164, 180, 194, 197–8, 203–4, 226, 235, 245–6, 265–8, 274–6, 279, 288–9, 307, 316–17, 319, 324–5; question of union with Serbia 92–4, 138–41, 190–2, 282–4, 294, 308
Moskovljević, Živan 288
Muslims 20, 55, 56, 127, 232, 234, 286

384　Index

Musulin, Baron Alexander von 40, 67

Narodna Odbrana 5, 6, 24–6, 44, 49
Nation Serbe en France, la 170, 172
National Assembly (Narodna Skupština) (Serbia) 7, 95, 96, 113, 181–2, 188, 282, 287, 304–5, 312
National Council of Slovenes, Croats and Serbs 318–19, 321
Nationalbank für Deutschland 220–1
Nicholas I, King of Montenegro 2–3, 8, 37, 41, 51, 68, 69, 93–4, 138–40, 162, 176, 180, 190–2, 282–4, 294
Nicholas II, Tsar 46, 152, 159
Niš 52, 71, 83, 90–2, 94–5, 103, 113, 120, 200, 225, 240, 241–2, 254, 256, 260, 314
Niš Declaration (December 1914) 95–6
Novaković, Stojan 137

Obrenović dynasty 22, 23, 38, 232, 233
occupation of Serbia 193–277; *see also* Bulgarianisation programme; detentions; executions and killings; guerrilla warfare
Odessa 167–8, 297
Ohrid 118, 122, 130, 133
Orthodox Church 55, 58–9, 78–9, 224, 230, 231, 232

Paču, Lazar 43, 45, 46
Pallavicini, Janos Count 130, 132
Paris 162, 170, 175, 177, 278, 311–12, 325
Party of the Right 20, 286, 299–300, 302
Pašić, Nikola 7, 24–5, 42, 46, 48, 52, 60, 61–2, 70, 87, 89–94, 95, 106–7, 114, 115, 120–1, 133, 135, 141, 149, 158, 163, 176, 178, 181, 184–9, 280, 281–3, 288–93, 305, 310, 321, 322
Pavlović, Živko 162
peace treaties 279–80, 325
Pećanac, Lt. Kosta Milovanović- 248–55, 258, 261–9, 273, 317–18
Perić, Professor Živojin 115, 287, 288

Pešić, Colonel Petar 69, 138–9
Pester Ungarische Commerzialbank 212–13, 216
Peter, King 7, 24, 69, 93, 147–8, 154, 288, 323
Plamenac, Petar 8, 41
Pljevlja 69–70
Poincaré, Raymond 34, 43
Popović, General Damnjan 114, 121–2, 133, 146, 183, 185
Popović, Professor Pavle 290
Popović, Lt.-Col. Vojin (Vojvoda Vuk) 165, 187
population 55–6, 58–9, 326
press 7, 20, 64, 114, 230, 304
Princip, Gavrilo 5–6, 25, 26, 77
prisoners of war 71–3, 81, 82–5, 109, 111, 167–9, 238, 277, 324
Priština, Hasan 128–9, 131–2, 134, 234
Prokuplje 256–9
Protić, Stojan 24–5, 48, 60, 290, 318, 322–3
protivchete forces 267–74
Protogerov, Colonel 257, 262
Putnik, Vojvoda Radomir 42, 68, 69, 70, 83, 103, 107, 147, 162

Radical Party (Old Radicals) 23, 65, 114–15, 181, 184–6, 281–2, 305
Radoslavov, Vasil 86, 124–7, 201, 202, 218, 260
Radović, Andrija 138, 191–2, 282, 283
railways 57, 109, 110, 199, 200, 202, 207–9, 215, 219–21, 249, 258, 264
Reed, John 83, 102, 105–6, 108, 109, 111, 117
refugees 71, 80, 109, 145–6, 148, 151–4, 158–61, 169–77
Reiss, Archibald 104, 111
relief work 111–13, 160–1, 235
Remen, General Adolf Baron von 16, 203, 227, 233, 235, 243, 247, 251, 256, 257, 262, 276, 277
resistance 245–77; *see also comitadji*
retreat of 1915–16 149–54, 158–61, 182
Rijeka 143, 144, 324

Romania 34, 97, 146, 164, 168–9, 227, 247–8, 308, 320
Russia 24, 28, 30, 33–8, 39, 45, 46, 47, 53–4, 62, 83, 84, 105, 110, 111–12, 118, 142, 147, 159, 167–9, 191, 269, 279–80, 292, 295–9, 308

Sabri, Ayub 130, 133
Salis-Seewis, General Johan Count 203, 226, 232, 233
Salonika, Salonika front 109–10, 112, 147, 148, 164, 167, 182–9, 202, 248, 264, 266, 269, 297–8, 313–21
Sandžak (formerly of Novi Pazar) 54, 201–2, 234
Sarajevo 18–19, 130, 191, 285, 323; *see also* Franz Ferdinand, Archduke, assassination
Sarkotić, General Stjepan 66, 71
Sava 70, 72, 85, 108, 136, 144, 319
Sazonov, Serge 45, 47
Schacht, Hjalmar 220–1
Serbian Relief Fund 105, 174, 175
Serbs in Austria-Hungary 15–21, 59–60, 67, 284–7
Seton-Watson, R. W. 104, 116–17, 291
Skadar 54, 128, 139, 141, 151–3, 157, 159
Skopje 146, 148, 201, 216–17, 242, 249, 257, 269
Slavonia 78
Slovenia, Slovenes 19, 21, 66, 75–6, 143–4, 287, 299–300, 319, 324, 325
Social Democrats 21, 36, 64, 79, 114, 115–16, 117, 189, 304, 311–12
South Slavs in Austria-Hungary 15–21, 28–30, 59–60, 63–8, 74–92, 94–101, 117–18, 136–8, 141–4, 176, 194–5, 279–81, 284–9, 299–304; *see also* Yugoslav idea/movement
Srem 65, 78
Štadler, Josip 18, 286, 302, 304
Stanojević, Stanoje 136, 137
Starčević, Ante 19, 20, 75, 286–7, 299–300, 302

Steed, Henry Wickham 104, 291
Stepanović, Vojvoda Stepa 103, 147, 313, 323
Stork, Wilhelm von 8–9
Stoyjanović, Nikola 90, 95, 309
Stresemann, Gustav 206, 214
Sunarić, Josip 286, 302
Supilo, Frano 79, 80, 99–100, 142, 291, 294
Šušteršić, Ivan 19, 20, 21, 66, 76
Switzerland 45, 174–6, 180, 288, 308
Szechenyi, Count 243
Szögyény, Count László 3–4, 11, 124

Tankosić, Vojislav 5–6, 23, 25–6, 44, 46, 50
Temešvar (Timişoara) 97, 321
Thallóczy, Ludvig 203, 234
Tirana 130, 135
Tisza, Count István 10, 39, 42, 65, 194–6, 198, 203, 205
Toplica 249, 252, 255, 268–9, 270, 275
trade restrictions 237–8
trials (political) in Austria-Hungary 77–8, 285–6
Trifunović, Miloš 175, 177
Trumbić, Ante 79, 100, 141, 142, 143, 278, 290, 292, 293, 298
Tucović, Dimitrije 116
Turkey 54, 122–3, 125–7, 129–33, 204–5, 206, 209–10, 234, 279, 319
Turnu-Severin 169
typhus 110–13

ultimatum of July 1914 40, 43–51
United Kingdom of Serbs, Croats and Slovenes 321–6
United States of America 84, 112, 142, 167, 280, 292, 294, 207, 325

Valjevo 90, 111, 113
Veljković, Vojislav 233
Vešović, Brig. Radomir 245–6, 266–7
Vlahović, Capt. Milinko 246, 250, 253, 273

Vlorë 134, 159, 170
Vojinović, Kosta 246–74
Vojvodina 65, 89, 95, 301
volunteers for Serbia 77, 80, 81–5, 107, 142, 163, 165, 166–9, 187, 188, 292, 295–8
Vranje 239–40
Vukotić, Janko 68, 147, 155, 156, 157, 266
Vulović, Major Ljubomir 24–6

war crimes, *see* atrocities
White Hand 184–8, 323
Wiener Kreditanstalt 212–13
Wilhelm II, Kaiser 3–4, 10, 11, 41, 50, 53, 193, 197, 214

Yugoslav Club 299, 302, 308
Yugoslav Committee 94, 141, 166–7, 180, 279, 283, 290–2, 321
Yugoslav idea/movement 20–1, 62–3, 66–7, 75–6, 79–80, 86–101, 117–18, 136–44, 166–7, 278–312, 318–26

Zagreb 16–17, 303, 318, 323–4
Zemun 49, 70, 74, 78
Živković, General Mihailo 295–7
Žujović, Professor Jovan 170–2